BASIC
ECONOMICS

BASIC
ECONOMICS

Second Edition

Rudolph W. Trenton
Oklahoma State University

**APPLETON
CENTURY
CROFTS**

Division of Meredith Corporation   NEW YORK.

to Marybeth

PREFACE TO THE FIRST EDITION

Economics is not an easy subject. It requires the analytical power of a mathematician who is used to thinking in terms of abstract logic; it demands a wealth of factual, institutional information which is the raw material of the subject; it also relies greatly on the experience and observation of economic life which no young student is likely to bring to his first course in large measure.

The introductory textbook in economics traditionally accepts this difficulty as an inevitable feature of the basic course. It confronts the student with problems which are often beyond his grasp, and it presents its information in a technical language which for the beginner appears to have little in common with his own life experience. He proceeds, therefore, to memorize required theories without much understanding and to reproduce them on demand during an examination. He also makes up his mind not to have any more of this subject than his advisor and the college catalogue require.

This book is directed to the student who does not consider economics to be one of his major interests. It hopes to demonstrate that a meaningful survey of major principles and issues in economics can be presented to the beginner without the full apparatus of the technical toolchest usually offered at this time.

This text is intended to be a first exposure to economics in non-technical language for that vast majority of undergraduates who have never heard of the subject and do not desire to pursue it beyond minimum requirements. The book has been kept short enough to permit complete coverage in one semester. Even the student who is committed to the typical two-semester introduction will view the subject with less foreboding if his first exposure is kept on a level of understanding which is no more demanding than the rest of the freshman or sophomore work.

Brevity in an economics textbook requires ruthless pruning of much valuable material. The reduction of size has been accomplished here largely by eliminating the technical details of the principles and by explaining them instead broadly in simple language. The principles are all here, both in the macro- and micro-economic fields, but they are not presented with the technical precision of a more advanced course.

Descriptive material is included in every chapter since the majority of the students is not familiar with the factual information which is inseparable from the principles which we like to emphasize. The beginner needs to know, for example, not only what the Federal Reserve System is expected to accomplish, but also how it conducts its operations.

The non-technical language adopted for this book is responsible for the avoidance of all mathematical exposition. Graphic analysis has been confined to simple supply and demand figures. All figures and statistical tables are fully described in the text on the assumption that many beginners are likely to skip them. The tables summarize the information of the text, but the discussion does not rely on them exclusively.

This book is the result of a long period of gestation. Several drafts have been tested in the classroom in mimeographed form. The comments of the users have contributed importantly to the coverage and to the form of presentation. The frequent misunderstanding caused by such simple terms as "perfect competition" and "equilibrium" was a real surprise to the writer as I am sure it will be to most economists.

The writer hopes that this simple introduction may whet the appetite of the student and motivate him to take another more technical course voluntarily after his first experience. Though he may hear no more of the subject, he should leave the course with a broadly comprehensive view of the operations of the American economy. If he tunes in to the next TV discussion of economics by presidential aspirants without feeling an urge to switch channels, this effort will not have been in vain.

Every basic textbook reflects in large measure the contribution of others and this book is no exception. Ben Lewis and Kenneth Strand, Oberlin College, helped to prevent errors and misunderstanding in several chapters. My colleagues at Oklahoma State University, Julian H. Bradsher, Ansel M. Sharp, Frank Steindl and Larkin Warner read the chapters concerned with their particular fields of interest. I am grateful to Dean Eugene L. Swearingen and Professor R. H. Baugh, Head of the Department of Economics at Oklahoma State University who never tired of encouraging the progress of this book and cheerfully cooperated with my requests of mimeographing earlier drafts of this manuscript.

My special thanks go to Professors Joseph J. Klos and Richard H. Leftwich, who read the entire manuscript and improved the final product with their incisive comments. To Mrs. Vera Milburn goes the credit of streamlining obscure passages into readable language; her careful editing greatly eased the reader's task. My wife, Marybeth Trenton, cheerfully typed the manuscript several times and suggested many editorial improvements. Her unfailing good nature created the atmosphere which made the completion of this task possible.

A large burden of indebtedness remains to my students and assistants, who suffered through years of experimentation and whose candid comments influenced the final product more than they may ever realize. To all of them I am most grateful, but the responsibility for the final product remains, of course, entirely my own.

R. W. T.

PREFACE TO THE SECOND EDITION

An introduction to the study of economics which integrates institutional information and economic theory needs to be brought up to date after a short time span. Data must be kept reasonably current to reflect the economic developments of the time, but more importantly, new trends present new issues of great economic interest to the beginner who associates economics with what he reads in the newspaper.

This revision not only brings the book up to date but includes major changes in areas where new concepts have become popularized to an extent that requires their understanding by the beginner. Medicare, the "war on poverty," and the war in Vietnam are examples of events which are treated in this revision.

At the same time, I am taking advantage of this opportunity to correct and to clarify wherever readers have brought this need to my attention. Their helpful comments are gratefully acknowledged. As a result of their interest, I hope that this new edition will become a more useful tool for an introduction to economics.

R. W. T.

CONTENTS

xi

PART II
PRICES AND THEIR APPLICATION

INTRODUCTION

Economics is everybody's business. Without becoming specialists in this field, we need a working knowledge about the operations of our economy. We learn to read and write in school without regard to our future occupation in life. The use of economic information is equally common to everyday life. The housewife goes to the store to do her shopping, her husband gets his do-it-yourself kit, but both are only partially aware that they are making economic decisions.

Some decisions are made by habit or instinct; we can buy the blue package rather than the green one without finding out what it contains, and we discover at home, regretfully, that we bought apricots instead of peaches. Important economic decisions are sometimes made with no more thought. A man buys a life insurance policy with an obligation to pay a premium for the next twenty years without ever reading the fine print. He does it because the salesman is a nice fellow who invites him for a drink and tells good stories. A newlywed couple contract to build a house in a suburban development because the bride enjoyed the sunset when the realtor drove them out to show the lot. The unhappy results that can follow such impulsive actions show that a hunch is no longer a satisfactory substitute for economic information.

ECONOMICS AS A SOCIAL SCIENCE

Economics belongs to the social sciences, the study of human conduct. Economics concentrates on that part of man's behavior which is concerned with the eternal struggle of making a living. Economics can be described as the science which studies the methods of using scarce resources for the best satisfaction of human wants. These resources comprise everything needed to make more and better goods and services available.

The problem of scarcity is as old as mankind, but its solution is always new. Change is a striking characteristic of economic life; the goods desired and the methods used in their production shift continuously. The effectiveness of an economic system depends on its ability to adjust to ever-changing conditions and to adapt its dynamic forces to the promotion of economic growth, a goal frequently identified with the idea of progress.

1

In their effort to find ways of improving our material well-being, economists draw heavily on the information supplied by other branches of the social sciences. History, sociology, psychology, and political science all contribute to the improvement of economic knowledge.

History teaches us how similar problems have been solved in the past. An inflation cannot be started in a country as an experiment to see how people are hurt by it and who will be affected most; this would be intolerable. However, the past supplies a sufficient store of experiences to render such experiments unnecessary. Therefore, economics depends partly on the historical method. Much can be learned from a study of the mistakes of the past, which frequently have been preserved in detailed records. History supplies information to document a long list of economic follies.

Information about local culture, which must be taken into account when making economic decisions, is supplied by sociologists. There may be, for example, a country where the production of beef cattle could flourish, but this innovation would not be a wise move if the local population had a strong religious conviction prohibiting the killing of cows.

Psychologists can enlighten us about the popular reactions which may follow specific economic decisions. Will a drop in income tax rates lead to an immediate boost in car sales, or will this sudden windfall be deposited in savings accounts? Or should we expect other consequences? The psychological impact of such a measure on the population must be evaluated in advance to avoid undesirable surprises.

Political scientists suggest what economic solutions are feasible within the existing political framework. Frequently economists, who are technical experts in their special field, suggest solutions too far advanced to be acceptable; sometimes their recommendations simply lack the political appeal necessary to command a majority vote. When economic principles are applied to political problems, we refer to them as *political economy*. Decisions of this nature represent a blend of economic wisdom with the art of knowing the limits of political reality.

ECONOMIC TOOLS

The use of data and numerical information in many forms is of particular importance to economics. Statistics, accounting, and mathematics are three areas of knowledge economists study to gain better insights into their own field.

Statisticians engage in the collection, analysis, interpretation, and presentation of numerical data. A data collection of the number of people employed and the compilation of index numbers are examples of statistics used as an economic tool. Statistical information, however, requires some technical knowledge for proper interpretation. Empirical data, isolated by themselves, have no clear-cut meaning. A headline announcing that the gross national product exceeds $600 billion means very little unless one knows how much it was last month, last year, or five years ago, and how much it usually fluctuates. Statisticians bring order into this chaos and make the scientific use of data by economists possible.

Accountants furnish useful information on the state of business, which is reflected in the accountants' balance sheets. Costs, prices, profits, inventories, and turnover rates are just a few significant accounting data on which economic conclusions are based.

Mathematicians, with their precise logic, may seem to be far removed from the flexible approach of the economists. However, economists more and more avail themselves of the abstract symbolism of mathematical methods. It sharpens their techniques and permits the reduction of involved problems to manageable proportions. Mathematical computing machines now make it possible to gather vital information about our economy where an educated guess would have had to suffice in the past.

All the numerical information we can gain is very helpful, but it cannot make economic studies so exact as the physical sciences. The human element renders such precision impossible. Fortunately, mathematical perfection is seldom needed to reach valid economic conclusions. Usually our interest is limited to discovering the general direction, the trend of economic developments. Are prices rising or falling? Is there a steady shift of people from agriculture to industry? Is employment increasing as fast as new workers become available for the labor force? These are the kind of questions frequently answered by economists.

THE ROLE OF THE ECONOMIST

The economist ascertains facts, then analyzes and interprets their meaning for the economic life of society. Facts never speak for themselves and can lead to very different explanations. When confronted by rising prices, one man may call this event a "price increase" while another calls it "a drop in the value of the dollar." Both describe the fact accurately, but their choices of expression emphasize the difference of interpretation.

The subject of economics touches closely on man's emotions. Many people find it quite possible to look objectively at the results of a chemical experiment, but their attitudes change when their own pocketbooks become involved. Economists are just as subject to emotions as the rest of humanity; no book on economics remains entirely free of the personal bias of the writer.

Economists have learned, however, that the solution of a problem requires objectivity even though the result may be unpleasant. Wishful thinking is likely to cause disastrous consequences when it intrudes into the making of policy. Actually, economists are in broad agreement on a large body of principles which are generally accepted regardless of personal prejudices. These principles form the basis for a better understanding of our economy.

The objectives for the national economy are established by political decisions. These objectives are the goals which the people determine in national elections. Economists may show how to reach the goal, not what the goal should be. They are trained as technical specialists to point out the available alternatives that will accomplish a desired result. Since economists are also people with strong emotions about the objectives of economic efforts, they may not always resist the temptation to substitute their own ideas for those of the society they serve. When an economist raises his voice in defense of specific objectives, such as building more power plants or helping the farmers, he may be able to point out the economic implications of these goals more clearly than others, but he has no more competence to determine them than any of his fellow men.

A popular criticism of our economic system is the indisputable fact that in this system the rich man's dog can afford to eat a steak which the poor man's health needs so much more. The economist is not the culprit who caused this result. His tools are neutral and can be applied with equal efficiency for good or evil. The social structure of our society determines the priority by which wants are satisfied. If society prefers night clubs to good books, jazz music to symphonies, or fat dogs to healthy people, we shall have night clubs, jazz, and fat dogs.

The economist does not judge how worthy these ends are; he simply accepts the priority list society itself furnishes. He does not pass judgment on the ethical content of people's wants. His advice concerns ways and means to reach a goal, but he does not appraise the value of the ultimate objective.

THE HISTORY OF ECONOMIC THOUGHT

Although man's preoccupation with economic subjects is as old as recorded history, the formal recognition of economic studies dates back only to the year 1776, when Adam Smith, a wise Scot, set forth the economic knowledge of his time in a systematic and readable book called *An Inquiry into the Nature and Causes of the Wealth of Nations*.

Smith was followed by a long line of colorful writers. David Ricardo in the beginning of the nineteenth century had much to say about the operation of a pricing mechanism. Thomas Malthus, a clergyman, tried to explain the economic difficulties which would arise from overpopulation, and issued such dire predictions about the future of the human race that economics of his brand could fittingly be called a "dismal science." Almost a hundred years later, Alfred Marshall used the precision of mathematical analysis in the study of economic phenomena. John Maynard Keynes, who died in 1946, turned the study of economics to a more optimistic search for progress through dynamic change. His hopeful legacy to a world which vividly remembered the depression-plagued 1930's had a profound impact on modern economics.

Many others in Europe and the United States could be mentioned in any review of economic thought. Robert L. Heilbroner called them the "worldly philosophers" in an unusually interesting book.[1] Browse through it for the full story, and you'll never again think of economics as a dull subject!

WHAT TO EXPECT

Will you find out how to make more money in a business or the best method to beat the stock market? A better understanding of economics may prove helpful in any venture, but the main objective of this book is to impart basic principles which will serve as guidelines and help you take a more informed stand on the many problems which confront the people of this country as citizens and voters.

Economics as a science has only recently reached the brink of great discoveries. Today it finds itself in a position which medicine passed at the turn of the century. How exhilarating must have been the first knowledge that the plague was not sent periodically from on high to destroy the doomed sector of humanity! A little knowledge and a harmless vaccination frees us from this fear. Economic science has just begun to learn that poverty is an avoidable economic disease, that excessive business fluctuations are controllable, and that nothing prevents us from improving our lot every day.

The study of economics developed on the following pages will sketch broadly some principles in all major areas of interest to the layman.

The function of prices and incomes will be discussed. Depression and inflation, competition and monopoly, money and the government, the role of special interest groups, and many other topics will be considered.

A general overview of an economic system is followed by a development of microeconomic concepts. Microeconomics refers to the behavior of individuals, families, and business firms in the give-and-take of the daily struggle

[1] Robert L. Heilbroner, *The Worldly Philosophers* (New York, Simon and Schuster, 1953).

for a larger share of earthly goods. It includes a discussion of producers and consumers and their interaction on each other. This foundation, with its emphasis on the conduct of each participant in the economy, is followed by an outline of a modern monetary system, which permits a discussion of macroeconomic principles. Macroeconomics focuses on the total performance of an economic system with changing total incomes, employment, and activity of business as a whole. The last section combines micro- and macroeconomic considerations in a look at the problems we face in the world around us.

This book concentrates on principles which are largely noncontroversial If the writer's own bias creeps unavoidably into the unfolding story, his prejudice is an optimistic one. Conceding from the outset that reality is never perfect, the American system of free enterprise regulated in the public interest has proven to be a remarkably efficient instrument for the material satisfaction of an ever-growing number of people. The progress of the past has brought us to the dawn of a still better era with a potential for economic growth limited only by our inability to use it to the fullest. To step forth into the discovery of economic principles which open up bright new horizons will become, I hope, a fascinating adventure.

PART I

AN OVER-ALL LOOK AT OUR ECONOMIC SYSTEM

Human wants and their satisfaction through the production of goods and services concern every economic system; scarcity of the fruits of such production has always interfered with man's ability to enjoy all he wants. The overview of our economic system looks first at the problems and choices which all social organizations have in common. A modern economy, however, is a more sophisticated instrument which cannot exist merely on the primitive methods of a traditional barter system.

The specific characteristics which distinguish the American economy from other modern systems form the content of Chapter 2, while the far-flung role of government in our economy is explored broadly in Chapter 3.

THE MODERN ECONOMY

Economic problems would exist if man lived in complete isolation. Even a hermit stranded on some forgotten island has to make economic decisions. He has a very limited amount of resources and he must decide how to use them. He is forced to make decisions involving the production and consumption of goods. He must make up his mind about the best way to take advantage of the things he has available. He may use wood either to build a cabin or to light a fire, or he may work longer hours cutting wood to have enough for both purposes. He must allocate his resources in the form which suits him best. Should he work extra hours today so that he can afford to sleep longer tomorrow morning? Should he spend some of his time making tools to ease his work, or should he limit himself to gathering food by hand? All these are economic decisions and no man can avoid them.

WHAT IS ECONOMICS?

To economize means to avoid waste, to obtain the best possible results from one's efforts. Why should we avoid waste? An economic system tries to satisfy human wants; to do a better job of satisfying these wants, we need more goods and services. We can never fill the limitless list of our desires because there are never enough goods and services for all of us.

It is the task of the economist to study these desires for goods and services so that the best approach can be found for satisfying them. Resources are always relatively scarce and must be assigned first to the most urgent demands. Economists do not tell people to work more; rather, they point out the best use or allocation of scarce resources on the basis of efficiency. We may say, therefore, that *economics is a science intended to discover the most efficient means of allocating scarce resources for the purpose of satisfying human wants.*

ECONOMIC WANTS

Human wants in the broadest sense cover many areas beyond the reach of economic satisfaction. Many desires are of a purely emotional nature.

Courage, love, and wisdom are examples of wants for immaterial objectives. The young man who wants a date with the blonde who just left the building is facing a noneconomic problem. It may, however, have economic implications if he lacks the needed cash to take her to the movies.

Some people honestly believe that they will be happy and want no more as soon as they buy the new automobile that has tempted them for some time. But the new automobile creates a want for seat covers and for more gasoline. It is fun to go places in a new car, so the car owner next wants a boat, outboard motor, fishing tackle, and accessories. With all this equipment he catches some fish and wants a deep freeze to store the surplus. This insatiability of human wants results in a need to economize since there is never enough to satisfy everybody.

Many facts when commonly observed seem to contradict the idea of limitless wants. The newspapers are full of stories of excessive inventories of automobiles forcing cutbacks in production, or of an unmanageable wheat crop demanding government action. The main problem for many producing firms is apparently the exact opposite of a shortage of goods for sale. They must try to find more customers who want the goods which flow from the assembly lines in such abundance. Some people feel that the main task of the economy consists not so much in producing more goods as in disposing of the mountain of products modern technology has learned to manufacture so efficiently.

ECONOMIC SCARCITY

Scarcity is not an absolute concept but refers to everything for which someone's desire must go unfulfilled. Society as a whole has never enough resources to satisfy all the wants of all the people. Therefore, we must economize and carefully allocate the available resources to the most urgent needs.

The abundance of automobiles in dealer showrooms may be an indication that a mistake has been made in the allocation of resources, or simply that the customers find the price too high for the product. If nobody had to pay for these cars the showrooms would empty overnight, and the shortage, or scarcity, would be felt severely. Scarcity is not merely a visible lack of goods; it describes the many desires which could not be satisfied if goods were free.

Economics discovers the most efficient methods for overcoming the ever-present scarcity of goods and services. These methods try to channel resources in such a manner that the right products will be available at the right time in the right place for the greatest satisfaction of the people.

To accomplish this task, a long list of services is needed. Beef on the hoof does not satisfy the appetite for hamburger. The farmer has to raise the cattle, the butcher must slaughter it, and the grocer will package and sell it to you. The list is particularly long when we keep in mind the transportation and marketing services which all have to enter the production stream to bring the hamburger to your table.

Scarcity is the cause and curse of human deprivations. The bulging inventory in the store downtown indicates a managerial error: the wrong goods in the wrong place at the wrong time, most likely at the wrong price.

ECONOMIC SATISFACTION

Satisfaction of human wants is the objective of all economic efforts. This statement is quite ambiguous. How does one measure satisfaction? If it is impossible to satisfy everybody, who should be taken care of first? Will a thousand added television sets contribute more to the satisfaction of humanity than a hundred automobiles? Does more production always mean better satisfaction, as some people who are fascinated by statistical tables seem to feel? Satisfaction is far too complicated to be measured by any numerical yardstick!

What satisfies people most depends at any moment on what goals society has assigned to its economy. Whoever happens to make the rules— Congress, the city commissioners, or the voters who decide on spending money proposed by the school board—establishes in fact the economic objectives. When we approve the expenditures needed to build a new schoolhouse, we give the school board the necessary funds to bid for steel and wood and cement over others. We implicitly have decided that this new school will do more to satisfy wants at this time than would other possible uses of these goods.

The objectives of economic effort undergo constant change. They may favor concentration on missiles for defense now and motorboats for better living next month. Even the length of time people care to work is subject to change. During a war the patriotic grandmother who works on the assembly line helps to achieve the goal of maximum output. In a peacetime economy it may be far more desirable for grandmother to retire to the joys of baby-sitting with her grandchildren. Her active participation on the production line is no longer desired.

UNIVERSAL ECONOMIC CHOICES

The scarcity of goods forces difficult economic choices. Every economic system must reach an answer to the following three questions:

What Shall We Produce?

Everything people want! This is an impossible answer because at any given moment our resources are limited and we must therefore choose between alternatives that leave some wishes unsatisfied. In practice we favor a compromise and produce goods that will satisfy all wants at least partly. There will be some refrigerators and some TV sets, and the question then boils down to a decision about what should be made first. The question of how much of each product shall be produced requires the creation of priority schedules which are likely to differ sharply with each personal viewpoint.

How Shall Production Be Conducted?

This may appear to be a purely technical problem which could be left safely for the engineers to decide. Such an opinion would be very much in error. Who shall take on any specific production job? It can be centered in small business just big enough to supply local demand, or the goods can be made by a giant enterprise for a national market. The production methods will differ widely depending upon the size of the producer and the number of people to satisfy. The best solution may be different in every case.

The resources used for the production process also involve economic decisions. A producer can choose his raw materials; he can knit a garment from wool, cotton, Orlon, Dacron, or some other fiber as long as it is technically suitable for the purpose. The choice among these fibers is mostly economic and depends on the relative scarcity of the alternative raw materials. This situation may change frequently with the cotton harvest, the wool crop, or the opening of a new Dacron plant, and requires continuous reevaluation.

The best economic techniques are not always the most advanced engineering methods. Many unused patents bear witness to the fact that technical progress is not the same as economic progress. Should homes be heated with coal or oil? Shall we wash dishes with human labor such as a housewife or with an electric dishwasher? The answer is not nearly so obvious as the ladies may think! Much manual effort can be changed to pushbutton techniques, but should it? Each change creates a need for adjustment: there may be a shortage of trained technicians; some narrowly specialized men whose jobs have been eliminated may find it difficult to learn a new trade. The final decision on how to produce goes far beyond the competence of any one activity and involves considerations which touch on many fields.

For Whom Shall We Produce?

This question has always attracted much attention and has been historically the cause of wars and revolutions. Whose wants should be satisfied first and to what extent? Should all production be channeled evenly to all people, or will the victor get the spoils? There has never been agreement on the relative merits of competing claims for the goods and services society can produce. Unlike the ancient rule for abandoning ship on the high seas, no such priority list as "women and children first" has ever been agreed on for economic satisfaction.

Our efforts can be concentrated on furnishing first the necessities of life for the greatest number of people. This bland statement misses its target on two counts. In the first place, it is grossly oversimplified and far from clear, since no two people are likely to agree upon what is really necessary. Secondly, although it may be possible by this principle to keep people from starving, a progressive economy must satisfy many more wants. Last year's luxuries become today's necessities. The automobile, the refrigerator, and the TV set are the results of an economic philosophy which tries to provide better want satisfaction rather than an even distribution of goods.

ECONOMIC ORGANIZATION

The wide variety of problems faced by a modern economy needs to be examined in orderly fashion. For this purpose the organization of an economic system can be conveniently arranged in four categories: production, consumption, distribution, and exchange.

Production

Production may receive the logical priority in this discussion because no other phase of economic activity can make itself felt unless we first produce the goods to be consumed. The amount of goods produced will not always indicate how happy people really are. Although it usually takes more goods to make people happier, production statistics do not necessarily reflect the satisfaction of peoples' desires

To produce more goods, resources must be used efficiently, but not all available resources can be applied at the same time. We mine only as much coal as we can conveniently burn at any one time, but the use of human labor, the most precious resource, cannot be postponed; human skill must be used in the present or it is lost forever. A shorter workweek which

leaves much leisure time may be a desirable objective, but involuntary unemployment renders it impossible for a man to do useful work when he
wants to do it. This loss of activity is pure waste and cannot be recovered
later. Human skills must be exercised constantly to remain sharp and alert.
An efficient production process will therefore avoid unemployment whenever possible.

Consumption

The consumer's satisfaction is the final objective of all economic activity.
His wants need to be satisfied, and a major task is to learn exactly what he
does desire. If we produce the "wrong" items—goods which consumers do
not like—we have compounded the waste of unemployment by adding to
it the waste of raw materials.

To keep people at tasks which are not constructive adds nothing to
the production that can satisfy wants. We may not wish to call these people
unemployed, and their activity may indeed have a beneficial effect on their
own morale, but the standard of living remains just as depressed as it
would be if they were doing nothing. When a large family cultivates a very
small farm, the resulting poverty can be attributed directly to the fact that
most members of the family are really unemployed since the farm could
be handled easily by one or two persons.

Economic activity can always be improved if we produce more articles
which will satisfy the consumer. To accomplish this, man's desires must be
studied so that the need for changes can be foreseen and the future wants
anticipated. An increase in marriages, for instance, permits a prediction of
increased needs for new homes now and for baby products and more class-
rooms a few years hence. But not all consumers' wants can be forecast with
the same confidence. Will the majority prefer smaller or larger automobiles
next year? Will they buy a sewing machine or take a vacation trip? The
most useful production, then, depends on a thorough understanding of consumers' desires and attitudes.

Distribution

Distribution problems arise from the need to forge a link between producer
and consumer in an integrated economy. As long as production is limited
to providing goods for specifically known consumers, distribution consists
simply in delivering the product. As specialization increases, however, and
as the personal connection between trading partners weakens, the middleman becomes a necessity. Today the services offered to facilitate distribution require an increasing share of human effort.

The entire field of marketing has been developed in an attempt to move the fruits of mass production to millions of homes all over the country. Research services try to discover what people want. Advertisers hope to influence man's desires by channeling them toward goods which are actually being produced. Transportation services widen the area of distribution for every product and give the consumer a broader choice of goods.

The efficiency of the distributive mechanism limits the degree of technical specialization which is practical for a manufacturing process. An industrial plant may operate best when producing thousands of mouse traps per day, but it wouldn't consider pouring out this amount unless the marketing department could sell them.

The seriousness of distribution problems is best understood when the system suffers a breakdown. In a depression we find closed factories and the waste of unemployment on the production side, and on the consumption side of the economy are the unsatisfied wants of millions of desperate people. An efficient distribution system is supposed to overcome these problems and prevent similar disasters in the future. With the help of an enlightened monetary and fiscal policy, better timing of production, more knowledge of consumption, and improved methods of distribution are the best safeguards against a repetition of the depressions of the past.

Exchange

Exchange problems cover the maintenance of a proper flow of money and credit in the economy. Two little boys may handle their exchange problem in a most elementary manner by bartering two marbles for a butterfly. A modern banking and credit mechanism offers more intricate methods to deal with the exchange problems of a complicated economy.

You may have solved your personal problem of exchange by depositing a monthly paycheck in the bank and sending checks to your creditors. It is difficult to realize how many involved arrangements are necessary to make your simple transaction possible. A good exchange system frees us from the need for direct barter—finding someone with just enough eggs to trade for shoes. But the function of the system goes a long way beyond merely simplifying the barter process. The institution of credit makes it possible to anticipate purchases or postpone them to a more appropriate time. In addition, capital is gathered from many small sources and used together by large business firms.

The value of the exchange function becomes most apparent when something goes wrong with it. Should you find yourself stranded in a town where nobody is willing to take your check, you might have to wash dishes to pay for your meal. Because a check is normally acceptable all over the country, you wonder what arrangements are necessary to make it possible.

A breakdown of the credit mechanism can lead to disastrous consequences. When usual credit facilities are disrupted because banks have become insolvent, normal trade is brought to a standstill. A consumer may still want to buy the same new car which the dealer wants to sell and both may agree on a price, but they need a banker to advance the credit to make the transfer possible. Without him there will be no sale. The depression of the 1930's demonstrated far too clearly the repercussions on the economy when such breakdowns occur on a large scale.

MARKETS

A market helps us in the distribution of goods and services. It is an arrangement which permits numerous buyers and sellers of related commodities to conduct extensive business transactions on a regular, organized basis.[1] Markets can be traced back in history to the earliest periods of mankind and have been rearranged over the centuries to fit changing economic conditions. They remain a major tool of any economy.

Markets may be physical arrangements such as the traditional village square, where fresh produce is sold to the housewife in a purely local attempt to facilitate the distribution of goods. Fairs and conventions are other traditional devices geared to bring together in one location the buyers and sellers most interested in the trade of specific products.

A market may be created on the floor of a stock exchange or commodity exchange connected by telephone and ticker tape with even the remotest parts of the country. At these exchanges men transfer pieces of paper which represent legal contracts. Their transactions are promptly reported and influence the efforts and decisions of people across the nation. A modern market mechanism no longer requires physical contact in a specific location. Chain stores, national advertising, and mail order facilities provide nationwide markets for goods and services and are important elements in the smooth operation of a specialized society.

ECONOMIC DEVELOPMENT

Economic development is an organized effort to reduce the relative scarcity of goods and to satisfy more of the limitless wants of humanity. The nature of economic choice changes considerably as society develops, though the basic problem of satisfying wants with scarce goods and services remains the same. Looking at the enormous mountain of products which flow in a

---

[1] Somewhat less descriptive, but more formally precise, is a definition of markets given by Henry H. Bakken, *Theories of Markets and Marketing* (Madison, Wis., Mimir Publishers, Inc., 1953), p. 34: "A market is an institution designed to facilitate the transfer of legal rights and titles to ownership in goods, services, and properties."

steady stream from modern assembly lines, one may wonder if the problem of a developed economy is not, in fact, of a different order. Professor Galbraith discusses these views in *The Affluent Society*,[2] a book which challenges the "conventional wisdom" of those who consider scarcity our eternal problem. The affluence of the electronic age in midcentury America has not eliminated the scarcity of goods for most people on this earth. On the contrary, the example of our industrialized society has greatly increased the demand for goods in all other nations and renders the problem of scarcity even more acute.

From the caveman to the explorer of outer space is a long road of evolution. In different parts of the world we still encounter examples of every stage of economic development. The political ferment of our times is due in part to the insistence of lesser-developed nations that they skip the slow process of evolution and receive immediately all the benefits of modern technology.

Stage 1: Self-sufficiency

The early dwellers on this planet had serious problems of survival which are of small interest to a modern economy. But even at the primitive stage, man organized his family in some fashion to "get the job done" more effectively. As tools were developed over the years, economic organization became more detailed. A farm family in the colonial setting of early America had gone a long way in technical development from the animal-like process of insuring survival. But the economy of the early farmer was still a self-contained arrangement where most want satisfaction resulted from the output produced by the family itself. Tasks were divided and assigned, largely by tradition, and handed down from father to son, with many of the tools made—or at least repaired—by the head of the household.

Stage 2: Division of Labor

The next stage of economic development is characterized by a division of labor that extends beyond the family in its broadest sense. This principle of dividing productive tasks into several separate functions in order to improve the end result does away with the self-sufficiency of a family economy. It creates instead a dependence on other people with whom we trade, thus involving the society in barter transactions. Rules for bartering must be established and some provision made for their enforcement. Consequently, a more elaborate social organization becomes necessary.

[2] John Kenneth Galbraith, *The Affluent Society* (Boston, Houghton Mifflin, 1958).

The advantage of the division of labor is the higher standard of living achieved by assigning each task to the best qualified workers and merging their combined efforts toward the production of more and better products. Even tribal societies today practice some form of the division of labor and barter, but along well-developed patterns which seldom change.

Stage 3: Specialization

A more advanced degree of specialization restricts an individual to the mastery of a small, but often intricate, task in a much larger production effort. The development of the division of labor, combined with the industrial revolution of the nineteenth century, so transformed production methods that it became necessary for many people to find new ways of earning a livelihood. In addition, industrialization forced an ever-increasing sector of the population into crowded urban surroundings, where they had to accept specialized jobs and depend upon these jobs for sheer survival.

The specialization of an industrialized society requires a different type of economic organization. A modern specialist seldom produces an entire product; he simply contributes a small part in its progress toward completion. This technique separates the producer from the consumer, creating a completely impersonal relationship between people who depend entirely upon each other. The quality of a man's effort no longer assures his proper reward in material goods. His place in society may depend largely on a lucky guess when he takes a job for the first time. His own fortune is tied up with the welfare of the firm for which he works, and yet he may have no more influence on the overall performance of his team than a baseball player watching from the bench. If management is capable and the business expands, there is plenty of room on top and promotions come easily. If the firm fails to grow, even an able employee may discover that his chances for advancement are poor.

The requirements of a specialized economy differ in substance from the simple methods prevailing in earlier stages of development. The economy must forge techniques to link production and consumption, since they no longer respond to each other directly. An old village tailor will fit a suit to measure. He knows for whom he is making the suit before he starts cutting it. Today, however, tailor-made suits are rather the exception than the rule. With mass production methods, large numbers of suits in various sizes and styles are manufactured by one firm, and will reach their consumers all over the country some months later. The specialized economy must develop a system of distribution with wholesalers and retailers, railroads, trucking firms, and banks before specialization can give us the desired fruits in the form of better products at smaller effort.

Why do we accept and even prefer the complications of a specialized economy? A jack-of-all-trades may be a lovable character, but a narrowly specialized expert renders a more valuable contribution to an involved production process. Better products are rarely the result of a single stroke of genius: they emerge as the conclusion of a carefully coordinated program of research executed by highly specialized technicians, and they are assembled in expensive laboratories equipped with intricate, special-purpose machines. A specialized production process requires a great deal of coordination and advance planning to insure positive results. Unfortunately, there is no simpler alternative to this means of continuing to improve living standards.

Stage 4: Diversification

Diversification is a modern attempt to combine the benefits of specialized mass production with the security enjoyed in earlier days, when a man did not need to put all his eggs in one basket. Diversification does not mean turning back the clock on specialization. Rather, a diversified firm combines several specialized products in the common effort of making and selling. An example would be an oil firm which originally produced only oil and gasoline. It now adds chemical fertilizers and plastics, and it may even enter the field of atomic energy.

This trend creates a new set of economic problems. In order to diversify, a firm must be so large that its success becomes a vital issue not only for those people directly connected with the business, but for a large number of others as well. This far-reaching involvement of outsiders causes an increasing need for public controls and brings about a still more intricate stage of economic development.

INDEPENDENCE AND INTERDEPENDENCE

The material advantages of specialization and diversification are obvious. They have made possible the high living standard of today—every housewife in her mechanized kitchen becomes a living testimony to the progress made since the time of the old wood stove. The advantages of the division of labor need no further comment.

Interdependence is the price we pay for this progress. Modern man has lost the rugged independence of pioneering days; he is now a small cog in a complex machine whose operation he cannot control, yet upon whose uninterrupted performance he is completely dependent. The specialist can no longer make a living on his own, and this fact has taken away his sense of security. The rapid increase of private and public insurance is the outgrowth of this changed situation. A city family can neither feed nor clothe itself, and a breakdown of the power plant can be a serious calamity unless promptly repaired. We all depend on the smooth performance of a well-organized economic system to furnish everything we need.

Is this too high a price to pay for progress? Some people make nostalgic speeches on Independence Day deploring the loss of self-sufficiency of of an earlier period; they would gladly turn the clock back. They seem to forget, however, that the individualist of the past was more often than not a poor and hungry man.

The integration of a modern economy has freed us from dependence on specific people, such as the tailor or the owner of the general store. A drought in one area no longer condemns its inhabitants to starvation. It is true that we must have electricity to light our homes and keep frozen foods from spoiling, but we neither know nor care if some particular engineer in the power plant is on the job or if he stayed home to nurse a cold. As long as the organization itself suffers no breakdown, the individual's performance is of negligible concern to his fellowman.

Modern interdependence has shifted the nature of individual independence rather than wiped it out entirely. Sears, Roebuck and Co. freed us from the dictates of the store on Main Street with the introduction of the mail-order business. Modern communications make it possible to be equally well informed in a small town or in a big city. Air transportation permits us to do business in person rather than depend on agents, even in faraway places.

Independence in an integrated economy has changed its characteristics and has adapted itself to the transformation caused by the technical conditions of our times. Specialization and diversification, interdependence and independence do not exclude one another. They all contribute to a continuous adjustment process which aims to allow the economy to use technical progress for the best satisfaction of human wants.

SUMMARY

An economic system develops appropriate methods to satisfy infinite human wants with goods and services; these remain relatively scarce even though at times they appear to be abundant.

Every society must make economic choices with regard to reducing scarcity. What to produce, how to produce, and for whom to produce present the key questions for which economic solutions must be found.

Problems of economic organization may be considered under four categories:

1. Production efforts must create more goods for more people with the least possible waste, particularly of human resources. The avoidance of unemployment is a major task.

2. Consumption studies aim to discover the consumer's wants so that the goods produced will contribute most effectively to his satisfaction.

3. Distribution links the producer and the consumer in a specialized economy. It provides the services which move the right goods to the right place at the right time.

4. Exchange techniques contribute a workable system of money and credit to facilitate the barter of a specialized economy. Markets are basic instruments in the operation of an economy in bringing buyers and sellers together.

Economic development has led humanity from the simplicity of the self-sufficient caveman to the division of labor and modern specialization based on the technical requirements of the industrial revolution. Diversification tries to mitigate the hazards of extreme specialization and to permit continued balanced growth in increasingly large business units.

Economic independence has given way to the interdependence of an integrated society. The compensation for the loss of pioneering independence is a new form of freedom which transfers the individual need for specific performance to the impersonal dependence on organizational performance.

Every modern economy operates within the framework outlined in this chapter. The nature of the solutions, however, will vary for each society in response to the specific objectives established by its members. These specific goals and the methods used to attain them are the subject of the next chapter.

Discussion Questions

1. Why are goods called "scarce" when the merchant's shelves are filled to over-flowing?
2. Are production and consumption decisions more important than the development of distribution and exchange systems?
3. Compare the advantages and drawbacks of modern economic interdependence with the self-sufficiency of an earlier period.
4. What is the role of the market in an economy?
5. The *most* goods do not always best satisfy *wants,* but reduction in output cannot by itself improve the situation. Why?
6. Is diversification a good solution to a firm's economic problems?

Suggested Reading

Many more detailed textbooks may be consulted throughout for reference. Only a few of the best known can be listed here.

BACH, GEORGE L., *Economics,* 5th ed. Englewood Cliffs, N.J., Prentice-Hall, 1966.
HARRIS, C. L., *The American Economy,* 5th ed. Homewood, Ill., Irwin, 1965.

MCCONNELL, CAMPBELL R., *Economics,* 3rd ed. New York, McGraw-Hill, 1966.
REYNOLDS, LLOYD G., *Economics,* rev. ed. Homewood, Ill., Irwin, 1966.
SAMUELSON, PAUL A., *Economics,* 7th ed. New York, McGraw-Hill, 1967.

2

THE FREE ENTERPRISE ECONOMY

THE SPIRIT OF FREE ENTERPRISE

The American economy is commonly called a free enterprise system. We point with pride to its accomplishments, to the mass and variety of earthly goods which enter the homes of an ever-increasing majority of the people. Most of us feel that it is a good system, but we would be somewhat at a loss to explain what is characteristic of free enterprise and how it differs from economies whose results are less satisfactory.

Profit and competition come immediately to mind. These require the right of private ownership of goods and the capital to run a business according to the ideas of private managers. The system must satisfy individuals both as consumers who choose what they want and as workers who decide individually how they are going to earn a living. Prices, incomes, and many other institutions are also important features in the operation of this economy.

Capitalism

In the past our economy has frequently been identified with capitalism. While it is true that this country has accumulated more capital than any other nation, the use of capital is not a feature unique to our society. All modern economies make heavy use of the industrial equipment that forms the capital of a nation. The concept of capitalism has such strong historical and political connotations that it spreads more emotion than enlightenment on the problem. The capitalists who served as models for Karl Marx's indictment in his famous *Capital* [1] of a century ago were a group of people who bear no comparison with the businessmen of our day. They owned the resources of the country, managed its business with autocratic arbitrariness, controlled weak governments, and were often in a position to dictate to their fellowmen.

To many people pure capitalism means absolute control of society by the "capitalist," the businessman-owner of industrial plants and equip-

[1] Karl Marx, *Das Kapital,* first published in 1867.

ment. It raises the vision of the robber-baron who made millions of dollars, paid little or no taxes, and shrugged off his social responsibilities with the philosophical comment that "the public be damned." This picture of capitalism is still carefully preserved by our enemies for propaganda in those areas of the world where hunger continues to be the most pressing problem, but it bears no resemblance to the American economy we know today.

Some of our representatives abroad have suggested that our economy be called a "peoples capitalism." This label hardly helps to clarify the concept. Too many people have learned to associate the term *capitalism* in any form with all the combined evils of colonialism and economic aggression. Our economy needs a better description.

A Mixed Economy

The American system incorporates many seemingly contradictory features. You may start a business at will, but in many cases you must first procure a state license or a city permit, or pass a special examination in order to qualify for the particular business you want to enter. Our economic organization has therefore been accurately called a *mixed economy* because of the many influences which help to shape this intricate system. It emphasizes the cooperation of private citizens, inspired by individual initiative, with democratically created public authorities, for the achievement of progress in a thoroughly interdependent economic system. The proper role of each of the partners in this progress may become occasionally a matter of dispute, but the need for a careful blending of public and private action has long found universal acceptance.

Freedom and Enterprise

The concept of free enterprise accents the two basic motivations which have been associated with our mixed economy and which deserve a large measure of recognition for its success. Individual freedom is a powerful force for economic progress. The man who picks his work, changes jobs in the light of his own wisdom, and improves his position whenever he can provides the innovating urge and restlessness on which economic advancement is based. Whereas a regimented economy relies primarily on the mental contributions of a few whose specific job is to have ideas, in a system of free enterprise the fertility and stimulation of a free exchange of ideas are a constant cause of improvement in every phase of life.

Enterprise is the driving force that urges us on in competition with others who are similarly motivated. We experiment with new ideas and new methods because there is no better way to improve our economic position, but we do so within the limits imposed by public authority in the interest of the welfare of all social groups.

THE INDIVIDUAL AND HIS SOCIETY

Each country has different laws to which its economy must conform. These differences can be grouped basically into two opposite categories that dominate the views of our times. One viewpoint maintains that the government is the servant of the people and exists to promote their welfare. The other contention is that the people are subordinate to those who govern. In this political philosophy the government represents the most important institution in the life of the individual, who learns from childhood to live, work, or even die if necessary in its cause. This organization may be called the Nation, the State, or the Party; it is conceived to be permanent, transcending the scope of an individual life span.

Philosophically, people believe either the state or the individual to be supreme. In its practical application, the dividing line is neither so rigid nor so easily drawn. A businessman may firmly invoke the principles of private enterprise, but he wants the government to protect him against his competitors; in everyday life, a compromise of principle with expediency cannot always be avoided. Some systems try to use the best features of both philosophies. A clear understanding of the two opposing views helps in a discussion of any specific compromise.

The Economy in a Dominant State

What is the task of the economy when it must serve the all-powerful State? The political leaders decide in the national interest what wants will be satisfied. Since they are not overly concerned with finding out the true wishes of the people, they may be inclined to order more guns instead of butter, tanks rather than passenger cars. If the eager consumer cannot buy that new car, he will simply have to wait. Economists contribute production quotas, rationing stamps, raw material priorities, and similar directives which are useful techniques in the pursuit of the totalitarian goal. The goals of society are defined by the ruling group, who dictate action in the name of the all-important Party which is assumed to rule forever.[2] The wishes of the individual can and must be ignored since his life span is relatively short. Man's main function consists in promoting the Party to add

---

[2] One of Hitler's leading philosophers spoke of the 10,000 years of projected party government. It lasted twelve years.

power and prestige to the permanent structure of the State. His own wants are satisfied only as they fit into the growth of the organization itself.[3]

The idea of seeing the economic goals of society determined, more or less arbitrarily, by a small ruling group may strike the reader as preposterous. The technique, however, is not completely foreign to societies which are free from dictatorship. During World War II Americans let the War Production Board decide economic priorities in the common interest of winning the war. Socialists also recognize the decision-making power of a few men who hold positions of authority.[4] Some business firms espouse a similar philosophy when they admonish their employees to dedicate their entire life to the firm. What is good for the Evermore Corporation is bound to benefit its workers.

In Russia the people learn to glorify the Party and its rulers. Want satisfaction means the completion of a five-year plan. If this plan is a little short on food and causes the population to be deprived of certain goods, this does not qualify as a serious problem unless food riots interfere with production. It has been determined that the Party requires more steel rather than well-fed people, and the economy promptly sacrifices individual hopes to satisfy the Plan. There can be no compromise with such a view of the purpose of life itself.

Economies Serving Individual Wants

The opposite goal of human effort is represented by the United States. We consider our government as a means to improving the well-being of the individual. The only wants that count are those of the people—all of the people and not just a narrow, self-perpetuating ruling class. The individual and his family cease to play a subordinate or temporary role like actors on the stage for only a few moments; their personal happiness becomes the purpose for which our social institutions have been created. The founding fathers of the United States committed this country to a philosophy which proclaims the "pursuit of happiness" to be a fundamental objective of the State. The practical application of this lofty goal encounters many pitfalls, but the philosophy provides a clear directive.

Economic techniques must fit the objectives of each system. The purposes of a centrally controlled economy require methods we would

---

[3] This philosophy was reflected with particular clarity in the basic law of Mussolini's fascist state in Italy. "The Italian Nation is an organism endowed with a purpose, a life, and a means of action transcending those of the individuals, or group of individuals composing it." See *Labour Charter,* official tr. (Rome, 1933), para. I.

[4] ". . . the equality of subordination to the common interest which is fundamental to modern socialism." See Fabian Tract No. 70 (London, Fabian Society, 1896).

not want to use frequently in the United States. Supervision and control must be ever present in a centrally directed system; ours thrives on individual initiative in an atmosphere of freedom. It would be a mistake to think of an economy serving the goal of individual happiness as one of simple *laissez-faire*,[5] as it was popularly conceived in the nineteenth century. Whereas our forefathers in the last century believed that the government "rules best which rules least," modern economists realize that individual freedom in an interdependent society requires public action of many sorts. What is the proper activity of a government in a free enterprise economy? The answer to this question has so many ramifications that the next chapter will be devoted to it entirely.

What are the goals of the American economy? No two men are likely to agree on the details of such a list, but in broad, general terms most people will express similar desires as the objectives of our economic effort. In the words of one of our foremost economists: "We want goods, well-distributed, security, greater equality (of some sorts, especially 'equal opportunity'), human rights (including rights of group action), justice, jobs. At present, we want all these things under a system of 'private enterprise.' "[6]

MAIN FEATURES OF THE AMERICAN ECONOMY

The American economy is distinguished by a bewildering array of seemingly contradictory features. Both freedom of private action and government control are prominently displayed; the chance for profit is extolled but profits are heavily taxed; competition is praised but monopoly is tolerated in many areas; the consumer is courted but the producer prevails in the legislature. What, then, are the significant characteristics of the American economy?

The tradition of private ownership of many, though certainly not all, resources is maintained. In spite of the severe restrictions on ownership rights, the principle of private control continues to be cherished as a cornerstone of our system. The consumer also plays a prominent part in the economy and influences with his purchases the direction of most productive efforts. Sellers and buyers of goods are brought together in free markets which are controlled primarily by the incentive to gain monetary profit and by the pressure to compete with the efforts of others. Prices and incomes serve as the main tools which facilitate the operation of the system.

[5] The term *laissez-faire* is a suggestion to the government to leave the people alone and let natural order prevail through noninterference in the economy.
[6] The late John M. Clark, *Guideposts in Time of Change* (New York, Harper & Row, Publishers, 1949), p. 55.

Private Ownership

The desire to own things is universal. Man's instinct to acquire more possessions is innate, somewhat akin to that of a squirrel. Our system enlists this self-interest motive to promote greater and more effective economic efforts, but unlimited accumulation of goods in the hands of a few lucky people does not contribute to the living standard of the majority. The privilege of private ownership in our society is therefore circumscribed by many obligations: The government has the right to relieve its citizens of property in the interest of the general welfare as long as suitable compensation is provided. Tax contributions are based in part on the size of private wealth. Inheritance laws make it difficult for too many possessions to be accumulated in too few hands.

The right to private property is not limited to items of personal use, but includes the right to own the means of production. This particular ownership privilege has been traditionally attacked with vehemence by socialist doctrine. Socialists feel that the ownership of capital goods confers too much economic power on the individual, who may abuse it to the detriment of his fellow citizens. In the evolution of modern business certain safeguards have been developed against the abuse of private power, without eliminating the incentive and responsibility which accompany ownership.

Consumers' Choice

To satisfy individuals, we need to know what they really want. The economic technique which discovers individual desires is called *the principle of consumers' choice*. We must try to refrain from the temptation to substitute our own judgment for that of others, as the human urge to tell people what they ought to want is great. To pass laws that favor some activities and hamper others seems perfectly right when it happens to fit our prejudices. People who don't like dogs feel that dog licenses ought to be expensive. The man who takes snapshots will agree with a tax on noisy record players, while the hi-fi fan thinks that taking pictures is a waste of resources and should be discouraged by higher taxes. Many people are inclined to feel that they know better what their friends and customers want than do the friends and customers themselves. A manufacturer with a product that doesn't sell is inclined to blame his salesmen and advertisers rather than his own bad judgment.

The freedom to demand satisfaction of individual wants includes the right to make a ludicrous choice so long as the freedom of others to do likewise is not interfered with. You may not use your home as a beauty parlor if your neighbors protest that your business interferes with their desire for a calm residential street. Special zoning regulations settle this conflict in most towns. You may think that your friend needs a new house most urgently because his present one is far too small for his growing family; but he prefers to trade his one-year-old car for a new Cadillac, and this is his privilege.

Few people will ever agree on the same priority scale for personal wants. Central planning of such wants is a contradiction of the spirit of individual want satisfaction. The seller of a product may try to influence you through an advertising campaign, but you have the complete and final authority to make your own decisions on the products that will best satisfy your desires.

Consumers' choice means more than just walking into a store and deciding between a green and a red shirt. Even in Russia one may have this privilege, but this is not consumers' choice at work. Let us assume Ivan, finds both the red and the green shirt available in his store. However, when he asks for a blue shirt which happens to be out of stock, the clerk simply informs him that the store has none. Ivan can buy either the red shirt or the green one, or he can come back next week and try again. If the blue shirt has still not arrived, he can write a letter to his district chief asking why there are no blue shirts in the local store. Maybe after some months he will get an answer, but probably he will not. The store manager won't bother his boss, who controls the supply, because his future depends on keeping the boss happy, not the customer.

Under the principle of consumers' choice, the store manager must try to satisfy you, the consumer, because his welfare depends on what he can sell you and not on what a distant wholesale firm in the capital happens to think of his work. His responsibility is to please you, not the person who sends out the merchandise.

Consumers' choice gives the customer the power to make the seller do his bidding. The store wants to keep its customers; it will not stand idly by and wait until new merchandise arrives. The manager will write, wire, or phone to be sure that the existing gap in his inventory is filled as quickly as possible. Resources are thereby shifted to the goods and services most wanted by the consumer. Each purchase is a vote for or against some merchandise, and this vote is vitally important to the manufacturer. There is a direct channel from consumer to store to wholesaler to manufacturer. If the manufacturer fails to heed the wishes of the consumer in a free enterprise economy, he will soon be out of business. He can never rest on past accomplishments but must adjust to ever-changing wants as often as the consumer changes his (or her!) mind.

The function of consumers' choice can be clarified by an example. Let us assume that some dictator decides to put all available resources into making raincoats—good, sturdy, army-type raincoats of olive drab color. The planning board concludes that production will be least wasteful when limited to one type, size, and color. The want for protection against a downpour is satisfied perfectly well even by an oversized raincoat. But when a woman buys a raincoat, she does not buy just protection against a downpour, she also wants a garment pleasing to the eye which makes her look attractive even when it rains. She may prefer to sacrifice the purely mechanical efficiency of a one-color, olive drab raincoat to a choice of bright colors and varied styles and sizes. For this reason, production figures alone do not tell the whole story of economic performance. The purpose of economic activity is not just to produce the greatest number of goods, but to manufacture the right mixture of all the things people really want.

Before a consumer can express a choice between several alternatives, he must receive offers from which to choose. Every individual has some basic wants which usually deal with food, clothing, and shelter; beyond these rudimentary needs, he may not be sure of his own desires. George Washington didn't miss the telephone, simply because he could not visualize such a gadget. Even today, if we were to go out and survey the man in the street to find out if he wants to make a trip to the moon, we would be likely to get some very puzzled answers. Nobody knows yet what the trip will be like, if it will be fun, if there will be suitable hotel accommodations upon arrival, or even if the reception will be friendly or hostile. Therefore, we are not aware of any desire for trips to the moon that would justify a producer's furnishing them. A principle that differs from consumers' choice must come into play in this case, in order to provide for wants which have not yet been established; we call this principle profit.

Profit

Profit is an incentive, a typical feature of a free enterprise economy. It adds the fuel to the engine and stimulates the advance to new horizons for a better life in the future. *Profit is a reward for taking chances in business.*

Economic profit is easily confused with normal income. People receive money for services rendered, but such payments are better described as wages, or salaries, which remunerate the work of the recipient. Economic profit also differs from the normal income of a firm. Accountants consider profit the difference between the cost of a product and the amount received from its sale, but the amount required for dividends to stockholders who furnish the firm's capital is not called profit by economists.

In essence, economic profit is a reward for going beyond routine business. A normal effort can be obtained from most people without any special profit incentive—even a dictatorship like Russia's has no difficulty in generating good, routine performances from its hordes of civil servants.

But it finds it so difficult to inspire these same people to exert initiative and try new methods not ordered from above that it has decided to adopt, cautiously, the Western profit motive. Routine performance receives an income, not a profit; only the American insistence on growth and change make the use of the profit concept essential.

The consumer votes for or against a product *after* it is introduced and offered on the market. Then the manufacturer knows what to produce. But how do we get a producer to take a chance and try something new when the consumers' reactions are not yet known? The daring individual needs an opportunity for gain before he is willing to depart from the established routine. Our economy provides this special incentive in the form of profit.

The function of profit in a free enterprise economy is easily misunderstood. Profits are sometimes described as the ill-gotten gains of unscrupulous operators, something they got for nothing, by taking advantage of less fortunate citizens. This is a mistaken view and one that overlooks the beneficial effects of profit on the economy.

It is always easier to continue on a well-worn path; to leave the road involves the risk of the unknown, and without special incentive few risks will be taken. Some exceptional people like to take chances out of a pure sense of adventure. The man who climbs a high mountain does not do so for money; he is just curious enough to try and see if he can do it. He feels sufficiently rewarded by the view from the top and the feeling of satisfaction from his accomplishment.

In our daily routine, many small risks present themselves without the glamour of the mountaintop. They frequently consist in small changes from an existing pattern. This is all part of the job. The buyer of shoes for a department store can be expected to order the same safe styles that have sold so well in the past. Why should he take a chance on a new color unless he benefits personally? He will do so only because of the bonus he will receive or the commission he hopes to gain from the larger sales.

Profit can take many forms although it is typically a monetary reward. Even nonprofit economies discover a need for incentives and substitute medals, or promotions, or larger living quarters for monetary profit. The advantages of a monetary reward, however, are great. If the incentive is a bigger house, it would not be of interest to a bachelor; money, on the other hand, is something everyone can convert to satisfy his own desires. Promotions, prestige, better working conditions, an office with a carpet, or a title of First Vice President are incentives commonly used to stimulate greater effort, but they lack the flexibility of the monetary reward.

A small, independent businessman takes more chances than most other people. He does so in the hope of a profit, which can be any amount of money. Frequently he earns no more than the normal salary he would receive if he were working for another firm, and the real profit may exist only in his imagination. The incentive function of profit is fulfilled whenever the opportunity to gain causes people to take chances. This function of profit—motivating people without necessarily rewarding them—is clearly understood by the sponsors of contests when the chance for one big prize moves thousands to work for nothing.

Monetary profit reaches its goal most completely as a reward for innovation. The multi-million-dollar facilities of a private research laboratory would not be built without the profit motive. The risks in this field of innovation are immeasurable. Without the chance for a big profit to make up for many losses, these risks would not be taken and research would become entirely a public function, with its inevitable emphasis on products only vaguely related to consumers' desires and living standards. Our hope for raising individual want satisfaction with a growing economy is firmly anchored on the rock of profit.

Competition

Competition acts in the economy like a pressure cooker in the kitchen. It exerts pressure on people and speeds up results by forcing them to make greater efforts even when profits cannot motivate them. This unpleasant function of the competitive influence is closely linked with but not identical to the profit incentive in the growth of a free economy.

A private enterprise economy faces the difficult task of obtaining the best possible performance without compulsion. A dictatorship may issue government orders under threats of punishment. A democratic system uses different and more effective methods. We know from raising children that some do their best when promised candy as a reward. Others respond better when they see how Johnny does it, and then want to do the same. The first group is motivated by profit, the other by competition.

The opportunity for greater profit becomes a less effective incentive as businessmen reach a position of comfort and satisfaction, and when the danger of loss outweighs the chances for gain. When a successful man grows older, he may be perfectly satisfied with his business. He hopes to continue reaping rewards from his earlier ventures but considers a quiet life his greatest gain. Although this attitude is understandable, it interferes with the progress of a dynamic economy. Competition prevents this danger to the continuous advancement of our economy—established profits will be reduced by new firms copying the successful methods of the old, and profits will disappear entirely as more aggressive competitors advance better, or at least different, products.

Competition and profit form a push-pull technique which drives the economy toward better want satisfaction. The hope for profit exerts its push on the producer to undertake something new that appeals to the consumer and makes the producer rich in the bargain. As soon as he reaches his goal and takes it easy, others imitate him and pull his profits down until they are wiped out.

Competition satisfies several objectives. It prevents profits from continuing after a risk has been reduced by experience, and it permits imitation at a lower price. Competition also causes the introduction of improvements which can produce the same output more cheaply. Profit may help to overcome the risk in making something new, but it is rarely a sufficient incentive to force management into a revision of outdated operating methods. Only the constant pressure of competition will force business to streamline production, reduce costs, modernize its thinking, and maintain this effort even when it is firmly established and no longer looks for new horizons. Competition is an uncomfortable element. It challenges our hard-earned positions to give way to the improvements of the leaders of tomorrow. It is an essential ingredient in the progress of free enterprise.

THE TOOLS OF FREE ENTERPRISE

The forces of consumers' choice, profit, and competition are translated into practical application in the market with the help of two major tools: price and income. Other economic systems may, and sometimes do, use these tools in a manner quite similar to our own. But in a centrally controlled economy their function is restricted, whereas they are essential to the operation of a free enterprise economy. In our system the key questions relating to a purchase are: Can we afford it? Is it worth it? In a planned economy, the chief problem for the buyer consists in obtaining a permit or a ration stamp.

Price

In our economic system, prices are paid for goods and services and for the resources needed to produce them. Prices perform the following four functions:

1. Price is a *yardstick*. People always compare values of different products. However, an individual's idea of value is a matter of personal opinion not likely shared by others. When, after many years of excellent care, we try to trade in the family jalopy for a less ancient vehicle, we become painfully aware of the difference of opinion concerning the value of our precious antique. The function of price takes over at this point. It provides an objective yardstick which indicates the relative desire to buy or sell on the part of everyone trading cars in the used-car market at a given time.

This method creates a basis of fair comparison between products which have nothing in common except a price.

2. Prices help to *determine production techniques.* Should we install oil or gas to heat the furnace in the new house, assuming that both methods are workable? The answer will be provided by a comparison of the prices of these two fuels based on their relative scarcity at the particular time and place. This example shows the beneficial effect of prices at work. But the fuel that is cheap today may not be so next year. As more and more consumers elect the same fuel, their demand may reach the point where the relative scarcity of this product is likely to bid up the prices for the preferred resource. An alert user of fuel will change his production techniques whenever the higher price for the old resource makes it advisable.

3. Prices *establish priority schedules* and help to determine what should come first. Should a firm produce color-TV sets immediately with meager existing facilities or hold back until automatic mass production methods can be constructed and put into operation? To make a few sets largely by hand will be an awkward operation and will result in a high price that only a few will be willing to pay. The majority will impatiently, but thriftily, struggle along with black-and-white sets until an improved assembly line can mass produce the new product and allow the price to drop. This choice between the use of resources for current or future production is determined by the price of the product.

4. Price serves as a *rationing tool.* When eighty people want to buy five sofas, we need a practical method of deciding who the five lucky owners will be. The final decision can be arrived at by various methods. We can sell the merchandise to the first five who walk into the store, or we can give them to five preferred friends. We can charge $320 each for the sofas and discover promptly that half of the potential customers don't care to pay that much. The shortage of sofas is much smaller at the high price. If we decide now to sell the sofas by public auction, we can really observe how prices ration scarce goods to the would-be buyer. The remaining purchasers start to bid on the sofas. As the price rises, one after the other drops out of the bidding until only five buyers are left to pay the auction price for the merchandise.

The rationing function of prices makes it possible to deal simply with the problem of shortage or surplus of goods. A changing price makes sure that the existence of only a few goods for sale does not become a shortage in the market. When a product is sold to the highest bidder, a buyer can always get it if he is willing to pay enough. When the housewife complains about the shortage of orange juice after a crop freeze in Florida, she does not like the higher price which moves the orange juice out of her budget range. By contrast, when there is a surplus of goods at the old price, the seller will have to offer the product for less and less, until enough people are willing to buy it.

To sum up, the main advantages of the pricing mechanism in the economy are the simplicity and efficiency of its operation. It works automatically without the need for human intervention. It requires no rationing board, planning committee, priority advisers, or other red tape. It works speedily, causing needed adjustment as fast as prices fluctuate. The efficiency of this technique is demonstrated by its ability to register millions of separate, individual decisions and coordinate them without a master planning board, bringing order into chaos and permitting resources to flow to where they are most urgently wanted by the individual consumer. To do this complicated job properly, prices must be allowed to remain flexible and to fluctuate freely, ready to signal a need for change whenever it may occur.

Income

Prices influence a man's answer to the question, "Is it worth it?" Income decides the other half of the problem and determines whether he can afford it or not.

Little children discover early the harsh realities of making painful decisions concerning resource allocation. They want to watch two cartoon programs on TV at the same time and realize that "Both" is no answer when mother asks "Which one?" But they also discover that the choice of one or the other is not always the only alternative and that there are cases where both desires can be satisfied. The total command of goods by each individual depends on his income, and the total quantity of all available goods is determined by the national income.

Personal Income.   The amount of income available to the individual decides what kind of economic package he can afford. It tells us little about the total want satisfaction received from his purchases, because his desires invariably increase when he sees what his friends buy. This comparison of personal incomes leads easily to dissatisfaction. The lady's new dress satisfies her wants perfectly until her neighbor comes home with a fur coat. A $50 raise is wonderful when nobody else gets one, but it will be unsatisfactory when others receive a $100 increase. Income from inherited wealth also becomes the subject of envy by those who have to work for a living.

The disparity in the distribution of goods on the basis of income is inherent in our system, with its higher rewards for those who pursue them.

There is strong opposition by some people, however, who protest against a technique which distributes goods only to those who can pay for them instead of assigning products according to need. This philosophy of equal distribution sounds fair and just, but in daily application "need" proves to be a slippery yardstick. During World War II, this country created rationing boards whose task it was to assign civilian goods to the people on the basis of their needs. The administration of these boards was very complicated, and they frequently favored people with eloquent lawyers. The final result did not necessarily reflect fairness in distribution.

Other countries assign priorities for goods on the basis of political loyalty to the ruling party. In some older societies a man's birth decides his rights to goods in life, and such a system leaves little opportunity for the demonstration of personal merit should the parents fail to belong to the upper class. The distribution of worldly goods by the income yardstick lays no claim to perfect justice, but it does constitute an effective tool to move goods to where they are wanted.

National Income.   National income represents the sum of all incomes earned by the entire population. This sum must be identical with the market value of the total output of goods and services produced by the nation's economy.

National income is not money in the bank, but a measure of the performance of the economic system as a whole. It also helps us to realize that incomes earned and the value of goods produced are identical measures by definition. If a book sells for $5, its contribution to the sum of values of goods produced is obviously $5. This amount is received by the seller who in turn pays wages to the printer, royalties to the author, rent to the owner of the plant for leasing his facilities, and interest to the banker who advanced the needed funds for the production. What is left becomes the sellers' own income. This total must be the same $5, its market price.

A properly functioning economic system registers a steadily rising national income. A healthy income trend is usually accompanied by a rising population. In order to feed and clothe more people as well as before, the total output must increase. To better satisfy more people, the value of the output must grow even faster than the population. A fall in the total income is always a sign of trouble in the economy.

In contrast, not every rise in the national income is a sure indication of progress. When all prices rise, the higher income may indicate not more goods for the people but the same amount of goods with bigger price tags.

National income measures the level of output, not the satisfaction given to the consumer. When people are free to buy what they want, a higher level of output is likely to correspond to improved living standards.

But during the regimentation of war, an increase in output will probably be concentrated on war goods which may help the feeling of national security but contribute nothing to the level of living of the people.

ECONOMIC GROWTH

National income is commonly used to measure economic growth, or the absence of it. The concept of economic growth has become very popular but it can easily be misunderstood. Human efforts are divided between two interrelated goals:

1. People want more goods now. This poses a problem of dividing the existing output at any given moment.

2. People want more goods produced in the future so that everyone can receive greater satisfaction later even though his relative share may not increase at all.

The choice between more goods now or later is a difficult one for individuals and nations alike. Present desires seem so urgent that people are usually reluctant to wait for satisfaction in the hope for a better future, particularly when the reward for present sacrifices is far removed.

The growth of an economy is based on present sacrifice. Plants built for future production use up construction materials now and may thereby force postponement of their building plans for new homes. The growth of our economy requires a careful balance between the immediate satisfaction of wants and plans for future satisfaction. Whatever compromise is reached, the full use of available resources is necessary for most effective growth.

A centrally controlled economy can assign a larger share of the national effort to the pursuit of future growth and impose a greater sacrifice on the people than they would accept voluntarily. In fact, growth rates of total output are often larger in dictatorial nations than in democratic countries, but they are not accompanied by a proportionate rise in living standards because the compulsory efforts of the citizens are often misdirected.

Growth is just as important to our own system since we always hope for more and better things tomorrow. In the past, beyond the willingness of individuals to save and wait voluntarily, there has been no attempt to sacrifice present satisfaction. Even without compulsion, the growth of our economy has been a remarkable achievement. Any choice for faster growth at the expense of individual freedom can be made only by the majority in a democratic country. In peacetime this nation has not been willing to sacrifice more consumption for speedier economic growth.

Growth rate comparisons between countries have little meaning. There is no magic rate of growth which every sound economy must achieve. Just as healthy children grow at varying rates until they finally become adults, so do economic systems differ in their rates of development. Economies must not stop growing, since none has ever reached its full potential.

THE HUMAN ELEMENT IN THE ECONOMY

A machine, regardless of how automatic it may be, is no better than the human brain behind it. The description of the tools and techniques of a free enterprise system shows in highly simplified form the functioning of the mechanism itself. People influence this operation and try their best to make it work to their advantage. This human pressure on the economy is exerted on three levels: the individual, the organized group, and the government itself.

Individual Influence

Individuals, families, and household units are a major force in our economy. Their influence is felt in the market where as consumers they vote on future production. As citizens in an election booth, their influence may seem to be remote, but it is actually more significant than one might realize. Many laws passed by our legislators have a tremendous impact on our economic lives. When Congress passes a highway program, the resulting boom in the road-building machinery business will be a direct consequence. Most laws have economic repercussions which favor some people and hurt others. The specific pattern of our economic system reflects the wishes of the people as the lawmakers understand them.

Organized Groups

Organized groups are sometimes called pressure groups or lobbying organizations, and these labels generally indicate our dislike for the way such forces operate. The action of some lobbyists and their organizations certainly cannot be defended, but we must not confuse individual misconduct with the unavoidable fact of group pressure. These forces are at work not because of some sinister scheming, but simply because the common interests of many people will make themselves felt. Their community of interest stems directly from modern industrial organization. We must recognize the existence of these forces, since they are inevitable, and we need to direct their influence to the benefit of the economy.

Who composes these organizations? They vary considerably, and we may find some people or firms engaged in more than one of them. One's status in the struggle for a livelihood may determine membership in a farm organization, labor union, trade association, or professional society. Geographical interests are defended by the local chamber of commerce and are reflected in the votes of representatives in Congress. On specific economic issues, several groups may combine their forces even though they remain otherwise sharply divided. The only thing which the members of a protectionist group have in common is a fear of foreign competitors. Retailers of different products may unite only in a common attack on retail sales taxes.

Influence of Government

The third major force engaged in shaping our economy is government itself. Whether we like it or not, the government occupies a major role in our economy today. The strong interdependence which is so typical of our economy continually creates new functions for a centralized authority. Modern communications and transportation make it possible to influence millions of people at the same time. The repercussions on the entire economy from the actions of a few are more far-reaching than past generations could have imagined. The many ramifications of government influence will make themselves felt throughout this book. Indeed, the position of the government in a free enterprise economy, dedicated to the satisfaction of the will of the people, is so broad that the following chapter is devoted entirely to the examination of this role.

SUMMARY

The free enterprise economy, sometimes called capitalism, is a mixed system in the sense that the government has a substantial influence on all economic matters. In order to maintain the freedom of choice so typical of our system, government must cooperate closely with the forces of private enterprise.

The free enterprise economy does not regard man as a cog in the wheel of progress for the glorification of the omnipotent state; rather, it is a mechanism constructed to serve the philosophy that the satisfaction of the individual and his wants is the objective of society.

Chief characteristics of a free enterprise economy are private ownership, consumers' choice, profit, and competition. The choice of the consumer is expressed by his vote in the marketplace when he buys one product rather than another. This vote has immediate repercussions on the producer, whose decisions are based on the wants of the consumer and who thus depends on his customers for his livelihood.

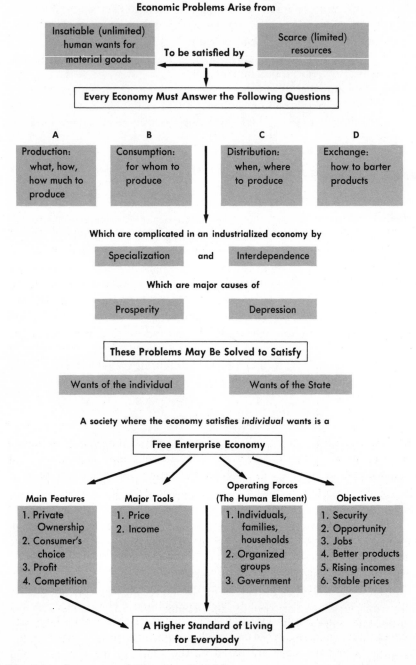

Fɪɢ. 2-1.　Summary of Chapters 1 and 2

Profit is a monetary incentive to encourage risk taking and innovation. It is the chief stimulus used in our economy because of its excellent adaptability to rapidly changing circumstances.

Competition provides economic pressure for continued improvements where the profit motive does not stimulate greater efforts. It prevents the stagnation which might set in when the most successful businessmen have accomplished all they want.

The main tools in the operation of a competitive economy are price and income. They help to channel individual wants toward possible fulfillment by answering the basic questions of all people: Can we afford it? Is it worth it?

As a yardstick, prices measure relative value and determine production techniques; as a rationing tool, they establish priorities for want satisfaction.

Income limits the total satisfaction of wants and forces a choice between alternate desires. It also measures the overall performance of the economy. Although a rise in income is a necessary condition for continuous growth, it is not always a sure sign of progress.

People exert their influence on the economy through individual decisions, organized group interests, and the government itself. The human element appearing in all these forms may not always act in the interest of economic progress, but people are the basic ingredient of society and their actions in the economy need to be studied and taken into consideration. Only through men and for men can we reach the goal of economic growth under conditions of free enterprise. The actual performance of the economy is not as smooth and easy as the broad outline of this chapter may have indicated. What we have seen here is a rather idealized pattern which we must examine in greater detail.

Discussion Questions

1. Why is the American economy considered a *mixed economy?*
2. What are the major features which distinguish a free enterprise economy from other systems?
3. Why is the existence of retail stores no assurance of consumers' choice?
4. Why are profit and competition together essential tools of a free enterprise economy?
5. How does the Russian view of society differ from that prevailing in the United States?
6. Why do economists concern themselves so much with the concept of economic growth?

Suggested Reading

CLARK, JOHN, M., *Alternative to Serfdom*. New York, Knopf, 1948.
————, *Guideposts in Time of Change*. New York, Harper & Row, 1949.

HEILBRONER, ROBERT L., *The Worldly Philosophers,* rev. ed. New York, Simon and Schuster, 1961.

KNIGHT, FRANK H., *The Ethics of Competition.* New York, Augustus M. Kelley, Inc., 1951.

SMITH, ADAM, *The Wealth of Nations.* New York, Random House, Modern Library, Inc., 1937.

3

GOVERNMENT IN THE AMERICAN ECONOMY

In an economic system which considers individual freedom a major objective, the proper role of government has long been a matter of heated controversy. No simple answer like being "for it" or "against it" will do in the complicated involvement of interdependent modern life. The action of public authorities will enter the discussion of virtually every major topic in this book. The present chapter will outline the conflicting approaches toward collective action in a free enterprise system; it will present a frame of reference for the classification of specific governmental actions and sketch very briefly the main areas where government activity has become important.

HOW MUCH INTERVENTION?

This discussion of the role of government presupposes agreement that freedom of enterprise is a worthy goal. Most people of the United States favor individual freedom to the greatest practical degree, and this freedom cannot be maintained in an economic system of governmental regimentation. Most people have to earn a living, and whoever controls their livelihood has a predominant influence on all their thoughts and actions. A man will not dare protest when he knows a public manifestation of disagreement may cause him to lose his job and leave him without opportunity for other employment. The risk of being fired by your firm when you disagree with your boss remains a serious deterrent to individual self-expression. However, this risk is reduced by the knowledge that other firms will want your services. When the government is the largest employer, the possibility of working for others is sharply limited. When all jobs are controlled by the same employer, individual freedom disappears entirely. Private business faces similar restraints when the government becomes the largest customer and can dictate a firm's basic policies.

The Case for Less Intervention

The restraint to individual freedom which is a by-product of public enterprise has led some people to a violent reaction against all government activity. They would like to turn back the clock and return to the simple prescription of *The Wealth of Nations,* first published in 1776. Adam Smith, the grandfather of modern economics, made some statements in this book which guided policy makers for many generations.

He observed that a working price system kept markets functioning automatically, prevented chaos in spite of millions of unrelated individual decisions, and reduced surpluses and shortages faster than any government action could accomplish. He realized that the economy did not always operate quite as smoothly as his theory pictured it, but he felt that on the whole it would be wise to leave well enough alone. Such an extreme view of *laissez-faire* limits the government to the minimum task of providing protection against bodily harm to its citizens at home or abroad. As Smith told us, every individual "neither intends to promote the public interest, nor knows how much he is promoting it. . . . He intends . . . only his own gain, and he is in this led by an *invisible hand* to promote an end which was no part of his intention. . . . By pursuing his own interest he frequently promotes that of society more effectively than when he really intends to promote it. . . ." [1]

This famous comment, which concerns the action of the invisible hand that guides the economy toward a natural order, accurately expressed the philosophy of the time. Smith realized that an economic system was an intricate instrument and that it was dangerous to tamper with its mechanism; natural law was likely to show better results than could be achieved by people who failed to understand how the economy operated.

Considering the absence of economic knowledge 200 years ago, Smith's advice was sound for his period. In the meantime, we have increased our knowledge in many areas. Hybrid corn and grapefruit are two products which illustrate how we have improved on nature. We have also increased our economic understanding and have learned to create far greater wealth than an economic system can produce when left to itself. An economic mechanism serves its own ends; it does not change from an established pattern, and if it grows at all, it grows slowly.

The Case for More Intervention

A government which takes no action is far from neutral; a hands-off attitude in a competitive fight favors the strong competitors against the weak

[1] Adam Smith, *The Wealth of Nations* (New York, Random House, Modern Library, Inc., 1937), p. 423.

ones, the "ins" against the "outs," the rich against the poor. The result of such a stand will not usually satisfy the economic goals of the majority. Noninterference can be a powerful action; a man who stands idly by and watches a twelve-year-old boy beat up a six-year-old decides the outcome of the fight just as surely as if he had hit the younger child himself. In the same way, we must use our acquired economic skill and adapt it to promote our goals.

Some economists feel that public action has lagged behind the rise in private want satisfaction. They point to the increasing number of motorboats and compare this spectacle with the overcrowded and undermanned conditions of many school systems.

Acceptance of the need for collective action may lead the unwary to the opposite extreme. They may conclude that, given some broad goals of society, the economy must select the most efficient technique for accomplishing these goals and disregard other considerations as irrelevant. Such a philosophy would assign to the government a virtually limitless range of tasks. Many people could improve their financial well-being and at the same time raise the level of performance of the economy if they were more efficient or just not so lazy. Should it really be the job of public authority to force the citizen, presumably for his own good, to do more than he wants to do?

A realistic approach to the role of government forces us to accept a compromise between several conflicting goals. In the pursuit of freedom, public authority needs to be kept to a minimum, and liberty is worth the sacrifice of topmost efficiency. However, the freedom of the individual is not the only goal of our society. It must accept restrictions in order to reduce poverty and promote stable economic growth, which alone can render the individual rich—and free!

The justification for collective action which underlies the compromise between economic freedom and restraint can be expressed most simply: we want incomes to rise while prices remain stable so that we can all buy more for our money. Unfortunately, incomes and prices have a tendency to move up and down together in response to the *invisible hand,* and it takes public action to prevent this from happening.

THE GROWTH OF GOVERNMENT IN THE ECONOMY

Regardless of our personal preference, the economic impact of government today in the United States is very large. About one out of every five dollars earned in the United States is collected and spent by the federal government. If we add together the revenue raised by all levels of government (federal, state, and local), the portion of the nation's income controlled by government exceeds one out of every four dollars earned.

This fact is well worth remembering in any discussion of governmental influence. The involvement of public agencies in the economy has become so great that for reasons of practicality it cannot be eliminated. Our only choice is in influencing the trend toward more, or less, collective action. The federal government is today both the biggest employer and the largest customer in the free world. Every step it takes carries a powerful economic wallop. When someone in Washington decides to switch to a new missile instead of a manned airplane, the change in defense contracts creates a boom in the community where the missile will be built and an economic crisis in the town where the airplane contract has been cancelled. The lucky owner of stock in the missile firm is many dollars richer overnight, while the shareholder of the airplane company loses. Many private firms have come to depend on the government, and any sudden change from the existing arrangement would do a great deal of harm.

The upward trend of government involvement is clearly shown in Table 3-1. The amount of money collected by all types of government has risen faster than the number of people and now totals over $1,000 for every person in this country. World Wars I and II sharply increased the share of government action in spite of rising incomes, and the Great Depression did the same simply because bad times did not reduce public functions in the same ratio as private income dropped. For the last twenty years the rise in government activities has matched the growth of the nation's income.

TABLE 3-1.   The Growth of Government in the U.S. Economy

Year	U.S. Population (*millions*) (1)	Total Income (GNP) (*billions*) (2)	Total Gov't. Revenue— U.S., State, Local (*billions*) (3)	Gov't. Share of Total Income (3)/(2) = (4)	Gov't. Revenue per Capita (3)/(1) = (5)
1902	79.2	$ 24.2	$ 1.7	7.02%	$ 21.46
1913	97.2	40.3	3.0	7.44	30.86
1922	110.0	74.0	9.3	12.57	84.55
1927	119.0	96.3	12.2	12.67	102.52
1932	124.9	58.5	10.3	17.61	82.47
1938	130.0	85.2	17.5	20.54	134.62
1946	141.4	210.7	61.5	29.19	434.94
1952	157.0	347.0	100.2	28.88	638.22
1956	168.2	419.2	119.7	28.55	711.65
1960	180.7	505.0	153.1	30.3	847.26
1964	192.1	631.7	192.4	30.5	1,001.56
1966	196.8	739.6	225.6	30.5	1,146.34

SOURCES: U.S. Bureau of the Census, *Historical Statistics of the United States.*
U.S. Dept. of Commerce, *Survey of Current Business.*
U.S. Bureau of the Census, *Governmental Finances in 1965–1966.*

Why has the economic function of government grown so much? The increase in population combined with the farm-to-city movement and changes in technology share the main responsibility for the trend toward more public action. This gradual increase of government involvement receives an additional boost in times of war when the role of the federal government becomes much larger than usual. When the war is over the share of the government in the economy usually drops again, but it never returns to the lower level that prevailed before the war.

A growing population needs regulation to prevent one man's attempt to earn a living from interfering unduly with the same desire of his neighbor. As the country becomes more crowded with ever-larger numbers of people, it develops the characteristics of an anthill—requiring even more regulations and controls.

The steady movement from the old country homestead with its self-reliant family to the dependence of city life also contributes to a demand for increased public service. Not only does urbanization demand more roads and commuter trains, but the city worker also needs financial protection in his old age, since he can no longer live off the farm.

Technological innovation is equally responsible for the rise in government action. The automobile, for example, requires an efficient interstate highway system for its best use. The limited number of airwaves makes public allocation of channels inevitable if we want to avoid the confusion of competing sounds on the radio or TV set. Then, too, mass production on a giant scale causes giant-sized problems which no single individual can solve. When a village shop with only a few workers suffers a lull in business, an unneeded man may find something useful to do if he makes a little effort to adjust; but when the automobile industry experiences a bad model year, we have a national unemployment crisis on our hands.

Life has become so dependent on certain technical services that we cannot function if they are interrupted. The supply of electric power must be continuous because a candle is no longer an adequate substitute, and without it the food in the refrigerator and the freezer will spoil in a few hours. The patients in a hospital also depend on electrical appliances for their care. It is the function of government to make sure that such services remain available at all times.

OBJECTIVES OF GOVERNMENT ACTIVITY

The reader may begin to wonder how he can practically apply the philosophy of public support in a free enterprise economy. He may be approached for the support of better public schools, lighted streets, foreign aid, or a higher sales tax. What yardstick can he use to make a logical decision?

Some goods are social goods. This implies that such goods and services as a city police force are generally considered essential for our society and would not exist unless provided by the government. Other goods largely benefit the individual but have a *spillover effect*. This term signifies that there is additional benefit to the community in a way which cannot be precisely determined in dollars and cents. For example, if we provide for public inoculation against cholera, the protection is not limited to the person who is immunized, but extends to all citizens with whom he comes into contact.

Let us divide government activity into five categories. The first two comprise social goods; the third group largely covers goods with a social spillover effect; and the last two categories constitute a more interventionist policy, which may have beneficial results desired by many but which is often criticized as unnecessary public activity.

Government in Defense of the People

The government may limit itself to activities essential to all social organization. Such functions have been assigned to public authority because no individual can exercise them alone. The best example of this is the defense against internal and external enemies. Indeed, most traditional tasks of government belong in this category. They have not changed in nature, only in costs.

Defense.   The most expensive function exclusively assigned to the government is the defense of the country against its enemies at home and abroad. The rising cost of modern weapons, and their continuous replacement by more efficient means of annihilation, accounts for about half of the cost of the federal government. While the number of dollars needed may be open to discussion, few people will argue for a weakening of the national defense.

Justice.   The administration of justice is also a traditional task of government. Its influence on the economy rises as court decisions shape the pattern of business behavior. The use of private economic power frequently becomes the subject of court verdicts, and judicial interpretations of the law have far-reaching consequences on the nature of business transactions.

Collection of Revenue.   The tax collector is a traditional figure in governmental action. Funds to cover public services must be raised, and as these services increase in number and size, the task of collecting the needed revenue becomes more important and influences economic decisions to a greater degree.

Public Action in Support of Private Initiative

The give-and-take of economic life often requires clear-cut rules of the game which individuals cannot formulate or enforce without the backing of public authority. This is a case where collective action enhances individual rights and makes it possible for the citizen to use his property most advantageously.

The city fathers approve a master plan showing the location of streets, schools, hospitals, and other facilities. They pass a zoning ordinance designating the type of buildings which will be permitted in each part of town. Without such an overall plan, private initiative might be stymied. A man will hestitate to build his home on a particular site until he knows that a road will connect his property with the city streets, and also what kind of neighbors he can expect to have. He certainly would be shocked to discover one day that his expensive dream house was located right across from the city dump.

Some permissive rules are also required on the national scene. Television manufacturers will hesitate to mass produce receiving sets until they know what type of transmission process will be licensed for broadcasting on the airwaves. Standard rules of flying safety must be national in scope before airplane manufacturers can deliver a generally acceptable product. Regional flood control projects release vast areas of land for productive use.

The first two classifications deal with the type of public action that is not likely to arouse many arguments on the basis of principle, even though few projects will stir more controversy in a community than the relocation of a highway. The following categories include projects which often lead to the opposition of noninterventionists.

Public Support of Nonprofit Projects

Arguments concerning the use of public funds for nonprofit projects go back to the early days of the country. The construction of public roads for the free use of all citizens was the cause of a prolonged national debate in the nineteenth century. Railroad construction in earlier days was considered a nonprofit venture unless it received a federal subsidy. Airport construction is still supported by public funds.

The principle of free public schools has always been defended as fundamental in providing the equal opportunity to which every young American is entitled.

The real difficulty with projects in this category is twofold:

1. Many nonprofit services could be undertaken at a profit; however, a large number of the users would not be able or willing to sacrifice a

sufficient share of their income to buy these services. This is particularly true in the area of education. Public action makes sure that the child becomes exposed to the learning process regardless of his parents' circumstances or wishes.

Public health services are in the same category but present a much more controversial problem. Should every citizen be entitled to the best care modern medicine can provide, without concern for his financial position, or should he pay for its cost? The existence of Veterans Administration hospitals, Medicare, and free immunizations for children indicates that the people want to classify certain health services in the same category with education. These examples show that Congress has legislated some preventive medicine for all and full health services for some.

2. Other nonprofit services may be considered desirable but too expensive for what they are worth to the majority. Dam-construction projects are very popular in their region, but few people really know how much tax money they absorb. We have noted already that all goods are scarce and thus necessitate choices. Do we prefer to spend the larger share of our income individually or collectively? Whenever the decision favors collective spending, we are implicitly voting for higher taxes, since the new project has to be financed. There is no such thing as a free lunch!

Public Projects for Greater Efficiency

Some people favor public services over private activity whenever the public operation can be more efficient. Public power projects are the most widely known examples in this category. The case for this type of collective activity argues that the systematic use of the country's water resources and the most efficient development of a distribution system can be assured only by broad public planning and management. The opposite viewpoint challenges not only the presumed facts of greater government efficiency, but the principle of maximum efficiency itself. More individual freedom may be worth some loss of efficiency within the limits of reasonable compromise.

Central Planning and State Control

Projects in this last category are often incompatible with the normal operation of a free enterprise economy. They are introduced and conducted only where defense requirements have dictated special procedures, such as in the field of atomic energy.

Occasionally these procedures become part of a traditional pattern even though they can no longer be justified under the principles which rule our economy. The U.S. Post Office started as a centrally managed operation when the mail was needed to open up the country and promote the spread of literacy with the subsidized distribution of the written word. The original purpose has long been accomplished, but the federal post office continues as an example of an interventionist economy.

Whenever some new government service is suggested, it may be well worth pondering into which one of these five classifications the project will fit best before making up one's mind for or against it.

MAIN AREAS OF GOVERNMENT ACTION

Let us now glance briefly at the tasks which are most prominently assigned to the government today. A more detailed discussion of each of them will be found in later chapters.

Maintenance of Competition

Competition has been featured as a major characteristic of our economic system. The interests of competing firms will often render it advantageous to reduce competition among them by agreements, particularly where modern technology makes it possible to produce more goods than can be sold at a profit.

The government assumes the task of defending the individual against actions intended to eliminate competition. Congress has passed legislation for this purpose since 1890. Many laws have modified competitive patterns since that time, but the principle of maintaining competition with government assistance has been firmly established.

Federal action in this area may use various techniques. It may prohibit specific types of business action considered harmful to the competitive principle—price discrimination, for example. It may directly support small firms in fields where a few large concerns occupy a dominant position. Giving credit to the smaller firms at favorable terms or assigning defense orders to them in preference to bigger competitors are examples of these efforts.

Regulation of Monopoly

Monopoly practices are inevitable in many phases of a modern economy, in spite of a strong desire to maintain competition. Such a monopoly arises when only one firm furnishes a product or service—such as the maintenance of local waterworks—on which the general public depends.

If the business of the company holding the monopoly can be handled by several competitors, the task of the government lies clearly in the promotion of competition, as we have seen before. In several fields it is not practical to permit the operation of more than one firm: a duplication of power lines or water pipes would be wasteful and render the service needlessly expensive. Two telephone companies in one town would reduce the value of a telephone to the subscriber, since he could not reach his friends who used the services of the competing firm. The natural limitation of television channels makes it inevitable that each licensee exercises some control in his area.

Where business activities are allowed to remain monopolistic, collective action is necessary to avoid abuse of this power. The exercise of monopoly control can take two forms: (1) The government can take over the business and manage it. (2) The government can leave the business in private hands but reserve the right to approve major policy changes, such as higher rates to consumers or the abandoning of a service. The relative merits of the two approaches are a matter of considerable discussion, and strong arguments are made on both sides. It should be clearly understood that no collective action, regardless of its form, can abolish the characteristics of monopoly which are inherent in the nature of the service.

Government-Operated Business. The case for direct public ownership and management of monopolies rests on the philosophy that the citizen should never be forced to depend on a private firm for essential services. He has no influence on the operation of a private business; only a public official will pay sufficient attention to the people's desires. Examples of public businesses are numerous. The Tennessee Valley Authority is such a government operation, and one which is frequently praised or vilified for its actions.

The foes of public ownership base their opposition on the claim that actual government management of a business is inefficient and usually hampered by political interference. They would limit direct administration to activities which, for security reasons, cannot be conducted in any other manner.

Economists are inclined to favor the most efficient process, even for a monopoly business. As we shall see later, monopolies easily become inefficient, and no clear case can be made for the greater effectiveness of either private or public management of them.

Government-Regulated Business. The prevailing form of public control over monopolies leaves the business in private hands for day-to-day management, but reserves approval of major decisions to supervisory agencies. These administrative agencies appear on all levels of government and are no longer limited entirely to monopolistic aspects. The Interstate Commerce Commission is the oldest federal agency. It was created in 1887 for the purpose of regulating the use of monopoly power exercised by the railroads in the field of transportation before the advent of automobiles and airplanes.

The restrictions on firms under public control involve many aspects of their business. In the first place, to engage in regulated enterprise requires a license by the government agency in charge. This license is frequently a most valuable asset; the agencies have broad discretionary powers in granting permission to do business. Violation of rules may lead to a loss of the license. The type and price of services offered are also subject to public control. The regulatory agency is frequently under attack from many sides, but its political durability usually outlasts all objections.

Minimum Standards of Economic Security

The protection of the citizen against becoming destitute is a more recent function of government, at least on the large scale practiced at the present time. As long as this country was predominantly rural, private charity took care of the occasional cases where men were unable to survive otherwise.

Traditionally, the family has assumed the responsibility of providing a livelihood for those without means of support. The employer of a few people in a small shop would not lay off his men as readily as would occur in a modern assembly line. The slaveowner in the Old South did not turn out his people in winter to collect unemployment insurance.

Modern technology has transformed the pattern of rural living. An efficiency apartment is too small to add parents, aunts and uncles, and other relatives to the household. Even the three-bedroom homes in the suburbs aren't large enough for Grandpa or Aunt Mathilda. In addition, by lengthening the life span medical science has increased the relative number of old people in our society.

All these changes have brought about a strong demand for collective action, and Congress has passed a number of laws in the field of social security. A special department of the federal government directs these activities, which center on providing protection against loss of income due to old age, accidents on the job, and during periods of unemployment. Widows and children receive some support in the case of the death of the family breadwinner. The worker is also protected on the job by laws that specify certain requirements for working conditions, such as minimum wages, minimum age, or maximum hours.

Issue and Control of Money

We have already mentioned the importance of a smoothly operating exchange mechanism for the proper functioning of our economy. The monetary crises of the past indicated a need for improvement, and this led to the creation in 1913 of a central bank with the exclusive right to issue money. The Federal Reserve System integrates the private commercial banks of the United States so that the needed money and credit flow readily to every remote village in the nation.

The right amount of credit influences the sale of goods, the decision to expand a business, and in general the level of economic activity of the entire country. Central control of this flow can help to keep business on an even keel, or it can do much harm. When public authority indulges in an excessive issue of money, the value of each dollar is reduced. On the other hand, the opposite policy may cause a shortage of money and credit, hamper the growth of the economy, and even develop a chain reaction of failures that depress the level of output.

Money and credit must reach the right places at the right time and in the right amount to permit the stable growth of our economy. This circulation can be compared to the blood stream of the human body, whose continuous pulsating allows all the organs to function properly. The government here behaves like a doctor who hopes to keep his patient's blood pressure at the desired level; and just like any doctor, it may err at times in its diagnosis and permit too much or not enough money to circulate.

Fiscal Policy

The management of government income and expenditures for the purpose of influencing the level of national income is called fiscal policy.[2] Its main objective is stable economic growth under conditions of full employment. Fiscal and monetary policies are closely linked because both aim at the same goal—to avoid the boom-bust cycle of the past. While no one individual or single firm has much influence on the total well-being of the country, the wide economic power of the government makes it possible to take appropriate action.

The effect of fiscal policy is not always so beneficial as it should be, since its efforts are often diffuse and contradictory. The President exercises general direction with the assistance of the Council of Economic Advisers. The Treasury Department pays the government bills and has the power of decision concerning the promptness of these payments. The Bureau of the Budget exercises some control over expenditures by timing the specific projects that require its approval. The power of the purse string, however, rests ultimately with Congress itself, though all too often decisions are delegated directly to numerous agencies, which may even embark on conflicting policies.

[2] *Fiscus* is a Latin term meaning the national treasury. Today the concept includes a wide range of economic measures directed by the federal government.

In order to stabilize the level of economic activity, a policy is needed which will keep the flow of production as high as the natural scarcity of resources will permit. When the nation's resources are fully employed, fiscal policy must decide the relative priority of private or public projects. It may postpone some public activities or cause the delay of private ventures since both compete for the same scarce goods. During a slump in business, federal policy can rush new programs into action, or it may prefer to stimulate and rekindle private initiative. Fiscal policy pursues its objectives with several different techniques, which are quite often used together:

1. Expenditure levels may be raised or lowered, mostly through the timing of orders which can be delayed or accelerated.

2. The methods of raising funds for meeting obligations may vary between tax collections and bond sales, with significant repercussions on economic activity.

3. Private business may be stimulated into greater activity with public loans and by insurance covering various financial risks. This last method is occasionally overlooked even though it fluctuates as sharply as direct revenues and expenditures.[3]

Bad times have been to former generations something like the bubonic plague was to the Dark Ages. The disaster came and went, leaving havoc in its wake. We have conquered the plague, and we have, as well, learned a great deal about the management of our economy in order to prevent another bad depression. In the thirties even the most rugged individualist discovered that we are all in the same boat. The shrewdest businessman cannot prosper when his customers lose their jobs and the economy ceases to function properly. The task of fiscal policy is to prevent similar disasters in the future.

LIMITS TO GOVERNMENT ACTION

This list of government functions in our economy does not pretend to be complete; but it has already become so long that the reader may wonder, Where is the limit? If a free enterprise system needs such a vast contribution from public authority to function properly, is there any difference between our economy and a socialistic state? The question is well worth asking.

Many government functions result directly from the demands of modern technology, and similar methods of centralized action become necessary in every industrialized country. The difference between the socialistic

[3] See Raymond J. Saulnier *et al.*, *Federal Lending and Loan Insurance*, National Bureau of Economic Research publication (Princeton, Princeton University Press, 1958).

and the free enterprise approach to collective action is one of degree. The socialist state favors governmental operation and control except where private action is the only workable method. Free enterprise, on the other hand, favors public action *only* where private business could not be effective.

In practice we have not always been consistent. Occasionally, historical accident may decide if some needed function should become a private or a federal project. New housing near an enlarged army camp represents an urgent need. Whether these facilities spring up through the efforts of private builders or as a military undertaking will depend largely on the relative demonstration of initiative by local contractors or by the officers in charge of the camp.

Federal action is constantly subject to two conflicting types of pressure: citizens who want more service, preferably at no cost to themselves, and those who protest further encroachments from a tax-collecting authority. Too few people evaluate public projects as soberly as they do their own, and they often fail to compare total benefits with total costs in order to separate the desirable from the less justifiable projects.

SUMMARY

The role of government in the American economy has many facets. It can be summarized as the task of supporting a growing standard of living for the whole population in an environment of individual freedom.

The increasing complexity of a modern economy requires more services by government authorities. One fourth of the economic activity of the nation is channeled today through many forms of government departments and agencies. This rise follows a trend of long standing and recognition that a modern society combines private initiative with public functions.

The growth of our cities and industrial regions is the result of the steadily increasing numbers of people who have to struggle for a living in a limited space. Their closeness requires more regulation. Technological innovations make it necessary to create new rules in many fields which were formerly of no economic significance.

Government's traditional role in the areas of defense, justice, and the collection of revenue reaches new importance as the dimensions of these functions increase in response to the demands of the missile age.

Private action begins in many cases only after the government sets the rules which permit the citizen to operate. Zoning ordinances and transportation patterns are examples of this rule-making function.

The government must see to it that sufficient competition in business is preserved so that the benefits of the free market can continue to improve the position of the consumer.

Technology dictates in some cases the use of monopoly operations. The government has to make sure that these monopoly positions benefit the economy and not lead to the abuse of this privilege. The desired result can be obtained either through public management or through regulation, depending on the circumstances of each case.

The fierce struggle for economic growth heightens the individual's feeling of economic insecurity. The government needs to provide a floor which relaxes destructive fears and provides a minimum insurance of survival to those who are not able to take care of their own livelihood.

The high degree of specialization of our economy depends on a smoothly operating exchange system. A centrally controlled monetary system can form the basis for a well integrated economy; the government provides this through the Federal Reserve System.

The fiscal policy of the federal government actively promotes the growth of the economy, which is necessary to absorb the increasing number of people who join the working force every year. The maintenance of full employment is a primary task of this policy function.

The market mechanism has shown sufficient flexibility to maintain a high level of prosperity since World War II. Private decisions covering three-fourths of the nation's business in conjunction with public support have achieved the continued growth of real income. More collective action to improve on this performance may sometimes be indicated in the interest of the general welfare. We must, however, remain alert to the fact that a continued trend toward enlargement of the government sector brings with it the two-pronged danger of too little freedom and no enterprise. The proper balance between the two sectors is always changing and must be redefined by each generation.

Discussion Questions

1. How can we evaluate the proper function of government in the American economy?
2. Why has the role of government grown so much during the past half century?
3. Discuss the specific reasons for action in each of the main areas of federal activity.
4. Why are some people afraid of any additional government services?
5. Under what circumstances would you be in favor of a federal project of residential construction?
6. Discuss the case of private versus public power plants.

Suggested Reading

FRIEDMAN, MILTON, *Capitalism and Freedom.* Chicago, University of Chicago Press, 1962.
GALBRAITH, JOHN KENNETH, *The Affluent Society.* Boston, Houghton Mifflin, 1958.

SAULNIER, RAYMOND J., *et al.*, *Federal Lending and Loan Insurance,* National Bureau of Economic Research publication. Princeton, N.J., Princeton, 1958.
WALLICH, HENRY C., *The Cost of Freedom.* New York, Harper & Row, 1960.

PART II

PRICES AND THEIR APPLICATION

The broad view of the objectives and the main features of our economic system which were covered in the introductory chapters will be followed now by more specific explanations. This part of the discussion concerns the principles underlying individual action and the tools used in the process. The behavior of the family, the basic unit for economic activity, and of the individual firm in pursuit of business occupies the center of our attention. Prices are the major tool which regulate their action. Economists call this sector of their discipline the study of microeconomics, a concept derived from the Greek word describing "small" units. Microeconomics is the subject of Part II, in contrast with macroeconomics, the study of overall economic performance, which we shall encounter in Part III of this book.

Chapter 4 will introduce and classify productive factors whose skillful combination helps us to overcome the law of scarcity. Chapter 5 presents a brief sketch of the way American business is carried on. Chapter 6 introduces the principles of pricing. Chapter 7 studies the impact of competition, while Chapter 8 focuses on the problems created by monopolies. In Chapter 9 the need for security of the individual will be discussed. Chapter 10 considers wages and workers, and Chapter 11 deals with the problems of the farmer. Chapter 12 ends this discussion by showing what individuals as consumers do with their earnings.

4

PRODUCTION

Scarcity is the reason behind the need to economize. Goods are scarce, raw materials are scarce, human skills are scarce, and time itself is scarce since we are not willing to wait forever to see our dreams come true. This lack of resources is frequently invoked to excuse the economic backwardness of a town or a region. Of course, it is easier to develop a wealthy city when it happens to be near an oilfield. Let us not, however, blame nature for all our troubles. Resources in the ground have not much economic significance until man develops them for his use. Countries with an abundance of valuable resources have at times shown only slight economic growth, while others without similar natural wealth have prospered to an impressive degree.

A bewildering array of factors enters into calculations of growth, and it is up to the people themselves to make the most of each situation. The best machine cannot be built without the right materials, and it won't work unless operated with the proper skills. The right piece of equipment correctly handled can greatly speed up the flow of materials to help reduce the scarcity of goods. Whatever action we take, the problem of choice confronts us. A given amount of steel can produce automobiles or can openers. The relative scarcity of all resources going into the productive process determines what will be produced and how we shall go about it.

The most efficient combination of factors may not automatically cause the most satisfaction of human wants. More and better products pouring from our factories without interruption are fundamental ingredients for better satisfaction, but goods not wanted by the consumer are a wasted effort.

FACTORS OF PRODUCTION

Many decisions are necessary in the creation of even the simplest product. A manufacturer needs a place where he can operate. He must give some thought to the kind of building he wants, its size, location, accessibility, railroad connections, and so forth. He makes many choices in the construction of the building, the selection of the equipment, the hiring of workers, the materials used, and the details of the finished product. The number of factors entering his deliberations seems endless.

To bring some order into this chaos, we group all factors of production into three categories and call them land, labor, and capital. This classification follows an old tradition, but the terms themselves do not give us a broad enough understanding of what is included in them. Most goods contain elements of all three categories, but each one of them has specific characteristics which deserve our attention.

Land

The term *land* not only stands for the good earth we till, but includes all the raw-material resources in their natural state. The coal in the ground, the trees in the forest, the uranium in the rock, and the water in the stream are all resources provided by nature and covered by the term *land* in its broadest sense. One objection to this classification points out that nature alone does not produce many things which satisfy human wants. Natural resources become productive agents only when they are transformed by man's effort. Coal in the ground is useless until it is brought to the surface and shipped to a destination where it will provide needed heat. Once it reaches a steel mill many hundreds of miles away, the coal is no longer a free factor given by the earth itself—the application of human effort is necessary to extract it from the earth and transport it to where it can be more useful.

Nature's contribution to the productive process has some distinctive features of special importance to the economy. Natural resources are limited both in their absolute amount and in their location, and the production process must seek to adjust itself to these accidents of nature. In some areas people have become prosperous because their land was more fertile, or because they discovered a gold mine or an oil field. The distribution of natural resources appears to be a matter of sheer luck. Although this does have some bearing on the economy of a given area, let us remember that other factors of production are quite as important for the final result as the gifts of the earth. There is oil to be found in Venezuela and in Brazil. In Venezuela it has been pumped out for years and has raised the living standard of the population; in Brazil the oil is still in the ground. Nature's gifts alone may give us an opportunity, but people's action determines the final economic result.

Labor

Labor is a very broad term which includes every kind of human effort exerted in the production process. The brawn of the ditch digger and the brain of the mathematician, the work of the youngest apprentice and of the president of the company are all classified under the concept of labor.

A Dual Role. We may think of labor as exercising a dual role because people are both producers and consumers of goods, sometimes even of the same goods. When Mr. Jones works in a factory which produces cereal, the factory manager looks at him as an expense item and determines his value to the operation strictly from the viewpoint of production costs; if another worker or a machine can produce equally well for less money, Mr. Jones is out of a job. In this case, we look at the worker in the same way as we do an oil well or a herd of cattle. However, when Mr. Jones stops on his way home from work and buys cereal in a grocery store, he becomes a consumer, an individual whose satisfaction remains the prime concern of the economic system.

Labor as a *cost of production* should be kept low, but labor as a *source of income* must be as high as possible to increase the satisfaction of the worker. In this respect labor differs from all other resource factors. We do not worry about the satisfaction enjoyed by an oil well when we try to get the most out of it. But in a discussion of human effort, the determination to get more output is always modified by the realization that the objective of an economy is not goods, but happy people. Wants are satisfied sometimes by products, but quite frequently by taking it easy.

Work or Leisure. On the want list of humanity, the desire not to overwork oneself looms large. Efforts to provide food and shelter have priority for most people; beyond these elementary needs there is a choice. To some men the accumulation of riches is all important, but others may feel that a fishing trip is worth a considerable loss of output.

The economic development of the past 100 years shows clearly how this principle has operated. The industrial progress of America has been matched by an equally astounding improvement in working conditions. The length of the workweek has dropped gradually from over seventy-two hours to about forty hours. Will it drop further? How many hours do people like to work? Only trial and error in the future can give a conclusive answer to this question.

Recent trends seem to indicate that wants may be satisfied better by improved conditions than by further reduction of working hours. An air-conditioned shop, soft music to soothe the nerves, or the more common practice of a coffee break are examples of this theory. In a modern firm these niceties may improve actual performance, as people work more effectively in pleasant surroundings. The reason for these expensive improvements is, at least in part, a desire to satisfy the employees in order to attract and keep as good a crew as possible.

Physical Versus Mental Labor. Human effort directed toward making a living can be either physical or mental. Physical labor is needed to trans-

form nature's offerings into usable products. The man who digs the ditch,
swings the hammer, or tightens the bolt on the assembly line is engaged in
physical labor. The toils of a lawyer or a corporation executive are mental
labor. Of course, every kind of activity requires some mixture of these two
types of effort. The arm of the assembly-line worker is controlled by his
mind, and if he lets his thoughts wander he is likely to have an accident. But
the thought process in this case is rather subordinate. A corporation president incurs considerable physical exertion dashing from town to town to appear at meetings, dictating a stream of communications, shaking hands
with countless visitors, and so on. The mental effort of his job is the controlling part of his position. Since both types of exertion often become
necessary, the two categories blend into each other.

Capital

The word *capital* has many meanings. To most people, it is simply a certain
amount of money; to an accountant, it may represent the value of the shares
of a firm. In an economic discussion of productive factors, capital means
the fruits of past productive efforts which have become available to help
future production.

You may own a tract of land in a boom town ideally situated for the
erection of new homes. Unless you can get construction equipment, such
as excavating machines and concrete mixers, your houses will not be ready
when they are needed. Fortunately, this equipment is available and the
houses can be started without delay. The availability of resources, which
have previously been combined into usable tools, is the essential ingredient
of capital. But we must not overlook the essential element of proper timing,
which is an important part of the production process.

Capital is the most elusive concept in our classification of productive
factors. A highly simplified example may help to clarify its meaning. Let us
assume that a man is stranded on an island where he is the only human
being alive. He exists by eating coconuts which he gathers and opens with
his bare hands. Working seven hours a day, he collects enough to stay alive,
but no more. Obviously, even a crude tool forged from stone would greatly
simplify his job. If it takes him a day to shape such a tool, he must work
an extra hour every day for a week and store the daily coconut surplus to
accumulate some food for the day when he will be busy making a tool. He
gives up an hour of his leisure time and refrains from eating the extra food
collected in the last hour in order to be able to produce his tool. The food
accumulated by his special effort is his capital, and the tool produced with
its help is a capital good.

Capital Goods.   Capital goods are such things as factories, machines, office
buildings, tools, and similar products which do not by themselves satisfy the

wants of the consumers. These goods result from spending time productively in the creation of useful items and refraining from their immediate consumption. This abstinence makes it possible to dedicate the time saved to the creation of new tools. The help provided by these new tools permits a sharp increase in production with no additional effort. The expectation of this happy result is the reason why a man is willing to sacrifice and refrain from immediate consumption.

Time and Capital. We must not confuse time itself with capital. If a man spends a free Saturday afternoon nailing together pieces of wood and building a ladder needed for his job, he is creating a capital good. But if he spends the same time in front of a television screen watching a ball game, he may enjoy himself, but he is not creating anything economic.

Sacrifice of Present Consumption. The sacrifice involved in abstaining from consumption to produce capital goods is harder to see in a modern economy than in a primitive system, but it is just as real. Every step of a production process builds on the results of past efforts. The factory which will house a new assembly line was constructed years ago. The machines were built by other people at some earlier time. Groundwork for the present effort has always been laid before; nobody starts from scratch. If a man can buy newer and better machines, and if he adds more trucks and cars to his operations, he is acquiring definite advantages for the production process. This *fund of goods accumulated by past effort,* which is used and renewed continuously, is the essence of what we mean by capital.

Accumulation of Capital Goods. Capital as a productive factor is as important as land and labor. Human effort, combined with natural resources, provides us with a hand-to-mouth existence as long as we consume everything produced. The idea of economic growth rests on the creation of an environment which permits the accumulation of capital goods. An economy can grow only when it produces more than it consumes at the same time. The reason we might forego present consumption is the hope of receiving more and better goods later on. In substance, economic growth is supported by the accumulation of capital goods, which makes possible a better combination of land and labor over a period of time.

The real significance of capital becomes clear when we think about why people in the United States have so much more material goods than do people in the rest of the world. We may be inclined to feel that we are smarter (or maybe just luckier) than others, but the evidence does not seem to confirm such a happy notion. The American worker produces a larger output than his foreign counterpart because of the expensive tools available to him. With the help of these capital goods, even a modest effort creates a stream of consumer products which represent our high standard of living.

A workman abroad must use physical effort, whereas the American worker avails himself of mechanical equipment to do the same task better and faster. The American worker uses on the average over $12,000 worth of capital equipment, while most other countries do not approach even half this figure at present.

Obstacles to the Creation of Capital.   Many obstacles are encountered in the creation and accumulation of capital goods. The poor cannot afford to save, but they are the people who most need capital to overcome their poverty. Once they acquire capital goods, which make them productive enough to enjoy a high living standard, they can afford to sacrifice some consumption and thus create more capital for the future. The ancient saying is still valid: "To him who has will more be given . . . but from him who has not, even what he has will be taken away." [1]

How do we break into this vicious circle and accumulate initial capital? The problem of mobilizing sufficient capital plagues many countries. The United States solved it successfully in the nineteenth century: The initial capital equipment was to a large extent borrowed from more advanced countries who were willing to lend to us, at a profit, the necessary goods until we could afford the time to produce our own. The rapid development of our economy in the nineteenth century followed the railroad tracks. The tracks were imported from Europe, and payment for them was not completed until the end of World War I. Although it would have been possible to develop this country even without foreign capital goods, it would have taken more sacrifice and a longer time. We would have had to withdraw from current consumption all the capital goods needed for the building of railroads. By borrowing a large number of the materials for our initial plant, our forefathers were able to subsist and still advance the economy of the country at a rapid speed.

MANAGEMENT

Management is a productive factor which belongs to the broad category of labor. Its function is of such importance to the economy, however, that some specific comments should be made. The productive contribution of management is decision making.

Dependence of Labor on Management Decisions

Man's physical effort in modern business makes only a modest contribution to the final product. In this respect human labor is used on a par with a

[1] Matt. 13:12 (RV).

machine, which gradually tends to supplant man in routine activities. The volume of his output depends on the speed of the assembly line and the ease of operation provided by the engineers. The quality of the product results from the materials used and the care given to the finishing touches. All these conditions remain entirely beyond the control of the individual worker.

The management function provides this control. The final result of any production process is more than the sum of various factors applied toward a given goal. The skillful organization of all available resources determines the quantity and quality of the end product. Of course, without resources no management can go very far, but the lavish use of factors alone cannot guarantee a satisfactory product. The number of bolts tightened by an assembly-line worker per hour depends on his equipment, the distance from one bolt to the next, the speed of the assembly line, and the efficiency of the tool used.

A secretary taking dictation may present a more familiar case to illustrate the dependence of results on the quality of management. A good secretary may produce ten letters in one office and be able to complete with equal skill and effort thirty letters in another office. In the first office she takes dictation in shorthand, waiting through innumerable interruptions and retyping each letter once or twice after her boss makes corrections in the original. In the other office, the boss uses a dictating machine and formulates letters which need no rewriting. The secretary does the same amount of actual work in both offices, but the final accomplishment in one case is three times as great as in the other.

Management Responsibility

The function of management is frequently misunderstood. Nobody seems to work hard enough to be worth the fabulous salaries we read about in the newspaper. There is widespread feeling that a managerial position is gained by sheer luck (or by marrying the boss's daughter) and that managers have very little to do except bark orders and occupy some fancy office. Why do firms pay managers large salaries? Scarcity of applicants does not seem to be the answer. Many people would like to be boss if the job were offered to them. College graduates dream of managerial positions in the near future, hardly realizing the preparation it will take and how many will fall by the wayside. There is no lack of applicants for management jobs, just a scarcity of qualified people—and they, too, are a resource.

Many people are brilliant in analyzing a problem by pointing out the various alternatives open for action. A firm can hire specialists who will furnish long and careful studies of all the possible answers to a question, but they do not have the responsibility for making the final and often difficult choice between available alternatives.

The key function of a business manager is his *responsibility for action*. He must make up his mind to the best of his ability, often on the basis of incomplete information, and learn to live with his decision, though he clearly realizes that he may have been wrong, and quite frequently is. It is not an easy thing to commit the savings of thousands of people or the livelihood of hundreds of employees, or to commit the future of an operating enterprise to an expansion project or to some new product that may or may not find acceptance with the consumer. The scarcity of people able and willing to make such decisions is the main reason for their high incomes.

POPULATION

Population trends influence the welfare of every individual. Not only is the absolute size of the population important, but the ages of the people and the numerical trend also strongly influence economic development.

Size of Population

The number of people in the United States has reached 200 million. This number is large enough to accommodate a high degree of specialization. Modern technology becomes most efficient when it mass produces identical goods, and only a large population is likely to have enough people with the same needs to make a large output practical. Highly specialized skills can be used only where enough people require similar services. A specialized surgeon with a unique technique of operating on men afflicted with a rare disease is not likely to remain in a small country where only a few such cases occur each year.

Population Trend

A steady, slow increase in the number of people in a country provides an effective stimulus for an economy as long as it does not lead to overcrowding. More people require more goods of every type, and this encourages business expansion. Optimistic firms may set their goals too high, but an increasing population will eventually absorb the higher output. Growing numbers reward an optimistic view of the future and penalize the more conservative manager who avoids excessive risks.

The population of the United States has shown a steady increase throughout its history. This rise was boosted by immigration before World War I and slowed down sharply in the depressed thirties. World War II caused a new upswing, but this trend has slowed down slightly since then.

Age Composition

The age of the population has economic significance. A bumper crop of babies causes a boom in the toy business and requires the construction of new schools. A concentration of people in their twenties brings about a rise in marriages and a heavy demand for wedding rings and housing.

The sharp rise in recent years in the number of older people has been the most noteworthy development of our population. Due to the advances in medical knowledge and the wider availability of medical care, many people live much longer than was the case in the past. All the implications of this phenomenon for the economy are not yet fully understood. The repercussions of the trend on housing, medical services, retirement plans, and many other areas of economics indicate a need for future adjustments in living patterns.

THE LAW OF DIMINISHING RETURNS

Economies of Scale

Modern equipment usually makes it possible to produce goods more efficiently now than in the past. Much of this equipment is so expensive that it cannot be used by very small firms. A modern metal press can stamp out car bodies in a few minutes, but its superior efficiency is useful only when thousands of automobiles can be produced in a continuous operation—when only one car is wanted, it costs less to hammer it out by hand, even if it takes all day. To keep the assembly line operating most efficiently requires many workers and a large marketing department with nationwide sales coverage. Only when the size of the whole firm lends itself to the use of expensive, high-speed equipment can modern technology pay for itself.

The principle involved here is known as *economies of scale*. The largest or most costly factor which cannot be made smaller determines the minimum size of the most efficient operation. This may be a small machine shop with a few tools or it can be a large, nationwide firm located in many cities.

A large business will probably enjoy true economies of scale, but it would be a serious mistake to assume that a firm cannot become too large. Just as there is a minimum size for efficient operations, all combinations of factors eventually encounter an upper limit as well.

At first glance such a statement may seem to be unreasonable. If a man discovers the perfect mixture of factors for a profitable hamburger palace, he will open a second and third outlet in neighboring towns and continue his success. At this point economies of scale will help him because he can buy his supplies cheaper by the truckload. Why should he not add new restaurants in more towns until he covers the whole country? Because he is likely to encounter difficulties of supervision and control. His early success was based on his own managerial skill, but he cannot manage each additional eating place as carefully as he did the first one.

Diminishing Returns

The law of diminishing returns states the universal principle which governs the best mixture of factors. It recognizes that not all factors can be changed with equal ease—some factors must be considered fixed while others can be varied. Of course, if we have enough time, all factors can be changed. The hamburger tycoon might be able to train palace managers to smile as expertly as he does and to conduct their business just as efficiently; but he cannot hire them now. Therefore, for the time being supervision is a fixed factor in his business. Diminishing returns refers to a time period which is short enough that some factors cannot be changed.

Assuming that a product is made with one fixed factor (a machine) and one variable factor (workers), the output will rise more than proportionately as additions of the variable factor take advantage of the economies of scale. Eventually, however, the *increase per worker will diminish* as the machine reaches its point of best utilization. The total output continues to rise at a reduced pace as more workers are used with the same machine. *The law of diminishing returns shows that the addition of units of a variable factor to a mixed factor will eventually lead to ever-smaller increases in output.*

In Table 4-1, the fixed factor is a brand-new, fully automated machine recently purchased by a mouse trap manufacturer. His variable factor is human labor, since he can easily vary the number of workers he wants to

TABLE 4-1.   The Law of Diminishing Returns

Fixed Factor (*Machine*)	Variable Factor (*Workers*)	Total Units of Product	Average Units of Product per Worker	Units Added by New Worker	
1	1	50	50	50	
1	2	120	60	70	
1	3	210	70	90	
1	4	260	65	50	⎫
1	5	300	60	40	Dimin-
1	6	330	55	30	ishing
1	7	350	50	20	returns
1	8	360	45	10	⎭
1	9	351	39	—9	

hire. He starts out operating the machine with one man and produces a modest output of fifty units since the single worker cannot keep the machine running continuously. Hiring a second worker is a distinct advantage which leads to a much improved operation. This causes increasing returns per worker. The addition of a third worker leads to a still greater jump in output and to a peak performance for each man.

Each additional worker contributes to a higher output until eight men are hired. By the time seven people help the machine to do the job, only little chance for improvement is left by hiring number 8. A further addition, of a ninth worker, would be self-defeating since he is strictly unneeded, gets in the way, and causes breakdowns. The firm operates the new machine under conditions of diminishing returns when it adds workers 4, 5, 6, 7, and 8. The first three workers cause increasing returns. The ninth worker adds nothing, but causes a loss of output.

How many workers should this firm hire? The first three are responsible for the sharpest rise in output as the machine is used more efficiently. It would be a mistake, however, to halt production short of the area at which workers labor under conditions of diminishing returns. The fifth worker still adds to the total output of the machine and should be hired. Although the output *per worker* is diminishing, the total product is still rising.

The exact point where the hiring of more workers is stopped depends on the profits to be made from additional production and is not concerned with the principle of diminishing returns. If the profit from selling the additional output is greater than the additional wage costs, more men will be hired. The law of diminishing returns simply assures us that the best use of the machine requires not less than three and not more than eight workers. As long as the addition of a variable factor causes a rise in total output, a firm will consider adding this factor though the increase is diminishing. The exact moment to stop adding a factor is determined by the price of the factor and is not considered here. Diminishing returns always means an addition, though a smaller one, and never a loss.

The law of diminishing returns is frequently misunderstood. When the disappointed manager of a firm tries to get across the idea to his even more disappointed stockholders that in the past year he made no profit at all but suffered a considerable loss, he is likely to couch this unpleasant statement in the most palatable form. He may be inclined to say something like this: "Your management has made strenuous efforts to improve the position of your firm, which is showing great hope for the future. However, the law of diminishing returns forced us to operate last year under such conditions that no profit can be reported at this time." In spite of the flowery language, this acknowledgement of a loss has no connection with the law of diminishing returns.

MALTHUS' PRINCIPLE OF POPULATION

Robert Malthus, an Englishman, wrote a famous book, *Essay on the Principle of Population* (1798), which was based on the law of diminishing returns. His doctrine had an enormous impact on the thought of past generations and is even now considered by some as a guide to population problems. Malthus observed that the land which produces the food is limited by nature, while people seem to grow in number without limit. Even though a greater population tills the soil, the additions to the food supply will become smaller and smaller until they no longer suffice to support the needs of the tillers.

Malthus suggested that this dwindling increase in the food supply would eventually limit the size of the population and cause the starvation of those who could not be fed. Was Malthus right in his dire prediction?

When we observe the increasing millions of well-fed Americans and read about the problems caused by surplus crops, Malthus' fears may strike us as absurd. His apprehensions certainly do not apply to the present generation—he failed to imagine the long list of new techniques which human ingenuity has devised to boost the food supply.

However, when we look beyond the horizon at the teeming masses of Asia, where the improvements in the use of the land have been much slower and the population rise more rapid than in this country, we see Malthus' principle in operation. The waves of starvation not uncommon to those countries seem to prove out Malthus' prediction.

PRODUCTIVITY

Productivity measures efficiency of performance by comparing various combinations of productive factors with their final output. The amount of goods produced is a measure of the efficiency of the productive effort. The degree of efficiency is the effort spent in obtaining products in relation to the result obtained. A worker may weave two baskets in one hour just using his hands. With a suitable tool he will weave twice as many in the same time; his productivity has doubled. We usually measure productivity in terms of *output per man-hour*.

The law of diminishing returns has taught us that it is not enough to just add more factors to the production process in order to obtain better results. The skillful combination of resources, with due consideration of their relative scarcity, will provide the best result which circumstances permit.

People's living standards depend primarily on the productivity of their efforts. Higher standards require more goods. Additional output can be obtained only if more capital goods of the right kind are placed in the hands of the workers.

The best use of available resources does not follow any simple, standard formula. We strive to use all possible manpower since unemployment is unproductive, but difficulties arise when not enough tools are available for the work. A new machine does not necessarily solve this problem; on the one hand it might make its attendant more productive, but on the other hand it may replace a hundred men who stand to lose their jobs. Unless some other constructive employment can be found for the displaced people, this technological improvement is a mixed blessing.

The right mixture of factors changes constantly and presents a real dilemma. The attempt to stop progress by guaranteeing the same job to every employee for his lifetime leads to the poverty observed in the world's least developed nations. The opposite approach confuses change with progress. What is new is not always better—the best result is frequently obtained by trial and error. In the eternal struggle for better things, last year's solution may not be good enough.

ECONOMIC GROWTH

Economic growth flows from improved production. Total output must rise to permit economic growth, and it must rise faster than the increase in population. Growth is usually measured on a *per capita* basis; the average amount of goods per person must rise.

This growth is sometimes hard to maintain. Unless the higher rate of output consists of goods presently wanted by the consumer, the growth becomes a mere statistical illusion. If manufacturers produce cars faster than the public is willing to buy them, cars are added to the inventory in storage, but nobody receives greater satisfaction. Moreover, if larger output is limited to war goods, such as tanks or ammunition, living standards are not raised. Production of the right goods at the right time is the right road toward economic growth.

A most difficult thing to determine in the production process is what ratio of capital goods to consumer goods will obtain the most favorable results. Should firms add new plants or work overtime whenever consumers want more goods? It takes the experienced judgment of shrewd management to make a wise decision, one which will not confuse a temporary spurt in the demand for a product with a long-run rise of the consumption level.

A healthy economy always grows in some direction. When the economy slows down and fails to use its resources to best advantage (as has happened so often in the past), wants are not being satisfied as well as they could be. A certain amount of involuntary unemployment may at times prove to be unavoidable, but its persistence for many months constitutes an unjustifiable weakening of the economic process. The record of performance of our economy since World War II indicates that we have learned to avoid depression unemployment, but we have not yet discovered how to find a job for all those who want one.

SUMMARY

Production of the goods on which the economy depends is the result of a combination of many factors which can be grouped into three broad categories: land, labor, and capital.

Land signifies the earth, the raw materials found below and the crops grown above. The entire contribution of nature to the production process is covered by this category.

Labor refers to all human efforts to transform natural resources into usable products. It includes both mental and physical work in the same classification.

Capital consists of the results of past efforts which are now available to facilitate future production. Capital goods are the plants, machines, and tools which do not serve to satisfy consumers directly, but which help to make more and better products tomorrow. While these goods are being built, some present consumption is necessarily sacrificed for more effective production in the future.

Management has the function of making key decisions in the production process. It exercises control over output and the methods of reaching the desired results. It is responsible for the final product.

Population trends have a significant impact on production decisions. A steady increase in the number of people provides a powerful stimulus for an expanding economy. The age composition of a population determines wide changes in production patterns.

The law of diminishing returns describes the effect on total output when the amount of one factor is altered while all others remain unchanged. An increase of this variable factor will at first cause a more than proportionate rise and then smaller (diminishing) rises until an output peak is reached, beyond which further additions would result in a loss.

Malthus' principle of population is an application of the law of diminishing returns. He pointed out the danger of the population's (variable factor) multiplying faster than the food supply which must be won from the earth (fixed factor).

Productivity measures the efficiency of performance of the production process by comparing various combinations of productive factors with their final output.

Economic growth is the major objective of the production effort. It is obtained only when a rising number of people receive more and better products per capita. This growth is reflected in increased productivity, permitting a higher standard of living and better want satisfaction.

Discussion Questions

1. There are thousands of productive factors. Why are they grouped in three categories?
2. What is the main feature of capital goods?
3. How much should a firm pay its president? Why?
4. Should a firm ever operate under conditions of diminishing returns?
5. Will Malthus' prediction of starvation of the human race come true?
6. Why is productivity the key to economic progress?

Suggested Reading

LANDSBERG, HANS H., *Resources in America's Future.* Washington, D.C., Resources for the Future, Inc., 1963.

MARSHALL, ALFRED, *Principles of Economics.* London, Macmillan, 1890.

VILLARD, HENRY H., *Economic Development.* New York, Holt, Rinehart & Winston, 1959.

WOLLMAN, NATHANIEL, *The Value of Water in Alternative Uses.* Albuquerque, N. Mex., University of New Mexico Press, 1962.

5

BUSINESS

A free enterprise economy relies to a large extent on the initiative of individuals who are organized in search of profit. The nation's business is conducted by millions of separate units we call firms, each pursuing its own best interest. The interpretation of this interest rests in the hands of business management, which may or may not own the firms.

THE SCOPE OF BUSINESS ENTERPRISE

The purpose of a business varies as much as the people who operate it. Some firms take special pride in their growth; others are more concerned with the benefits to the owners, employees, or the managers themselves. None of these considerations rivals the basic goal of every business in our economic system—to show a profit.

Some businessmen who spend a great deal of time helping others in charity drives will challenge the statement that profit is at the heart of business. A man can afford to devote his time to public welfare so long as his own firm continues to report an annual profit. When red ink takes over, however, he will find it necessary to resign the chairmanship of the United Drive and put his own house in order. He may have forgotten that it is the profit of his enterprise which permits him to engage in the other worthy activities he values so much.

Profit is the first job of any private business. It results from many causes, but one of its major influences is efficiency. The importance of efficiency is well understood; in fact, we often call an efficient operation a "business like" one. Beyond the need for efficiency, business firms have few common interests. Retailers differ from manufacturers, small firms from big ones, exporters from importers, and so on. Unlike a pressure group demanding specific legislation, business cannot speak with one voice. Their very differences reflect the opinions of the infinite variety of people who work for a living.

This chapter will sketch briefly the economic significance of the various legal forms of business organization in the American economic system. We will look at the shift of power from owners to professional managers.

Some of the problems arising in connection with the need for accumulating large amounts of capital will be discussed.

Over eleven million firms were estimated to exist in the United States in 1964. About 3.3 million were farmers, and 2.5 million people were engaged in independent services of all kinds. All other industries together conducted their business in over five million firms. This number experiences a slight, long-run growth, particularly in prosperous times. The turnover rate of business is high; every year about 400,000 new firms try hopefully to make a fortune, or even just a living, while over 300,000 old firms quit or sell out, and disappear as separate units. The bulk of business' deaths occurs in new firms whose owners discover in the first two years many difficulties they never expected. Often their attempt in business was only halfhearted and is gladly given up when someone offers a job with a modest but safe paycheck.

Sole proprietorships are most numerous, including most farmers and accounting for over nine million businessmen. Active corporations handle the bulk of the nation's business in a little over 1.3 million corporate firms. Partnerships are not so widespread and account for the rest of the business population (922,000 in 1964).

Number of Firms

The number of business firms is distributed unevenly over many fields of enterprise. Manufacturing firms are responsible for the bulk of production, but their number is smaller than those in other activities. Manufacturing also requires the heaviest accumulation of capital goods, which makes the average firm in this field relatively large. Retail and service establishments account for the largest number of firms, but they are usually quite small in size.

Size of Firms

Business enterprise is frequently associated in our minds with fairly large-sized operations. It may come as a surprise to realize that companies employing not more than four people constitute three-fourths of all American firms. Fewer than 7,000 are large enough to be classified as big business employing over 500 persons each; the total employment of this group provides jobs for about 18 million people.

The wide variety of sizes is related to the nature of different business activities. Modern technology has a tendency to force firms to be larger than they were in the past. The minimum size for an efficient manufacturing plant is frequently so large that its output exceeds the needs of the locality. Even a modest firm of this type must therefore aim for regional, or even national, distribution of its product. For example, a small automobile manufacturer is necessarily a very large firm.

Even traditionally small-firm activities, such as grocery stores, have felt the impact of modern technology. Large display areas, self-service counters, and an increasing variety of frozen foods with their need for continuous refrigeration mark the tiny corner grocer for early extinction. The cost of equipping a small modern grocery store has become so great that supermarket operations are needed to earn a profit.

Financial requirements often dictate the size of a firm. When the owner is not able to secure any capital beyond his own savings, the size of his business remains severely limited. The large, well-known firm has a chance to expand because its credit is sufficiently established to attract the capital needed for a new venture. Even the best small business grows slowly so long as it is restricted to its own savings.

LEGAL FORMS OF BUSINESS

There is considerable variety in the legal arrangements used in the operation of a business. The most common legal forms, however, are the single owner, the partnership, and the corporation. These three types of business enterprise will now receive more detailed attention.

The Single Ownership

The single, private owner (also referred to as the *sole proprietor*) represents by far the most usual type of legal organization in business. Most farmers, individual service organizations, and small retailers use the single-ownership form. Sole proprietors prevail numerically, but their size is so small that they do not rank very highly as employers of other people or as contributors to the total output of the nation.

No legal restrictions prevent the single owner from building a very large business; the Ford Motor Company remains the best-known example of a proprietorship which did not change its legal form during the lifetime of its founder. However, Henry Ford was a rare exception; the typical sole owner is more limited in his ability to manage and finance a business.

Advantages of Proprietorship.   The most obvious advantage of the sole proprietorship is its simplicity. There is no red tape—no forms to file, no reports to make. You wake up one morning determined to buy something and sell it at a profit, and you are in business. You need to consult no one for advice and you make your decisions (as well as your mistakes) when you please; the profits are all yours, as are the losses. You have no problem of communication; you issue orders to your employees and they won't argue, not even when you are wrong, because you are the boss and sole owner.

Disadvantages of Proprietorship. The very simplicity of this arrangement creates its own limitations. The success of the business hinges upon one individual—on his health, his energy, his wisdom, and his luck. If the owner is a good and trustworthy man, people may take a chance and enter into continuous transactions with him. Their contracts, however, will be for relatively short periods, since the risks over the years are great in a one-man business, and credit transactions are kept low enough to avoid a long-run commitment.

Importance of Proprietorship. The real importance of the single-ownership form to the economic system defies statistical measurement. The key function of the proprietorship is the freedom it affords the individual to make a living without asking for permission or punching a time clock. It translates into practice the right to be different and to demonstrate to oneself and to the world that this difference can be profitable.

Although some inventions become famous success stories, many more original ideas fail to show a profit. The single owner has the right to take a chance and try his luck; he may try without a license, without permission, without special knowledge, and all too frequently, even without money. A man has a bright idea which all his friends think absurd: he invents hair curlers no established firm will touch. So he manufactures them in his bathroom and sells them directly to the people until the skeptics realize that his idea is practical. The proprietorship provides a training ground for the venturesome; they may not be able to persuade a board of directors to take a chance, but they can convince the customer to accept their innovations.

Some people want to be sole proprietors in order to do as they please. The man who wants to become independent so that he can go fishing whenever he feels like it winds up working fourteen hours a day to earn no more than he did as an employee on his old job. Don't feel too sorry for him! He satisfies his own urge for independence, he does not really like to go fishing—he just treasures the feeling that he *can* go if he really wants to, without asking anyone for permission. His overtime hours are the price he is willing to pay.

Most modern managers follow a different pattern to success. They start with a college degree and are promoted steadily on that long ladder which leads through the years to the upper echelon of large-firm leadership.

The single-owner route provides an alternative for the nonconformist. The fact that many try and only a few reach their goal shows just how severe a selection is exercised by the market. Regardless of the chances of failure, the opportunity to try your luck in business is an essential feature of a free enterprise system.

Partnership

A partnership is an agreement between two or more individuals to own and operate a business together. In his business transactions, each partner commits not only himself and the firm, but all other partners as well.

In its simple informality a partnership resembles the proprietorship in that it is a very personal form of conducting a business. Only a verbal agreement between the owners is needed to set it in motion. Even the most elementary wisdom, however, dictates the need for a written contract between partners before misunderstandings arise. One partner buys a new truck; if the firm fails to pay on time, the other partners are just as responsible for the bill as the one who arranged the purchase. Since each individual can commit the other partners, none of them can drop out or sell his interest without permission from the others. This intimate link is the strength that permits informality in the management; but it is also the basic weakness which limits the use of partnerships to few areas of business.

Partnerships are often seen in the professions. Lawyers, doctors, accountants and architects find them well-suited to their needs. Brokerage firms and investment banks were conducted as partnerships until legal obstacles to incorporation were removed in the 1950's. The partnership form is also well-suited to a large number of special situations usually expected to last for only a limited time. As can be expected, the rate of turnover in partnerships is great.

The main features of a partnership become apparent when we look at its use by a group of doctors who want to practice medicine in a common clinic. The partners in this arrangement are specialists in different areas and respect each other's competence. The concentration of knowledge permits easy consultation and better service for the client; each doctor has his own patients, but substitution can be arranged readily in case of absence. Few decisions require managerial agreement. The partners must hire a secretary to serve the whole office, and they have to agree on the color scheme of the waiting room; beyond this point each doctor treats his patients according to his own best judgment.

Most merchandising partnerships are not able to separate management functions quite so neatly. One brother may do all the buying while the other is the sales manager of the firm. All is well until a large shipment remains unsold and the brothers start blaming each other. They soon learn that two managers second-guessing each other cannot create a profitable business, and if their venture has not yet failed, they find it wise at this point to change their firm into a corporation.

THE CORPORATION

The modern corporation has a long history; as an institution it goes back to the Roman Republic, and it is now the prevailing legal form of business in the United States. As a form, the corporation is used for ventures of all sizes but represents almost the only type adopted by large firms. Corporations conduct most of the business, employ the majority of all workers, borrow the most money, and largely control what products may be bought.

They are creations of the law. Upon application, the state grants a charter to a firm and confers on it the rights of a legal person. Long ago charters were special privileges granted by the king; they were expensive and hard to come by. Today they require only a filing fee of a few dollars and a properly drawn legal document, which lawyers will provide at a modest cost.

The legal personality of the corporation makes it possible to separate its own affairs from the other activities of its owners and managers. The funds of the firm cannot be confused with those of its owners. Stockholders have no right to speak for their firm; only the registered officers may do so. The corporation as a legal person may sue or be sued in its own name, as well as engage in contracts not limited by the life of any person connected with the business at the time.

We shall now consider the characteristics of the corporate firm from the viewpoint of liability, fund raising, continuity, taxation, and management and ownership.

Limited Liability

The single owner of a business is responsible for his firm's entire activity. When the firm encounters a loss, he is fully liable for the debt, not only with the assets of the business but also with his personal belongings. In a corporation, the owners are not personally involved in the daily transactions of the firm and cannot be held responsible for them by law. Only the officers and managers of a corporation are personally accountable for their actions in the name of the firm; the stockholders have only limited liability, and their responsibilities are restricted to the amount spent on purchasing stock.

Why should the law allow stockholders the rights of ownership without the corresponding responsibilities? The purpose of limited liability is not primarily their protection, but rather the promotion of capital accumulation for industrial enterprises. To raise large sums from many small contributors would be impossible if the stockholders were not assured that their involvement would remain limited to the amount of money they put into the stock. The man who owns 100 shares in a huge corporation neither knows nor cares how the business of this firm is conducted. He places a modest amount of money at the disposition of the corporate managers in the expectation of future profits. If he should become responsible for debts of this firm beyond his voluntary contribution, he would refrain from any involvement at all. Large firms must gather funds from thousands of stockholders in order to operate their business. Limited liability helps in the accomplishment of this task.

Financial Arrangements

The possibility of mobilizing small contributors for the accumulation of large sums does not imply that a firm solves all its financial troubles as soon as it incorporates. A small proprietor of unknown reputation finds it difficult to raise funds. Should he decide to change his firm into a corporation, he would discover that his credit has not improved. He is still small and unknown. He may now try to sell stock, but who will buy it? The firm may sign a note to the bank, but a weak balance sheet may deter the bank from accepting it. The banker may actually prefer to lend to a partnership when he knows that the private wealth of the partners represents a guarantee for repayment.

One of the real advantages of a corporation in financing a business becomes apparent only when a long-established firm wants to raise additional funds. The strong reputation of a well-known enterprise, rather than its legal form, makes the sale of stocks and bonds feasible. The growth of corporate business is financed largely by the earnings of the firms themselves, as is shown in Figure 5-1 later in this chapter.

Length of Life

The corporation has the legal advantage of eternal life. The death of the largest stockholder or the president of the firm does not terminate the legal contracts, obligations, and operations of the business. Even in a partnership, such a changeover may proceed smoothly, but the possibility of a crisis caused by the litigation of heirs is much greater.

The legal form becomes important in family enterprises dominated by a father who built the business over a lifetime. When many relatives hope to take over the reins, the future prospects of the firm become uncertain; creditors may hesitate to engage in long contracts because they cannot tell what might happen when the owner dies. Prompt cash payments to heirs and the sudden impact of estate taxes may weaken the business beyond any chance of recovery. The corporate form prevents the use of funds for such purposes, and this strengthens the confidence of creditors in the firm's future. The heir who does not want to keep his shares has to find a buyer.

In firms without efficient management by more than one person, the eternal life of the corporation provides little help. When the "old man" runs the business completely on his own without acquainting the younger generation with managerial responsibilities, a crisis becomes inevitable sooner or later, and creditors will take such a hazard into account.

Taxation

Some taxes are the same for every legal form of enterprise, but taxes on the income of a corporation differ substantially from those for other types of business. If the single owner plans to spend the entire income of his firm for his own personal use, he will not want to use the corporate form. In addition to corporation income tax, he would have to pay a personal income tax on the amount left that he pays to himself in dividends. The situation would be different if all the profits were spent by a corporation on the growth of its business and no dividends were handed to its stockholders.

A tax specialist will need to evaluate each case before it is possible to conclude whether or not taxes can be saved by changing the legal form of a business. The most advantageous arrangement depends on the objective of the management and the stockholders, the size of the profit, and the capital needs of the firm. No generalizations are possible.

Management and Ownership

The owners are usually the managers of proprietorships or partnerships. Some owners may not spend all of their time with the firm, but their responsibility for the business makes it advisable that they not lose touch with its operation. Partners may split their managerial assignments, but some overlap remains inevitable since the law holds each of them fully responsible.

The corporation has a clear advantage in this respect. Ownership and management are completely separated. In large companies the managers may own very little stock in the firm, but they alone are liable for corporate actions. The names of the officers and their areas of responsibility are a matter of record. The hierarchy of decision-making follows clearly understood lines, and the confusion that can easily occur in a partnership, where everybody is boss, can be avoided by the corporate structure.

WHO CONTROLS A CORPORATION?

The separation of management from ownership in corporate business has been a development of great economic significance during the last hundred years. The law has been slow to recognize this change. The stockholder is the owner, and he, legally, controls the corporation. This legal arrangement does not fit firms of all sizes equally well; economic reality differs in many cases from the dictates of the law.

The Family Corporation

Small firms frequently incorporate for many of the reasons discussed earlier. Management, ownership, and control are combined in such a business. The meeting of the board of directors is a family gathering, and the most forceful member runs the show, regardless of any possible legal safeguards. The corporation mechanism is rather ponderous for this type of firm, and its widespread use results from there being nothing better available. All the stock is held by family members, who are actively engaged in the management of the firm. The strongest member of the family controls the business.

Medium-Sized Corporations

The laws of corporate control in the nineteenth century assumed a situation where a limited number of wealthy citizens pooled their resources for a larger venture. They were in control of the enterprise: they elected the directors of the firm and knew the managers personally; and while they were not involved in day-by-day decisions, they were well aware of the policies and the fortunes of their corporation.

Stockholders were both legally and practically able to control corporate policy. If they did not like the management, they held a meeting and voted for a change. Most of the stockholders lived within a short distance and owned enough stock to make participation at a meeting both practical and wise. This type of firm, for which corporation laws were developed, is less common today. Its control usually rests with the board of directors who remain in touch with stockholder opinion.

Large Corporations

Large firms with over a thousand stockholders and millions of dollars in assets are fairly typical of corporate business. A few firms count over a million stockholders. In an enterprise of this size there is complete separation of control and ownership. Stockholders own a financial asset in hopes of receiving dividends and in the expectation of selling the stock later at a higher price. They neither know nor care who manages the firm or how good a job the management does. For them, attendance at stockholders' meetings a thousand miles away would be a total waste of time.

In practice, the rights of the stockholder in such a firm are narrowly limited. If he does not approve of the management, what can he do? "Sell or sue" is a concise but true summary of his alternatives, and since lawsuits are expensive, he will usually prefer to sell his stock and forget the unhappy experience.

Proxies. What has happened to the voting right, the traditional legal attribute of ownership? It has lost much of its value to the proxy device. A proxy is a legal grant of authority to vote stock, usually given by a stockholder to a management representative by simply putting a signature on a card mailed out by the firm. The inevitable absence of most stockholders from meetings has made it necessary to assemble a quorum by mail. The president of the firm has the duty to make sure that enough shares are represented at the meeting to conduct business, and this majority vote is exercised by a man he appoints and whose actions he controls.

The chances of a successful proxy fight against the management of a firm are exceedingly slim. Many stockholders may disapprove of managerial actions; they can always refuse to send in their proxy. Such a protest is ineffective, and someone must actively organize the opposition and offer a better alternative to stockholders before an established management can be ousted.

Such a battle of proxies is very expensive, since it requires repeated mailings by the opposition and a great deal of publicity to acquaint stockholders with the case against the managers. Only when the opposition is led by very wealthy men does it have a reasonably good chance of victory. The cases of the New York Central Railroad and of the Allegheny Corporation in the 1950's are rare examples in which managers were changed as a result of proxy fights at a cost of millions of dollars.

Corporate Control. The board of directors supervises the corporation. Its members are nominated by the management (subject to legal election by proxy votes) and are not likely to gain excessive independence from their source of power, the president of the firm. The board in turn "elects" the officers of the corporation and decides on the use of profits earned. The stockholder is not automatically entitled to collect all profits in cash—he receives only that part of the earnings which the board decides to distribute as dividends. Undistributed profits are often held for future use in the growth of the company.

The control of the large firm rests with its top management. This small group is largely self-perpetuating and not subject to any outside control; when a member resigns or retires, his successor is nominated by those left in charge. This vast accumulation of power in the hands of a few individuals presents a real problem in connection with the giant-sized firms, whose fortunes involve not only managers and stockholders, but millions of people all over the country.

Impact of Giant Firms.   The names of some firms are known to virtually every American. General Motors and General Electric are represented by their products in every town. They are private corporations which are treated like all others under the law, but their economic impact differs considerably from that of smaller firms.

The welfare of the average firm concerns comparatively few people. If a business fades, its competitors will be glad to move in and take over customers and employees alike. On the other hand, an economic crisis of a giant involves many people who have no direct connection with the firm itself. The towns in which the plants of the sick giant are located cannot cope with mass unemployment, and many supplier industries find it hard to cushion the shock. As a result, the entire nation's economy suffers from the upset of one firm.

The giant business remains a private firm, but the public has considerable interest in its performance since whatever it does will affect many people who have no direct ties with it. The law has never stated it specifically, but the economic impact of giant firms renders their management a public trust.

FINANCING A CORPORATION

A well-known firm decides to add a new, modern plant to its business at an estimated cost of $50 million. Where does it find the money? The largest share of the financing of a corporation comes from internal sources, sometimes called corporate savings, and consists of profits which have not been distributed to the stockholders and depreciation funds which become available for new purchases. A smaller share comes from external sources. Some of these consist simply of trade debts—bills which have not yet been paid to suppliers. Loans of many types are also used to raise funds for corporations; the best known sources are stocks and bonds, which play a relatively small role in financing, as shown in Figure 5-1. Four sources of funds for financing a corporation will be considered here: loans, stocks, bonds, and corporate savings.

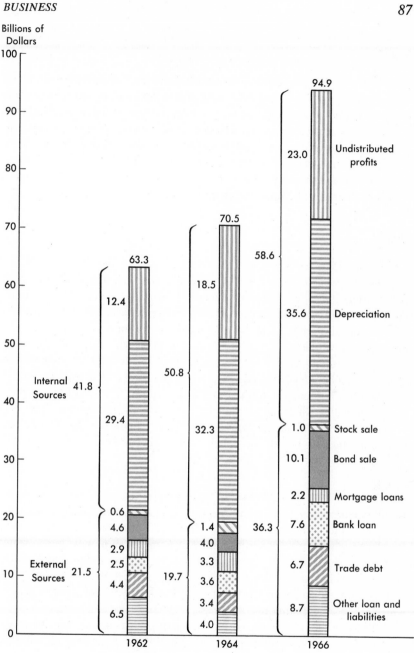

SOURCE: U.S. Department of Commerce, *Survey of Current Business*.

FIG. 5-1.   **Sources of Funds for Corporations**
(Nonfarm-Nonfinancial firms only)
(*billions of dollars*)

Loans

Short-term-fund requirements of a corporation are satisfied with bank loans. When a firm expects to use borrowed money for several years, it is likely to prefer a lending arrangement with a different type of financial institution, such as an insurance company, which does not want repayment within one year. Mortgage protection is often arranged in connection with such loans of a longer duration. When a manager feels that he will need more funds permanently to take care of a growing operation, he looks for still other means of financing; he may, for example, decide to sell more stock.

Stocks

The stockholders are the legal *owners* of a corporation. Stock certificates are readily divisible, with each share representing a fraction of ownership rights. Sometimes these rights are called the owner's "equity", but a nominal value printed on some certificates has no economic meaning. The fortune of the firm decides what each share is worth. If business is good, the value of the stock will rise; in case of losses, the price will drop. Should losses lead to bankruptcy, stockholders receive what is left after all creditors are paid; the stockholders in such cases are called the *residual claimants*.

When a corporation wants to raise new funds, it may try to sell more stock certificates. Since an additional sale reduces the percentage share held by the prior owners, the corporation will usually favor the old stockholders and permit them to buy the new shares before they are offered to the public.

Bonds

Bondholders are *creditors* of a firm; they lend their own funds to the company until the *maturity* date of the bond, the day slated for repayment. Bondholders are entitled to receive the exact amount of money due, as stated on the certificate, but no more. Their claim is paid before stockholders receive anything, and the interest due is not subject to a decision of the board of directors, because interest must be paid with the same regularity which applies to all other bills.

The bondholder seems to enjoy a much safer position than the stockholder. He knows how much money he will receive, he is sure of collecting interest, and in bad times his claim against the firm is stronger than the owners' claim. The stockholder, however, will often profit from his uncertain position. In good times the value of the stock is likely to rise, and dividends may increase where bond interest remains unchanged. Particularly during an inflation, when all prices rise, the price of stock will reflect this and rise also. Bond prices will fluctuate less over the years than stock prices. However, they are not always safer when it comes to maintaining capital values, because in case of bankruptcy the firm may not be able to pay the owners of either bonds *or* stocks.

Corporate Savings

The savings of a corporation are usually the major source of funds for its future growth. Just as an individual may refuse to spend all his income, the board of directors may do the same for a firm. Frequently board members save more enthusiastically in the business than they do at home, since their interest may be more in the expansion of the company than in cash dividends.

When profits are earned, some part is usually distributed to the shareholders. Many firms are slow to change the established pattern of dividend payments. When profits are low, they prefer to maintain the usual dividend rate; this makes it necessary to raise dividends slowly in good times, leaving a huge surplus for corporate savings.

Most corporations save additional funds for replacing and expanding facilities by means of depreciation allowances on capital goods. We shall hear more about this type of savings in Chapter 15.

THE HOLDING COMPANY

The separation of control from the ownership of a firm has inspired the creation of the holding company, a single firm which owns other companies for the main *purpose of exercising control* over the management. It is widely used by public utility firms and banks. When the managers of several firms find it advantageous to cooperate closely with each other without giving up their identity, they may create such a firm to control them all. While 51 percent of stock ownership insures absolute control, a much smaller amount will usually suffice to secure enough influence over a firm. A company that needs to attract a lot of capital may require more funds than it can raise alone. If it is linked to other similar firms, it may be able to mobilize enough money for its projects.

The holding company device led to widespread abuses in the twenties. Certain enterprising salesmen would create a firm and sell stock to the unsuspecting public, keeping enough stock for themselves to maintain a working control of the company. The funds collected by the stock sales were used to create another firm controlled by the first one, but much larger and ready to sell even more stock. This technique continued until enough funds had been raised to buy control of the one firm the manipulators really wanted. The complicated organization of such a business jungle permitted fraud to remain undetected for quite some time, occasionally leaving innocent stockholders with a worthless piece of paper.

The Public Utility Holding Company Act was passed by Congress in 1934 for the purpose of preventing a repetition of the abuse of holding companies in the field of public utilities. Existing organizational structures had to be simplified so that stockholders and bond buyers could know who was in control. Much detailed publicity became required by law.

COOPERATIVES

Cooperatives are firms whose business is managed for the benefit of the users. Members are entitled to the profits at a rate corresponding to the volume of their transactions rather than to their share of ownership rights.

Producers' cooperatives unite farm groups primarily for the purpose of processing and selling crops. Consumers' cooperatives are organized in the hope of buying many articles cheaper by eliminating the middleman. Present legislation favors the continuation of the cooperative method for doing business, but their success depends largely on the ability of their managers.

SUMMARY

Business represents all economic activity and speaks for many conflicting interests. The only feature all business has in common in a free enterprise economy is the search for profit, which supports its continued existence.

The number and size of firms vary widely. Their distribution is uneven and follows the ever-changing needs of our society.

Three legal forms of business—the single owner, the partnership, and the corporation—dominate the American economy. The sole proprietor is numerically predominant, but the bulk of employment and output comes from corporations.

The single ownership provides a necessary training ground for many future leaders, who gain valuable experience by managing a small operation before they move on to increased responsibilities. This form of business permits the venturesome nonconformist to prove to himself and to the world the merits of his unorthodox approach. The single ownership is an expression of individual freedom, of the right to make a living without following the orders of any boss. This precious right is a necessary feature of a free enterprise economy.

The partnership permits the informal combination of different talents for a more effective operation, particularly in connection with the professions. In other fields of activity, the value of this legal form is reduced because of the rule which renders each partner fully responsible for the action of all other partners. It is therefore best suited as a temporary arrangement.

The corporation is created by the grant of a charter and acquires legal personality with its own rights and obligations. Financing is facilitated by means of selling securities, provided that buyers can be found. The stockholders have limited liability and are not responsible for corporate action. This permits the gathering of funds from many small owners, whose sole interest in the firm is their annual income in the form of dividends, as well as gains from a higher price when they decide to sell.

Funds are also raised by borrowing, selling bonds, and by using the savings of the corporation itself.

A corporation has a permanent charter and continues to exist beyond the life of its officers and owners. Its stability eases changeover in management and enhances the credit of the firm.

The organization of the corporation provides a relatively simple and clear-cut line of command, with a chief executive officer in charge of its operations. He controls the management of the firm, particularly when there are many stockholders with no single one owning a large interest. He commands a majority by proxy vote; he nominates the members of the board of directors and creates his team to be in charge of the firm. The stockholder is entitled to his dividends after they are declared by the board of directors, and he may sell his stock when he chooses to do so.

In small and medium-sized corporations, the power of the professional manager is not as great and may be shared with a group of influential stockholders and the board members who represent them.

The tax structure may constitute an important factor for or against the use of the corporate form. Each case must be examined separately; generalizations are dangerous in this rapidly shifting field.

Holding companies hold stock in other firms for the purpose of controlling their management. They are widely used in public utilities and banking. Cooperatives distribute their profits on the basis of the volume of business of each member rather than on the amount of ownership. They are well established in the area of marketing agricultural products and are popular with some consumer groups.

Discussion Questions

1. Why are there more retail businesses than any other kind?
2. Why should a firm incorporate?
3. The separation of management from ownership in the modern corporation has caused an economic revolution little recognized in the laws. Comment on this statement.
4. How can a holding company control firms with more capital than its own?
5. Why is it difficult for a large stockholder to oust the management of a firm?
6. To gain the independence of being the sole owner of a business often imposes much sacrifice. Discuss this statement.

Suggested Reading

BAZELON, DAVID T., *The Paper Economy*. New York, Random House, 1963.

BOULDING, KENNETH E., *Principles of Economic Power*. Englewood Cliffs, N.J., Prentice-Hall, 1958.

GALBRAITH, JOHN KENNETH, *American Capitalism,* rev. ed. Boston, Houghton Mifflin, 1956.

HACKER, ANDREW, ed., *The Corporation Take-over*. New York, Harper & Row, 1964.

6

PRICE

Price is the expression of the irrevocable law of supply and demand. This frequently heard statement encompasses for some people all the problems of an economy. Such a broad generalization is quite meaningless.

Prices are essential tools of a free enterprise economy because they enable millions of individuals to engage in orderly and purposeful business activity without a government directing their every move. Prices are used to measure economic values as they influence both demand and supply factors; they are the gears in our system of distributing products. They operate to increase efficiency in the production and consumption of goods and serve as both cause and effect in the unbroken chain of interdependent economic activity.

This chapter intends to shed some light on the way prices are determined in the market, on the function of demand and supply in the pricing process, and on the necessary conditions which must be met to maintain the efficiency of the pricing mechanism.

VALUE

Why does a new television set cost $159.95? Is it worth that much? Should it cost more or less? Individual estimates of value are largely subjective opinions. People may feel that some goods are very vaulable, but do not particularly want to own them. A rare bird on a special diet, or a painting by an old master that requires constant attention to avoid decay, may have great value but few possible buyers. On the other hand, some goods might have little value and still be of great interest to certain individuals; a rock without special significance may yet be important to a rock collector who lacks that very specimen.

Broad generalizations concerning people's value estimates have little meaning. We may assume, however, that a man who decides to buy a TV set feels that the value to him of this appliance is greater than any other combination of goods he can buy for the same amount of money at the same time. This estimate may be purely temporary, valid only for the moment of purchase. After watching the programs for a day, he may be sorry about his decision to get it. We do not know why this person wants a set.

He may desire to watch movies without leaving home, or he may simply wish to keep his family happy; another man might buy a TV to keep the children quiet while he reads the evening paper, or maybe just because his neighbor bought one.

Social philosophers have advanced several theories which try to explain the cause of individual value decisions. Some refer to the intrinsic utility of a good as a basis of its value. But the facts of everyday life contradict such a view; water is far more useful than diamonds even though it can be bought cheaply. Another idea bases value on cost—on the sacrifice required to obtain goods. Again, there are numerous situations which make this unlikely; a building site on main street has great value even though it costs nothing to place it there.

The nature of individual value judgments has not yet found a universally satisfactory explanation. Our economic system operates without delving into motivations and instead focuses its attention on the results of people's actions in the markets for goods and services. The market registers only *objective* valuations; these take the form of prices based on actual offers to buy and sell.

DEMAND

Demand describes all human desires for economic goods for which people are willing to give up something in return. We can look at demand in two different ways: The individual consumer has a demand for many goods, but he has to choose among them since he seldom can afford to buy everything he wants. The business firm looks at demand from the opposite viewpoint and tries to discover how many people will want to buy its products. In the first case we speak of individual demand, while in the second we total all the individual demands for a product to arrive at the market demand. The sum of goods demanded represents the sales of that industry.

Individual Demand

A man's wishes, like his dreams, can be vague and without limit. When he tries to single out those desires he wants satisfied, he creates a demand. Some of these things he may want strongly, seemingly regardless of price, while others will be considered only if they can be bought at a bargain. No demand is completely independent from price. A person may go out to eat at a restaurant with his appetite set for a steak, for which he will pay $3, or even $4. But when he sees the steak marked $8, he has a sudden change of mind and feels that chicken might be preferable (considering the much lower price on the menu).

All individual demand is a matter of choice, of reaching for the best alternative offered by the market. People do have some priority schedules for their purchases, but in most cases these plans are not rigid and can be strongly influenced by changing prices.

Changes in income will also exercise an impact on buying habits. When income fluctuates sharply, price differences become less important. Within a given unchanged income, the relative price changes among different products cause the greatest influence on the demand. Rising prices of beef and a drop in the price of pork will switch many families from an extra meal of beef to one of pork as long as the housewife has to keep her purchase within a given weekly budget.

Many different influences help to shape demand and to determine price. A young, single man in college may dream of a racy sports car; ten years later he would rather have a station wagon with room for his wife and four children. One general rule applies, however, to the demand of nearly all products: more units of a good will be bought at a lower price than at a higher one.[1]

People will buy additional units of a good at lower prices not only because they like bargains, but on account of a simple principle which is familiar to everyone. A hungry man will give a great deal for a loaf of bread to satisfy his appetite. A second loaf, however, will look much less attractive to him, and a third loaf may appear to be almost useless. Correspondingly, he will be willing to pay only a smaller price for additional loaves of bread. This principle is known as the *law of diminishing utility*.

Market Demand

Market demand is the sum of all individual demands. Not all people want to pay the same price for a given product. Some men will pay $5 for a shirt; others won't spend more than $4. The store owner who wants to sell shirts is faced not by a demand for 100 shirts, but by something more complex called a demand schedule.

Demand Schedule. A demand schedule is an estimate of quantities which consumers would purchase at several different prices. This list exists mostly in the mind of the seller and contains a number of possible prices at which he expects to find customers willing to buy the product, and an estimate of the number of items that would be bought at each price. A main street store may estimate the demand of its customers for shirts as shown in the following schedule:

[1] The numerically minor exceptions to this rule refer to the case where a good is bought at a high price because of the prestige attached to its expensiveness. The high price marks the buyer as a man of wealth. Champagne, Cadillacs, and caviar might lose their glamour and desirability in the eyes of potential buyers if their prices dropped to a point where everybody could afford to buy them. Goods that are bought *because* of their high price rather than *in spite* of it are few.

TABLE 6-1.   **Market Demand Schedule for Shirts**
(*Estimated by Owner of Dry-Goods Store*)

Sales Price (1)	Estimated Number of Shirts Demanded (2)	Total Revenue Obtainable from Sales (1) × (2)
$5	20	$100
4	40	160
3	60	180
2	80	160
1	100	100

Assuming that the store's estimate is correct, at what price will it want to sell the shirts? A casual glance may give the impression that the store will receive $5 from those who are willing to pay that much, and a smaller amount from others. However, this approach is not possible. The store will have to mark the bin with the shirts at one price only. Even a customer who is ready to buy a $5 shirt will not do so when other people get exactly the same product in the same store for less. The seller must decide on one price for all shirts of the same kind. The estimated sales of forty shirts at $4 include the twenty shirts for which a higher price could have been obtained and twenty shirts demanded by people who will not pay more.

In the demand schedule faced by this store, the price will certainly not be set below $3 per shirt. It is true that more shirts could be sold at $2, but it does not pay the seller to price them so low, even if the shirts cost him nothing. The total revenue from shirts shrinks when the price drops below $3. The firm would be better off to throw away its surplus merchandise!

What price will the store place on its shirts? To keep the problem as simple as possible, let's disregard for the moment all costs or alternative choices which may come to mind and concentrate only on the number of shirts which can be sold at each price in this example. With these restrictions the firm will sell sixty shirts at $3, because this combination of price and sales volume creates the largest profit for the store.

Actual pricing decision are likely to be much more involved; they may be influenced by tradition or by the unwillingness of a businessman to change too radically from a customary pattern. The seller may have only the haziest idea of the demand schedule he is facing; his pricing decision will therefore be hesitant and uncertain. There is only one rational yardstick to determine which price is best when a series of alternatives is available: the net revenue from the total sales of a product is highest at the best obtainable price. The sales price is the one which creates the largest total profit.

Profit maximizing. A low price of a good may benefit those customers who cannot afford to buy when the product costs more; a high price may reduce the number of people who ask the salesman for his services. Neither of these considerations can be used as a suitable yardstick for a pricing decision, because prices are determined with the objective in mind of creating the largest net revenue or total profit. We realize, of course, that businessmen do not spend their days wondering whether or not a 10-cent rise or drop in price would cause total revenue to increase. There is, however, a logical objective to business efforts; their main goal is maximum profit.

Profit means here the difference between revenue and cost of the merchandise. When costs are assumed to be zero, total profit and total revenue are the same. Do not confuse the greatest *total* profit with the desire of some store owner to make the largest possible profit on each shirt sold. He may not sell very many. Still other firms may be so keen on expansion that they try to sell all the shirts they can, almost regardless of price. They will be very busy as they go bankrupt!

Pricing errors happen quite readily. A firm traditionally sells shirts at $5; conditions change and revenue would be increased substantially if the price dropped to $3. The manager, however, hesitates to lower the price because he can see only how much he would lose on every shirt and not how many more shirts he could sell profitably at the lower price. Another firm may concentrate so heavily on its efforts to increase the sales volume, even at repeated price reductions, that the total income will drop below its best level.

The fact that all sixty shirts will be sold at $3 by the store in our example reveals an important feature of a pricing system. Forty people would have been willing to pay at least $4 for their shirts. But they got them cheaper because nobody needs to pay more for a product than the lowest bidder, whose demand is still necessary to sell the available goods. At $4 twenty shirts would have remained unsold, reducing the total revenue of the store. Only at $3 was it possible to lure enough customers into a purchase of these shirts.[2]

Why did the price fail to go below $3? There was a potential demand for shirts at $2, but at anything below the $3 price the store would lose revenue. Consequently, it refuses to make shirts available at this low price, and the people who would like to buy a $2 shirt will have to refrain from doing so in this case.

---

[2] In the terms of technical economics, the lowest bidder needed to dispose of the available shirts is called *marginal* since he provides the difference, or margin, between selling and not selling a product. The marginal demand at which goods are sold determines the price for all sales of this type.

Demand Curve. A demand curve is a graphic presentation of a demand schedule. Some people prefer a picture to a table; we can help them by plotting the information contained in the demand schedule on a graph, as seen in Figure 6-1. The sales price per shirt ($/q) is shown on the vertical

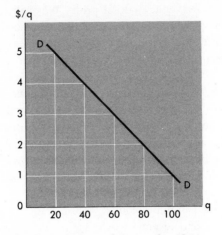

Fɪɢ. 6-1. **Demand Curve for Shirts**

axis; the number of shirts which are estimated to be sold at each price is marked on the horizontal axis (q = quantity). The result illustrates the same information contained in the demand schedule, and again shows that more shirts are sold at lower prices and vice versa.

ELASTICITY

Elasticity is a widely used concept in economics with a very special technical meaning. Economic elasticity has no relationship to rubber, but, like the bounce of a ball, it does measure a degree of responsiveness. The elasticity of the demand for a product measures the responsiveness of buyers to a change in price.

Every demand schedule represents a list of alternatives. The seller must decide at what price he hopes to reap the greatest benefit. As long as a price reduction raises his total profit, he will prefer it under any given set of circumstances. What raises the revenue when he cuts the price? The number of units sold rises at a faster rate, at a greater percentage, than the price reduction. When the shirt price is dropped from $5 to $4, the reduction equals 20 percent; [3] the number of shirts sold rises from twenty to

---

[3] Twenty percent is the difference based on $5; the same difference becomes 25 percent based on $4. The distinction shows that comparisons of price and output changes can be meaningful only if they are small.

forty, doubling the sales. This increase in the number of units sold at the lower price represents a higher percentage than the relative drop in price. The demand for shirts at these two prices is said to be *elastic*.[4]

The opposite holds true when sales increase at a smaller percentage than indicated by the price drop. When a 10-percent reduction in price results in a 5-percent rise in goods sold, the demand is *inelastic*, or unresponsive to a lower price. The number of shirts sold is greater at every price drop, but it is not always large enough to compensate for the loss of selling each shirt more cheaply. Compare the sales estimates for shirts at $3 and at $2; at the lower price eighty shirts can be sold, as against sixty shirts at the higher price. The price drop causes a loss of $1 for sixty shirts ($1 × 60) which is not compensated by the twenty extra shirts sold at the $2 level ($2 × 20).

This elasticity principle presents some interesting insights. A store manager cuts his price 10 percent, and the result is excellent. He jumps to conclusions and now wants more volume at any price. He cuts his price again and again; of course his sales volume goes up each time, but he is puzzled because his dollar revenue is not rising the way it did after the first reduction. He is learning the important lesson that he must not generalize about the result of price changes. The elasticity of the demand for a product will differ for any two prices he compares.

Businessmen are sometimes inclined to underestimate the elasticity of the demand for their product. A fountain pen may have been priced traditionally at $2.95, and the store is unaware of the many sales that might be added if it sold at $2.50. When you ask the manager why he does not lower the price to sell more pens, he will tell you that it won't pay. This is his way of saying that he does not believe he can add enough sales volume to make up for the loss of 45 cents on every pen sold.

A price so high that only a few units are sold will frequently encounter an elastic demand. When a new product is introduced for a few customers at a very high price, the seller will frequently try to find a way to mass produce the item and cut the price sufficiently to reach a broader market. He expects the demand at the lower price to be elastic. When sales of a product are already very large, a price reduction will probably not boost the demand for a product sufficiently. This is one reason why firms often produce less than their most efficient output if added units will have to be sold in a market with an inelastic demand.

[4] For the mathematically inclined reader, the formula for demand elasticity reads:

$$\text{Elasticity} = \frac{\text{Output difference}}{\text{Output}} : \frac{-\text{ Price difference}}{\text{Price}}$$

$$= \frac{20}{40} : \frac{-1}{5}$$

$$= \frac{20}{40} \times \frac{5}{-1}$$

$$= -2.5$$

Elasticity of Demand of a Firm

How elastic is the demand for household refrigerators? This question needs some clarification. In general the demand is very inelastic, since people are usually ready to buy a new refrigerator only when the old one breaks down. When this unhappy day arrives and the owner is assured that the old box is not worth repairing, he wants one promptly, and the price does not seem to matter very much.

The unsolved issue in the refrigerator demand is not that one icebox will be sold, but who will sell it. The repairman will assure the customer that he can have a very good one installed this afternoon for $399.50. The housewife may, however, think of calling some other store and learn that she can purchase another brand for $280. It is difficult to compare several brands, all with different features and prices, but a price difference may easily switch the refrigerator sale from one store to another. The demand for refrigerators sold by *any one firm* is likely to be very elastic even when the total demand for refrigerators does not fluctuate much with price changes.

Elasticity of Demand of an Industry

A firm gains sales largely at the expense of its competitors. If one service station sells gas for 5 cents less than any other station in town, it will get so much business that it is worth the reduction in price. If all gasoline stations drop their price at the same time, no one will sell much more gasoline than usual. The total demand for gasoline sold by the entire oil industry increases very little when a price war breaks out. A few teen-agers buy an extra gallon or so for their jalopies, but most people go about their business as usual. The nationwide demand for gasoline rises for other reasons which have nothing to do with price; a business boom means extra driving for many people and more sales of gasoline. But the price elasticity of the demand for gasoline for the whole industry remains inelastic.

CHANGES IN DEMAND

The discussion so far has been limited to the sales of one unchanging product. We have estimated how many more units of the same product can be sold at a lower price. Each price-quantity combination presents an alternative, and the seller will offer to the public what he hopefully expects to be the best alternative available to him. What happens when we broaden our viewpoint and permit the manager a different solution to his problem of reaping the greatest profit from shirt sales? He may decide that a price reduction will not help much and he would rather spend some money on advertising. Or he may switch over to a different type of shirt.

In any event, we realize that the old estimate for shirts will not hold true any longer. A stock of different-style shirts is certainly a new product, but an advertised shirt is also as different from the unadvertised shirt as one with a different collar. We are no longer comparing the possible sales of the old shirt at $4 or $3, but we are estimating a whole new demand schedule for each different product.

Should we try to show this change graphically, d would represent the same demand curve as before, flanked by other curves to the right (d_1, d_2) or left (d_3) depending on the new sales estimates.

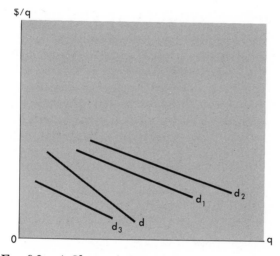

FIG. 6-2. A Change in Demand

Sometimes people refer to the elasticity of demand without knowledge of the specific prices of a demand schedule. What do they mean? A businessman may say, for example, that the demand for his product is rather inelastic. He is comparing not any two prices of the same product, but the entire demand schedule for this product with the demand schedule for other products. Let us assume that prices of wheat and automobiles are lowered by 10 percent. More wheat and automobiles will be sold at the reduced price. If the increase in sales is twice as high for automobiles as it is for wheat, the demand for wheat is relatively less elastic.

The distinction between the two different views of demand has considerable practical importance. When a firm looks at its sales opportunities, it pictures the possible demand for its product. The firm may contemplate improvements along two different, though related, lines. On the one hand, it will try to discover how to make more money by selling the same product at prices which differ from its current practice. This is an effort to find the best price on the demand schedule for one product.

The manager, on the other hand, will try to discover a means of making a more acceptable product, comparing the possible sales of the new item with the sales opportunities of the one now marketed. A product need not be entirely new to encounter a different demand at every price. A colored shirt is not the same article as a white one. A piece of costume jewelry packaged in a fancy box is different from such jewelry available unwrapped on a dimestore counter. Each separate product with different characteristics has its own demand schedule.

SUBSTITUTION AND COMPLEMENTARITY

The rise in sales which results from a drop in prices differs widely for different products and circumstances. What is the cause of this difference? Why is a reduction in the price of lounge chairs likely to boost sales much more than a similar drop in the price of wheat? The answer to this question is found in the principles of substitution and complementarity.

Substitution

The concept of substitution refers to a buyer's opportunity to do without a given product either because he can buy one similar to it or because he does not need the product at all. *The easier it is for a buyer to find a substitute, the more elastic becomes the demand for the product.*

The demand for wheat may be relatively inelastic because people are unable or unwilling to change their wheat consumption in the daily diet. The alternatives that are available as wheat substitutes are not very attractive. A 10-percent increase in the price of bread will cause few people to switch to rice or potatoes. Conversely, a drop in the wheat price will not reduce most people's reluctance to substitute an extra slice of bread for a helping of meat. When a man wants fresh fruit, he may be willing to pay 30 cents for a pound of peaches when there is no other fresh fruit in town, but he may change his mind if he can buy grapes or plums more economically in the same store.

The most common substitute a buyer may choose is simply not to buy at all. The demand for furniture may be quite elastic because many people may not need another chair nearly as much as they need another meal. Others may consider buying more furniture if they can get it at a bargain, but otherwise might be perfectly willing to spend their money on a vacation trip. To some extent all products are substitutes for each other in their competing claims on the consumer's pocketbook.

Complementarity

Goods are complementary when they are bought and used together. The demand for golf clubs and golf balls will rise and fall in a similar pattern. An increase in residential construction will be accompanied by a greater demand for brick, windows, and floor covering at unchanged prices.

When two goods are used together, the rise in the demand for one good will cause an increase in the demand for the other. It does not matter why the demand for one of the products becomes greater, the favorable effect on the demand for the complementary product will take place automatically. For example, a drop in admission fees to a tennis court creates more demand for its use; although it may not always mean more profit for the owner of the court, it will certainly boost the demand for tennis balls even if their price remains unchanged.

Causes of Change

The interdependence of all business is emphasized by the multitude of influences which may change a demand schedule and prove it wrong in spite of the most careful estimates. A sudden boom in automobile sales will raise the demand for steel. The opening of a new motel on the outskirts of the city will reduce the demand for rooms at the old hotel downtown.

The success of a businessman depends largely on his ability to realize the continuing need for change and to understand the exact nature of the influences on the demand for his products. He may sometimes work only with one clearly established fact: His sales have dropped. Should he change his price, his product, his service, his advertising? The answer will differ in each case with his estimate of the reasons underlying the changes in consumer demand. No simple prescription will work in every situation.

Some firms underestimate the importance of price changes. Rather than cut the price of their product by 20 cents, thereby hoping to attract more customers, they will spend this amount on an expensive sales campaign in the hope of gaining more buyers at the old price. Their sales effort may consist in changing the model each year to tempt people into a new purchase though their present product is still usable. For some goods, such as automobiles, this approach seems to have worked well. But others who use the same technique might have increased their profits more if they had reduced prices without expensive model changes.

SUPPLY

The word *supply* may mean many things. When giving a party, a hostess may be concerned about her supply of ice cubes being sufficient. Automobile dealers speak about a thirty-five-day supply of new cars. Economists use the term with a more specific meaning.

Supply refers to the number of goods or services offered for sale at specific prices. There is no such thing as a supply of 5,000 shirts, but only a number of shirts offered at different prices. The supplier of a product must make some estimates concerning the price at which his product may sell and then decide the number of units he wants to offer. He would like to produce more units to sell at a higher price, of course, but he realizes that frequently he has little control over the sales price. His only alternative is to decide how many units he wants to offer at the price at which he thinks he can sell them; his estimates of the market situation will include the offers of his competitors together with his own. Only a consideration of the total market-supply situation makes it possible for him to come to a practical conclusion about the size of his own output. This estimate is called a supply schedule and may read like this:

TABLE 6-2.   Market Supply Schedule for Shirts
(Estimated by Shirt Manufacturer)

Sales Price	Estimated Number of Shirts Offered
$1	20
2	50
3	80
4	110
5	130

The supply schedule has much similarity to the demand schedule. It provides a list of alternatives where the larger number of shirts offered at $2 includes those offered at $1 and is not an addition to the $1 offer. Any manufacturer will be glad to sell at $2 instead of $1 if he can get the extra money. The one price at which shirts are offered depends on the number of units that need to be supplied to satisfy the demand.

Why does the number of units offered increase so much as prices rise? At a low price, only a manufacturer who can produce the product very cheaply will be willing to offer it. The other producers concentrate on more remunerative items. At higher prices more firms will supply to this market; as prices rise, they become more willing to work overtime or drop some other activity to increase the supply.

Supply elasticity closely resembles demand elasticity. Supply is considered elastic when a small increase in price is accompanied by a more than proportionate rise in units offered. When a 10-percent price rise boosts the amount offered by 20 percent, the supply is elastic.

For those who like diagrams, we can draw the supply schedule of Table 6-2 in the form of a supply curve:

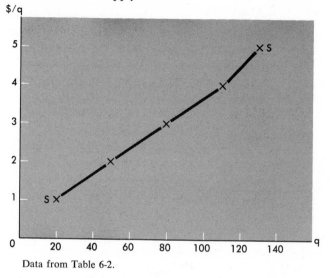

Data from Table 6-2.

FIG. 6-3. Supply Curve for Shirts

The discussion of supply has been confined so far to a comparison of price and output alternatives. Many other influences make themselves felt that change the picture and the supply estimates. A new machine that cheapens the production process will increase the number of units offered at every price, a business tax will have the opposite effect.

All change takes time. A change of price will cause more response in the number of units offered if there is enough time to adjust production schedules. Demand follows wants, and changes in wants can occur rather quickly; but supply changes often require production changes or movement of goods and people. These are more time-consuming adjustments. The implications of this time factor will be examined further when costs are considered.

MARKET PRICE

The list of alternatives reflected by a demand or a supply schedule fails to indicate at what prices actual business will take place. Let us now consider demand and supply together, and we shall make an important discovery.

There are many demand prices at which people like to buy, or supply prices at which others want to sell, but at any given moment there can be only one price at which the amount offered and demanded will be exactly equal. This is the market price.

TABLE 6-3.   Demand, Supply, and Market Price of Automobiles

Demand	Unit Price	Supply
250	$2,000	50
200	2,500	100
150	*3,000*	*150*
100	3,500	200
50	4,000	250

Table 6-3 shows that at the low price of $2,000 the demand is great and 250 cars could be sold, but that the suppliers are unwilling to satisfy the demand. They would be glad to deliver 250 automobiles at $4,000, but only fifty people are willing to consider a purchase at this price. A satisfactory compromise is reached only when 150 cars change hands at a price of $3,000. At this level, the decisions of buyers and sellers match.

A market price is the compromise arranged by our economic system to reach the difficult decisions with regard to the production and distribution of goods and services. We have seen earlier that every economic system must decide what to produce, how to produce, and for whom to produce. The market price is the primary tool for reaching the appropriate decisions in a framework of free enterprise. Governmental influence may have much to do with our preferences, but the ultimate verdict is rendered in the marketplace.

What happens if the suppliers refuse to drop the price below $3,500 per automobile, hopefully lining up 200 cars for sale? They discover that they guessed wrong and that something will have to be done to clear the market. They will take action on both the price and the number of cars offered. They will gladly relinquish cars to dealers in other areas in order to reduce their own supply, and they will probably make price concessions as well.

Price changes may escape the eyes of the casual observer. The official list price for an automobile remains the same for the model year. It is common knowledge, however, that the actual prices paid are constantly adjusting to market conditions. The dealer may add some accessories without charge or offer a better trade-in for the old jalopy. He will complain of a *surplus* of cars when he cannot get the price he is asking; when he has more orders than he can fill at the moment, the customer learns promptly that there is a *shortage* and he will have to pay the full price asked, or else wait.

The continuous matching of demand schedules and supply schedules causes an ever-changing series of market prices. It pushes the market price up when demand exceeds supply and pulls it down when the situation is reversed. Shortages and surpluses are not tolerated by a fluctuating market price. A shortage causes the price to rise, reducing the number of units wanted and encouraging suppliers to offer more units at the same time so that demand and supply are matched again.

A graphic presentation of the demand and supply curve in the same diagram will show a market price at the crossing point. Such a graph is a flash picture of one moment of a market situation and cannot reveal the changes which occur continuously.

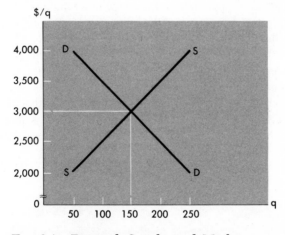

Fɪɢ. 6-4. Demand, Supply, and Market
Price of Automobiles

A word of warning may be in order at this point. In the daily course of business, neither buyers nor sellers have so clear a picture of the market situation as was just described in a simple example. The market price is largely the result of trial and error where a good hunch, born of practical experience, may prove an invaluable asset. Many familiar products follow a pattern of minor price changes which will usually suffice to clear the market of the total output.

A free pricing system maintains the balance between buyers and sellers. When this mechanism works without hindrance, there can be no surplus or shortage of goods—the number of goods supplied can always be sold at some price.

The role of the market price is of considerable importance to a free economy. Price is not only the result of all the forces of demand and supply, but also the cause of major shifts in the production and consumption patterns. A rise in the market price of a product will cause new facilities to be directed toward its production. At the same time, however, demand is discouraged at the rising price and will find a substitute. A drop in the market price may eliminate the inefficient producer whose costs are too high and stimulate the search for cheaper production methods by those who continue in this line of business. Price changes cause a continuously shifting allocation of resources.

COST

The discussion so far has ignored deliberately the cost of the goods bought or sold. This oversimplification helps to clarify the nature of the interaction between demand and supply forces. Let us see now what modifications must be introduced in the description of the operation of the market price when we remember that most goods have a cost.

The very first step in this investigation presents a surprising discovery. The flash picture shown by supply and demand schedules for any given moment of time remains unchanged by cost considerations. This statement is likely to be challenged by many people who will argue that you can't sell at $1.50 something you bought for $2. Their objection is in error. Once you have bought merchandise for sale, you must sell it at whatever price you can get.

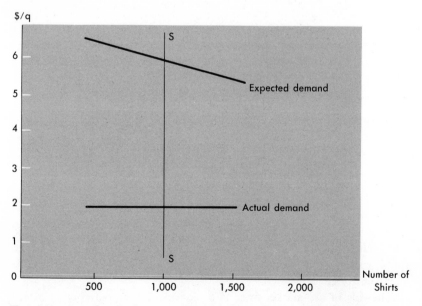

FIG. 6-5.   Supply of Shirts and Expected and Actual Demand

Let us clarify this important point with an example. A dry-goods store owns 1,000 wool shirts bought at $2.50 and priced to sell at $5.95; the owner has paid the invoice and cannot return the shirts to the manufacturer when he realizes that this item was an incredibly bad purchase. He sells ten shirts at the original price. He puts the rest on sale, reducing his profit margin slightly, and sells a few more without making much of a dent in his stock. He reviews the situation and concludes that he can dispose of the shirts only by selling them to a factory for use as workshirts at $2.00 apiece. His estimated demand schedule indicates no large sales to move the shirts at any higher price in the near future.

What shall the shirt owner do now? If he remembers their cost to him and refuses to sell below that price, the shirts pile up; they become dusty, shopworn, and moth-eaten; they tie up storage space and clerical time for periodic inventories. They represent unusable cash which must be recovered from customers. The owner would be wise to forget the cost completely and dispose of the shirts, even at a loss, as fast as possible. Then he can use the money, space, and effort on new merchandise where he may have better luck.

One of the most essential lessons learned by a beginning sales manager is the principle that he must not fall in love with his merchandise, but keep it moving. Once a product is ready for sale by the manufacturer or bought by the retailer, it must move on to its final destination regardless of the costs of the past.

Cost and Time

The impact of cost on the market price can be seen only when the passage of time is taken into consideration. The current demand and supply situation reflects the hopes and errors of the past; but costs incurred in an earlier period are best forgotten—they no longer influence the present supply. When goods or services have been supplied and their sale cannot be postponed, the amount of goods offered is fixed as this moment, and the market price will be determined entirely by the demand. When a singer has agreed to perform in an auditorium at 7 P.M. for a percentage of admission receipts, he will sing whether the audience holds fifty people or 5,000. The ticket price will reflect the demand, not the cost. If the room is half empty, rates will be reduced for students or any other group that can be induced to fill the space. If the auditorium is sold out, however, scalpers will sell tickets at a higher price than charged originally at the box office. Cost does not matter any more; the present supply cannot be changed.

Cost becomes important when we discuss what will be offered in the future. The singer who was disappointed by an empty auditorium will not return without a guaranteed minimum fee that will at least cover his expenses. The future supply of goods depends on future costs. "Future" may mean here the next few hours, next month, or ten years from now. Some of the costs of a business belong to the past, while others occur in the future. The length of time available before completion will make a difference in the goods actually offered.

Let us assume that in the earlier example of the 1,000 shirts only fifty have been actually delivered. With the order approaching completion, the store may not be able to cancel shipment of the rest, but it can ask the manufacturer to convert the unfinished material into sport shirts, or make some other arrangements to prevent a loss.

To clarify the role of cost on future supply, we must distinguish between short-run cost, when some costs are fixed, and long-run costs, when all can be changed.

Short-Run Costs

The short run refers to a time when some costs which we call fixed belong to the past and cannot be changed, while other variable costs, which will be spent only in the future, can still be avoided. In the short run, for example, a firm may not be able to alter its plant significantly, but it can decide how much material will be fed into the machines to produce more output. The factory may be operated for a few hours a day or around the clock.

What determines in a short-run cost situation the number of units which will actually be supplied? Before more units are produced, the supplier will expect to sell them for more money than he must spend for additional costs of production. When a firm has sold 10,000 backscratchers at $2 each and is ready to stop production of the item, a new order for 200 units at $1.50 as a special promotion will be accepted only if the additional cost of making and delivering them is less than $300 total. The added revenue from this new order must exceed the additional costs. Of course, the firm hopes to gain more than all its costs, past and future, in order to reap a profit; when this is not possible, however, it can continue to supply a product as long as additional revenue exceeds additional cost.

Long-Run Costs

The long run refers to a period of time which is long enough to allow a firm to change all its cost factors. The length of time involved depends on the nature of the business. A firm with a plant full of machinery can produce for many years before its equipment wears out and needs replacing, but a service institution operating in rented quarters can make a complete change as soon as its current contract expires. When one looks far ahead, all costs become variable and belong to the future. An entire plant needs replacement and modernization eventually; even the president of the firm can be replaced in the long run.

It may be helpful at this point to summarize the relationship of cost and price. *Cost has no direct bearing on the demand for a product.* When costs rise, the seller may no longer care to offer a good pair of shoes at $8, but the buyer continues to want them. The demand schedule for a product may be wishful thinking by many frustrated buyers, but their eagerness to buy at the same price is unaffected by the costs of the seller.

The market price is not affected directly by the past cost of the existing supply. Once the product has reached the market, it must be sold. The price fluctuates with the changes in demand, while the supply remains fixed —a principle which can be observed best at an auction. If several bidders want the same item, the price will rise. If nobody shows much interest in the product, the sale will be concluded at a price which may be even considerably below the production cost of the product. As long as the seller is better off with a sale than he would be by throwing away the product, he will part with his merchandise.

Not all goods need to be sold immediately upon completion. The rule that demand determines the price applies chiefly to products whose sale can't wait. Fresh fruit may spoil unless sold today if refrigeration is not available at the time. Some goods are so expensive to store that it would not pay to keep them around. Only when the time pressure is acute will the supplier have to accept whatever price he can realize.

In the short run, additional costs will determine the supply for the near future. The present market price serves as a guide toward estimating the demand for a product as it approaches the market. If added costs are expected to remain below the added revenue, the supply will continue to flow toward the consumer.

In the long run, costs will dominate the supply picture. A new plant will be constructed only when demand estimates exceed all possible costs by a comfortable margin. The supply two years hence is a new commitment, and the outlook for future sales must amply justify it.

Cost considerations will often become much more involved than this brief sketch has been able to show. The many refinements of different circumstances are more properly left to the technical experts.

APPLICATIONS OF MARKET PRICES

A market price is completely impersonal. Registering the forces working through demand and supply, the price is the result of the combination of all these influences. Quite often we may dislike the result presented by the market; what can we do about it?

The simplest answer comes from people who like the particular price to which others object. They will tell you that this price indicates the true interaction of demand and supply, which renders it untouchable and beyond the reach of human influence. This popular view is wrong. The existing market price is precisely determined by those willing to buy or sell, but the forces motivating buyers and sellers can be influenced and changed in many ways. These forces are not the result of natural law, but simply reflect human expectations.

The opposite reaction to an unfavorable market price comes from those who dislike it most strongly. If the price is too high, the consumer clamors for a price ceiling or for police action against speculators, a popular scapegoat for high prices. If they have dropped extensively, hard-pressed businessmen go to Washington and ask their congressmen to stabilize the unreasonably low prices which ruin their firms.

Market prices can be altered in many ways. If we do not deliberately interfere, a high price will reduce demand and stimulate supply and eventually will provide its own rectifying forces.

Perhaps the nature of the product makes it unwise to sit idly by until the situation corrects itself. Assume that the price of milk rises sharply due to higher cost. Milk is necessary for the health and strength of our children. A high price of milk will particularly injure families having the most children—a socially undesirable result. To bring the price down, we can stimulate the milk supply. By offering cheap credit to anyone who wants to raise cows, more resources will be available for milk production. Or, in order to reduce costs, research may be undertaken to increase the productivity of the milk industry. Both of these methods are used in several fields.

Another alternative would be the direct interference of public representatives in the milk market. The government could guarantee milk producers a higher price, which would stimulate an increased supply. In Figure 6-6, if milk has a tendency to sell at $1.00 per gallon, 1,000 gallons will be sold. If the government assures milk producers of $1.20 per gallon, the result will be an increased supply of 1,100 gallons. To sell the additional milk, the price must drop to 80 cents. The consumer is happy because he gets lots of cheap milk; the producer enjoys his increased sales of expensive milk; and the taxpayer eventually pays the difference, because he presumably favors plenty of milk for all.

Some people will object to this use of government power, but the example illustrates that supply and demand can be influenced to conform to the wishes of the majority—if it wants to pay the difference in taxes.

A demand for a legal ceiling price to be enforced by the government has repercussions which its sponsors may fail to appreciate fully in advance. If the market price for milk reaches $1.00 and the ceiling price is higher, such a ceiling becomes unnecessary and ineffective. If the ceiling is placed below the market price of 80 cents, a milk shortage can be predicted. People will want to buy 1,100 gallons at this price but will discover that only 900 gallons have been offered for sale.

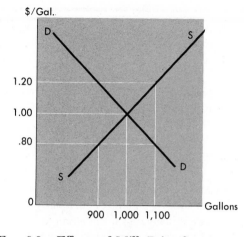

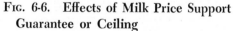

FIG. 6-6. Effects of Milk Price Support Guarantee or Ceiling

At the lower ceiling price, the producer has no incentive to supply more milk. It does not pay for him to concentrate on milk production, and so he shifts his efforts to ice cream for which no legal ceiling has been established. The law that guarantees cheap milk also causes a permanent shortage of the product. A stubborn price-control agency will then probably add a ceiling price for ice cream in order to push production back to milk. But the not-so-surprising result is a rise in cheese output, because the producers will keep on looking for profitable business where initiative and imagination will continue to pay.

Only during times of war is it possible to enlist the cooperation of virtually all citizens for centrally controlled prices and production goals. We are willing to forego individual want satisfaction to save the nation, but we do not want to sacrifice a smoothly working price mechanism for lesser goals. When prices are too high, we need to learn a lesson—not unlike the little boy who associates his mother's fever thermometer with her stern order for him to stay in bed. He doesn't like to be confined, so he decides to break the thermometer; he still has the fever, however. We may not like high prices, but hiding them under a legal ceiling does nothing to relieve the shortage of output with respect to the current demand.

FLEXIBILITY

An examination of the forces shaping demand and supply has revealed that at some price both will be equal and the demand for a product will just clear the market. How long will this market price remain the same and accomplish its function of equating supply and demand?

Fluctuations of price level differ for each product. The prices of stocks traded at the New York Stock Exchange vary with every transaction although they may be less than a minute apart. The prices of goods sold in a vending machine may not change for years. Is the pricing mechanism doing an equally effective job in both cases?

Prices are intended to act like a very sensitive recording instrument and register all changes surrounding business transactions. Fluctuations in price are important clues for business decisions and exert a strong influence on future production. When the price does not react promptly to a change in demand or supply conditions, one of the major advantages of the pricing mechanism is lost.

For some products continuous change of price would be impractical. When a store prepares a new shipment of merchandise for sale, it marks the price tags, which won't change until the store gets ready for its annual (or seasonal) sales to clear out remaining inventory. This system insures the customer that he will pay the same price regardless of the time of day he picks for buying or the number of people crowding the store. Imagine our reaction to a grocery store that would change prices with the length of the line at the checkout counter!

The balance between supply and demand is frequently restored without a prompt change in price as long as there is enough time to change the volume of production; the output of goods will thereby be brought in line to match the ever-changing demand. If a car model does not sell well, production schedules will be cut, some workers laid off, and others given a certain number of days of involuntary and unpaid vacation. Such curtailment of output may be inevitable in order to adjust production quickly; but people, plants, and materials need to be used to contribute to the growth of the economy. Fluctuations in output at rigid prices are accompanied by waste and unemployment. The maintenance of output at fluctuating prices is one of the basic prescriptions for a healthy national economy.

SUMMARY

Price is an essential tool of a free enterprise economy. It registers the ever-changing wishes of millions of individuals and transmits the information promptly to those who must act upon it.

Value is translated into demand for a product when one is willing to buy. High prices will result in a demand for few units, and low prices will sell a large number. A demand schedule lists the possible alternatives of price and input combinations as they appear to a firm.

A small price reduction accompanied by a proportionately larger sales increase indicates that the demand is elastic at this price. The reverse holds equally true.

Changes in demand occur constantly. Tastes may shift, incomes can rise or fall, or the outlook for the future may cause different needs.

Good substitutes will reduce sales of the original item, while a supplementary good rises in sales with the one it matches.

Supply describes goods offered at varying prices. A supply schedule shows the volume of output which can be expected at different prices. Higher prices will cause a larger flow of products to be offered; the opposite holds true for lower prices.

Market prices are the result of the interaction of supply and demand forces, and fluctuate in order to match an equal number of units offered and bought. At the same time, the price is a signal to the producer of the best opportunities for future sales.

Costs are a controlling factor in the supply of future products, but they have no influence on the demand or the present market price. The immediate market situation is dominated by the desire for available goods. In the long run all costs must be recovered.

The application of pricing principles shows that supply and demand can be influenced in order to reach a market price acceptable to a majority. Whatever means are taken to affect supply and demand, they are more acceptable than measures which supercede the pricing system, such as ceiling prices.

Prices must fluctuate in order to reflect the actual market forces and to signal the results speedily to buyers and sellers. Where freely fluctuating prices are practical, neither shortage nor surplus can develop.

The price mechanism has proved its efficiency. It is an impersonal system which directs goods to the highest bidder and rations them while at the same time calling for more supply. The application of a system of flexible prices, however, is not often as smooth and simple as the description in this chapter may indicate. This ideal sketch of prices will be investigated in its various forms in the next chapter.

Discussion Questions

1. How would you rank the relative elasticity of demand for the following products: penicillin, salt, cigarettes, filter-tip cigarettes? Why?
2. Does the supply of a product depend on its cost?
3. "The market price of a product is the result of demand and supply and cannot be changed." Comment on this statement.
4. What effect, if any, will a drop in the price of motorboats have on the sale of boats? on the sale of life preservers? on the sale of competing products?
5. When you suggest to a merchant that he cut the price of an article which does not sell well, he may often tell you, "It does not pay." Why does he feel that way?
6. How flexible do prices need to be for full use of resources? Why can't we fix a price and let the supply adjust to the demand?

Suggested Reading

BOULDING, KENNETH E., *Economic Analysis,* 4th ed. New York, Harper & Row, 1966, 2 vols.
LEFTWICH, RICHARD H., *The Price System and Resource Allocation,* 3rd ed. New York, Holt, Rinehart & Winston, 1966.

7

COMPETITION

Changing prices are primary tools for the adjustments of free markets. Prices, however, do not change automatically in response to economic influences; human decisions, and the suppliers' and buyers' willingness to transact business determine at what price goods can be traded. The demand and supply of a product can be matched in two ways:

1. The market price may rise or fall and change the minds of buyers and sellers so that their wishes coincide. Excess demand will be discouraged by rising prices, and slow demand will be stimulated by lower prices.

2. The supplier may announce a seldom-changing price and adjust his output to meet the number of units demanded at that price. An automobile manufacturer, for example, determines his price for each car model when the new model season opens, and afterwards he adjusts his production schedule to the estimated demand every month.

The commonly observed facts of fitting output to demand seem to contradict the claim that flexible prices regulate a large segment of economic life. Actually, a powerful force is needed to motivate people to do business under conditions of frequently changing prices. In our economy, the stimulus is supplied by competition.

WHAT IS COMPETITION?

Competition is a word of many meanings. In its broadest sense, life itself is a chain of competitive events. Babies compete for their mother's attention, children compete in school, and adults compete for work, for rewards, for goods, and for recognition. Competition as a form of rivalry is ever present. The United States has traditionally recognized competition as a major source of strength for the operation of an economic system. The competitive system becomes part of an educational system which trains children to push on as far as they can go. When we compare our idea of unlimited opportunity for the young competitor with the traditional outlook in other lands where children are trained to follow in their fathers' footsteps, we recognize one of the basic differences which exist between the United States and most other nations.

Economic competition, characteristic of our free enterprise system, partakes of all the broad aspects of human rivalry, but its features can be narrowed down to more specific points. Economic competition exerts pressure on the individual to take actions he would prefer to avoid: it forces him to work when he would rather play, to take less money when he wants more, to give a service he does not care to provide, to be efficient when he prefers to relax happily.

Let us not jump to the conclusion that competition is always a good and positive force! Be that as it may, economic competition causes efficiency by motivating people to produce the most wanted goods with the most readily available resources. Its determination of wants has its own biases; it favors productive action over relaxation; it favors, in many cases, appearance over substance and quantity over quality.

Competition is an abstract concept, but it is far from neutral in its impact. The competitive principle has contributed significantly toward shaping the mind of Western man. The affluence of the United States' economy is due to a large extent to the maintenance of competitive pressure over a long period of time.

In this chapter we shall describe first an abstraction—a pure form of price competition with its prerequisites and results. We shall compare this unrestricted form of competition with its opposite, an equally pure form of monopoly. Such abstractions furnish a helpful frame of reference for the more limited kinds of business rivalry which are found in everyday life. The determination of the form and the degree of competition suggests a compromise which is known as *workable competition*.

UNRESTRICTED COMPETITION

What conditions force a firm to reduce its sales price? What are the circumstances that lead a firm to pay more for its raw material than it has paid in the past? The answer to either question implies that the company has no control over its market as a seller or as a buyer. The conditions which deprive a firm of its market control are the characteristics of absolutely unrestricted competition. They will now be discussed from five points of view: (1) the size of competitors (relatively small), (2) the number of competitors (relatively large), (3) the addition of new competitors, (4) the sameness of competitors' products, and (5) the completeness of competitors' information of market conditions.

Size of Competitors

Competing firms must be small to be deprived of control over the price of their product. How large is a small firm when it comes to influencing price?

The answer depends on the nature of the product, the extent of the market area, and the size of its competitors.

If a product requires servicing of any kind, its seller has a greater share of market control than do those where service does not matter. On the other hand, the company whose product is serviced entirely by others must meet the price dictated by the market. A small appliance store, for example, may compete successfully with a discount house if it has a reputation for good service. However, if the small merchant limits his activity to delivering the merchandise and must depend on the factory warranty for service, he will have to meet the competitive price.

The size of the market area has a large influence on the relative smallness of a firm. A wheat farmer can grow a big crop and still remain insignificant in terms of the whole country, while a local lumberyard may be very small but exercise definite market control if the nearest city is far away.

The size of a competitor can be evaluated only in relation to the rest of the industry. One or two firms which are much larger than all others in their line of business may exercise considerable influence and leadership—even though they might be considered small in many other industries. The size that a company must reach in order to be freed from the dictates of unrestricted competition is never an absolute measure.

Number of Competitors

The number of firms needed for a pattern of unrestricted competition is also indeterminate. There must be a large enough number to convince any one competitor that the others are too numerous to worry about; neither his nor their individual actions make any difference in the outcome. Farmer Jones may use his 500 acres for the production of wheat or corn or alfalfa. His decision has no influence on what Farmer Miller does in the neighboring county, because 500 acres more or less makes no difference in the total estimate of the wheat harvest. The number of farmers runs into millions, and the production decision of any single one of them loses significance. Of course, when all farmers are organized so that they reach the same decision, the situation changes materially. They no longer represent small owners, whose individual, independent actions form the basis of unrestricted competition.

The number of firms which must be involved to approach unrestricted competition varies with each product and the size of the market. Automobiles compete in a national market; so do mail-order houses, while do-it-yourself laundry services compete on a purely local basis. A small number of competitors may vie strongly in a narrow market, while a broad market would require a much larger number. We may think of a national market for gasoline, with many thousands of small filling stations competing under conditions where no single station is very important. But if we consider the market for specific brand-name fuels under the control of large firms, each competitor has a distinct influence on the market.

Free Entry

Another condition required for unrestricted competition is the opportunity to start in a line of business and leave it again. This principle of free entry is necessary to prevent the "ins" from coming to agreements with each other and providing themselves with a collective influence on the market. Any number of competitors is not by itself sufficient to insure that they will refrain from an effort to reach agreements; a continuous influx of new firms and the exit of some old ones will render concerted action impossible.

Identical Products

Competition is unrestricted only when all competitors are selling the same product. The competition of cigarette makers may be intense, but it is not the unrestricted abstraction discussed at this time. People neither produce nor smoke cigarettes as such; they prefer Camels, Kents, Luckies, Chesterfields, or any other brand whose skillful advertisements have convinced smokers that one or another of them is better, or at least less hazardous to the buyer's health.

As soon as one encounters brand differences, products are no longer identical and the competition falls short of being unrestricted. Only when the products are undistinguishable can they be called identical. An open barrel containing salt of several producers would represent a type of identical, unidentifiable product; but as soon as the salt is packaged in handy containers and labelled "Morton," the producer gains some influence over the price and output of Morton's salt.

Complete Information

Competition is frequently restricted by the ignorance of the competitors and of their customers about the existing market situation. A merchant may be able to sell a shirt at $3.95 when his competitor sells the identical shirt at $3.50 just because his customers are not aware of it. Occasionally, a firm may sell a product at an old price after the market price has risen and competing firms are charging more for it.

It is a rare situation when buyers and sellers are fully aware of the status of the market and have the same information. A stock exchange is an example of a market which comes close to furnishing full information to all traders. When a sale of stock is completed, the details of the transaction (number of shares sold and price) are flashed on the board as fast as modern electronics permit, and the same information is quickly distributed through wire connections with every stockbroker in the nation.

The complete information needed for unrestricted competition refers to the market of a product. Buyers and sellers may know nothing about each other, but ignorance along these lines does not matter; they will avoid mistakes as long as they are fully aware of the market situation and know what they can get at any one price.

OBSTACLES TO UNRESTRICTED COMPETITION

Unrestricted competition creates pressures which eliminate all market control, and its prerequisites are seldom encountered in economic life. The reality of business, conducted by human beings with peculiarities and weaknesses, reveals a type of competition which includes many obstacles and restrictions.

Firms differ greatly in size; they shrink or grow depending on the wisdom and hard work (or good luck) of their managers. In modern manufacturing industries, small firms may be impractical and inefficient because of the need for large and expensive machines. When each firm must be large, the number of enterprises is necessarily limited and cannot be increased significantly. There may be opportunity for ten car manufacturers instead of four, but there is certainly not room enough for 1,000 firms producing automobiles in order to approach unrestricted competition.

Many industries are not open to the free entry of new firms since the obstacles here are numerous. Lack of money for a new operation is a common difficulty. Even more often, government rules prohibit the start of new firms without special permission, which is frequently hard to get. Public transportation, banking, and dry cleaning are examples of areas of restricted entry because of license requirements.

Most products of competing firms are not identical, and differ from each other at least in the minds of the customers. Physically, two products may be identical, but they are not the same in the marketplace if the customers distinguish between them. The information available to the buyers, the sellers, or both, is usually quite incomplete.

This list of market obstacles should reemphasize that unrestricted competition is an abstraction, not a description of business as we usually find it.

COMPETITION AS A YARDSTICK

Why do we consider in so much detail what unrestricted competition would do in an economy, when such a system is extremely rare in practice? The characteristics of unrestricted competition provide a very useful yardstick for the evaluation of actual business performance. Competition in business takes many forms. Some are highly desirable; others are certainly destructive. To clarify the picture of a competitive system, let us classify all business competition along a scale ranging from 0 to 100 percent.

The use of a scale to measure competition may sometimes lead to a serious misunderstanding. The 100 percent, or unrestricted competition, of this yardstick is called in the technical terms of the economist *perfect competition,* just as he refers to the zero as *perfect monopoly.* Many people feel that monopoly is bad and competition is good. Therefore, it is easy to jump to the conclusion that perfect competition is the best there is. The reader will certainly realize at this point that such a conclusion is unfounded. When a chemist isolates in his laboratory 100 percent perfect alcohol, he does not imply that anybody should drink this potion. Similarly, when economists study how unrestricted competition would operate, they do not suggest that the purest form is most desirable for all business in everyday life.

HUMAN REACTION TO COMPETITION

One hundred percent competition is not necessarily the best point to reach on the competitive scale; although people favor some characteristics of competition, they do not want it to become too severe. All of us would like to have a certain degree of influence on what we supply to the economy. The helplessness of the small fish in the big pond may be unavoidable at times, but it certainly is not the goal of the individual.

Unrestricted competition is a perfect device to cause the efficient operation of the economy. But efficiency is not life itself. Less perfect methods may have a noneconomic appeal which is occasionally more important to the satisfaction of wants than a higher efficiency rating. The coffee break has become an accepted custom in many offices in this country even though there may be some doubt about its justification in terms of efficiency improvement. Under conditions of unrestricted competition, a competitor who introduces the wasteful coffee hour in his firm might force others to do likewise. This aspect of competition is not popular with many employers, and some of them make persistent attempts to prohibit such actions. State legislatures often debate Sunday Closing Laws so that no competitor can offer a service which others would have to match to keep their share of the business.

Most people's attitude toward competition reveals a split personality. They favor more of it for others but less in their own business—the same person approves of competition as a buyer, but dislikes the excessive pressures which confront him as a seller. A store owner is glad if he can select his purchases from many suppliers, but as an earner of income, his outlook changes and he wants no strong competitors who might spell trouble. The consumer becomes a very important person who is offered a wide variety of choice to satisfy his wants. We approve of employers who fight for our services when we need a job. When these services gain in value, the opportunities offered by other employers can assure us that we will receive all we are worth. However, as we climb the ladder of success, our attention focuses increasingly on holding onto the place we have obtained. Our main concern becomes the defense of a good position against attempts by others to take it away rather than climbing still higher. Security emerges as an important goal when the competition becomes tough.

Economic views of life are influenced more strongly by man's income-earning activity than by his role as a consumer. He votes as a farmer, a worker, or a small businessman. As long as he feels moderately well-off, he votes for measures to keep his position unchanged. He applauds a luncheon speech by a great defender of free enterprise who extolls the virtue of competition, but then returns to his office to write his senator about the "chaotic" price conditions in his industry, asking Congress to pass a law to stop these wasteful price wars.

Let us not condemn the businessman who wants Congress to maintain some order in his market. Competition is pressure exercised by powers beyond our control; it forces competitors to take many steps—good and bad—which they dislike and hope to avoid. Their reaction is a natural one; they try to create every possible obstacle to the full impact of competition upon their own actions.

THE VALUE OF COMPETITION

The human reaction to competitive pressure is largely negative. Only a short step leads from grumbling about unbearable conditions to active opposition, and finally to the view that competition is bad for the economy and should be replaced by something more systematic and carefully planned which won't hurt anyone. Actually, such arguments are frequently used, even by businessmen whose strong adherence to the doctrine of freedom of enterprise cannot be doubted.

A typical case will find a businessman trying to convince the government that it should take action to keep him solvent. The cause of his troubles varies. He may be undersold by a foreign firm, by a discount house, or by a new competitor near his old market. Whatever the reason, he fails to see why he should make a change in a business which has flourished for years using the same style and technique. He wants the government to place a tariff on the foreign merchandise, pass a law against "pricing below cost," or subsidize directly his own "depressed" operations.

He rationalizes his request by pointing out that the economy is not helped when his firm shuts down and his workers lose their jobs. Of course, he is mistaken. The difficulties of his firm signal a call for change; it may need engineering improvements, new sales methods, or even a different product. It may need, most of all, new management. The competitive pressure has caused financial losses which the firm cannot ignore.

The value of competition should be quite clear from our example. Competition forces progress and causes economic change. It hurts all who refuse to change with it. It disregards social status and remains immune to the most convincing alibis; it judges only on the basis of accomplishments. In brushing aside the objections of even the very best citizens, it impartially promotes economic progress. Societies which have passed laws to protect existing firms from competitive change have slowed down the economic advancement of the community. Their people may have fewer ulcers, but they certainly will have fewer automobiles!

The economic value of competition is reflected in the high living standard of the United States. Competition cuts prices far below the level a seller would suggest; the competitor must remain efficient to keep his costs low, and he has to be willing to accept new ideas for a better tomorrow. No one can stop progress for his own personal comfort.

CHARACTERISTICS OF MONOPOLY

Monopoly is the opposite of competition. The word *monopoly* means that there is only *one seller* in the market. In its extreme form, monopoly indicates complete control over the market—the power to fix the price and to sell at this price all a firm chooses to produce.

A pure monopoly situation is as rare as one of unrestricted competition. Very few goods are such that people must buy them regardless of price. Even though a person may need a monopoly product, he usually has a choice in the amount he will buy. At a higher price he will buy less, and this indicates less than complete monopoly control in the market.

The city water plant is a fairly close approach to a monopoly business. People must have water, and there is no other convenient source for getting it. You can go to the nearest river and dip your own, but this is not usually a practical alternative. Even in this case, however, monopoly control is not complete. If the water prices rise beyond the level consumers are willing to tolerate, they will reduce their nonessential water use—they will quit watering the lawn and washing the car. To some limited extent rainfall might prove to be a substitute for the city water supply.

In a discussion of monopoly business, the economist is not thinking of a situation where a customer cannot do without the services of the monopolistic firm. Only in a few examples of heavily regulated public utilities do we approach this extreme. More commonly, we observe a monopoly situation whenever the customer finds it sufficiently inconvenient to purchase a substitute that the firm can charge a little more and adjust the amount produced to the selected price without losing a significant amount of business to competitive firms. The most typical effect of monopoly power is *reduced output* sold at *higher prices* under conditions of *slower changes* than would be expected otherwise.

Market Control

Unlimited power is not necessary, but a working monopoly implies substantial market control. A monopolist is in a position either to set the price for his product or to decide on the amount of goods he wants to supply to the market. If he insists on a given volume of production, for example 1,000 units, and places them on sale at $500 per unit, he may find only 600 people who can and want to buy his product. In this case a firm will sell only 600 units and not the 1,000 contemplated. Characteristically, a monopolist has a choice which permits him to determine the best combination of price and output.

A firm with monopoly power frequently determines the price of its product and then produces at this given price whatever amount the customers are willing to buy. If times are good and the demand rises, a monopoly business does not always raise its price, but often increases its output to fill the rising demand. The prompt price changes that are typical for a competitive market will be delayed, if they occur at all. When the boom recedes, the firm will cut its production and still maintain the same price.

Monopoly Profit

A frequently held belief is that the power of influencing price assures a firm more income than it could hope to earn otherwise. This added wealth goes under the name of *monopoly profit* and becomes an easy target for harassed legislators in search of new tax revenue. In fact, a monopoly has an opportunity to reap much added profit by skillfully adapting price and output to a fluctuating market demand.

Prices of products sold under monopoly conditions are frequently higher than they would be if numerous competitors were supplying similar goods.[1] This does not always mean a greater profit, however. The higher prices may well indicate the higher operating costs of a firm which is not forced to become as efficient as an enterprise that has to maintain standards comparable to those of its sharpest competitors. Only efficient monopolists are likely to reap monopoly profits.

Rigid Prices

Under monopoly conditions, the maintenance of rigid prices is more prevalent than high profits; a firm loses many customers when it tries to find the highest possible price for a product. A firm with limited monopoly power is not likely to take a chance on raising prices so high that its customers decide to do without its product. The price decided upon by this firm will reflect a consideration of cost plus a possibly more generous markup than would prevail under competitive conditions. This price may be equally as far removed from the minimum necessary to stay solvent as it is from the maximum the market will permit. Changes in cost or in customer demand does not usually cause changes of the monopoly price, which remains quite remunerative in good times or bad.

Lack of Pressure

The greatest advantage of monopoly power is not so much the opportunity for excessive profits, as it is the chance for an easy life without the constant alertness demanded by competitive pressure. This particular advantage of monopoly control is often reflected in the management's attitude toward its employees. Working conditions are frequently more pleasant, demands for performance less stringent, and the atmosphere on the job more relaxed than is customary under more competitive conditions. The firm is known as a good place to work and its employees are considered particularly fortunate. Few people stop to realize, however, that all this pleasantness is due to monopoly conditions which raise the price of the product for the rest of the population.

---

[1] In a *seller's market* in time of war or in other periods of prolonged shortages, it is possible that a monopoly price would remain below the competitive price because the monopolist may be slow to adjust to "all the market will bear."

Objections to Monopoly

The economist objects to excessive monopoly power because of its detrimental effects on the economy as a whole. High and rigid prices can be maintained because monopolistic firms are immune to demands for change. Unused plant capacity is quite common under monopoly conditions and results in a *waste of resources,* which produces a *smaller output* than the technology would permit and fails to give the consumer as many goods as he would be able to buy under competitive conditions. A drop in the demand for a product does not generally result in lower prices or a changing product, because monopolists may be inclined to meet a lower demand with a cut in production, layoffs of productive factors, and reduced sales at unchanged prices.

A firm might actually reap greater profits if it lowered its price and sold more products; without competition to prompt this, the manager may never find out what opportunities he is missing. The sales price is based on the volume of output the firm feels fairly sure to sell without special effort. A businessman who is used to an existing sales pattern rather doubts that sales can be boosted very much by price reductions. He prefers to wait for better times rather than borrow trouble and will lower prices only if *a competitor undercuts his old price and forces him to experiment.*

Since businessmen seldom feel that a cut in the price of their product would cause higher profits, we need enough competition to force such experiments. Mass production for mass markets is the beneficial result of cost-reducing, competitive pressure.

COMPETITION VERSUS MONOPOLY

A comparison of the two extremes of the competitive yardstick—100 percent competition and 100 percent monopoly—reveals some surprising similarities.

Completely unrestricted competition will be reflected in identical prices, because all buyers find out the lowest price and will not pay more. No wheat farmer can get more, or has to accept less, per bushel than any other wheat farmer. In the monopoly case, the one seller has only one price for all who need his product.

Identical prices may have several causes. Occasionally people become suspicious when they inquire about the price of a product and receive the same quotation from several firms. This similarity can, of course, result from an agreement between competitors who are tired of competing. If such a practice is uncovered the conspirators may be jailed because they are violating the law.

More commonly, identical prices result from an accounting technique which is standardized for the whole industry. When every firm uses the same rate book, only an arithmetical error can lead to a difference in quoted prices. The fact that many firms charge the same price for a product is, therefore, by itself no sign of competition or monopoly.

In extreme cases of monopoly and competition, there are no special services, no advertising, and no efforts to impress the customer. The competitor will refrain from needless effort and expense because he can sell all he wants at the going price. Why should he advertise "Buy Jones's wheat"? The monopolist sells with ease at his own price to all who need his product.

The difference between competitive and monopolistic operations is sometimes hard to see. While both extremes lead to one and only one market price, under the pressure of competition this price will probably be lower and the number of transactions will be greater than in a monopoly, because more people can afford more goods at the lower price.

Competitive forces lead to change where monopoly avoids change. Continuing innovation demands unrelenting efforts to maintain a competitive position with the favorable effects these efforts produce for the consumer.

Competitive Rivalry

The world's business takes place somewhere between the extremes of the competitive yardstick. When competitors know and influence each other and are able to exercise a noticeable influence on the result of the struggle for more income, competition becomes a form of economic rivalry.[2] This type of competitive situation forms the normal pattern of business behavior. Usually several firms compete with each other, but seldom are there so many that they lose all control over the market. Competition becomes personalized when a firm is able to give its customers more of what they want than its rivals do. This gives the public a choice not offered by the extremes of competition or monopoly.

The rivalry of healthy youngsters on evenly matched football teams helps to build healthy bodies. Young minds are improved when sports rivalry is linked with a spirit of fair play. It is fun to win and no tragedy to lose. However, when winning the game becomes a matter of extreme importance the play gets rough and results in broken bones instead of

---

[2] Formal economic analysis distinguishes between imperfect competition, monopolistic competition, and oligopoly, which refers to the competition of a few firms that are keenly aware of each other's actions.

healthy bodies. When practicing for next Saturday's game takes up all study time, the beneficial effects of the sport becomes doubtful. This example in athletics tells us something that holds true in all competition: rivalry can be much fun, but it is easily overdone.

Characteristics of Restricted Competition

Economic rivalry takes many forms. A business may concentrate its efforts on improving quality, novelty, consumer persuasion, price cutting, or individualized services. Most successful firms aim at several of these objectives at the same time. They all have one goal in common—to remove the firm as far as possible from the rigors of unrestricted competition.

Quality. The competitive struggle will concentrate on the improvement of quality only when the customer wants to buy higher quality and is in a position to know the difference. A manufacturer of precision gauges or airplanes will try to produce the best possible product. But the quality of the invisible parts of consumer goods is likely to be kept at the minimum necessary to prevent an early breakdown during the producer's warranty period. The popular opinion that competition will always improve the quality of a product is often contradicted by the evidence.

Novelty. Novelty is a major objective of rivals selling consumer goods. Newness itself attracts customers although the latest thing may not be always or necessarily an improvement. Something different appeals to people's constant desire for change in the satisfaction of their wants. If the product turns out to be disappointing, something still newer is likely to take its place. Many durable consumer goods, such as cameras, are discarded long before they wear out because an electric-eye model has rendered the older product obsolete.

Consumer Persuasion. To persuade the consumer of the special value, or the uniqueness of your own product is a most effective way to reduce competition. Presumably buyers will not compare prices too closely when they are convinced that your product is better than all others. This accounts for the widespread use of advertising in many forms. Under very competitive conditions, the single firm has not enough influence on the market for its products to justify advertising expenditures. At the other end, a complete monopolist would not spend money on advertising because his customers have no choice except to go to him if they want his product. But advertising can help a firm to move from too much competition to something closer to monopoly conditions.

The creation of trade names plays an important part in this effort to remove a product from the area of unrestricted competition. The name makes a product appear different, though such an appearance may be quite deceptive. Particularly when a product differs in looks from others sold for the same purpose, the persuasion of the advertisers may successfully sell one good at a much higher price than similar ones. Examples are numerous and well known. Home appliances are sold by trade name; cigarettes, beer, and many other products use the same technique.[3]

Price Cutting. The oldest form of rivalry used is cutting a price to gain a better market position, a technique often associated with the idea of extreme competition. A firm under conditions of unrestricted competition can sell its total output at the going market price and therefore has no reason to charge less. Price cutting is most typical for an industry with greater output capacity than the market demand will absorb at a profitable price. Since not all rivals have the same ability to produce, the low-cost firms can cut their prices to drive the high-cost firms out of business. Gasoline price wars are an example of such action.

As long as the more efficient producer earns a profit at the lower price, the elimination of weaker firms becomes the sacrifice an economy must make to continued progress. Should, however, these temporary price cuts prove to be so unprofitable that they are maintained only until several competitors have been eliminated, then competitive rivalry becomes a cutthroat method which is hard to defend, since it leads ultimately to less output and higher prices.

Individualized Services. The exercise of rivalry flourishes most readily where services are involved. Price cuts can be met by one's rivals immediately, and advertising can be matched with similar speed. Personal services are not copied with equal ease. The success of many firms rests largely on their ability to render a service which the bigger or low-cost rivals cannot immitate. These services take many forms—individual advice on the best use of a product, prompt and effective repair service, free delivery to the home, gift wrapping, and many others. Some services have become so widely accepted that all competitors have to furnish them, such as cleaning your windshield when you buy gasoline.

All these forms of rivalry attempt to reach two objectives for which most businesses strive:

1. They must continue to compete effectively and sell their product at a price dictated by market conditions—this is the competitive aspect of business.

---

[3] *Product differentiation* is the technical term for a market situation in which like goods are offered as different products.

2. They try to obtain a position in their field which permits them increased market control and restricts competition in that particular area— this is the monopolistic aspect of business.

Unfair Methods of Competition

Price cutting below cost has been mentioned before as a possible method of unfair competition when the objective of the price cutter is a higher future price after some of his competitors have been eliminated. Cutthroat competition and other devious methods are symptoms of too much rivalry and do not help to maintain a competitive system.

What are unfair methods of competition? It is less difficult to agree on examples of unfairness than on a general definition. Fraudulent advertising, misleading labels, and meaningless warranties are examples of competitive methods which few people approve. But it is not necessarily unfair to take advantage of opportunities which competitors cannot match. One firm may be financially strong enough to give credit to its customers while others cannot afford this service. Is this unfair? When a lady buys perfume, the fancy package may cost more than its liquid contents. Should she object to this "fraudulent" packaging? Or does she admit that an impressive-looking gift package is what she really wants just as much as the scent of its contents? Public opinion must determine to a large degree what will be considered unfair in the market.

Workable Competition

Workable competition is a compromise of competitive and monopolistic elements. The practical arguments about the nature of workable competition are numerous, and some of these discussions will be presented in the following chapter on monopoly control. Whereas the businessman who tries to reduce competition in his industry places most emphasis on the word *workable,* the student of economics must realize that the essential element remains *competition* (which may be mitigated but is still necessary). "Workable" in this sense is as much competition as any line of business can stand.

The exact point on the competitive scale which is best for the economy cannot be determined arbitrarily, and must be judged separately case by case. There are clues, however, which indicate the presence or absence of competitive practices. An industry which abounds in innovations, cost reductions, and product improvements operates in the competitive framework. Its price structure may be less revealing. People frequently disagree on whether or not a price is too high, too low, or just right. However, some indication concerning the degree of competition in an industry is furnished by the frequency of price changes. Prices do not have to change continuously, but if they always change long after similar products have fallen or risen, they demonstrate a "stickiness" which tells us that competition in this area is substantially reduced.

Rigid prices and lack of growth combined are a clear signal that competition in a particular industry is insufficient and that stagnation has set in. These are the firms most likely to turn to the government for help, clamoring for support to maintain the existing situation in the name of free enterprise. Nothing could be more harmful than to assist these firms. Their lack of competitive adjustment and their inability to help themselves are an indication of the need for the most disagreeable feature of free competition—the elimination of firms which fail to keep up with changing times.

Workable competition steers a narrow middle course through dangerous waters. On one side there is too much competition for the competitor to bear, and on the other there is too little of it to maintain a progressive economy. We need to feel secure enough to keep our mind on future progress rather than on avoiding a present disaster. But let us not become so safely enshrined in our economic position that we sit back and do nothing! The best point on the competitive scale cannot be determined in abstraction. We have to discover it anew every day.

SUMMARY

Competition in its purest and most unrestricted form describes a type of business which is characterized by many firms, relatively small in size, none of which are large enough to influence the market with their decisions. It is easy to get in or out of such an industry, which is assumed to make the same product for customers who have complete market information.

This extreme concept of competition serves only as a yardstick for the measurement of actual business performance, not as a goal to be reached by the economy.

The praise of competition as a tool to promote economic progress is tempered by the fact that most people as producers of income would prefer less competitive pressure in their own business.

Monopoly describes the opposite condition of competition. The monopolist controls the market of his product. He sets the price and, to some degree, the amount he wants to produce, and exerts the power necessary to exclude potential competitors. Monopoly profits can be larger than most, but more often the monopolist uses his power to keep prices rigid, letting the output and the profits fluctuate instead. The lack of pressure to adjust promptly to changing market conditions is a major characteristic of monopoly control.

Competitive rivalry is the degree of competition usually found in everyday life. The competitors have some influence on their market; they may know each other and make their decisions on the basis of personal information. They compete by emphasizing the differences of their wares and by trying to persuade the customers that their own product has some special advantages over the others.

While most forms of competition are accepted as necessary for more efficient performance of the economy, some practices are condemned as unfair. Efforts to eliminate competitors for the purpose of creating a monopoly position are considered detrimental to the economy.

The practice of a free enterprise system is a form of workable competition. Enough rivalry must prevail to promote the growth of the economy, the introduction of improvements, and the search for more efficient ways to produce better things for more people. These efforts cannot be taken for granted. Constant alertness is the price we pay for the maintenance of workable competition.

When an unchanged product is delivered in diminishing volume by firms actively engaged in eliminating the weakest competitors, and when prices are fixed at the expense of the consumer, it is evident that the competitive system requires improvement. The next chapter will show how the law has come to recognize the need for workable competition, and how the courts try to maintain a competitive structure and a progressive performance in those industries which come to their attention.

Discussion Questions

1. Why is competition often praised so highly and attacked so viciously by the same people?
2. Nothing short of perfect competition is good enough for the progress of our economy. Comment on this statement.
3. Competition irks most competitors. What is its value to an economy?
4. What are the main features of monopoly operations? Why do economists oppose these operations even though many people like to work for such firms?
5. Why does economic rivalry take many forms in addition to changes in price?
6. How does workable competition differ from unrestricted competition or from total monopoly?
7. What makes competitive methods unfair?
8. Is vigorous competition compatible with identical prices of all competitors? with unchanging prices?

Suggested Reading

CLARK, JOHN M., *Competition as a Dynamic Process*. Washington, D.C., Brookings Institution, 1961.

MACHLUP, FRITZ, *The Economics of Seller's Competition*. Baltimore, Johns Hopkins, 1952.

MANSFIELD, EDWIN, *Monopoly Power and Economic Performance*. New York, Norton, 1964.

MONOPOLY CONTROL

Monopoly is a bad word to the majority of the American people and has never been socially respectable in the United States. Although they may not always be too sure of the nature of monopoly business, most people are against it in principle. They object to the idea that any person, business, or other organization can dictate economic actions to the public.

This national attitude has been responsible for the passage of legislation designed to curb monopoly power. It has also led to a broad suspicion of big business and large organizations in general, a situation that places every huge institution on the defensive. Our position differs substantially from that of other nations toward the monopoly problem. While the operation of competitive business is far from perfect, strong public support of competition has contributed significantly to its continued survival in this country. In fact, competition is more vigorous here than in most other nations, which pay lip service to the idea but cannot practice it without popular support.

The broad defense of the competitive ideal is rather surprising when one considers the numerous benefits individuals gain from monopoly operations. Many people prefer to work for a firm with substantial market control; such a business can afford to offer better working conditions, job security, and other advantages to its employees. The more competitive and cost-conscious a firm becomes, the less security it has to offer. Also, as consumers we prefer to buy the products of well-known large firms, because we feel that such giants cannot afford to sell bad merchandise or fail to make good on an occasional error. In this case the consumer is confusing national importance with monopoly power without realizing that a firm with true monopoly control could safely ignore his wishes.

For a less emotional approach to monopoly control, let us look at the sources of monopoly power and the methods used to render this power harmless to a free economy. Many laws have been passed to restrict private monopolies and the courts are constantly reinterpreting the statutes to cope with novel methods aimed at the elimination of competition. Limitation of monopolies by law, regulation of private monopolies by public agencies, and public operation of monopolies for the general welfare are the techniques of monopoly control to be discussed in this chapter.

SOURCES OF MONOPOLY POWER

The sources of monopoly power are many and varied. Some of them can be traced to the accidents of nature which place a firm in an advantageous location or give it control over raw materials. Economic causes of monopoly positions are the large size of a business, financial strength, experience, and knowledge of difficult operations. A famous research team is hard to duplicate; its advanced knowledge may confer enough power on a firm to discourage serious competitive challenges.

An important source of monopoly power has always been the government itself. Whenever the government grants exclusive rights to a firm, it establishes a monopoly position. The grant of a license to transmit television over specific airwaves creates a monopoly, and conferring a patent which others are not allowed to duplicate has the same effect. The most complete type of monopoly control, however, is direct government operation. The U.S. Post Office, for example, excludes all others from similar activities. We shall now discuss these sources of monopoly power in more detail.

Natural Advantages

A good location may place a firm in such a strategic position that its competitive advantage will discourage all potential rivals. The owner of the busiest corner on Main Street in a small town may dominate the business of the community. A plant located in a spot where substantial savings can be made in transport costs has some control over the price of its product. A restaurant overlooking Grand Canyon can charge higher prices because of its unique location and its strong appeal to tourists.

Ownership of raw materials can become the source of monopoly power. Assured access to the most desirable bauxite deposits may permit control of an aluminum industry, for it would be difficult for other firms to match the advantage of a low-cost raw material. A firm does not need to own all sources of the raw material; control of the most desirable low-cost deposits is sufficient to assure the maintenance of a dominant position in the industry.

Economic Advantages

Economic power is both a cause and an effect of monopoly control. A dominating firm may exercise its leadership so vigorously that others in the industry prefer to follow the leader without challenge, thus making it possible for the firm to become even stronger. Not every large firm exercises monopoly control, but the inherent advantage of large size has forced the courts to deal with the problem repeatedly as we shall see below.

Finance.   Financial strength is a source of monopoly power. The known ability of a firm to outlast potential competitors in a test of power discourages challengers. Suppliers can be brought to terms when they know that their customer is in a financial position to build his own plant unless they deliver on his conditions. The possibility of a challenge from new competitors diminishes when several hundred million dollars are needed to give a new firm a reasonable chance of success. This is the case in the manufacture of automobiles.

The wealthiest citizen in a small town sometimes controls the economic life of the community. Since he is a major owner of business and real estate as well as a prime source of credit, few people will dare challenge his monopoly position. They realize that this leading financier can influence so many people that a new business must obtain his stamp of approval in order to operate profitably in the community.

Organization.   Economic power is vested also in organized groups; trade associations, labor unions, and professional organizations create a monopoly position for their members. The strength of their control depends on the effectiveness of the organization, its ability to regulate membership, and the aims of the group. It is sometimes hard to define the borderline between an informal association of kindred spirits for the purpose of exchanging ideas and an organization asserting efforts to control the field for its members. We shall return to this problem later.

Knowledge.   Limited access to special knowledge, such as the results of electronics research, creates an economic advantage on which monopoly power can be built. Until other firms gain the same information, the leader has the controlling position. This type of monopoly, however, will be short-lived unless this special knowledge can command legal protection.

Legal Advantages

The law is an important source of monopoly power. Legislation covering patents and trademarks has the objective of conferring limited monopoly control to its beneficiaries. The goal of patent legislation, which protects the owner of an invention for seventeen years, is to encourage and promote research and technical progress; a monopoly position may result when one firm owns numerous patents.

Modern research is very expensive and requires the systematic use of well-equipped laboratory facilities. Only wealthy firms or public agencies can afford to mobilize sufficient funds for the organization of skilled research teams. The fruits of the inventors' efforts are assigned to their employers from the start of their employment, which explains why one firm often owns many patents. The law protects the patent owner against unlawful duplication of the invention.

The patented results of successful research enjoy enough monopoly power to command a very profitable sales price. This monopoly profit must be sufficient to pay for all the research facilities, including those used on projects that fail. Patent rights channel more funds toward such risky investment. These rights are not unlimited, however, and they will be supported by the courts only so long as they are used for continued technical progress.[1]

Licensing requirements are a widespread form of monopoly control. Government agencies are empowered by law to restrict the entry of new firms into many fields to a number adequate for "the convenience and necessity" of the public. The interpretation of this broad, discretionary rule leads frequently to the protection of previously established firms by a regulatory agency.

ATTACKS AGAINST MONOPOLY POWER

Any attack against monopoly power must first define its exact objective. Are we opposed to economic monopolies in every form because of the inherent *inefficiency* of these operations? If such an all-out attack were intended, much of it would have to concentrate on the local level. In a small town the services of the plumber, barber, or electrician are as likely to be governed by monopolistic practices as any large operation anywhere.

A few owner-operated firms can reach an agreement on prices and on a division of a small-town market without major difficulties. The partners in such an agreement will do quite well, provided the entry of new firms can be controlled locally so that there won't be too many competitors to divide the pie. This type of monopoly operation does not usually cause widespread opposition since the majority seems to accept such a lack of local competition as an inevitable fact of life. Men who refuse to conform will leave town. Without showing undue excitement or indignation, we may refer colloquially to the situation with the comment that "someone has sewed up the town."

Our opposition to monopoly is apparently more restricted, focusing

[1] A popular description of the development of the American patent system, which goes back to Colonial times, can be found in a pamphlet in the U.S. Department of Commerce series Do You Know Your Economic ABC's?, *Patents: Spur to American Progress* (1965).

only on large regional or national organizations. Even here it is not clear whether the attack is directed against monopoly as such, or against some other feature of business operations. Frequently we hear it suggested that some important business is a monopoly and should be taken over by the government. Such a view indicates a serious confusion of thoughts. A private firm does not become competitive when the government takes over its operation. In fact, government-managed business exerts an extreme form of monopoly control since it can prohibit the appearance of any potential challenger.

The question arises whether we are opposed to all monopoly or only to privately owned monopoly. The philosophy of a free enterprise system leaves no doubt that competitive, private operations must be maintained whenever possible. The nationalization of private business which has been laggard in actual competition is the typical solution of the socialistic state. Government management does not restore competition; it acknowledges the absence of competition and makes the monopoly permanent.

ANTITRUST LEGISLATION

The popular attitude opposing monopoly power has found its strongest expression in antitrust legislation. These laws are intended to discourage and suppress, when necessary, the use of monopoly power by private firms in competitive industries.

The laws against monopoly business go back to the nineteenth century, when public demand forced Congress to take action against the ruthless practices of a few firms whose power had grown rapidly after the end of the Civil War. Strong industrialists had welded together some powerful firms by transferring the voting rights of several owners to one *trust*.[2] The Standard Oil Trust under the rule of John D. Rockefeller was the best known at the time. The monopoly power resulting from these combinations became the prime target of popular ire.

Sherman Act

The basic federal statute to prevent monopoly is the Sherman Antitrust Act of 1890. The law is brief and broadly worded, which made it possible for succeeding generations to reinterpret its spirit in the light of the requirements of changing times. The two main sections of the law are quoted here:

[2] These trusts, which have long ceased to exist, must not be confused with modern trust agreements. A trust company, usually a bank, administers the management of a family fortune in the interest of widows and children who are not judged capable of handling their own affairs by the man who accumulates the fortune.

Section 1. Every contract, combination in the form of trust or otherwise, or conspiracy, in restraint of trade or commerce among the several states, or with foreign nations, is hereby declared to be illegal. . . .

Section 2. Every person who shall monopolize, or attempt to monopolize, or combine or conspire with any other person or persons, to monopolize any part of the trade or commerce among the several states, or with foreign nations, shall be deemed guilty of a misdemeanor, and. . . .

The interpretation of such terms as "restraint of trade," "monopolize," or "conspire" was left to the courts. The initial impact of the law on business practice was minor; only in a few cases did the courts find fault with the growing power of firms resulting from many forms of combination. Secret agreements of pipe producers were held to be in violation of the law; the creation of a holding company to control several railroads was prohibited by the courts; the Hatters Union was found to violate the Sherman Act by calling a strike.

The true significance of the Sherman Act became clear only much later, when the broad wording of the law permitted the courts to stop practices never thought of at the time of its enactment. The success of this law is not measured by the number of indictments and the percentage of cases won by the attorney general, but by the high degree of competition which is still in evidence in the American economy. Many businessmen continue to compete without attempting to reach monopolistic agreements simply because it is the law; their number cannot be measured by statistics.

Clayton Act

Several unexpected judicial interpretations of the Sherman Act, particularly its use to punish a striking union, led a majority in Congress to the enactment of the Clayton Act in 1914. The purpose of this law was to clarify the legal intent of the Sherman Act in certain areas. The use of the antitrust laws for strike breaking was prohibited, and several specific forms of monopoly practices which had previously been found lawful were declared illegal. The attempt to legislate against specific practices, however, proved to be quite unsuccessful, since clever lawyers promptly found other ways to accomplish the same objectives without violating the detailed prohibition of the law. For example, Section 7 of the Clayton Act ruled out the purchase of shares of competing firms when it would create a monopoly position for the surviving company. The provision had no practical effect— the same objective could be accomplished by other means.

Celler Act

Only in 1950 was this loophole in the Clayton Act closed by Congress with the passage of the Celler-Kefauver Act. The new law has made it possible to stop mergers which tend to create a monopoly. When two competitors try to combine into one firm and the resulting organization would be likely to control more than about 15 percent of the market in which they operate, the courts will reject their merger attempt.

Robinson-Patman Act

One of the more controversial clauses of the Clayton Act was its Section 2 prohibiting price discrimination. There was confusion over its interpretation until it was clarified by the Robinson-Patman Act in 1936. This statute makes it unlawful, among other things, to sell identical products to different customers at different prices unless the price reflects a cost differential. The provision was directed against large and powerful retailers who would be able to buy at lower prices than smaller firms. The sellers might agree to special price reductions for fear of losing the trade of those big customers otherwise.

Pricing practices are often subject to court review. The Supreme Court prohibited the so-called basing-point system of pricing in a decision involving the cement industry in 1948. The cause of the complaint in this case was not price differences, but identical prices. The trade associations in several industries, such as steel, cement, corn syrup, and others, had developed a pricing technique used by all competitors, whereby each firm would reach the same price quotation for the same order regardless of the location of the supplier. This elimination of the geographical differential was considered a form of price discrimination under the law.

Different sellers may charge identical prices to the same customer as a result of keen competition; in addition, if every seller uses the same accounting standards in figuring costs, their quoted prices will probably be the same. The courts, however, are very reluctant to accept such an explanation. They assume that identical bids by many competitors are the result of conspiracy; if basing-point pricing produces the same bids from all firms, the courts prohibit the use of this technique. The Robinson-Patman Act requires identical prices for all customers from one seller, but expects a different price quotation from each seller.

The Federal Trade Commission Act

Congress created the Federal Trade Commission (FTC) as an independent federal agency in 1914, the same year in which the Clayton Act became law. The new agency was given the task of preventing unfair methods of competition before they hardened into monopoly positions requiring intervention by the Department of Justice. In practice, the FTC found it difficult to prevent trouble. Consequently, its activity developed a tendency to parallel and occasionally duplicate the efforts of the antitrust division of the Justice Department.

The Federal Trade Commission had the task of deciding which competitive methods were unfair and to issue cease and desist orders to stop such practices. These orders, however, could not be enforced by the Commission without recourse to the courts. Further, judges often took a different view of commercial practices and failed to support the decisions of the FTC. The law was finally amended in 1938 with the passage of the Wheeler-Lea Act, whereby all cease and desist orders of the Commission became binding after sixty days unless they were appealed before this period had expired. The law also permitted the FTC to prohibit deceptive practices and launched the Commission on an investigation of complaints against advertising techniques. This led to specific legislation on the labeling of many products, such as the Wool Products Labeling Act (1939) and the Textile Fiber Products Identification Act (1958). Although more accurate information helps to protect the consumer, its effectiveness in reducing monopoly practices is remote.

ENFORCEMENT OF ANTITRUST LAWS

The true meaning of any law is revealed only through its interpretation in the courts; particularly the decisions of the Supreme Court of the United States which carry great weight in influencing the future behavior of business firms. The broad features of the antitrust laws make it possible for the courts to change their impact with changing times.

Rule of Reason

During its first twenty years, the interpretation of the Sherman Act by the courts was narrowly literal and not very effective. The demand for amendments to the law was strong enough to promote the enactment of the Clayton Act in 1914. Three years before this legislative action, the Supreme Court had rendered two key decisions in the Standard Oil and American Tobacco Cases.[3] Both firms had been found to violate the Sherman Act and were ordered to split their firms into several smaller and independent companies—they had used methods to monopolize their industries which were considered illegal.

The major impact of this decision, however, was the new meaning given to the term *restraint of trade*. The Supreme Court proclaimed the

[3] *United States* v. *Standard Oil Company of New Jersey*, 221 U.S. 1 (1911); *United States* v. *American Tobacco Company*, 221 U.S. 106 (1911).

"rule of reason," pointing out that not every restraint was a violation of the law; only an *unreasonable* restraint was forbidden. In the oil and tobacco cases the Court condemned not the degree of monopoly achieved, but the practices which were applied to reach a monopoly position. The rule of reason required proof of (1) actual injury of a competitor in his ability to compete, and (2) deliberate action to reduce his competitive strength. A violation of the law was present only in a case of deliberate injury of a competitor. If a firm could monopolize an industry without such flagrant violations, the courts would not disturb it.

Is Bigness a Crime?

Many people associate monopoly with large size. Hardly a year passes without headlines concerning the monopoly practices of a large firm, for which it is brought into court. It is natural, therefore, to jump to the conclusion that big firms are monopolistic by nature and should be reduced in size; in fact, proposals to this effect have reached Congress occasionally in the past. This assumption, however, is not necessarily well founded, for every court case against a huge business makes the headlines; indeed, it returns to the front page with each new legal move. Du Pont, for example, has been defending its actions in courts for over fifty years.

The national attitude toward big business has received changing interpretations in the courts. The oil and tobacco cases mentioned before led to the dissolution of big firms, but because of their practices, not their size. The Supreme Court was even more explicit in a famous case against the giant U.S. Steel Corporation (1920).[4] It declared bigness per se not to be a crime under the law. This was confirmed by other decisions which limited the antitrust laws to a prohibition of bad *conduct*.

This interpretation, however, was reversed in 1945 with the final decision in a case charging the Aluminum Company of America (Alcoa)[5] with a monopoly in the manufacture of newly refined aluminum. The courts found no deliberate wrongdoing on the part of Alcoa, but because the firm controlled 90 percent of aluminum production in the United States, its dominant position was sufficient to discourage potential competitors from any attempt to enter the industry. For the first time, the court found the *structure* of the industry itself a violation of the law. When large size creates a dominant position for a firm, the courts consider such a potential monopoly a cause for demanding reduction of the firm's power.

The decision in the Alcoa case has been reinforced several times. In 1957 the Supreme Court forced du Pont to sell its 23 percent of General Motors' stock, because this partial ownership gave du Pont a monopolistic

---

[4] *United States* v. *United States Steel Corporation,* 251 U.S. 417 (1920).
[5] *United States* v. *Aluminum Company of America,* 148 F. 2d 416 (1945).

advantage in selling paint to General Motors.[6] The heart of the case rested in the giant size of the two firms, which created a potential monopoly power without any proof of wrongdoing.

Growth, Mergers, or Agreement

Until the Alcoa decision by the courts, the defenders of competition were helpless in their attack on firms whose monopoly position was the result of growth. Even now the big three in the automobile industry seem to be safe from attack under the antitrust laws as long as vigorous competition is maintained between them. When two large firms try to merge, however, the courts are likely to stop them. A merger is a combination of two existing firms into one larger and more powerful unit. Not all mergers are prohibited, but only those which tend to create a monopoly. For example, an attempt in the 1950's of two large steel companies to unite was promptly halted.

The interpretation of the law is even more restrictive against agreements among competitors. Trade associations in an industry are permitted if their practices do not interfere with the competitive rivalry of their members. In 1961, when several executives of competing electrical equipment manufacturers were found to have engaged in fixing prices, they were sent to jail. It was the first time that anyone had been jailed for an offense of this type.

To sum up, the courts are firmly opposed to agreements among competitors; they are fairly quick to stop mergers; but they will interfere with firms that have grown large only when the structure of the industry becomes clearly monopolistic.

Structure, Conduct, and Performance

What constitutes a sufficient degree of workable competition in the eyes of the law? The answer changes with the times and with the judgment of the courts; in the 1960's it is based on an appraisal of the market structure of an industry, its behavior pattern, and the performance of the firms involved.

The structure of an industry is determined by the number of firms, their relative size, the existence of barriers against the entry of new competitors, the regional distribution of plants and sales, and other similar considerations. A firm may hold a dominant position in the industry without exerting a monopoly if there are close substitutes for its products. For example, a firm may completely control the field of gas refrigeration; but electric refrigerators are such close substitutes, and the companies making them are

[6] *United States v. E. I. du Pont de Nemours & Company,* 353 U.S. 586 (1957).

so strong and numerous, that vigorous competition does exist in the refrigerator business.

The structure of an industry cannot by itself tell the story of its competitive vigor. Firms furnish important indicators for the evaluation of competitiveness in their behavior patterns. Is there a pattern of similar pricing? Do all firms follow the same leader when prices change? Do prices remain inflexible for long periods? Do the strongest firms engage in predatory practices to reduce the number of firms in the industry? Any one of such actions may persuade the courts of monopolistic conduct by the accused firm.

When structure and conduct of an industry leave the result still in doubt, the actual performance of the firms will permit a final judgment. The courts will appraise the growth of the industry and its willingness to change and to experiment with new ideas. The application of these criteria, however, is usually a difficult task, since there are no generally accepted methods by which to measure performance.

Under such flexible rules, each case will be judged in the light of the peculiarities of the industry and not necessarily on precedents established in different circumstances. While lawyers deplore the legal uncertainty surrounding the competitive practices of their clients, the opportunity of reinterpreting the law permits the courts to render broad economic judgments to preserve the competitive system.

EXCEPTIONS TO ANTITRUST LAWS

The numerous attempts by Congress and by the courts to preserve a large measure of competition in American business have suffered occasional setbacks when specific industries were exempt from the full impact of the antitrust legislation. Numerous examples of partial exemptions are found in farm-based industries, labor unions, railroads, and others. Some of the more important exceptions to the competitive rule will now be discussed.

Defense of Small Business and Fair Trade Laws

Popular opinion favors small business. Laws declaring the support of small business as their main purpose have been numerous, though they do not always accomplish this objective. Some provisions supposedly in support of small firms are in fact designed to reduce competitive pressure, such as *fair trade* legislation. This attack against the normal operation of a competitive price mechanism was passed by Congress originally in the depression days of the thirties and was later amended. The law [7] granted permission to each

[7] The Miller-Tydings Act on retail price maintenance, passed in 1937 and amended in 1952.

state to authorize manufacturers to fix minimum retail prices for their products and force all retailers to abide by them. Price competition was eliminated wherever such a law could be enforced.

Fair trade laws were supposed to help the small retailer against the large department store, which could afford to sell each item at a smaller profit because of its large volume of sales. The result of this interference with price competition, however, failed to favor small business in general. It shifted the rivalry from price differences to other considerations, such as services, which those firms most in favor of restrictive legislation could not match. While the laws are still in existence (though challenged in many states), most manufacturers have ceased to avail themselves of the opportunity to fix retail prices.

A more positive approach to the defense of small business favors measures to strengthen the competitive position of many firms. For example, they have been supported by access to improved credit facilities, and the inclusion of small firms as suppliers of the federal government is another step designed to help their survival.

Not every law passed in the name of small business is necessarily a boost to the competitive system. Each measure requires careful scrutiny in order to avoid the use of a popular label for monopolistic purposes.

Monopoly in Organized Groups

An individual alone is frequently unable to accomplish some of the economic objectives he shares with many others in similar circumstances. He will combine with them for group action and depend on the weight of their number and the skill of full-time representatives to achieve what he cannot do separately. The popular reaction to organized pressure groups by nonmembers is frequently hostile. Such a general attitude is not always justified, because these organizations arise inevitably out of the community of interests of their members, rather than from the scheming designs of a few leading organizers.

Organized groups take many forms. Some represent only a few common interests of a very large number, such as the National Association of Manufacturers or the national headquarters of the labor union movement. Due to the many conflicting views of their membership, these organizations can take a strong stand only on a few issues.

Smaller, homogeneous groups defend specific interests more forcefully. For example, trade associations for specific products examine every law from the narrow viewpoint of its possible influence on one industry. Their efforts to reduce competition in their particular business can be quite effective. A producer association may attempt to regulate prices, output, imports, or competitive innovations.

Organizations of owners of professional services or skilled labor may restrict the number of members in the profession through careful regulation of admittance. A labor union may stipulate long apprenticeship requirements, while a professional organization, such as the American Medical Association, may specify lengthy and expensive academic studies and difficult examinations as conditions for membership.

The code of the organization serves to maintain high professional standards. At the same time, such a philosophy renders any attempt for change more difficult and reduces the number of new members. The maintenance of high standards is praiseworthy for every profession. This effort, however, may take the form of excessively difficult entrance examinations in order to exclude new members and preserve a strong monopoly position for those previously admitted. Legal attempts to eliminate only the monopoly aspects of such organizations are generally unsuccessful, since it is impossible to distinguish clearly the good effects from the monopolistic ones.

REGULATED MONOPOLIES

Business firms must compete with each other in order to earn a profit. This basic philosophy cannot be applied to those cases where the nature of modern technology renders the duplication of services impractical or prohibitively expensive. Under such circumstances, our economy permits the exercise of monopoly operations in private hands under the control of a regulatory agency of the government that has final authority over major policy decisions.

The use of the airwaves for broadcasting purposes must be restricted; otherwise two firms would use the same wavelength competitively, with the result that neither could be heard clearly. Two telephone systems competing for customers in one town would prove to be awkward, confusing, and expensive. River water cascading from a mountain cliff can provide electric power—but not for just anyone who wants to tap it for this purpose. These examples show the types of activities which do not permit the free exercise of competition.

Regulatory Agencies

Regulatory agencies are created by the representatives of the people on a local, state, or national level. The law creating an agency sets forth its purpose and the means by which it plans to achieve it. Usually the agency has authority to grant firms permission to operate under its jurisdiction in accordance with rules formulated by the agency. This absolute power over the existence of firms in an industry includes a detailed control over the nature of the service rendered and the rates charged by each firm. Even when some aspects of service may involve a loss, the firm cannot discontinue them without permission.

A new agency or control commission is created by a legislature to protect the public against specific abuses of monopoly power. This purpose will be carefully stressed in the infancy of the commission, when dedicated crusaders, who want to eradicate all bad monopoly practices, are first appointed commissioners. After some years the atmosphere of the agency changes. The original zeal has given way to a well-functioning routine; new commissioners are appointed for political reasons, rather than for their burning desire to improve the national economy.

Agency representatives now act more and more like public spokesmen of private monopolies. They have learned so much about the problems of the industry that they cannot help but identify themselves with the welfare of the firms under their jurisdiction. They are in daily contact with industry managers and develop a feeling of responsibility for the welfare of "their" firms. The views of the public are seldom presented with as much force and knowledge as are the demands of the firms furnishing the service. Under these circumstances, it is not surprising that commissioners often side with the industry viewpoint. The members of the commission will frequently see no reason to oppose the suggestions of its controlled firms and are inclined to identify the public welfare with the prosperity of the particular industry. Obstacles to new firms, new ideas, and improved services are an inevitable result of this attitude, which is only partially corrected by a frequent rotation of commissioners. Should a regulated firm lose money on its services, it may blame the agency, or the public for not using the services with more enthusiasm, instead of making attempts to improve the service and stimulate greater demand.

Regulated Industries

Regulatory commissions are intended to carry on a wide variety of activities, but they prevail in fields offering services of a public utility nature. State agencies which are frequently called railroad commissions, or corporation commissions, control the rates for electric power, gas, and telephone service. In oil-producing states, these agencies also determine the amount of oil which can be extracted from the earth every month. Other consumer services, such as dry cleaning or barbering, are regulated by boards in some states.

Controls exercised by the federal government are primarily in the fields of transportation, communication, power, and finance.

Transportation. The Interstate Commerce Commission (ICC) was the first federal regulatory agency, created in 1887 to control the chief means of transportation of the time, the railroad. Later its authority was extended to include trucks, buses, and other means of transportation (except ocean and air carriers). It saw the growth and glory of the expanding railroad reach its peak in the 1920's. The era of railroad decline, caused by the technical advancement of road and air traffic, introduced a strongly competitive element into the transportation business.

The ICC lacked the needed flexibility to adjust quickly to the new competitive pressures. While the technical progress of railroading has continued at a rapid pace, the economic position of most railroads has deteriorated to a point where they are unable to attract sufficient capital for needed improvements. The proper function and usefulness of a regulatory agency in an area no longer monopolistic in character have become a matter of much controversy. Learned commissions have studied railroad problems in much detail and have suggested many changes in present operations; in 1966 Congress ordered a major change with the creation of a new federal Department of Transportation.[8] The act left the traditional agencies with their roles unchanged, but it created hope and expectation of a new approach to transport problems in the future.

The Civil Aeronautics Board (CAB) was created in 1938 for the purpose of controlling the air lines and air routes. It is not charged with purely technical aspects of flying, such as issuance of pilots' licences or inspection of aircraft, as these are functions exercised by the FAA in the Department of Transportation. The CAB assigns routes to each airline and approves all rate changes. Its reluctance to accept changes in existing flight patterns postponed the introduction of cheaper flights for years; it still remains a retarding factor to experimentation.

Communications. The Federal Communications Commission (FCC) was created in 1934 for the purpose of regulating the use of the airwaves for telephone, telegraph, radio, and, more recently, television. The assignment of a television channel to a specific firm confers an extremely valuable monopoly right. The FCC has refused to utilize the pricing mechanism of a free enterprise economy, which would assign each channel to the highest bidder. It gives these properties instead to the best qualified applicant, a criterion which exposes the Commission to heavy pressure and much embarrassment. While the users of airwaves are necessarily monopoly enterprises, it is not always true that competitive rivalry cannot be used in determining who may broadcast and what programs will be permitted. The quality level of programming is deplored by many, including members of the Commission.

---

[8] The Department of Transportation Act, Public Law 89-670, October 15, 1966.

The Commission is confronted with a particularly long list of thorny issues typical for a young industry in the process of sharp technical innovations. The insufficient use of many frequencies, the selection of the best means of color television, and the experiments with pay-TV are only some of the questions which the Commission must answer without the benefit of observing free competitive choice. Under the circumstances, no group of men could avoid public criticism, and some of this agency's difficulties must be attributed to its very perplexing assignment.

Power.   The Federal Power Commission (FPC) was created in 1920 to regulate the use of water for the production of electricity. The control of natural gas was later added to its duties.[9] The FPC must decide not only the location of power projects and the firm receiving the license to build them, but also the price of power to consumers in states which do not produce it.

Natural gas has presented the FPC with some extremely difficult issues because the public welfare is hard to define. The courts held that the commission must regulate gas prices from the wellhead to the consumer. States without gas wells insist that the lowest possible price promotes the public welfare because it causes the greatest use of cheap energy. The producer-states prefer that the largest amount of total revenue be retained in the state, because this revenue provides not only income to its people, but also large funds to operate the state government. Such issues can never be resolved to the satisfaction of everyone concerned.

Finance.   Private banks operate under the control of several agencies. State licenses are required for the start of a new bank, and states have their own regulations concerning bank inspections. More important, however, is the control of the Federal Reserve System over its member banks, as we shall see later.

The private securities markets are controlled by the Securities and Exchange Commission (SEC), which protects the buyer of stocks and bonds against fraudulent statements and misinformation. This agency was created in 1934 in order to prevent a repetition of the stock market collapse which ushered in the Great Depression.

GOVERNMENT-OWNED MONOPOLIES

Private monopolies under public control are used chiefly for activities which are intended to be profitable. In such situations private enterprise is preferred because in spite of its monopoly position it may be expected to im-

---

[9] The Natural Gas Act of 1938, The FPC's duties were greatly enlarged by a Supreme Court decision of 1954: *Phillips Petroleum Company* v. *Wisconsin,* 347 U.S. 672 (1954).

prove its efficiency in order to reap better profits at the publicly controlled rates. In some instances, however, the legislature may decide that some services should be performed without charging the full cost to the user. In this case the service is paid by the taxpayers, since no service can be obtained without cost to the public. The reasons for furnishing services without profit reflect objectives approved by the majority—such as the right to education regardless of the financial position of the child's family.

Nonprofit Operations

The American system of public schools is intended to raise the educational level of the population, not to show a profit. The principle of public education is so widely accepted that it is usually taken for granted. The same principle of public support becomes more controversial in other fields.

The United States Post Office is one of the oldest federal business operations. Its mail deliveries to remote rural areas at a deficit were justified by the Congressional desire to spread the written word in the days before modern transportation had solved this problem. The need for a public monopoly in the handling of mail today is due to a chronic deficit, which makes the mail operation unsuitable for private enterprise. The deficit, however, is caused now by Congressional reluctance to adjust rates to the point where all mail pays its own way, notwithstanding the fact that it seems doubtful that many taxpayers really desire to subsidize the advertisements found in their mailbox by permitting such delivery below full cost. Also, the political nature of many post office appointments is a serious obstacle to cost-cutting attempts and modernization.

Public operations become a necessity when the secrecy of national defense is involved. The Atomic Energy Commission (AEC) controls all efforts in this area because of military implications. The National Space Agency directs a multibillion-dollar operation in its efforts to produce more effective space vehicles. The need for a federal monopoly in this area is well understood.

Public monopolies in other fields arouse much controversy. Public power projects, such as the Tennessee Valley Authority (TVA), are strongly defended as a means of developing a sparsely settled area by furnishing cheap power. Their opponents point out that public power exercises a function efficiently managed by private business and should not become a charge to the taxpayer under any circumstances. Regulation of private power had failed, however, to open the TVA area to large-scale industrialization, and the defenders of public power projects point with pride to this successful venture which, they claim, has not become a burden on the taxpayer. Similar arguments arouse strong feelings for and against the still undecided power projects in the Rocky Mountain States.

Profit-Earning Operations

Some public operations are conducted at a profit. This favorable develop-ment, however, is only incidental to the main task of furnishing a service which would remain unavailable otherwise. The New York Port Authority is a monopoly business which has managed tunnels, bridges, airports, and other facilities of a noncompetitive nature in the New York area without need for assistance from the taxpayer. Its attempt to construct a giant world trade center in competition with comparable private buildings has created much controversy, however.

The Federal Reserve System is a nonprofit operation which never fails to reap a profit. The World Bank is an international institution helping the less-developed nations of the world. While it must be careful to com-mand the confidence of investors in its solvency, it was not intended to show a profit—but is, in fact, a very profitable organization.

Which are more successful—publicly controlled private firms, or out-right government operations? The answer seems to depend on the par-ticular circumstances of each case, and examples of success or failure can be shown on both sides. Individual preference for private or public control of operations will depend on the personal views one holds with respect to the proper role of government.

The very nature of a free enterprise ideology presents an obstacle to unnecessary expansion of collective enterprises. There are some who con-sider this view of modern capitalism obsolete and demand a larger share of public services to match the growing affluence of the American people. They object to the fact that people can buy new cars without considering the wisdom of such expenditures, while every school bond issue must be defended with sufficient eloquence to command a majority at the polls. This difference in treatment is largely responsible for a greater upsurge of auto-mobiles than of educational facilities.

The issue goes beyond the technical competence of the economist, who is limited to satisfying the goals established by society regardless of his personal preferences.

SUMMARY

The American majority is traditionally opposed to monopoly in business. Monopolies arise from many sources. An advantageous location, raw-material control, economic strength, or government action may become instruments for the creation of monopoly power.

The citizen objects to unwarranted economic power as an interference with the freedom of the individual and his rights to a better life. The principle of workable competition in a free enterprise economy is defended in three ways:

1. Whenever possible, private firms must compete. The courts and the Federal Trade Commission have the mandate from Congress to strike down any attempt to monopolize any line of business.

2. When only one firm can furnish a service with reasonable efficiency and at a profit, a government agency is created by the legislature to protect the public against abuse of this monopoly power. This procedure is designed to let the industry approximate the operations of competitive business as closely as possible. This objective is occasionally thwarted when the regulatory agency identifies itself too closely with the fortunes of the firms under its control.

3. Noneconomic reasons may persuade the legislature to provide a service or create a product without consideration of costs and profits. In this case the government operates its own business at the expense of the taxpayers in general. Public corporations do not necessarily show a financial loss, but their main objective is to render a service, not to show a profit. Occasions do arise, however, where government activity becomes businesslike in nature, but in a free economy, collective services of this nature are usually confined to ventures which private initiative fails to provide.

Big business is not a crime in itself, but the potential monopoly power of a giant firm can become too great for the survival of small competitors. When this happens, the courts will reduce the power of the leading firm, though there may be no evidence of wrongdoing on its part.

Small business is favored by the law because it is assumed to be more competitive. Not all measures advocated in support of small business help the maintenance of competition; some laws strengthen the competitive position of small firms, and others reduce the fierceness of competition through interference with the pricing system.

The total effectiveness of the American system of monopoly control cannot be measured by statistical comparisons. The continuing vigor of a growing, competitive economy is a real mark of success, which challenges all its critics.

Discussion Questions

1. Why is monopoly power an ever-present issue though most people are opposed to it?
2. Do you agree with the statement that big business is bad business? What reasons prompt your answer?
3. Do we need more laws to protect the competitive system?
4. In the first seventy years, no monopolizing executive was jailed under the provisions of the Sherman Act. Does this fact show that the law is ineffective?
5. Distinguish the objectives of the Clayton Act from those of the FTC Act.

6. Firms may grow big as long as they do not merge big. Comment.
7. Structure and performance determine the decisions of the courts in antitrust cases. Interpret this statement.
8. Why are many industries regulated by federal agencies?
9. Should the mail-handling business in the United States be sold to the highest bidder? Would someone be likely to buy it? What specific conditions would your answer assume?

Suggested Reading

ADAMS, WALTER, ed., *The Structure of American Industry,* 3d ed. New York, Macmillan, 1963.

BAIN, JOE S., *Industrial Organization.* New York, Wiley, 1959.

CAVES, RICHARD, *American Industry: Structure, Conduct, Performance,* Englewood Cliffs, N.J., Prentice-Hall, 1964.

DIMOCK, MARSHALL E., *Business and Government,* 4th ed. New York, Holt, Rinehart & Winston, 1961.

MASSEL, MARK S., *Competition and Monopoly.* Washington, D.C., Brookings Institution, 1962.

9

RISK AND SECURITY

Life itself is full of hazards; total security exists only for the dead. Risks must be accepted as an inevitable and necessary part of living. "Nothing ventured, nothing gained" is a fairly accurate description of the risk inherent in all human enterprise.

Security is also a basic goal of humanity. Adventures are fine, particularly for the young, but the large number of people who do not feel quite so venturesome in spirit long for more security. This urge for safety is not entirely economic—emotional security is an important factor in smooth family relationships—but a feeling of safety is impossible whenever the basic means of livelihood are missing.

ECONOMIC SECURITY

Our economic system uses risks as a challenge, and rewards the successful risk taker with a profit. All of us have to face the normal hazards of life, and even greater ones in business ventures if we want to get ahead and climb the ladder of success. Competitive business offers a reward and threatens a loss; both are fundamental ingredients of a free enterprise economy.

Some risks, however, fail to contribute to the constructive advancement of society. A firm competing effectively in its regular line of business can be wiped out by a fire. There are certain hazards just too large or unpredictable to be shouldered by an individual alone; they create a desire for more security and do not serve as a challenge.

"Security," or protection against *excessive* hazards, is approved by most people, while "monopoly" is a bad word with unfavorable implications. Unfortunately, the greatest degree of security for a business or a worker derives from a position of monopoly. The demand of an industry for "stabilization of chaotic market conditions to insure an orderly flow of goods to the consumer" may be the sign of a desperate effort to prevent widespread bankruptcy and provide minimum security; or it may indicate an organized attempt to enrich a monopolistic group at the expense of the consumer.

Measures promoting economic security must steer a perilous middle course. The pressure of competitive rivalry is needed to keep people on their toes, but it should not be allowed to lead to economic ruin, the shutdown of plants, and no output. The assurance of a guaranteed income, on the other hand, may promote loafing and carelessness; but the threat of losing one's job and income upon completion of the current task leads to a slowing down of the worker and is not a constructive contribution to the economy. Destructive insecurities must be avoided without eliminating the constructive pressures which form the essence of a competitive system.

Involuntary risks can be reduced in three ways: private insurance reduces uncertain economic dangers to a known, manageable cost; speculators assume the burden of some business risks avoided by others, and public insurance fills the vacuum of insecurity created by the urbanization of an aging population.

PRIVATE INSURANCE

The perils of life confront us as soon as we rise in the morning. We may slip on a banana peel, cut ourselves with a razor blade, or have an accident with the family car. As long as damages remain minor, we hardly give them thought, but in some cases their economic impact endangers our livelihood. Insurance eliminates or reduces the danger of financial disaster caused by these involuntary risks.

Purpose of Insurance

An insurance system exchanges a large uncertainty for a small and certain monetary outlay in the form of a premium. Many people are willing to pay a moderate fixed price for the feeling of security gained from protection against unforeseen financial demands. By insuring a house against fire, we can convert an unavoidable risk into a mathematically certain cost. We don't know whether or not our house will burn; neither does the insurance company. But the company pools the risks of many people by protecting their houses; experience gained from long observation tells the company how many out of 10,000 insured houses are likely to burn, on the average, every year. This mathematical probability is sufficiently exact that the insurance company is not taking any risk either. The distribution of the fire hazard over 10,000 home owners results in the small and certain premium paid for our security and peace of mind.

Insurance is the opposite of gambling. A gambler hopes to gain and is willing to take a chance of possible loss. The man who buys an insurance policy gives up the amount of the premium in order to avoid the possibility of a loss.

Principles of Insurance

Not all involuntary risks are insurable. They must conform to some definite criteria in order to become suitable objects for insurance. Let us look at these limitations.

1. *A large number of people must need protection against perils which can be compared.* The certainty of the insurance company rests on the mathematical probability of the law of large numbers. Unless many people are in a similar position and require protection, private insurance is not practical. Fire in a home constitutes a hazard which is incurred thousands of times in comparable form, and many insurance firms are willing to protect owners against this risk. However, only in a few places, like the famous Lloyd's of London, are a sufficient number of odd risks collected to permit insurance—such as a beauty queen who needs protection against the possibility of a scar on her face, or a trapeze artist who worries about a fall and a broken leg.

2. *Risks need to be similar* to permit grouping in definite categories for insurance purposes. All healthy twenty-year-old men have a similar chance of reaching the age of seventy. But a man of the same age who is known to be afflicted with an incurable disease cannot be grouped with the others, because his mathematical chance of reaching old age is much smaller.

3. *Chances of possible loss need to be independent of each other.* A large number of similar dangers are still not feasibly insurable if the mishaps are likely to occur at the same time. An insurance firm would be most unwise to concentrate hail protection in one town only. Even though the firm might hold a large number of separate, small, and similar policies, it would be liable for a gigantic, combined loss in the event a hailstorm struck this one town.

The same number of people can be protected safely when the policies are spread over independent perils throughout the whole country. A hailstorm in Texas is not likely to cause damage in Ohio. Conversely, private insurance is not practical against the threat of atomic warfare or against the hazards of unemployment in a depression. The so-called unemployment insurance provided by federal and state legislation is not really insurance, but a form of social benefit for the jobless.

4. *Uncertainty* is a necessary element of an insurable risk. You cannot insure against a sure loss. Even in a life insurance contract, we never know when the loss of life may occur, even though all men die sometime.

Homeowners in a flood area discover much to their dismay that their policy excludes insurance against this sort of loss; the necessary uncertainty is missing. People in a high location would never buy flood insurance, while those in designated low areas must expect this disaster at regular intervals. Only a few homes would be located in a spot where the expected damage to their fixed property could be considered uncertain.

5. *Only a financial loss* can provide an insurable interest. The reason for such a restriction is obvious. A house has a market value of $20,000, and the owner decides to insure it against fire at $40,000. The temptation for the owner to play with matches would be too great. Regardless of the size of the insurance policy bought, the company will never pay more than the actual amount needed to restore the house to its previous condition.

One cannot insure an expected profit; this principle is illustrated in a contract that protects the concession stand at a ball game against losses due to rain. This contract may cover losses incurred from spoiled supplies, the payroll of vendors who had no customers, rent payments, and similar expenditures. His contract may stipulate payments up to 50,000 hot dogs, but the insurance company will not pay for more than the number that are actually spoiled. The company will also refuse to pay more for the supplies than the actual cost; what the owner hoped to sell is not an insurable risk.

6. *Control of the risk by the insured* renders it uninsurable. A college student cannot buy insurance against failing an examination. But a financier who makes a loan to a student to help him through college might conceivably be able to insure against nonpayment of the loan due to scholastic failure.

This condition is not absolute, and it acquires particular importance with regard to the protection of life and health. A person can terminate his own life at will, but insurance firms know that people value life more than money. Suicides are not planned far in advance; life insurance policies will therefore pay in almost all cases of death, except for suicide during the first year after the policy has been purchased.

Health insurance offers a more difficult problem. Most people consider surgery too dangerous and painful to undergo just to collect an insurance payment, but abuse sometimes occurs in cases of hospitalization without surgery—mostly in the form of unnecessarily long occupancy of hospital facilities. We should, however, hesitate to label every extra day of hospitalization an abuse. A patient may be in physical condition for dismissal without impairing his health, but an extra day or two of hospital care might be advisable to help him recover his strength much faster than he could if he were back on the job.

Insurance covering visits to the doctor's office presents serious difficulties. Some people simply like to visit and can imagine a variety of symptoms to justify consulting a doctor, and only the financial punishment of a monthly bill prevents them from unduly wasting his valuable time. Insurance coverage is not practical in such instances because the insured controls the risk to an unreasonable degree.

SPECULATION

Speculators are traders who are willing to buy or sell the same commodity in the expectation of making a profit on the difference in price. Most businessmen buy one kind of product and sell another, but speculators offer to buy or sell the same product because they believe the price will soon change in their favor.

Speculation is not a friendly word in our dictionary of ethical values. Boys may be encouraged to become doctors, engineers, business executives, or even teachers, but speculators will hardly be included in any list of recommended occupations. A popular view considers them gamblers who waste their time, if not their money, in a wholly unproductive fashion.

A speculator is a trader in risks. Every business contains some elements of chance. The owner assumes those risks that are the essence of his business: he must make sure that his product is satisfactory, that his services please the customer, and that his costs remain within his estimates. There are other risks in business, however, that are beyond the control of its owner, and these call for protection. The ever-present danger from the elements has been mentioned before as a suitable risk for private insurance. An equally unpredictable hazard for a firm may be the fluctuating price of raw material, but no insurance company offers protection in such situations. This is when the professional speculator who is willing to gamble enters the picture.

Wherever the nature of the peril permits, the professional speculator voluntarily assumes business risks that are uninsurable. When prices fail to follow a predictable pattern, somebody has to gamble, and hope for a profit while relieving others from the danger of a loss. The area of unpredictable price fluctuations is best suited to the operations of the speculator. In the process of taking chances on the shifting price of commodities or stock certificates, speculators exercise two necessary functions in the economic process: they relieve others of uncertainty, and they provide a market for the exchange of ownership rights.

Voluntary Risk Taking

The economic role of the speculator becomes clear when we observe his actions in commodity markets such as wheat. Wheat is plentiful at harvest time, when farmers need to dispose of it. Also, its price is relatively low. As time passes and wheat disappears through consumption channels, the price can be expected to rise until it reaches a peak shortly before the next harvest. The farmer knows this very well, but he is often not in a position to wait for a price rise, particularly when he also realizes that storage and credit involve added costs. He does not want to gamble on the future price of wheat, not knowing if the increase will be sufficient to compensate for extra costs.

The miller wants to make sure that he gains his usual profit from transforming wheat into flour; he, too, prefers to avoid taking any chances on changing wheat prices.

The speculator helps everyone concerned. He buys wheat at harvest time, insuring a better price for the farmer because of his added demand. Later in the year, the speculator sells the wheat, thereby preventing the price from rising as much as it would otherwise. In this regard, speculation exercises a stabilizing influence. The speculator is also prepared to sign a contract with the miller covering the delivery of wheat several months later. As a result, the miller is protected against fluctuations and can calculate his costs with certainty.[1]

The speculator hopes that the price changes will favor him and enable him to show a profit. Although he has no personal contact with the commodity, his willingness to buy or sell wheat at any time, even before the crop is harvested, is of great benefit to those who actually deal in it.

Unfortunately, there is another side to speculation. A rumor of a crop failure may cause many people to buy wheat hastily at rising prices. Speculators may do the same thing and buy wheat when they should be selling it. In this case, the price fluctuations are aggravated by speculation, and not reduced as in the previous example.

Providing a Market

The speculator exercises another useful function when he helps to provide a market. People who buy corporate stocks instead of real estate with their available funds do so quite often because of the greater liquidity of their assets. They may feel that a piece of local real estate would indeed be profitable, but that it is not always easy to sell at short notice when cash is needed. The owner of 100 shares of General Motors can dispose of his property within a few hours of his decision to sell. The speculators in the market are willing to act as both buyers or sellers for the same stock at only a small difference in price. To match buying and selling orders without them would be difficult, and it might even be impossible to arrange trades. The assurance provided by the speculator protects people who otherwise would not dare to buy stocks for fear of purchasing unsalable pieces of paper.

Speculators make a constructive contribution to our economy when they assume risks voluntarily which other people do not want. This function can be and has been abused in the past when speculators tried success-

[1] This business operation is called *hedging*.

fully to influence the market to their advantage. Many rules have been adopted to prevent such misuse. Federal law created the Securities and Exchange Commission to prevent fraudulent practices involving securities. Of course, unprincipled men can cause trouble in almost any activity, but it would be unwise to confuse the undesirable practices of a few, with the much-needed function of risk taking inherent in speculation. We should be particularly cautious about blaming speculators for every major drop in market prices. As a group they may be a popular scapegoat, but they are seldom the cause of the trouble.

SOCIAL SECURITY

Private insurance can relieve the individual of worry concerning losses of many types, but the gravest danger to the economic security of most families is a sudden disappearance of income. The demand for a minimum amount of income security is as old as man's effort to establish some sort of social organization. The custom whereby many members of a family live together and share the available means of support is a rather rudimentary form of social security. The tradition that grown children should take care of their parents and the unmarried women in their family follows a similar pattern.

Changes in the social habits of modern society have dissolved ancient economic bonds and accentuated the insecurities connected with the maintenance of income. In the past, the poor laws and private charity were considered adequate to prevent the starvation of those few unfortunate individuals who did not have a family able and willing to take care of their kin.

These changed circumstances have created a demand for public action to protect a large segment of the population. The economic security of a wage earner is indeed precarious, since his income depends upon his being employed by others. Regardless of his personal performance, the worker's job is beyond his control, and he may face sudden dismissal when his position is moved to another town or abolished completely.

The living standard of many who work today is far above that experienced by past generations. A sudden loss of income, therefore, causes a much sharper downward revision in the established expenditure pattern, and effects a need for more painful adjustments. A high living standard usually creates an equally high level of fixed monthly expenditures—from utility bills to installments due on the automobile—which cannot be reduced overnight. The basic insecurity of the modern employee is due to the fact that his expenditures are patterned for a period of one to three years ahead, whereas his income is assured for only one week at a time.

Other causes endangering security are part of an ever-present pattern. Disasters may happen to any family; long illness will wipe out savings accumulated by years of careful budgeting, and occasional periods of unemployment will exhaust savings in a short time. In addition, the economic insecurity of old age has become more pronounced, because:

1. Medical science has succeeded in prolonging life beyond the normal retirement age of sixty-five years. Only a generation ago, a worker could expect to live only a few years after he retired. Today, life expectancy at the sixty-fifth birthday exceeds fourteen years.

2. Compulsory retirement from work at about sixty-five has become standard procedure for many firms.

3. Systematic savings during an active lifetime, through bond purchases and life insurance policies, have been reduced to an inadequate income by public policies of continuing inflation.

These causes combined create a definite need for public action toward providing a minimum income. Opposition to social security frequently centers around the amount of this income. Some people feel that government payments are far too high, while most congressmen still believe that a vote for greater benefits wins friends back home.

The issue of the proper level of benefits has a tendency toward self-adjustment. As the cost of payments rises, the contributions in the form of taxes on the labor force must rise also. The point may be reached where the worker on the job will revolt against ever-larger paycheck deductions which are in favor of those who are not working, at which time some balance will become necessary. Higher contributions, lower benefits, or postponement of retirement are the three obvious solutions to the problem of old-age insurance. In a period of substantially full employment, the most constructive answer to the problem would be the continued use of still-able-bodied citizens for some additional years. These alternatives are all unpalatable to politicians who seek reelection. Congress has seriously considered, therefore, a change in the basic principle which has governed social security for its first thirty years—the direct connection between worker contribution and benefits. Senators promise higher benefits, but they are beginning to fear the wrath of wage earners whose payroll deduction becomes ever larger. They prefer, therefore, to use general revenue funds to pay for their promises; the same people will pay for them but the connection is less obvious.

Social security refers to a series of laws which furnish an income to persons in designated categories whose private source of income from work has either temporarily or permanently disappeared while the tradition of assistance to the indigent and helpless is still maintained, current laws on social security take a different approach to the subject. Everyone who belongs to a category covered by law is entitled to benefits regardless of his personal wealth or his need for added income. *Social insurance is a matter of right—public assistance is based on need.*

The task of providing social security as a right rather than a charity has been accepted by the federal government only since the Social Security Act of 1935. The law has been amended many times, and the most significant change was introduced by the law of 1965 which added health protection for the aged, popularly known as Medicare. In spite of some heated political debates, the role of government in this field commands broad bipartisan support in Congress today and leaves only the details to partisan controversy.

Old-Age, Survivors, Disability, and Health Insurance (OASDHI)

Some states introduced measures to protect elderly people financially as early as 1907, when Massachusetts created a commission to investigate the problems of old age. The Social Security Act of 1935 established the first federal program of old-age insurance. Although details of the law have been frequently changed, they maintain a similar pattern—the occupations included in the protection, the benefits which a person is entitled to claim, the income limit for which protection is provided, and the rate of tax contribution chargeable against the income of those currently working.

Coverage. The purpose of old-age, survivors, disability, and health insurance laws is the replacement with benefit payments of lost income from work. In order to qualify for such benefits, a person must have been engaged for some length of time in an occupation covered by the law.[2] Initially this coverage was limited, but it has been broadened by later legislation to the point where now over 90 percent of all workers are eligible for protection. The exceptions consist of groups for whom earlier arrangements of a similar nature (for example, railroad workers and federal civil servants) had already been made. Professional people are included in the law, and in some instances the inclusion is optional, as in the case of the clergy.

The number of persons entitled to payments rises constantly, because that portion of the population over sixty-five years old is rising much faster than the population as a whole. From 1950 to 1960 the increase in this age bracket exceeded 34 percent and included over sixteen million people. As of 1967, approximately twenty million people, or 10 percent of the population, are aged sixty-five or over. Social security benefits are of importance to the majority of these citizens. Numerically, they rank as the

---

[2] The principle that retirement pay requires some months of work during an earlier period was disregarded by Congress for the first time in 1966, when payments were extended to people over seventy-two years under certain conditions though they might never have worked before (Public Law 89-368, March 15, 1966).

largest interest group—larger than labor unions and farmers' organizations —and since they all have the right to vote, they cannot be ignored by any legislature. The political impact of the aged, however, has not yet been as powerful as that of other groups, since it developed only recently and still lacks effectively concentrated group action.

Benefits. The benefits of this federal insurance are paid to the insured when he retires at the age of sixty-two to sixty-five years, or at an earlier age if he is disabled. The payments are made to his widow and children in the case of the death of the insured. The detailed provisions of the law are quite involved, as they also take into consideration numerous exceptions to the basic rule—benefits may be paid at an earlier age in some cases, or to other survivors in certain other circumstances.

The total amount of benefit payments under the Social Security Act exceeded $20 billion in 1966. The importance to the economy of this largest payroll in the land is obvious: It fluctuates very little with good times or bad ones, since most retirement has become compulsory regardless of the state of business. Unlike most business expenditures, its influence is spread over the entire nation and is not concentrated in certain localities.

The size of each payment varies considerably. The maximum per month per family is $368. The average payment, however, is much smaller and does not exceed $100 per month. The size of the payments depends on the previous income of the insured up to a current maximum of $6,600 per year; income in excess of this sum is not considered by the law. Table 9-1 shows some examples of monthly benefit payments.

The payments schedule emphasizes family needs and is weighted in favor of the smallest incomes. The monthly benefits replace the income of a family with two children for the largest part up to $4,200 per year. At higher incomes, the likelihood of private savings and other income reduces the exclusive dependence of the beneficiary on federal payments. Even in the income brackets above $6,000, however, the social security payments are likely to be an important part of the family income.

TABLE 9-1. Examples of Monthly Payments Under OASDHI, 1966
(Selected Cases)

	Size of Average Annual Earnings			
	$3,000	$3,600	$4,800	$6,600
Retirement pay at 65	$101.70	$112.40	$135.90	$168.00
Wife's benefit at 65	50.90	56.20	68.00	84.00
Widow 62 or over	83.90	92.80	112.20	138.60
Widow under 65 with two children	202.40	240.00	306.00	368.00
Maximum family payment	202.40	240.00	309.20	368.00

SOURCE: *Social Security Bulletin.*

Contributions. Where does the money come from? Social security payments are linked to contributions by all people who work, in the form of a special payroll tax which will entitle them to qualify for benefits later on in life. Participation is compulsory and the contribution is a flat percentage rate of the employee's income up to a maximum of $6,600 (1967). The actual tax rate increases in later years as benefit payments require larger funds. In 1967 the rate was 4.4 percent, which must be paid both by the worker and his employer. For self-employed people, for example lawyers or accountants, the rate was 6.4 percent instead of the combined charge of 8.8 percent in the first case. On the basis of this percentage, the maximum deduction from a worker's paycheck in 1967 was $290.40, and the total contribution per person was $580.80.

The contribution for social security payments is a tax and not an insurance premium. The contributor does not acquire any rights in the amount of money he pays, as he would under a private insurance contract. Current payments are intended to suffice for benefits now due to those who have qualified for them. Since the exact amount of the taxes to be collected depends on employment conditions, the Social Security Administration has a sizable reserve fund which makes it possible to continue benefit payments in case tax collections fall short, temporarily, of the amount required. The continued rise in the percentage of retired people makes an upward revision of current tax rates inevitable in the coming years.

Unemployment Insurance

The depression of the thirties caused millions of people to lose their jobs, because the firms for which they worked had to close their plants or go completely out of business. The duration of this period of unemployment was so long that in many cases past savings were insufficient to maintain even the minimum requirements of existence. The demand for public action resulted in the first unemployment insurance law, enacted in 1932 by the state of Wisconsin. It was followed by federal legislation in the Social Security Act of 1935.

Characteristics. The main features of the unemployment compensation program concern its administration, coverage, eligibility, benefits, and taxes.

1. The administration of the program is the joint responsibility of federal and state governments. Because the federal law penalizes states which refuse to cooperate, all of them have enacted unemployment compensation laws. The provisions of the laws, however, vary widely and the administration of each program remains entirely in the hands of the particular state employment office.

2. About forty-five million workers were protected by unemployment insurance in 1965. Self-employed groups are not covered by the law; many states exclude also the very small employers, since federal requirements are limited to firms with four or more employees.

3. Unemployment must be involuntary in order to qualify a person for compensation payments. This principle seems to be simple enough, but its application is full of pitfalls. Presumably, a worker cannot quit his job and receive payments, but it is easy to get yourself fired when you do not want to work anymore. Is a man involuntarily unemployed when his union has called a strike? Most states say no, but this question has been answered differently in the past. To remain eligible for benefits under the law, an unemployed person must be available for work. In some states, this requirement means simply that he must register with the employment office; in other states, a person must accept any job he can handle.

4. The size of benefit payments varies widely. Maximum benefits per week in 1965 were as low as $30 in Mississippi and reached a high of $65 in California. State laws differ also with reference to the maximum number of weeks for which a person can draw benefit payments; twenty-six weeks is the maximum in most states. During the recessions of 1958 and 1961, Congress temporarily extended the maximum eligibility periods. The size of the weekly payment today is a smaller percentage of a normal paycheck than it was when the law was first enacted. An adequate level of unemployment compensation cannot be determined with accuracy, because the minimum needs of a family's only breadwinner are clearly much higher than those of a housewife who earns a second salary for the family to boost the total income to a more comfortable level. The law is not based on individual need and does not distinguish between different cases.

5. The total cost of unemployment compensation during the prosperous fiscal year 1965 amounted to $3.8 billion. This sum is collected entirely from employers through a payroll tax. Firms whose employment remains stable throughout the year are entitled to a lower tax as an incentive to keep people employed—an incentive, unfortunately, not strong enough to prevent many layoffs.

Objections to Unemployment Insurance. The present system of unemployment insurance, born in the Great Depression and continued without basic changes into the prosperous sixties, has been attacked from all sides. The proponents of one opinion consider present legislation wholly inadequate and feel that an economy as rich as ours should be able to keep all its people from the brink of starvation regardless of local job opportunities. The views of the opposite extreme point to the difficulty of finding good workers in a booming period. The spokesmen for this side feel sure that everyone who wants to work can find a job, and they consider the large number of unemployment payments a sure indicator of abuse by loafers and chiselers.

The Case for Unemployment Insurance. Most people will agree that it would be nice if unemployment insurance became unnecessary and everyone in need of income could find work to fit his talents. Unfortunately, even during the greatest prosperity, things will not always work out quite so well. Unemployment insurance is best suited to cases where a breadwinner loses his job for a limited time and needs financial help in order to make an adjustment.

In a changing economy, some jobs are always on a downtrend as new activities open up elsewhere. It is hard to move the older worker with strong ties to his community and train him for different work. Consequently, unemployment becomes inevitable, at least on a modest scale, and insurance payments simply help to cushion its effect.

The defenders of unemployment insurance do not believe that the very small payments will induce anyone to loaf. But in an institution of such large size, isolated cases of abuse are unavoidable. Their number is greatly exaggerated, however, by the opponents.

The suggestion that people should be put to work when they are unemployed is a good principle which, however, can be applied only with great difficulty. The cost of providing a job includes much more than wages and would render a large-scale effort of this kind by the government very burdensome for the taxpayer. To put people to work without modern tools simply to keep them busy is wasteful and inefficient. In some countries in Asia such practices are widespread and have thus contributed to a continuation of the poverty of those nations.

Unemployment compensation has a stabilizing effect on the economic system as a whole, as we shall discover in more detail later.

Cyclical Unemployment. The greatest difficulties connected with unemployment insurance occur in situations of cyclical unemployment. When the entire economic system slows down and millions of people find themselves without work, unemployment insurance becomes prohibitively expensive, and is inadequate at the same time. Such a disaster must be avoided at all costs. Much remains to be done in creating incentives for an employer to keep a worker on the payroll when business is slow. It is an ironical observation of our times that a firm must assume far greater responsibility for its capital equipment than for its workers. No practical solution for this problem has yet been found.

Labor unions have tried to inject an element of employment security into their contracts through the provision of seniority rights, which prevent an employer from firing a worker as long as more recently hired men keep their jobs. In some cases, efforts have been made to stabilize income on a yearly basis, with demands for a guaranteed annual wage to match the long-term obligations incurred by the worker. Some improvements in income security have been accomplished, but much remains to be done before every person in the country can be safe from ever becoming destitute.

Workmen's Compensation and Disability Insurance

Workmen's compensation and disability insurance protects workers against financial loss resulting from accidents and disease connected with their jobs. The protection against hazards connected with a man's work is a relatively old practice and is incorporated in state laws; the requirements differ considerably from state to state, however. Only in 1956 were disability benefits added to the federal Social Security law.

The claim of an injured worker is directed against his employer and not against the government. The law provides only that the employer make the necessary arrangements to be able to pay for such claims. Usually he buys private insurance to cover his liability.

Job-connected disability should not be confused with the total disability from any cause, which allows for direct federal benefits, as we have already seen.

Prolonged sickness of the breadwinner is often considered a major cause of poverty. Not only is the family deprived of income during a period of illness, but the cost of modern medicine looms large to a family whose income flow has been interrupted. Health insurance for workers is not covered by legislation today. Private insurance, with or without the assistance of employers, has shown a steady rise.

Medicare

After many years of controversy, Congress enacted legislation in 1965 to provide financial assistance for the aged in need of medical care. Earlier laws had made limited sick benefits available for those who were unable to pay. The amendment of 1965 to the Social Security Act established important precedents whose ultimate results will be fully realized only in years to come.

Medicare introduces the principle that the citizen is entitled to health care regardless of his financial position. The provisions of the law are limited initially to people over sixty-five years old. Since only through experience can we tell to what extent the medical facilities of the nation should be changed when the price of health care ceases to be the limiting factor, it seemed wise to embark on this new venture on a restricted basis. This new approach places health substantially in the same position as education, which has been a public responsibility from the early days of the nation. The present age limitation may be changed by Congress when the people feel that the new system will satisfy their needs.

Health protection has become part of the social security rights of those who are sixty-five years old. The law distinguishes, however, between benefits which accrue automatically, such as payments for hospital bills, and additional protection, for extra expenses such as doctor's bills. For the latter type, each beneficiary must make a modest contribution of $3 per month, which is matched by the federal government with an equal contribution out of general revenues. This monthly payment cannot be considered an insurance premium since it falls short of the expected cost of services rendered, but it introduces the principle of partial contribution by the beneficiary to the total cost of the service.

Another interesting innovation in the law is the principle of sharing costs with the beneficiary. The provision that the initial cost of hospitalization is charged to the sick (who pay the first $50 of the hospital bill) is intended to discourage the overcrowding of hospitals with cases that do not require such a service. The government pays the rest of the necessary hospital costs (not including TV) for sixty days, after which time the patient again contributes to the costs so that he has an incentive to leave as soon as possible. In addition, there are government payments to "extended care facilities" for those able to leave the hospital but too ill to go home —a provision also intended to relieve the burden on the hospitals.

The role of the physician in this new federal service remains a matter of controversy. The administration of the law is intended to leave the relationship of doctor and patient unchanged. Since the public has to pay the bill, some interference with charges for medical services becomes almost inevitable. It is likely that changes in the traditional pattern of health care and of the medical profession will occur in the future, but the nature of these developments cannot yet be determined.

SUMMARY

Economic security consists in the assurance of maintaining a minimum livelihood. While the pressure of competition is needed to counteract man's natural tendency to make his own position safe through attempts to monopolize, excessive fear of economic insecurity is not a constructive force for a progressive economy.

Private insurance can furnish protection against many risks in return for the payment of a rather small premium on a voluntary basis. Not all risks are insurable, however.

A risk is suitable for private insurance when many people need protection against similar but independent uncertain perils, the occurrence of which would involve a loss beyond the reasonable control of the insured.

Speculation may be wasteful, and at times deplorable, but it undertakes business risks which other people do not want to assume. Speculators also help the buyers and sellers of corporate stocks by providing a market which might not otherwise be readily available.

Social security encompasses those government measures which guarantee a minimum income where other forms of insurance are not practical or are inadequate. Federal legislation provides protection for the old, for widows and orphans, and for the disabled. Benefits are paid from the collection of a special payroll tax which is adjusted periodically to provide a sufficient flow of funds.

The sudden absence of income because of unemployment is cushioned by unemployment insurance. The program is paid for by employers and administered by the states within the framework of federal law. Job-connected disease and disabilities are insured by the employer in accordance with state laws. Medicare provides for the medical needs of the aged.

Security is a major goal of the American people; they dedicate a large share of their work effort to its achievement. The total cost of economic security absorbs a considerable part of the nation's income.

Discussion Questions

1. The techniques of monopoly serve the ends of security. Why do we approve of the one, but not of the other?
2. Why can't a person insure against any kind of hazard he does not want to risk on his own?
3. Some people buy insurance as a gamble in the expectation of receiving more than they pay, but the insurance company never gambles. Why?
4. Discuss the case for and against health insurance for the aged.
5. Should speculation at commodity and stock exchanges be permitted?
6. Are old age benefits under the law high enough? What criteria do you consider in a carefully balanced evaluation?
7. What are the main objectives of unemployment insurance? Who pays for it?

Suggested Reading

Economic Aspects of the Social Security Tax. New York, Tax Foundation, Inc., 1966.

KNIGHT, FRANK H., *Risk, Uncertainty, and Profit.* Boston, Houghton Mifflin, 1921.

TURNBULL, JOHN G., C. ARTHUR WILLIAMS, JR., and EARL F. CHEIT, *Economic and Social Security,* 2d ed. New York, Ronald, 1962.

WITTE, EDWIN E., *Social Security Perspectives,* R. J. Lampman, ed. Madison, Wis., University of Wisconsin Press, 1962.

10

ON HUMAN EFFORT

People contribute more to the state of the economy than any other factors of production. The role of man as a producer is the subject of this chapter.

MAN'S DUAL ROLE IN THE PRODUCTION PROCESS

Most people must earn a living, since they do not enjoy a sufficient inheritance of worldly goods to lead a life of leisure. To earn their daily bread, men use all their productive resources, of which the most important factor is work time. People try to sell this at the highest possible price; they want to earn as much as possible per hour and put in as many hours of work as are necessary to reach a high total income. As far as man the producer is concerned, wages are never high enough.

People are not only the producers of goods, but are consumers as well. Their interests are quite opposed to each other. The consumer wants to buy at the lowest possible price so that his income can satisfy more of his wants; the seller wants to receive the highest possible price for his services. This dual role presents a conflict because the income of the worker becomes part of the price he pays as a consumer of the product.

Man's split personality leads to strange contradictions. The use of manpower for productive purposes (like that of any other factor) must necessarily be governed by rules of efficiency. Coal serves to heat our houses if it happens to be the most efficient fuel. If natural gas will do the job at lower cost, the switch to the more economical method will take place as fast as is practicable. We are not concerned with the fate of the coal that remains in the bowels of the earth.

When human efforts at the market price become more expensive to the employer than a machine, man will be replaced for reasons of efficiency. The responsibility of the firm ends with the worker's dismissal, but society must still find income for the displaced man, because the satisfaction of his wants is part of our economic goal. Efficiency is only the means to an end, but want satisfaction is an end in itself. The firm's yardstick of efficiency is apparently in conflict with the broader view of social efficiency in this case. The firm's gain when it replaces a worker with a machine must be compared with the cost of this saving to society as a whole. The state must pay unemployment insurance; the worker loses purchasing power because of his sudden drop in income; and the retraining of a man whose skills have become obsolete may be far more expensive than any possible saving by the firm that let him go. This aspect of achieving the best use of all resources is frequently overlooked.

The individual at work and his protection will be our first concern. A discussion of wages will follow, and the role of the labor union in the American economy will conclude the chapter.

THE INDIVIDUAL WORKER

The need for security has concerned us already, but the discussion of insecurity was focused on the special problems of the unemployed. The individual worker with a job faces hazards of equal gravity.

Job Security

Some people suggest that society need not be concerned with workers' problems. A man is born free; he does not have to take any one job offered, and should he discover a dislike for his work he can quit and find other employment. Unfortunately, this ideal description of working conditions misses the mark in most cases. The average man in search of a job does not know what to expect from an employer, nor does he have any practical means of finding out. Besides, he needs a job immediately since he has no means of survival without one.

Lack of job security is the worker's gravest problem. He may like the job he holds right now, but he never knows how long this happy situation will last. A number of dangers largely beyond his control are lurking in the dark future. They all combine to create a pronounced feeling of insecurity and a desire to do something about it. Let us look at some of his fears.

Layoff. The possibility of layoff is ever present. If the firm lacks orders it shuts down operations until more orders are received. The worker is not at fault; he is simply a victim of circumstances. The length of the layoff is unknown, unemployment compensation is a pale substitute for a regular paycheck, and savings do not last very long. It is hard to find a new job under these conditions, because hundreds of other workers without a job are competing for the same limited number of employment opportunities.

Promotion. The chance for promotion may bear only a slight relationship to the employee's performance. Granted, that really bad work will probably not be rewarded by advancement, and that genuinely outstanding work will be recognized; but many good men may be blocked for years simply because there are more good men than there are good jobs.

Supervisors.   Arbitrary actions of supervisors contribute to a general feeling of insecurity. The idea of never knowing what is likely to be demanded next causes a most uncomfortable feeling, particularly when there seems to be nothing the worker can do to improve the situation.

Technological Change.   Technological change may eliminate the worker's job permanently. His special skill developed over the years is no longer needed. The seriousness of this predicament is emphasized by the impossibility of finding a similar job with other firms, because they will also be introducing the same technological change. Moreover, retraining an old worker to learn a new skill poses serious problems for an economy, not the least of which is the necessity of choosing a skill for which job openings can be found.

Sale of Firm.   Other difficulties may arise when the firm is sold to new owners—new superiors may change familiar rules, plants may be shifted to new and perhaps remote locations, or working conditions may be altered.

As an individual the average worker is likely to feel helpless and frustrated, quite unable to cope with the hazards of the business world surrounding him. He may be inclined to team up with others in a mutual effort for protection and for the removal of fears born from the insecurity of their position. In some cases this concerted action may result in new labor legislation. In other cases, it may drive workers to the organization of labor unions.

Automation

The large-scale replacement of workers by mechanical equipment is called automation. As with any other form of technological change, the greater productivity is gained at the expense of workers who know only the job they lost to the machine. The adjustment of the individual to the different tasks of a new job is always difficult, but it becomes a national problem when an entire industry automates and wipes out the jobs of half the population of a town. In the coal-mining industry the Push-Button Miner, a mechanical giant controlled by only three men, has been responsible for both a tripling of productivity by the mine worker and the unemployment and misery of Appalachia.

"Is this the price which America must pay for technological progress?

Must the American miner be plunged into a state of hopelessness in order to make mining more competitive?" [1]

The rest of the country may enjoy a prosperous year and experience little difficulty absorbing a few displaced workers, but the automated mining town will not feel the benefits of general prosperity. A systematic effort is necessary to avoid such disasters. Advance planning for replacing old jobs with new activity can prevent much trouble; special incentives for the firm to create new jobs, and direct help for the town's efforts to locate a new business need to accompany major technological upheavals. The disinterest in their workers shown by some modernizing companies in the past has been responsible for much unnecessary hardship and bitterness.

State Legislation

Governments have recognized for a long time the precarious position of the weakest workers, the fringe members of the labor force. State legislation has occasionally attempted to regulate the employment of women and children and of minority racial groups. Legislatures have formulated minimum standards of health and sanitary requirements for many occupations. They have controlled safety regulations for inherently risky jobs such as coal mining.

The use of child labor has been under attack for over a century; Pennsylvania passed a law in 1848 for the purpose of eliminating this practice. Such early legislation proved to be ineffective, however, because states with strong protection for workers became less attractive for employers. Regulatory laws stimulated the development of industry in those states which boasted the least supervision and the weakest legislation. Even today state action to improve work conditions through effective legislation is severely limited by fear of the loss of industry or the failure to attract new industry.

The impact of other laws which favor particular groups of workers has been even more controversial. Fair-employment-practices legislation has been pioneered in some states, but beneficial effects of these laws are sharply disputed. Some state laws try to defend the worker against unions and their officials. These measures will draw our attention in a discussion of labor unions.

The Fair Labor Standards Act of 1938

The federal government showed some concern for the protection of individual workers, particularly for the very young ones, as early as 1906, but

[1] *Labor Looks at Automation*, AFL-CIO Publication 21, December 1966.

the first protective legislation was passed by Congress in 1916. Yet the courts declared these child labor laws unconstitutional until Congress passed a Public Contracts Act in 1936.

The most important step toward federal regulation of the individual at work was the Fair Labor Standards Act of 1938. The law required a minimum age for employment in interstate commerce and provided for detailed accounting of all hours spent on the job.

It also required payment at higher rates for overtime work, which included all work in excess of forty hours per week. The practical impact of the law on the working habits of a large segment of American labor was considerable.

Large industrial enterprises with unionized labor were little affected by the new rule because in most cases their operating procedures were already quite similar to the new requirements. But smaller firms and office workers discovered a major change in working rules. Where it had been the custom never to leave the job before the boss did, the strict accounting and additional payment for extra hours abolished the overtime habit as too expensive. The wage-hour legislation has added more leisure time to the life of the American worker than many people realize.

WAGES

A wage rate is the price paid for human effort. A wage may be called a salary, a commission, a stipend, or any other name peculiar to specific types of work. Regardless of its name, *every wage is a cost to the employer and an income to the worker*. Wages still represent the largest share of all production costs and the most important form of income. Unless rising productivity permits better utilization of human labor, increases in labor costs are likely to be reflected in higher prices of finished goods. A rise in workers' income adds to satisfaction, but it does so only if the higher income buys more goods. Both aspects of wages—cost and income—are forcefully proclaimed by employers and workers when wage rates are in dispute.

What is the right wage? Do people always receive what they are worth? Why do similar jobs so often pay very different wages? Is any raise for one group likely to reduce the income of other people? Let us look for some answers to these often-heard questions.

Wage Rates Under Completely Competitive Conditions

The theoretical framework of unrestricted competition presented in Chapter 7 can prove helpful toward a better understanding of forces influencing wage rates. The two opposing views can be set out in simple terms: The employer will contend that labor should be hired at the lowest price available because labor costs will determine how competitive he is when he sells his product. The worker will claim that wages should represent what he is worth.

Under conditions of extreme competition, workers compete freely for jobs; employers do likewise in hiring men. The two opposing views of the right wage will surprisingly lead to the same result in the following theoretical case.

We shall make here the unrealistic assumption that both employers and workers know of all alternative opportunities and are ready to make a switch for a better offer. In such a situation, the lowest wage at which a worker would become available would be determined by his contribution to the production process. If one employer should try to pay less, he could not find people to work for him, since the worker knows where he can receive higher pay and is willing to take advantage of it. The competition of employers for his services would insure his receiving all he is worth.

This wage would also be the maximum because no firm can afford to pay a man more than he is worth. If the employer knows that an extra worker will add $10 more to the net income of the firm (duly considering all changes in other costs, including normal profit) he will not pay more than this amount. If the worker insists on $11, he will find himself without a job because he is simply not worth that much to any firm.

In these circumstances there is only one right wage for any worker at any given moment, and its amount is determined by the value the worker adds to the firm's production. As technological progress and improved organization make his services more efficient and his contribution more valuable, his wage will increase. Productivity is the unique determinant of the wage rate as long as there is no change in the product or its price. We discussed the need for ever-increasing productivity in Chapter 4. It becomes apparent now that a rise in productivity is not only an essential ingredient of continued growth; it also determines the income, and thereby the living standards, of the worker.

The logic of this abstract case is sometimes advanced in opposition to attempts by labor unions to advance wage rates. If there were only one right wage, paid automatically to each worker as a result of competition, a labor union would become totally ineffective. The real-life situation, however, differs considerably from our assumption of perfect knowledge of all opportunities on both sides of an employment contract. In the area of uncertainty surrounding an actual wage bargain, unions have a real function.

Wage Rates Under Moderately Competitive Conditions

In the ordinary course of business, workers may receive less than their full value or, at least for a short period, they may even be paid too much. Neither employers nor workers know exactly the value of each worker's contribution. The actual wage rate is the result of a bargain based on the personal estimates of the individuals who come to an agreement.

The lowest wage a worker will accept depends on the urgency of his need to find a job and on the other opportunities at his disposal. Fortunately, the going wage for routine work is not determined by the most desperate job seeker. In the continuous flow of people and jobs, the majority of workers never move. The wage rate for all is determined by the supply and demand for the type of workers needed by the firm. The amount offered to the last man to be hired tends to determine the rate paid to all other workers in a similar position who come after him. Some of them may well be willing to work for less, but they do not need to do so as long as the demand for labor is strong enough to boost the going rate. The principles of supply and demand are at work here.

The case of an employer's paying too much for his labor is not unheard of. When firms in different industries hire workers from the same labor supply area, the most efficient firm determines the going wage in the community. The rate may well be higher than the amount a less technologically advanced industry can afford to pay. However, in order to assemble a reasonably good crew of workers and not the misfits rejected by everyone else, the weaker firm must pay a competitive wage even though it may feel it cannot afford it.

The firm hopes to raise the price of its own products in order to compensate for higher wages. If it can sell almost as much at the higher price, all is well. Should the consumers find a suitable substitute, however, the amount of the product sold will drop, the firm must close, and the workers will be unemployed. The case of coal mining is a good example of an industry where ever-increasing wages and prices have shifted the demand for coal to other fuels. The number of coal miners passed its peak a generation ago, and the disappearance of mining jobs at the going wage rate continues to proceed faster than it has been possible to absorb displaced workers into other activities.

Wage Inequality

The difference in wages paid for similar work constitutes a common grievance. Why don't underpaid workers quit and take a job that pays better? If a sufficient number made a switch, the price of human labor could become as uniform as the price of wheat. It would not be necessary for all workers to quit their jobs, but only a number sufficient to cause a shortage of labor for the low-paying firm.

Lack of Mobility.   A worker may refrain from quitting a bad job because he needs continuous current income. The better position for which he could qualify may not materialize for some weeks. Unless he has something saved, he must continue to work every day in order to feed his family. He is caught in a vicious circle. The low pay of his present occupation makes it impossible for him to accumulate savings; without savings he cannot seek better opportunities; therefore, he continues in a low-paying job even though he would prefer to leave.

A highly skilled specialist is of course in a better bargaining position; his earnings are greater, and he knows he has opportunities not open to the nonspecialist. His mobility is considerable at the start, but after a few promotions he acquires valuable rights—in the pension fund, in longer vacations, and so on. Suppose for any reason he begins to dislike his established position—what can he do?

The man can quit, naturally, any time at all. But the operation of the seniority principle reduces this possibility for most practical purposes. Seniority has given him salary increases based on the length of time with the same firm. His income may compare unfavorably with the rates of another firm for the same number of years' service, but his current salary is still higher than the income of a new man in the better paying firm.

Seniority gives limited protection to a worker against being laid off. Seniority rules usually provide that those who join the firm last will be the first ones dismissed when employment opportunities shrink.

The hope of finding a more acceptable employer is seldom worth the real loss that goes with the surrender of seniority rights after long years with the same firm. Many a worker has discovered too late that he is married to his job much more irrevocably than to his wife.

Seniority rules constitute an awkward method of creating job security for the worker. They are of some help in certain cases, but ordinarily they do not apply when a plant closes completely or when its operations are moved to another town. Similarly, they are of no help when the worker's classification is abolished by the introduction of new equipment. Seniority may also become an obstacle to progress when it dictates the order of promotion in a firm and prevents the hiring of the best man for a particular job.

Differences in Productivity. Different wages are paid for similar work when the efficiency of two firms is far from equal. Better management may make the work of employees more effective in one firm than in another, and higher wages can be paid in such cases, as we have seen earlier.

Quality of Work. One of the main reasons for inequality of wages is so obvious that it may be taken for granted. The performance of different people on similar jobs may vary more than is readily apparent. Even where the actual output is mechanically controlled, the worker who is always on the job when needed is far better than the one with a record of many absences. The better paying job may well go to the more reliable individual. Two secretaries may be equally efficient, but one does her work with a smile while the other gives an impression of resigned suffering. Their salaries may well reflect the difference in attitude.

No claim should be made that there is automatic justice in our economic system, or that every worker receives his proper reward. Perfect justice is simply not of this world, and the tricks of fate can be exceedingly cruel. It certainly helps to be lucky; but the chances for better luck do increase with superior performance.

Wage Distribution

Workers want to increase their income without wondering who pays for it. Is it possible for everyone to improve his economic position simultaneously, or will one group of workers climb to the top at the expense of another? Will the combined pressure of all workers boost their income by taking it away from their employers, as Marxists like to proclaim?

There is a reassuring answer to these questions about the best distribution of wages. Incomes have, in fact, risen spectacularly in all the more advanced countries in the twentieth century, and the good things of life have become available to an increasing number of workers, particularly in the Western world. This progress has come about without any great shift in labor's share of the total income. Historically, about two-thirds of all income is paid in wages. Even in periods of spectacular progress, not much change in this ratio can be observed.

The wages of labor are not a fixed number of dollars. If they were, an increase in the share of one group would, in fact, reduce the income of others. Wages are, however, part of a growing income which permits everyone to receive more, though their share of the total may not change.

The size of the wage is only one factor in a complicated economic chain. Higher incomes buy more goods, which can be produced in larger quantity and therefore more efficiently. Improved efficiency permits the payment of higher wages and completes the circle. If improvements in productivity keep ahead of wage demands and allow for continued economic growth, a rising wage rate can be maintained without ill effects on anyone. When wages increase at a faster pace than productivity, the day of reckoning cannot be postponed for long.

Minimum Wage Laws

Legislation in 1938 introduced the concept of a federally guaranteed minimum hourly wage rate. The actual rate is subject to change by frequent

Congressional action; the law of 1966 (effective in 1968) pushed the minimum wage up to $1.60 per hour in several categories. Some forms of employment are not covered by the law. The largest number of jobs not included in the law are those not in interstate commerce. Since Congress legislates only for commerce beyond state lines, some local occupations are not subject to federal control. Few jobs are specifically exempt from compliance with the minimum wage requirements, and the legislative trend points toward broader coverage and higher rates.

Against the Law. The desirability of minimum wage laws is very controversial. Those opposing the law consider such legislation either ineffective or harmful for the beneficiaries. The minimum wage fixed by law is generally below the going rate; it is ineffective in that workers are paid more without the urging of the law. However, should the law insist on a wage rate above the market price for a specific type of labor, unemployment, will be the result.

No firm will knowingly pay a man more than he is worth. If the minimum pay is too high, the lowly individual in greatest need of a job cannot find one. A minimum wage law guarantees a wage rate if you find a job. The opponents of this legislation suggest that we concern ourselves more with employment opportunities for the lowest paid workers than with fixing an unrealistic wage rate at which many cannot qualify for any job.

The case against the law has been summarized effectively in this statement:

> Minimum wage laws reduce job opportunities for beginners, for people without developed skills, for seekers of temporary or spare time employment. Then there are the inevitable numbers who, for lack of industrious habits, have so little to offer a prospective employer that pay of as little as 75 or 90 cents an hour would be an act of charity.[2]

For the Law. The defenders of minimum wage legislation stress the lack of bargaining power of the lowest paid group of unskilled workers. These employees are usually not unionized and have no spokesman for their cause —they simply must accept whatever the firm offers. The minimum wage will in this case prevent the exploitation of the weak. Admittedly, some jobs may disappear as a result of the law, but people who favor this legislation point out that any job that is worth less than the legal minimum is really no job at all and should not exist. If a man can qualify for a job at the legal rate, he should be able to find one and not have to waste his time in an occupation that pays less. Should the worker be physically or mentally incapable of handling a job at the minimum pay level, he cannot be con-

[2] *The First National City Bank of New York Monthly Letter,* September 1960, p. 107.

sidered a member of the labor force and should be helped through public assistance or rehabilitation.

An example of work which is often not worth a legal minimum wage would be a neighborhood short-order delivery service from a snack bar. In days long past, children would be hired to remain on call for such deliveries into the middle of the night. Their wages were only a few cents per hour. Such jobs have been eliminated, and there is no doubt that the children are better off with more sleep and additional attendance at school. But not all cases are as clear-cut.

People in favor of a minimum wage law dispute the claim that it causes unemployment. They argue that a low wage makes a job unproductive because the employer has no incentive to utilize his workers efficiently unless he has to pay them more. If such a view were correct, the minimum wage would be a stimulant for technological progress and not a cause of unemployment.

Wage Rates and Unemployment

The relationship of wage rates and unemployment needs more clarification. Since the days of the Depression, national policy statements have always proclaimed full employment as a major goal. At times, economic policy has appeared to value high employment to the exclusion of all other considerations; actual practice, however, contradicts these lofty pronouncements.

The working reality of labor relations and of the laws governing employment contracts focuses almost exclusively on hourly wage rates and tends to disregard their effect on total national employment. The struggle for a labor contract centers on a few cents more or less per hour, but remains silent on the number of men employed. For most practical purposes, a firm in need of cutting costs has no alternative but to discharge people —a man on the job is protected by many rights, but not the essential one of keeping his employment.

Such an unfortunate wage pattern tends toward persistent unemployment. During a period of recession, unemployment may be hard to avoid in any case. During a boom, however, we ought to achieve substantially full employment; but unfortunately, an improved business outlook may lead promptly to higher wage demands. When times are good, a new machine replacing five workers appeals strongly to the employer, particularly when he considers, as he surely will, that the trend in wage rates points invariably upward. He controls his total cost by firing the workers.

The undesirable result of this institutional arrangement is often deplored by many people who make no serious effort to change it. The tradition of concentrating attention on wage rates is so strong that management, labor, and the public seem to accept the situation without question in spite of its unfortunate consequences. Policy decisions tend to be dominated by the majority of workers who keep their jobs even at higher wages and who disregard the fact that some people will be unemployed. Management also prefers to bargain over hourly rates, since this cost factor is familiar to the negotiators. A job guarantee would create new issues of unknown complexity—which all sides try to avoid.

LABOR UNIONS

Labor unions are organizations formed for the representation of the common interests of groups of workers. The community of interests regarding employment conditions shared by a large number of people is the source of union power. The main economic function of a labor union consists in securing the highest possible wage rates for its members. To reach this goal, a union must try to enroll all qualified workers in its membership and still prevent the number of members from becoming too large for the available job opportunities. The effectiveness of a union depends on its ability to control the supply of labor in its area of jurisdiction.

Historical Development

The first attempts at unionization in the United States were made early in the nineteenth century. Early unions proved to be quite ineffective and short lived. Not until 1881 was a lasting organization born—which a few years later became the American Federation of Labor. Founded on principles which insured its survival, it grew into the leading labor organization under the long-term leadership of Samuel Gompers. This union concentrated on improving the immediate economic conditions of its workers within the framework of a capitalistic society, avoiding identification with purely partisan politics. In the hostile atmosphere prevailing before World War I, the unionization of labor grew slowly.

The rise of mass production industries in the twenties accelerated the demands for worker representation. The plight of labor after the crash of 1929 led to increasing pressure for unionization, which found political recognition in Congress in the early thirties.

Legislation supporting the unionization of railroad workers in the twenties had already set a precedent for Congressional action. The rising tide of organized labor received its permanent legislative foundation in the Wagner Act of 1935. Armed with powerful legal support, labor unions penetrated most major industries with large concentrations of workers, particularly in the industrial areas of the North.

The managers of business were initially inclined to take a dim view of this new power group representing the workers. With public opinion and Congress solidly on the side of the unions, however, most firms adjusted after some hesitation and learned to live with the new rules of collective bargaining. Nonetheless, a minority held out much longer and engaged in a costly and bitter rear-guard fight against the unions.

By the end of World War II, the Depression which had helped unions to organize had receded in people's minds, while the abuse of power by a few union leaders had become glaring and widely publicized. The political pendulum was ready to swing in the opposite direction. In this mood Congress passed the Taft-Hartley Act (Labor-Management Relations Act) in 1947 and the Landrum-Griffin Act in 1959. The objective of this legislation was to curb abuses of union power, which had been exposed and disapproved by the public. As a result, current labor legislation, while far from perfect and exceedingly complex, is gradually becoming a more balanced framework for labor relations than it has been in the past.

The Structure of Labor Unions

The structural organization of the labor movement is headed by the AFL-CIO. It forms the parent organization for the majority of the unions in this country. As a group, only the railroad brotherhoods are not normally affiliated with the AFL-CIO. Other large unions, such as the Teamsters, may find themselves temporarily without affiliation when their policies or their leaders come into conflict with the parent institution.

The old American Federation of Labor had maintained an organizational structure which combined workers of the same craft in each union. The development of mass production on an assembly line brought large groups of unskilled and semi-skilled workers into fast-growing, new industries such as the manufacture of automobiles. The organization of an entire industry along traditional craft lines was no longer practical. The AF of L proved too slow to adjust to the changing requirements of the 1920's, and some of its most energetic leaders created a new parent organization called the Congress of Industrial Organization (CIO) in 1935. This association sponsored industrial unions—organizations which covered all workers in an industry regardless of their special skills. It proved most successful with the employees in the mass production industries, particularly steel and automobiles.

After twenty years of competition between AF of L and CIO, the two parent organizations merged into the AFL-CIO, combining the advantages of both groups in one large association representing the common interests of over sixteen million workers. There continues to be, however, much friction among competing unions over the right to organize particular groups of workers.

The function of the central headquarters of the AFL-CIO is highly restricted. It sets broad policies and acts as the public spokesman for the labor movement. Individual workers, however, belong to much smaller groups known as union locals, which exercise the representation in a plant or firm. Union power is concentrated in national unions, such as United Steelworkers, where many locals serving similar worker groups are combined. Individual union members do not hold membership in a national union. The connection between the local and the national union is a close one, while the link to the Federation is much looser. The affiliation of a national union with the AFL-CIO can be rescinded whenever the two sides disagree with each other. The Federation has no power to enforce its policies in any union. It may deprive the union of membership in the Federation, but this does not necessarily hamper the effectiveness of the locals involved.

Federation	*Combines Loosely*	National Unions	*Which Charter*	Local Unions
AFL-CIO		United Auto Workers		GM Local
		United Steelworkers		Ford Local
		Ladies' Garment Workers		Etc.
		Meat Cutters and Butcher Workmen		
		Plumbing and Pipe Fitting		
Railroad brotherhoods		Engineers		Railroad locals
Unaffiliated unions		Teamsters		Teamster locals

The national union determines the policy of union action for its own affairs and for its locals. Negotiation patterns for employment contracts are decided by the national unions, and they also furnish specialized negotiators and other highly skilled personnel whenever the locals need them. Minor issues, local problems, and individual grievances are handled on the local level.

The heart of union power rests with the leadership of the national unions. They charter and organize local unions when they consider such a step advisable. In many unions the rights of the rank-and-file members of locals are very limited with regard to the selection of national leaders. In general a union constitution, or by-laws, appears to be quite democratic, but in practice the members may not have much influence. Thus, candidates for offices in a local are often selected by the national leadership, a procedure which in turn assures the national leaders of a majority whenever problems of the national union come to a vote. Parts of the Landrum-Griffin Act attempt to increase the rights of individual members who disagree with their leadership. A serious problem arises only when the leadership of a union is captured by racketeers or other underworld figures who abuse union power for their own purposes and disregard the welfare of the union members.

The Functions of Labor Unions

Workers join unions for economic, sociological, and psychological reasons. To obtain the best possible compensation, they need experienced spokesmen for the defense of their economic aspirations. But unions also fill important noneconomic needs of their members. The tendency of large business operations to reduce men to insignificant numbers is counteracted by the feeling of "belonging" that goes with union membership. Being a good union man has social status for many a workman, and his feeling of security is increased if he knows he is part of a large and powerful group representing his interests.

Collective bargaining is the main technique used by a union to accomplish its objectives. The individual worker is usually in no position to put pressure on his employer in order to gain a raise in pay; he will be afraid of losing his job by being too forceful and insistent in his demands. The union representative, however, is in a much stronger position; he negotiates a contract for all the workers in a firm and is immune to pressure by the employer. The firm cannot play one worker against another, but must make an offer to all of them collectively. The right to collective bargaining is a real advantage for organized labor and has helped to make unions a permanent and powerful institution in the American economy. This right was firmly established by the Wagner Act and was reaffirmed by the Taft-Hartley Act.

Labor-Management Contract. A labor-management contract is a long and detailed document which covers, among other things, wage rates, hours, and conditions of work. Typically, the contract will include *fringe benefits.* These are valuable and often costly concessions by the employer in addition to wage payments, and they include paid vacations, pension plans, health insurance, recreational facilities, and so forth.

Working conditions are frequently spelled out in great detail by such a contract. Promotion and layoff rules establish the rights of a worker in connection with his job; detailed work rules protect the men against arbitrary actions by an employer. The contract governs the relationship between the firm and its employees for some length of time—usually from one to three years.

Labor-Management Disputes.   The interpretation of contract rules may occasionally lead to a difference of opinion. To avoid serious difficulties in such situations, many contracts provide for *arbitration*. When the firm and the union disagree on the interpretation of a contract clause, they refer the dispute to an impartial arbitrator who has been selected earlier for this purpose. His interpretation of the contract will usually be accepted by both sides.

Arbitration must not be confused with *mediation*. The arbitrator decides the right interpretation of an existing contract, while the mediator helps the union and management to reach agreement on a new contract which has not yet been accepted. The mediator helps both sides to arrive at a compromise, and suggests mutual concessions toward the speedy settlement of a labor dispute. Unlike an arbitrator, he renders no decisions.

Mediators are not always able to obtain agreement on a new contract. In this case the union may call a strike of its members in order to induce the employer to accept its contract terms. A *strike* is an organized refusal to work by groups of workers who maintain that they are not quitting their jobs, but who try to strengthen their demands on the firm by *picketing*. Pickets are union members posted outside the employer's place of business in order to advertise their disagreement with management and to discourage others from entering the plant. Sometimes the employer acts first, shutting down all plant operations and laying off the workers. This action on the part of the firm is known as a *lockout* and is intended to bring the union to more reasonable terms.

The strength of the union stems from three sources: the specific protection of the law, the financial impact built on the payment of dues by members and on control of insurance funds, and the community of interest of a large, organized group of voters.

The Law as a Source of Power

The Norris–La Guardia Act in 1932 strengthened union leaders in their relations with management, chiefly through two negative provisions. It abolished the yellow-dog contract and greatly restricted the use of injunctions by employers in labor disputes. Both practices had been most effective in curbing union power in the past.

A *yellow-dog contract* was a statement signed by the worker when he accepted a job. He promised not to join a union while employed by the firm, acknowledging that violation of the agreement constituted cause for discharge. The existence of such a document proved to be a handicap to union organizers, since even the most sympathetic worker usually did not care to lose his job.

An *injunction* is a court order directing the defendant to do or not to do some thing which might cause harm now beyond future legal repair. In earlier labor disputes, employers would stop attempts to organize strikes, or virtually any union activity, by petitioning the courts for injunctions, proving without difficulty that union activities would hurt their business. Union leaders found injunctions very harmful because they interfered with the proper timing of union pressure on management—an essential detail for success. A coal strike is effective in midwinter when coal demand is highest. If postponed by court order until the following May, a strike becomes an empty threat. The injunction is a powerful and necessary legal device, but in labor cases it was abused in the pre-1932 period.

The Wagner Act in 1935 strengthened union power positively. This law *proclaimed labor's right to collective bargaining* and created the National Labor Relations Board (NLRB) for its enforcement. This federal agency supervises elections to determine who will represent the workers in their discussions with management. It also handles numerous complaints and makes sure that the rights of labor are not violated. Under the impact of these and other laws, union power has grown rapidly and has become a major influence in the American economy.

The prohibition of injunctions in labor cases by the Norris–La Guardia Act tempted some union leaders to abuse their new freedom. Some strikes were primarily aimed at the profits of the employer, but others created serious inconvenience for the public, who had no part in the labor-management dispute. Some union leaders hoped that involving the public would exert additional pressure on management to give in to the unions and accept their demands. After some successful strikes of this type, however, the public reacted against the unions. This change of heart by the majority led to the passage of the Taft-Hartley Act in 1947. The most controversial provision of this law permitted the attorney general to ask the courts for injunctions in labor disputes where the public health and welfare required it. The right to ask for an injunction remained restricted to the attorney general rather than to the firm threatened by a strike. The courts could grant an injunction, not to protect private profit but to save innocent bystanders from the more harmful effects of strikes.

Arbitrary actions by a few union leaders led to specific legislation intended to protect individual union members against undue pressure by their officers.

The Taft-Hartley Act prevented the unions' charging unreasonable initiation fees and union dues for members. It prohibited jurisdictional strikes—a form of warfare between the leaders of different unions—in which one union would threaten a strike in order to force the employer to replace one group of workers with another by claiming jurisdiction on the job.

The law also tried to insure democratic control of unions with free elections by their members. These provisions were ineffective and were strengthened by the Landrum-Griffin Act of 1959. This law is very specific in its efforts to keep the leaders responsive to the real, common interests of the members. The effectiveness of this new law remains a matter of dispute.

Existing laws have not been able to prevent labor-management disputes from hurting both the public and the national economy. No court can make a group of people work when they do not want to do so; the law may provide for penalties, but these are effective only against individuals or small groups. The threat of discharge under the laws of the State of New York failed to keep the subway workers on the job in January 1966; the physical impossibility of replacing thousands of employees was obvious, even if it had been politically possible. An airline strike in the summer of 1966 was not settled for six weeks, in spite of its damage to the public welfare. Only the intervention of Congress stopped a railroad strike in 1967.

Financial Power

The financial power of a union is based on the regular collection of dues from the largest possible number of workers. To reach this objective, a union must receive funds not only from its most enthusiastic members, but from all workers who benefit from union efforts, particularly from collective bargaining agreements negotiated by unions and management. To exert complete control over all workers in a plant, unions used to insist on a *closed-shop* contract which stipulated that the firm would hire only union members. The Taft-Hartley Act abolished this type of agreement, which deprived nonunion workers of employment opportunities because the firm no longer could hire whomever it chose.

The *union shop* has generally replaced the closed shop. Under this arrangement management may hire any worker, provided that he agrees to join the union within a given period and to pay dues. Such a contract has proven to be adequate protection for union finances. In some states the union shop has been prohibited by right-to-work laws, a restrictive legislation whose promoters claim that no worker should be forced to join a union. In addition, they hold that a firm should recognize only an *open shop,* where union and nonunion workers exist side by side without distinction.

Unions object that open shops reduce the effectiveness of the union when a firm has enough nonunion workers to operate in a pinch, even without the union men. They further object to so-called *free riders*. These are workers who allegedly benefit from all the gains won by the union in its contract without contributing their proper share to the union treasury.

The erosion of the union's financial power by free riders has been avoided in some states by an *agency shop*. In this case the union does not require membership of all workers, as long as they are willing to pay the equivalent of dues to the union while they work in a plant covered by such an arrangement.

Financial power may be exerted in *featherbedding* practices, which provide for payment to the worker for work not done. The law prohibits such practices, but the courts have interpreted it quite narrowly. A union may insist, for example, that a small radio station hire local musicians at the same time that it carries the New York Symphony over a national network. Though the local music is not intended for transmission on the air, the courts have refused to consider this as featherbedding provided the musicians are present and are actually making noise with their instruments.

Not all labor unions have the same financial power. Some of them collect only enough for headquarters operations, while others have accumulated very large funds. In most industries the business firms dwarf the unions in financial power. In the textile field, however, the national union is financially stronger than many of the firms employing its members. Unions may engage in far-flung investments, they may accumulate pension funds for their members, and they can even make loans to the firms which employ them. Some own banks or buy stock in firms in order to influence the management. The Taft-Hartley Act provides for audits of union finances, but it has not set standards of stewardship for this great financial power.

Community of Interest

The real foundation of all union power rests on the community of interest of the workers who join. This interest covers all the details usually found in a labor contract, but it goes beyond the specific points of bargaining and includes the general recognition of the dignity of human labor and its importance to the production process. The exact extent of these combined interests is hard to define and may lead to exaggerated claims on the part of union leaders. It has been particularly difficult for union leaders to deliver the vote of their followers to any one political party, even when they claim that their members will follow their advice on questions which are only slightly connected with their role as workers.

After a generation of struggle and growth, labor unions are finding a permanent place in the economic organization of this country. They have been generally accepted by most people, and their function is recognized in most key manufacturing fields. Unionization varies widely. It is much stronger in heavy industry than in small service-type occupations; it is more widespread in the North than in the South, and in big cities rather than small towns.

The majority of the American labor force continue to belong to no union, and their average hourly wage rate is lower than that of organized workers. Conflicts and abuses of power still occur in the union in spite of much legislation. Some employers think wistfully of the good old days when the best use of manpower and the amount paid to each worker were dictated only by the wisdom and conscience of management. These days are gone forever, and unions are here to stay; their influence establishes new patterns to shape the rules governing human effort. The art of compromise must be learned by everyone involved to make it possible for people with conflicting interests to work harmoniously toward the common goal of higher incomes. Cooperation cannot be dictated by law, but depends on the wisdom and mature judgment of all participants.[3]

SUMMARY

Man occupies a unique position in the production process because he is both the most important cost factor in the creation of goods and services and the recipient of income which permits him to buy the goods produced.

The worker's job is surrounded by insecurity; this causes a demand for legislation and an incentive for unionization. His insecurity is based, among other things, on fear of layoffs, discrimination on job advancement, arbitrary action of superiors, and technological unemployment.

State laws have tried to protect the weakest groups of individuals in the labor force with provisions concerning health requirements, child labor, women, and minority groups. Federal laws regulate working hours, overtime, minimum wage rates, employment practices on federal projects, and other aspects of employment.

Wage rates cannot exceed the value of the job's contribution to the employer's business, and they cannot drop below the amount competing firms are willing to pay. In a normal business situation, the two limits may not be well known to the participants of a wage bargain and may allow considerable leeway for discussion.

Wages differ for apparently similar jobs because of the difficulty of moving job seekers to high wage areas, the restrictions in seniority rules, varying degrees of productivity, and differences in the quality of individual performance.

Incomes of workers will rise when the economy prospers. Disappearance of unemployment and efficient use of labor will contribute to the real income of the individual. Our institutional arrangements, however, focus too much on wage rates instead of job security, with the result that there can be unemployment even in prosperous times.

---

[3] The role of unions in a period of national inflation will be discussed in Chapter 16.

Labor unions have grown slowly from 1880 to 1930 and much faster since that time, particularly during the depression period before World War II. They are organized on three levels: the local union represents the worker in a plant or a firm; the national union combines a number of locals and furnishes guidance, assistance, and supervision to the locals; and the AFL-CIO acts as a parent organization for most national unions, which are loosely federated, and speaks for labor on broad, national objectives. The focus of union power rests in the national unions.

Major legislation covering union rights and obligations is contained in the Norris-La Guardia Act, the Wagner Act, the Taft-Hartley Act, and The Landrum-Griffin Act. The first two laws mentioned strengthened unions and their leadership; the last two were intended to prevent abuse of powers by those leaders.

The community of interest of its members is the foundation of union power. The accumulation of large funds insures the practical recognition of this strength. The recognition of union rights by the law renders the exercise of power lawful and respectable. Labor unions today are fulfilling a function and have become permanent institutions in the American economy.

Discussion Questions

1. Why does the modern factory worker lack job security?
2. How did the Fair Labor Standards Act help change working conditions?
3. Why can't people agree on a "scientific" wage rate?
4. What makes wage differences unjust?
5. State the case for and against minimum wage laws and right-to-work laws.
6. Why is the AFL-CIO not responsible for the action of a union local?
7. How did the Taft-Hartley Act deal with union members? with union leaders? with the general public?
8. The Wagner Act is sometimes called the Magna Carta of the labor movement. Why?
9. What makes labor unions strong?
10. Distinguish closed shop, union shop, open shop, agency shop.

Suggested Reading

The American Assembly, *Automation and Technological Change,* John T. Dunlop, ed. Englewood Cliffs, N.J., Prentice-Hall, 1962.

BUTLER, ARTHUR D., *Labor Economics and Institutions.* New York, Macmillan, 1961.

MORGAN, CHESTER A., *Labor Economics.* Homewood, Ill., Irwin, Dorsey Press, 1966.

REYNOLDS, LLOYD G., *Labor Economics and Labor Relations,* 4th ed. Englewood Cliffs, N.J., Prentice-Hall, Inc., 1964.

11

AGRICULTURE

FARMING IS A BUSINESS

Modern agriculture differs as much from farming at the turn of the century as a new factory does from the shop of sixty years ago. History tells us that this country has been a nation of farmers and that farming is a way of life. This tradition belongs to a past far removed from the realities of today.

Rapid technological advances, and increasing capital investment, have made it possible for fewer and fewer American farmers to supply the food and fiber needs of larger and larger numbers of people. American farmers have shown great initiative and competence in responding to the opportunity thus created. They have taken up the latest production methods with a speed that amazes the administrators of agriculture in planned economies.[1]

The technological revolution in agriculture has come somewhat later than in manufacturing, but it has been equally impressive. A smaller number of people are operating fewer but larger farms, which feed and clothe more of their fellow citizens today than ever before in history.

In 1959 the United States census counted 3,700,000 farms. They were operated by 3.1 million farmers and their families with the help of 690,000 hired workers. These are the smallest figures for the farm population since 1870. Today, fewer people can easily produce a harvest of abundance because they have learned to handle tractors and machinery with great efficiency. The modern farm has become a highly mechanized business with a huge capital investment.

Agricultural production has increased faster in the past twenty-five years than in the preceding seventy-year period. "In 1870, the U.S. farm worker produced enough food to supply 5 persons; in 1940, enough to supply 10.7 persons; in 1950, 14.56 persons; and in 1960, 26.1 persons. Behind these phenomenal advances have been rapid increases in scientific knowledge and technology, efficiently, and promptly applied." [2] The change in American farming methods is aptly illustrated by this comparison: in

[1] *An Adaptive Program for Agriculture* (New York, Committee for Economic Development [CED], 1962), p. 7.
[2] Ralph McCabe, *Agriculture's Role in the 1960 Decade: Food and People* (U.S. Congress, Joint Economic Committee, Subcommittee on Foreign Economic Policy, 87th Cong., 1st sess., 1961).

1918 United States farms used twenty-seven million horses and mules and 300,000 tractors; in 1960 the figures had changed to three million horses and mules and 4.8 million tractors.

The speed at which small farms disappear is directly related to their size. It is highest in farms of less than 220 acres, while those over 500 acres in size show a steady numerical increase. About 1.5 million efficient commercial farms, each selling more than $5,000 worth of products per year, provide 87 percent of total farm output. One-half of all sales of farm products comes from less than 10 percent of the nation's farms; their annual sales exceed $15 billion, or over $20,000 per farm. Most small farms have become part-time operations with some of the family members earning a livelihood in town, or they provide occupations for retired people who want to keep busy and supplement their retirement income. About two million small farm operators produce only 13 percent of all agricultural products. These small farmers are no longer needed to feed and clothe the nation and should be encouraged to move away from farming into more productive activity.

This introductory description of modern farming should make it clear that the statistical averages—lumping together a typical 1000-acre wheat farm and the forty acres operated by a retired factory worker drawing an old-age pension—are not very meaningful. The modern farmer is a businessman who manages a complex, highly specialized firm using a large amount of capital and knowledge. To be successful, he needs more information in a wider variety of fields than does the store owner on Main Street, because his operation is larger, more expensive, and often technically more complicated.

It is, indeed, small wonder that not all farmers are able to meet the requirements of a changing agricultural situation. Like his counterpart, the small businessman in town, the small farmer finds it difficult to keep up with changing times—to learn new methods fast enough, to utilize modern equipment most efficiently, and to make the wisest use of credit. However, there is nothing wrong with the big, healthy, efficient, competitive, and prosperous American farmer; he has no equal anywhere in the world.

THE FARM PROBLEM

The picture of the large, modern farmer is one of efficiency and progress, of growth and prosperity. He bears no resemblance to the poor, neglected, hopeless individual we encounter so often in political oratory when the discussion turns to the farm problem. Congress spends many billions of dollars on agriculture every year. What, then, is the nature of the farm problem?

What Is the Problem?

Poverty. The income of the farmer has in fact failed to rise as fast as that of the average American worker. While the nation's income has increased over twelve times since 1910, the net income of farmers is only three times what it was. The drop in farm population compensates only in part for this income lag. The average farm income was only half that of urban families in 1959. This statement is misleading, however, since it fails to consider nonfarm earnings of farm families. If everything is included, the farm average is much higher, but it still lags behind city families by 13 percent.

Since the large commercial farmers obviously are in a much higher income bracket, such a low average spells poverty for the majority of small farmers in the United States. *Poverty is the farm problem.*

The low-income farmer surely needs higher income. How can it be achieved? A federal subsidy to raise the lowest level of subsistence on the farm would be possible; indeed, laws that would guarantee a minimum income have been introduced in Congress several times. But they have never been accepted by Congress for the following reasons:

1. The beneficiaries of such a law, it is claimed, do not want legalized charity; they want to earn a living, not receive a dole. 2. An assured minimum farm income might stop the exodus of the small farmer and make the farm problem permanent; the large number of poor, young farmers moving to town is often deplored, but it will eventually eliminate the problem. 3. The large farmers exert more influence on the writing of farm legislation, and they have no interest in keeping the small operator in business.

Too Many Farmers. Technological change has rendered the skills of the small farmer obsolete without offering him a practical alternative. *The farm problem is also one of excess labor,* which has not been able to make the transfer to city life in sufficient number, nor soon enough. The small farmers are unable to control enough land or are unwilling to change outdated methods in their futile efforts to eke out a living. Other workers in fading industries face similar difficulties, from wool textiles in New England to the coal mines in West Virginia. But the farm problem involves more people, greater costs, and all regions of this nation; for sheer size it is more important.

Too much wheat or a cotton surplus may cause periodic headlines in the newspapers, but the key to the trouble is a surplus of farmers who are forced to exist at the brink of survival. These people should move to urban occupations, but lack of training and job opportunities keeps them on the farm. In addition, the cost of moving often seems too great.

In spite of all obstacles, the small farmers are selling out as fast as possible; but over a million full-time operators remain to form the core of the farm problem. They operate an insufficient acreage of poor land with cash sales (*not* net income) of less than $2,500 for a full year.

Young men and women who grow up on the land will move to town in search of work in industrial occupations. They are ready to give up the independence of farm life, and the poverty which has been their childhood companion, for the better paycheck of a city worker. Recent trends show clearly that the average age of farmers is rising as a result of the exodus of the younger men. As older farmers die, their small farms are sold (or leased) to larger operators who absorb them in their ever-growing business. But the movement away from the farm continues to be slow.

Causes of Low Farm Income

Slow Rise of Demand.   The demand for farm products does not grow as fast as the demand for industrial goods—food consumption rises only slightly faster than the population. Most Americans may want to switch their eating habits from hamburgers to more steak as rising incomes permit, but they do not choose to eat more total calories.

The demand for fiber grows faster than for food. But the increasing use of man-made textiles has kept wool and cotton consumption from rising in this country. A 50-percent increase in fiber consumption from 1958 to 1965 left wool unchanged and cotton just barely holding its own, whereas noncellulosic fibers such as nylon, Dacron, and Orlon showed a phenomenal increase in spite of their much higher prices. On the whole, the demand for farm products grows only slowly.

Lower Prices Have Little Effect.   A price drop in wheat fails to boost demand for it sufficiently that we can dispose of surplus products. People will eat about the same amount of food regardless of price. This lack of responsiveness holds true for cereals and, to a smaller extent, for other foodstuffs. A switch from cheaper types of food to more expensive ones will, however, be more strongly governed by prices.

Furthermore, a drop in the price of wheat does not cause a noticeable reduction in the retail price of bread. A loaf selling in a store for 21 cents contains only 2.6 cents worth of wheat paid to the farmer (1966); the rest of the price is the cost of transporting, milling, baking, and selling the bread. Even if wheat costs only half as much, bread will not drop more than one cent at retail, if it changes at all.

With cotton, price becomes a very important factor, since industrial users such as tire manufacturers will use cotton or rayon according to what they cost. When Congress boosted domestic cotton prices in the early 1960's to 33 cents per pound, users switched to rayon at 27 cents. After the passage of the law of 1964, the market price of cotton dropped to 24 cents and cotton sales recovered promptly.

Inflexibility of Farm Resources. The difficulty has been pointed out of moving farmers away from their land at the speed dictated by modern technology. Farm workers are actually leaving the farms as fast as towns are able to absorb them in better-paying jobs. Any rise in industrial unemployment retards this adjustment process.

Cultivation of farm acreage fails to respond sufficiently to price changes of crops unless the government intervenes. Low product prices may reduce the price of land, but the land will not be taken out of cultivation. The farmer will try to raise a crop year after year, even when it looks hopeless. When he can no longer manage to pay his bills, the banker may take over the mortgaged farm. He may sell it to another farmer or lease it back to the man who lost it in the hope of better luck next year—but the farm will continue to produce a crop.

Agricultural Competition. Farming is highly competitive; in fact, the example of a wheat farmer is frequently used to illustrate the operation of unrestricted competition. No single farmer can hope to influence total output or price through any steps he takes alone. He may even try to produce more when prices fall, in order to compensate with larger sales for any drop in income per ton. Such fierce competition becomes a predicament, because the manufactured goods bought by the farmer are not produced under similar conditions. In industry, if demand falls prices stay up, while output is reduced promptly to avoid selling at a loss. In agriculture, on the other hand, when demand falls farmers continue to produce, and farm prices drop drastically.

Technology. Technological development is a boon to mankind, but it has greatly aggravated the agricultural crisis. Farming was revolutionized later and faster than most other activities by the sudden impact of modern technology. The shift from manpower to machinery was so large and so rapid that adjustments simply could not keep in step, resulting in the accumulation of currently unneeded farm labor.

The Weather. Agriculture depends on the weather, which is more uncertain than anything faced by a company in town. A year's effort may be wiped out by one hailstorm or by a drought. Some farmers carry private insurance against wind and hail, but drought insurance is either impractical or too costly. The farmer thus feels that his unique position entitles him to special assistance by the government.

Not all people in town will accept this claim. Resort operators depend on the weather as much as any farmer, but they receive no help from the government. Businessmen selling fashion merchandise will claim that the tastes of the ladies are more capricious and change faster than anything nature can produce.

Differential Treatment of Industry.   The farmer points an accusing finger at industries which receive special protection to help keep prices up. A tariff wall against imported goods forces the farmer to pay more for what he buys, because the government secures the privileged position of the domestic producer. The farmer argues that it is not fair that he be expected to sell cheap competitive food in exchange for high-priced, protected industrial products. Labor unions are also guilty of raising prices of manufactured goods with their wage demands, for which the farmer eventually will have to foot the bill.

This demand for equity sounds reasonable enough. Little will be gained, however, for the progress of a free economy if we insist upon piling special privileges upon one group after another. Farming is not the only occupation where intervention can be reduced. A competitive economy must not compete to secure monopoly positions for everyone!

FEDERAL ACTION IN AGRICULTURE

Government assistance to agriculture is nothing new either in this country or elsewhere in the world. Farming has been the dominant occupation ever since men have had to feed and clothe themselves. Its political primacy has been such that farmers would not give up their influence on the government even after they ceased to represent the majority of the voters.

However, the days of this preponderance are fading away as city dwellers insist on more adequate representation, and the voice of the farmers is becoming weaker and more divided. Their interests differ as much as those of businessmen—grain farmers want high prices for crops, while meat producers prefer low-cost feed.

Many areas of farming benefit from some sort of federal activity. We shall consider first the type of legislation which is of undisputed help to the farmer, though the city worker may not be enthusiastic about footing the bill. Next we shall discuss price-support laws whose beneficial effects are sharply disputed. Finally, we must look at the cost and effectiveness of federal legislation in the light of possible alternatives.

Federal Aid for the Farmer

Soil Conservation. Soil conservation enlists federal assistance for partial financing of farming practices which will save the land for future generations. Many techniques advocated by the government appeal to progressive farmers because they are in the best interest of those who own the land. The help rendered by the Department of Agriculture makes soil conservation practices financially more attractive. This assistance contains, in part, an element of subsidy which is justified by its proponents in view of the generally approved objective of soil conservation.

Education. Federal aid to education of the rural population has a long history. The Morrill Act of 1861 provided for the creation of land-grant colleges, bringing the advantages of higher education within reach of farm families. While these institutions started with an almost exclusive concern for farm problems, they were able to change with the times and help successive generations of farm children to a smooth transition into the industry-dominated life of today.

Research and Extension Service. Government-financed research has been of major significance to the dramatic evolution of modern agriculture. Experiment stations, operating in conjunction with the land-grant colleges, are financially able to undertake the expensive research that individual farmers can not afford. The rise in farm productivity owes much to these research laboratories.

The application of new and progressive methods to farming is generally a slow process since farmers are inclined to be conservative by nature. The federally sponsored Agricultural Extension Service has contributed materially to speeding up the utilization of laboratory advancements in everyday farming.

One of the consequences of federally financed research has been an emphasis on the improvement of production, with less attention focused on advancements in the distribution and marketing of certain agricultural products. The result of this uneven rate of progress has contributed to the piling up of a burdensome surplus of many crops.

Electric Power. In a major program to help the farmer, electric power was brought to the farm through the Rural Electrification Administration (REA) created in 1935. The farmers received loans to bring power lines to sparsely settled areas where private utility services would have been prohibitively expensive. Modern living depends so much on power that the electrification of the countryside removed a major obstacle to agricultural living. However, the REA has received sharp criticism in recent years because of its efforts to expand into the suburbs in competition with private power.

Farm Credit.   The lack of farm credit has been an age-old complaint of agriculture, and with increasing mechanization the availability of cheap credit becomes even more important. To help fill this gap, Congress has authorized measures to create banking facilities designed to make loans in agriculture. Low-interest loans are now available for many purposes, from farm housing to flood emergencies. Although the need for federal action in providing cheap credit has been challenged, the benefit to the farmer can hardly be questioned.

Food Distribution.   The federal government buys farm products for distribution to schools under the school lunch program, and to foreign countries under a more recent "food for peace" program. The impact of these projects on total farm income may not be very large, but federal expenditures which increase the demand for farm products are certainly an advantage to the farmer.

Foreign Sales.   Under the provisions of Public Law 480, passed originally in 1954, the Department of Agriculture has systematically disposed of surplus food to foreign lands. The provisions of sale under the law do not require payment in dollars, but in the local currency of the buyer. These accounts are used in the foreign country for payments on which both governments agree.

The law has accomplished its basic purpose of reducing the surplus of farm commodities. In the case of wheat, heavy shipments to India in 1965 and 1966 were an important factor in eliminating unneeded grain in storage in the United States. The total cost to the American taxpayer of disposing of farm commodities abroad has reached about $15 billion in twelve years.

The continuation of this policy must be considered from a broader viewpoint. Sales under such lenient conditions of payment virtually constitute gifts which may, at least partly, replace normal sales from such countries as Canada. In this respect, our farm policy may hurt a friendly nation and come into direct conflict with our other foreign policy objectives. The reduction of the wheat surplus brings with it a request for more wheat acreage and may result in an increase in farm support costs. The right decision depends on our national objectives. If we want to feed the world, we should produce all we can and give away the surplus; but we cannot object to this form of foreign aid and at the same time favor an increase in land use which causes this costly surplus.

Price-Support Laws

The perennial debate over federal action in agriculture focuses primarily on measures to support the prices of farm products. Before we evaluate the long series of programs which have controlled the decisions of farmers for a generation, let us see how, exactly, the principal features of this system operate. The program is built on the concepts of parity, acreage control, and price support.

Parity.   The parity concept has dominated farm-price legislation during the entire period under consideration. Parity is supposed to be an expression of economic justice; it presumably entitles the farmer to a standard of living comparable to that of a man who works in town. Such a standard expresses a perfectly reasonable goal with which few people care to argue. Its translation into political reality, however, raises some thorny questions.

The ideal parity is essentially an income concept. We want farmers to have incomes which permit them to buy goods and services as can others who are equally productive in the economy. Parity legislation, however, has always focused on price. The parity law selects one year as the basis for comparison. The cost of the goods purchased by farmers is compared with the price per unit of each crop he sells during this year. The parity price for the crop is adjusted each year to reflect the same relationship with goods bought as existed during the period selected for comparison.

The number of units (bushels of wheat, bales of cotton) harvested per acre and per farm has increased rapidly, raising cash sales per acre far above the base year. This change is left out of the parity calculation, while, on the other hand, the increased cost of modern farm implements is duly noted. The effect of this one-sided adjustment is a parity price for farm products that will result in a far higher income per acre than existed in the comparison period. New fertilizers are responsible for more abundant crops; but the application of the formula assumes no change in output. Assurance of this legal parity price for an entire crop would result in a living standard far superior to any experienced in the past.

When determined on a parity basis, prices do not reflect market conditions. Moreover, prices are more unrealistic for some crops than for others, and the farmer therefore concentrates production on crops for which there are parity profits rather than on crops for which there is strong market demand. Thus the price system is not permitted to work. A price mechanism could correct such waste of resources, but rigid federal guarantees of high prices render this economic safety device inoperative and pile one surplus crop on top of another.

Acreage Control.   The unwillingness of Congress to permit a downward adjustment of farm prices in response to market conditions resulted in the federal accumulation of surplus products. A certain amount of excess crops may provide insurance against future crop failures or other sudden demand increases. But the amount of some farm products in storage has reached such dimensions that only gifts abroad can use up the surplus. In the meantime, the cost of storing these commodities continues.

The steady accumulation of unwanted plenty forced Congress to look for new means of controlling the surplus. In view of the political difficulty involved in a change of the guaranteed price, the law added new controls which told the farmer how many acres he would be allowed to plant in certain specific crops, such as wheat and cotton.

Acreage control proved ineffective, because farmers abandoned the least productive acreage and concentrated their efforts and their fertilizer on the land which they were still permitted to use. It is possible, of course, to reduce acreage so drastically that surplus crops can be prevented even in the best years, but Congress has always hesitated to order such a severe cutback.

An unwanted by-product of acreage control is a shift of land to new uses. When acreage is removed from its traditional crop and shifted to a product not yet restricted by law, this hitherto uncontrolled crop begins to experience a similar surplus problem. When the surplus is successfully donated to foreign countries, farmers promptly demand removal of acreage restrictions in order to avoid a shortage. The larger crop simply replenishes the storage and makes ever-larger gifts abroad a continuing policy.

Price Support.   The Commodity Credit Corporation (CCC) is a federal agency which manages the financing of farm programs under directives of Congress. It is authorized to borrow up to $14.5 billion from the U.S. Treasury for its many activities. It must return to Congress periodically for appropriations to refund the losses from various support programs. The management of the farm program is a multimillion-dollar operation.

The chief weapon in the government's effort to maintain high prices has been in the past the non-recourse loan. Such a loan is granted by a banker and repaid by the Commodity Credit Corporation unless the debtor does so before the end of the crop year. As soon as the farmer has harvested his crop on approved acreage, he places it in storage and borrows as much money as federal regulations permit in exchange for his warehouse receipt. Should too many farmers place their crop in loan storage and cause a supply shortage in the market, the price will rise above the loan level. At this point, some farmers will sell their crop in the market and use the cash receipts to repay the loan while pocketing the difference.

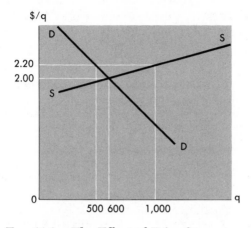

**FIG. 11-1. The Effect of Price Supports
in Agriculture**

On a graph, the market situation can be represented as shown in Figure 11-1.

In a free market, 600 units would be grown and sold at $2 per unit. The support price, however, is fixed at $2.20 per unit. As a result of this assured higher price, it pays to fertilize more and increase the crop to 1,000 units. At the same time, the quantity demanded at the higher price is cut back to 500 units. As the crop is harvested, enough of it will be placed under the loan to reduce the crop available in the market to 500 units and abandon the rest to the Commodity Credit Corporation for storage. If at the end of the season the loans are not repaid, the commodity is taken over by the government and the farmer's debt is cancelled.

APPRAISAL OF FARM POLICY

All farm legislation claims to help the small, poor farmer. The results show clearly that this is not the case and that, for the most part, the laws, enacted in the name of the poor, help the wealthiest large-farm operators in the nation. In fact, a cynical observer of the change in farming during the last thirty years may well claim that the laws have been very successful. While they have not reduced poverty, they are eliminating the small farmers altogether at an accelerated pace; and when these farmers have all died or moved to town, the problem will no longer exist!

Such a detached attitude prefers to disregard the very serious consequences which are the result of decades of neglect. Some poor people on the farm die quietly, but others move to the big cities where their lack of education and training condemns them to unemployment and life in the ghetto. The seriousness of the situation has been brought to national attention by the widespread riots of 1967.

As described by a reporter in the Delta region of Mississippi,

nearly 55,000 people are living on farms (in 1967) with practically no hope of employment there. Sixty per cent of the poor families in two Delta counties get less than two-thirds of a recommended "minimum" diet. . . .

The national implications of rural poverty, which has caused thousands of Negroes to move into big-city ghettos over the last 20 years, have received renewed attention in recent months. Furthermore, the growing problems of the agricultural South may send new waves of Negroes to the Northern slums.[3]

In 1965–1966 the United States sent more wheat abroad than its total home consumption. This dramatic removal of many years' surplus was welcome, but it promptly created new difficulties. The market price of wheat rose and acreage restrictions were relaxed to prevent still higher prices. As a result, this country faces even larger crops at guaranteed minimum prices. We can continue to send the surplus abroad, but our cost will rise as larger acreages produce bigger crops; or we can limit our international shipments and have the domestic surplus reappear, since the bigger acreage grows far more than we can consume.

Cost of Farm Policy

The cost of our farm policy is much greater than people generally realize. In addition to direct outlays by the U.S. Treasury, the cost consists of waste of resources, land converted to less suitable crops, and fertilizer poured on to receive parity payments, to say nothing of human effort focused on raising output no one wants.

A share of the cost of this program remains hidden. Because of price support in the market, the consumer probably pays more for food and fiber than he would without these measures. Although the total difference in costs to the consumer cannot be estimated very accurately, it must be remembered.

The actual cash outlay by the Treasury can be ascertained more precisely. These costs have been rising over the years, as is clearly shown by Figure 11-2. The total burden of the program has reached $6 billion per year.

The recipients of this flow of federal cash are not poor people, but

[3] Walter Rugaber, "The Delta: Poverty Is a Way of Life," *The New York Times,* July 31, 1967, p. 1.

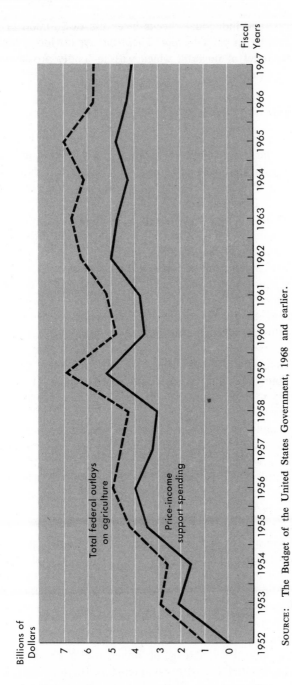

SOURCE: The Budget of the United States Government, 1968 and earlier.

FIG. 11-2. Federal Farm Expenditures 1952–1967

large farm operators, and individual checks in excess of $50,000 or even $100,000 continue to be an annual event. These outlays obviously have no connection with the relief of poverty, which was so loudly proclaimed as the aim of federal support.

Effects of Farm Policy

The technique of supporting the unit price of a farm commodity is uniquely designed to help the largest commercial operators. All farming involves a gamble with the weather; if a large percentage of a crop is lost, farm prices will be high even without federal action. This is of no advantage to farmers, large or small, because in a bad crop year they have little to sell.

Should the weather cooperate and produce a bumper crop, the market price will drop under the weight of the surplus. Government price support becomes effective and maintains the price at a higher level. The small farmer registers only a small gain, because even at best his crop is not very large. A peak year may compensate him for a bad one, but it can do no more. The large farmer, however, sells a bumper crop at a high price with a tremendous gain, which permits him to take several bad years in stride.

The result of this arrangement is a misuse of land. Some acreage is known to produce a crop only once in three or four years. Large operators protected by price supports will buy such land and gamble on it because one good crop in four is all that is needed to show a profit. If the good crop year were likely to depress prices, nobody would consider such marginal land for the type of crops actually planted.

The excessive land use for many crops forces broad acreage restrictions. The government cannot single out specific owners of land and tell them to stop growing wheat because their land is not really suitable for it. Instead, it orders all wheat growers to cut back wheat acreage by an identical percentage. Therefore, the best wheat land will not be allowed to grow wheat on some farms so that the owner with much poorer land has a chance to gamble on a crop.

The advantage of a large farm is magnified by this control procedure. A large farm is sure to contain both good and bad land. A requirement to cut back production can be satisfied by taking the worst acreage out of wheat, which had little chance for success anyway. The small farmer has no comparable alternative. What land he possesses he needs to work just for a living. Acreage restrictions hurt him severely.

One of the side effects of rigid support prices has been the steady increase in the price of land. Even acreage of limited usefulness increases in value when it can be counted as part of an acreage restriction. This distortion of land values, which assigns a higher price to a farm than its actual utilization could ever justify, becomes an inevitable result of a system of acreage controls.

The Law of 1965

Under the Food and Agriculture Act of 1965 the emphasis in farm commodity programs is shifted from high support prices through loans to direct payments to farmers. This system is more effective in forcing farmers to cooperate with acreage restrictions than what had been tried in the past. The direct cost of the new program was estimated at $3 billion for 1967. While the market price of the supported commodities has been permitted to change, a form of processing tax keeps the domestic price to the user up.

The fundamental weakness of price-support legislation is its resistance to change. The philosophy of a parity price is based on the idea that a farmer is entitled to continue the same activity as in the past regardless of changes in technology or in consumers' tastes. Imagine what might have happened if a similar philosophy had been marshaled in support of the buggy industry when automobiles started to take away their business!

The law has been rewritten constantly, but it has persisted in interfering more, rather than less, with each new step. When parity prices created a burdensome surplus, acreage control was added, rather than a reduction in prices. When acreage control in one crop caused a surplus in another, the controls were not dismantled, but the new crop was included in the pattern of restraint. Eventually, the restrictions became so tight that the farmers realized that they must comply with federal policies for the sake of self-preservation.

Alternative Solution to the Farm Problem

Few people suggest that the government drop overnight the entire system of federal interference and suddenly restore the farmer to the forces of the market. Such a step would certainly eliminate some problems, but it would also eliminate too many farmers, who would be unable to adjust to the new requirements. The dangers of a sudden reversal are pointed out in this presidential message: [4]

Acting individually, the farmer cannot shift readily away from commodities in surplus. Nor will lower farm prices automatically assure reduced farm output, unless those prices fall to disastrous levels and remain there. Historically, lower prices

[4] From President Kennedy's message to Congress on agriculture, January 31, 1962.

have been met by increased output in a desperate effort by the farmer to make his business profitable and to stay on the land.

The Committee for Economic Development suggested an adaptive approach which would use federal action to facilitate a gradual return to free market procedures.[5] Such a changeover can be speeded up by helping farmers move to town and by retraining them for jobs which may be available there.

The opposite solution has been suggested by Edward Higbee, who objects to the use of public funds for large farmers while the small ones are being driven off the land:

> There could be only two valid reasons for using public funds to encourage inefficient farmers to move out of agriculture. One would be if the country were short of food and needed to put its lands in more expert hands. This is obviously not the case now although as the population increases the situation may change. The other would be if agriculture's surplus manpower were needed elsewhere. Considering the high rate of urban unemployment that has persisted in recent years it would seem that the market for unskilled labor is already oversupplied. Until the nation needs their lands and labor, inefficient farmers may be better off where they are than if they were to head for the city's slums and welfare rolls.[6]

Another study [7] suggested that the "best" farm program depends on the viewpoint of the individual:

> If the objective is to minimize consumer food bills, the answer is unrestricted farm production. If the goal is low United States Treasury cost, the answer is mandatory controls—or unrestricted production under conditions which approach a free market. . . . If the goal is to maximize farm income . . . , the optimum program is not free markets.

The current program based on the law of 1965 is a very expensive solution for the taxpayer that does nothing toward curing the evils inherent in the price support concept. A compromise which would designate in advance the total cost of farm payments, leaving to market forces how this support would be split (between higher prices for products and incentives for not planting a crop), is not likely to be greeted with enthusiasm by big farmers; but the unfortunate result of a closely regimented farm economy illustrates how effectively the pricing mechanism operates when it has a chance to do so.

SUMMARY

The technological progress of American agriculture in the twentieth century has revolutionized farm life and made it possible for an ever-smaller

[5] *An Adaptive Program for Agriculture,* p. 12.
[6] Edward Higbee, *Farms and Farmers in an Urban Age* (New York, Twentieth Century Fund, 1963), p. 105.
[7] Earl O. Heady *et al., Roots of the Farm Problem* (Ames, Iowa, Iowa State University Press, 1965), p. 193.

number of commercial operators to feed and clothe the population. Farming has become a business which requires much managerial skill to be successful.

The farm problem stems from the difficulty of transforming a vast rural population to urban pursuits at sufficient speed to match technological progress. Too many farmers and too much poverty are at the heart of the problem.

The farmer claims a special right to government help because of the uniqueness of his position. His dependence on the weather, the lagging demand for his products, and the inordinate fierceness of competition in agriculture render his work more difficult. His inability to reduce output by lowering prices, coupled with an excessive acreage for many crops, creates a need for governmental price maintenance.

The federal government has helped the farmer with subsidies for soil conservation practices, with education for farm youths, with research by experiment stations, and with a distribution of knowledge through extension services; it supports rural electrification and cheap credit by special banking institutions created for this purpose, and it distributes farm products here and abroad.

The federal government supports high unit prices for many crops in order to raise farm incomes. This technique has proved unsuccessful, since it leads to large surpluses under government control and a high cost to the taxpayer.

The parity concept, originally intended to assure economic justice to the farmer, has become a formula to push prices higher than they were in the past. Parity loans keep crops away from the market in order to insure whatever price is desired. This induces farmers to adjust their production to the federal loans and not to consumer demand.

The surplus of commodities forces a system of acreage control which restricts the farmer by telling him how much he can grow on his land. These restrictions on producers cause a distortion in effective land use. They also stimulate the heavy use of fertilizer and other improvements which contribute to maintain the surplus.

Price-support legislation favors the big farmer against his small competitor, assuring him of sales at high prices even in a year of heavy surplus.

The farm policies of the recent past have failed to improve the lot of the poor farmer, while at the same time they constitute a heavy burden for the taxpayer. The emphasis on unit price and rigid restrictions comes into conflict with the ultimate goal of higher incomes and greater flexibility.

The current approach forces farmers to comply with acreage restrictions in order to receive support payments above the market price. The high cost to the taxpayer suggests several compromises to return farming slowly to free market arrangements. The failure of government intervention in agriculture presents a warning that we abandon a free pricing system only at the risk of worse solutions.

Discussion Questions

1. What is the farm problem?
2. Should the government help the farmer because he is a farmer or because he is poor?
3. Why is the adjustment of farm surplus difficulties not left to the free market system?
4. Can the farm problem be solved? Is it being solved?
5. What is the purpose of parity and acreage-control legislation?
6. How does prosperity and high employment in town help the solution of difficulties on the farm?

Suggested Reading

An Adaptive Program for Agriculture. New York, Committee for Economic Development (CED), 1962.

HEADY, EARL O., *et al., Roots of the Farm Problem*. Ames, Iowa, Iowa State University Press, 1965.

HIGBEE, EDWARD, *Farms and Farmers in an Urban Age*. New York, Twentieth Century Fund, 1963.

McCABE, RALPH, *Agriculture's Role in the 1960 Decade: Food and People*. U.S. Congress, Joint Economic Committee, Subcommittee on Foreign Economic Policy, 87th Congress, 1st session, 1961.

12

THE DISTRIBUTION AND USE OF PERSONAL INCOME

THE ROLE OF THE CONSUMER

Consumption is the objective of all productive efforts. To satisfy consumers' wants is the main goal of a free enterprise economy.

The consumer faces two barriers in his drive to reach the greatest satisfaction: (1) The size of his income limits the total amount of goods and services he can command. He tries to overcome this obstacle by persistent efforts to raise his income. (2) Within the limits of a given income, the consumer finds it difficult to select the mixture of want-satisfying products that he will like best. Since satisfaction is never complete, the consumer continuously shifts his manner of spending income, hoping to find a better solution tomorrow than he did today. His desires are insatiable, as we have seen before, and he economizes in order to reach the most acceptable compromise.

Income in this very personal sense is familiar to all of us. It controls many of our everyday actions. Economists also use the income concept for measuring the performance of the whole economic system. In this sense, the national income serves as a yardstick which indicates the gradual growth of total output, or the lack of it. The yardstick function of income will be clarified in detail in Chapter 15.

We shall discuss in this chapter the distribution of the nation's income among the people and the pattern of consumption created by their preferences. The changes in this pattern reveal the persistent effort of the consumer to get the most for his money.

CONSUMPTION IN A WEALTHY ECONOMY

The consumption problems of the United States today have little in common with those of our grandfathers, or with those of other countries whose standard of living remains well below ours. The majority of the world's people are still engaged in a struggle for survival. Their consumption is centered on the basic requirements of food, clothing, and shelter, leaving very little choice for individual desires.

The most significant characteristic of consumption in the United States today is its concern with wants which go beyond the necessities for physical survival. Historically, most countries have developed an upper class of a few families able to indulge their many desires, but only in twentieth-century America has the majority of the population reached a state of affluence where *over half of their income is spent on goods they do not need.* Although this new development creates its own problems, we would not want to reverse the encouraging trend because of possible complications at the other end. The goals of the economy continue to focus on achieving improved want satisfaction, even when it becomes more difficult to discover what these wants are likely to be.

The consumer today may purchase a wide variety of goods and services. They add to his comfort but are not needed for his survival. It is true that some groups of people lack even a minimum income and must depend upon public attention and assistance, but fortunately they are a minority. Many more people may feel dissatisfied with their standard of living; their urge for continuous improvement is a powerful force in the advance of economic progress. However, most of our present consumption problems are caused by the wealth of goods which presents a choice of what to consume and when to consume it. The new difficulties arising from this economic progress parallel the development of modern medicine. Progress in this science has sharply reduced the diseases which used to fell men in their prime; now doctors have the additional problem of old age to study, an area which formerly concerned only a few people.

PERSONAL INCOME

A person's total consumption depends on his purchasing power. He can buy only as much as his income or his creditors permit. This income varies considerably over a lifetime. A child starts usually with no income; as he joins the labor force, his income rises from a low beginning and increases during his most productive years. Finally, a drop in his income signals retirement and old age.

A man must fit his consumption to this income pattern. The amount he is willing to spend at any moment depends partly on his current income and partly on his expectations of future income. The assurance of a raise next year may induce him to spend his entire income now and even to assume added obligations for the future by buying on credit. If he has serious doubts about maintaining his income for any reason, the prudent man will not only reduce his expenditures to fit his current income, but he is likely to cut down still further to pay off a mortgage or save for a possible emergency. Old age is not the only cause for reduced spending; the fear of a depression with its threat of unemployment may cut consumer purchases even more suddenly.

How high is personal income in the United States? For the year 1966 per capita income was $2,940. This figure is obtained by adding up all personal income earned in that year and dividing the total by the number of people living in the country. This procedure has the advantage of being simple, but it has the disadvantage of possibly giving the false impression that this nation is poor. Such a figure does not mean much, since it averages income in terms of individuals, whereas it is usually spent by families.

Income data become more meaningful when they are calculated on the basis of families.[1] Average income per family amounted to $6,882 in 1965.[2] Incomes in the United States have been rising steadily. In 1957 only 8 percent of all families earned over $10,000; the same percentage had incomes over $15,000 in 1965. Table 12-1 illustrates the distribution of family income in 1965.[3]

TABLE 12-1.   Income of Families in the United States, 1965

Money Income Total	Number of Families (*millions*)	Percent of all Families
Under $2,000	4,415	9.2
$ 2,000–$ 3,999	7,389	15.3
$ 4,000–$ 5,999	8,385	17.4
$ 6,000–$ 7,999	9,160	18.9
$ 8,000–$ 9,999	6,952	14.4
$10,000–$14,999	8,342	17.3
$15,000 and over	3,636	7.5
Total families	48,279	100.0

SOURCE: U.S. Bureau of the Census, *Current Population Reports*, ser. P-60, no. 51, 1967.

These figures may surprise many people who feel sure that the number of very rich men with fabulous incomes must be much larger than it really is. The number of families in the lowest income category is still too large to be ignored; this indicates clearly that not all our citizens can avail themselves of the advantages of a wealthy economy.

[1] A family is any group of two or more related persons residing together.

[2] The average shown above is the "median income." This is the income of a family at the midpoint of all income-earning families, one-half of all families earning more and one-half earning less.

[3] The primary source for the data in this chapter is the U.S. Department of Commerce, Bureau of the Census. It publishes *Current Population Reports,* Series P-60, periodically.

INCOME INEQUALITY

The difference in incomes between rich and poor becomes frequently the focus of political argument. Some people favor the idea that incomes should be roughly equal; others hold that the American ideal is the equality of opportunity, not of income. Political pressure for a more equal distribution of income is widespread, since the poor are more numerous than the rich. Therefore, any scheme that promises to favor lower income groups has great vote-getting appeal. What does the evidence show about the equality of the income distribution in the United States? The statistics on this subject can support almost any view one cares to take.

Complete Equality

A yardstick might be based on a theoretical goal of complete equality, giving every human being exactly the same share of the available income. If this measure is used, the data will show extreme inequality in income. In 1965, the richest 20 percent of families shared about 41 percent of the income, while the poorest 20 percent received only 5 percent. The top 5 percent of families received 15 percent of the income that same year.

Arithmetic equality can hardly be considered a proper yardstick for fair distribution. Income changes with age, and differences in income will necessarily reflect the earning power of a ten-year-old child, a college student, a man at the peak of his activity, and a retired pensioner in his seventies.

Even within the same age bracket, complete equality of income is hardly a desirable goal. Some people work hard while others loaf; to assign the same income to both groups does not appeal to our sense of fairness. These examples show only how the selection of an unreasonable yardstick may lead to unwarranted conclusions. A measuring technique based on absolute equality may be interesting arithmetic, but it is not a good standard of the equity of income distribution.

Historical Comparison

A different approach measures the fairness of income distribution by comparing changes which have occurred over a period of time. We discover that in this country the share of income received by the families in the highest paid 5 percent of the population has dropped continuously since the 1920's. This means that the wealthiest segment of the population receives now only about half as much of the nation's income as it did at the earlier date. Regardless of which years or income groups are used in this historical comparison, the trend since the end of the First World War shows a marked drop in the share of the total income going to the highest income group.

However, this comparison may look a little too rosy. Life has changed so much during this century that a comparison over too long a period becomes rather difficult to make. Grandfather felt just as rich driving a surrey with a fringe on top as his grandson in a new Cadillac. But any automobile requires a higher income. Income levels cannot readily be compared in terms of modern automobiles and the products of horse-and-buggy days.

Geographical Comparison

We can attempt to measure the inequality of incomes by a comparison with the situation in other countries, but the problem here is that consumption patterns differ sharply between nations. In some countries goods are frequently assigned to families without payment being necessary, following some ancient tradition.

The most striking point of distinction in a comparison with other countries is the fact that all incomes in the United States are much higher than in the rest of the world. Average family incomes are almost twice as high here as in the wealthier nations in Western Europe, and about four times higher than in Russia.

Such statistical evidence should be interpreted with caution. People look at their income in terms of what their neighbors earn or what they themselves received last year. The standards of faraway countries with very different surroundings have little meaning to the majority of us. The present ferment of many poor nations can be at least partly attributed to their increased contacts with richer countries. They *do* compare income levels, and insist on raising their low standards with a speed which creates major national and international problems.

Income Gap

The difference between the highest and the lowest income groups can be measured and compared year by year. The change in the gap between the incomes of these two groups can be used to determine the relative inequality of incomes.

This yardstick, too, is open to criticism. It doesn't really matter if the richest individuals in a country add another $10,000 to their incomes once they earn far in excess of their ability to consume. These high incomes present an easy target for envious attacks. The income of a Vander-

bilt or a Rockefeller may be a colorful item for political speeches, but it is
not very significant to the problems of equality in the country as a whole.
High incomes for a few can also be viewed as an incentive which may
inspire some people to work harder in order to move into the select group.
The high-income group may be considered a suitable target for the income
tax collector, who exercises a leveling influence, but the changing incomes
of the multimillionaires have little influence on the living standard of the
majority.

Low Income Trends

A more meaningful measure of relative equality concentrates on the
earnings of the poorest group; a rise or fall at the bottom of the scale can
determine the inequality of incomes at any time. When the lowest incomes
rise, inequality is inevitably reduced. An increase in the family income
from $3,000 to $4,000 makes a big difference. It may mean a change from
insufficient meals to proper nutrition, or it may spell the difference between owning an automobile and doing without one. However, a similar
$1,000 increase in a family with a $25,000 annual income changes consumption habits too little to be noticeable.

WHO ARE THE POOR?

Even a wealthy nation has its poor. During the prosperous times of recent
experience, reactions to the poor by their more fortunate fellow citizens are
likely to reflect opposite extremes. Some feel that a rich country certainly
can afford to take care of its poor and that their continued presence is deplorable. President Johnson's "war on poverty" expresses the sentiments
of this group, though there is not necessarily agreement on all its details.
Others feel that many jobs are available in this country during a boom, and
that if the poor don't work, they must be blamed for their own predicament;
if a man is not just lazy, he ought to be able to get along without much
trouble. Neither view represents the real situation. Let us see who are the
poor.

Death of the Breadwinner

The early death of the man in the family often leaves widows and orphans
in precarious financial circumstances. Social Security payments to a widow
are seldom enough to cover the numerous debts for house, car, and furniture which are common to families with growing children. Life insurance is

becoming more popular, but a worker's coverage is usually too small to do more than cushion the initial shock caused by a death.

Ill Health

Prolonged sickness is usually an even worse financial blow to a family than death. No life insurance pays for the sick, and most health insurance policies are inadequate for long sickness or too expensive for low-income families. A breadwinner who cannot continue on the job loses three ways: he has no income because he is not working; he costs more because of the need for medical care; and he is likely to tie up another person (his wife) who might otherwise be working and earning income. This situation can be more desperate even than a death and, unfortunately, is not uncommon in the ranks of the poor.

Retirement

Old age is traditionally a cause of low incomes. Public and private pension arrangements are alleviating the economic position of those who have retired. But the steady decrease in the value of the dollar undermines the effectiveness of systematic private savings, and it causes hardships for many old people who do not want to be a burden to their children or to the community.

Our statistics show that the number of families without income earners is increasing in number and at the moment makes up approximately 7 percent of all families. This group is composed largely of retired people who live on savings and social security. The rise in the number of such families should not be misinterpreted, however. While their income is low, it shows much improvement over former periods when the old folks had no choice but to move in with their children. They may not have much money, but they are able to maintain their independence from relatives and are, therefore, counted as separate family units.

Lack of Skill

A good, modern job requires more skill than was necessary in former generations. Some people lack the innate ability to learn enough to acquire such skills—they simply cannot meet the requirements of the times. Moreover, education does not seem to be the answer for these cases, as the attempt to learn is likely to lead to sheer frustration on the part of the student who does not comprehend. With the increasing complexity of modern technology as an added barrier, this aspect of poverty is apt to become more serious.

Slum Environment

The deep roots of chronic poverty rest in the slums. Riots in recent summers have placed the spotlight on the problems found in some sections of our largest cities, such as Watts, Newark, and Detroit. The inhabitants of these areas are not all sick, retired, or unable to learn; they have little opportunity to make a decent living. Employers are not located in these areas of a sprawling city; their factories are too far away to reach without considerable expense; and management does not send hiring crews into slum districts. Young people who drop out of school are heavily represented in this environment of hopelessness. They have no education because they see no incentive for learning in their present surroundings; and without more education they are unable to successfully break away from their environment.

THE WAR ON POVERTY

In 1964 President Johnson declared a war on poverty. He was convinced that the causes of poverty could not be overcome by the poor themselves; prosperity would simply pass them by unless the federal government undertook direct action to eradicate the sources of the trouble. Congress passed legislation that consisted of numerous programs under the administration of a new agency, the Office of Economic Opportunity (OEO).

The antipoverty programs cover a wide variety of activities. The Job Corps trains school dropouts between the ages of sixteen and twenty-one so that they may be better able to find a job. Operation Head Start gives preschool training to children whose family background is likely to be a hindrance to their normal progress in school. Community Action programs are local antipoverty projects created through community interests and administered by the participants with the help of federal funds. Vocational training programs and adult education for job training are also given financial assistance. Other federal agencies whose relationship to the antipoverty drive is less obvious than that of the OEO have started their own projects under this popular label.

An evaluation of the fight against poverty is not yet possible. The administrative costs of some of the new programs are very high in terms of their early accomplishments. The further rise of the federal bureaucracy reflects additional costs which must be considered in any appraisal of results. But we must not close our eyes to the need for action in some cases. The one-third of the population described by Franklin D. Roosevelt as ill-housed and ill-fed has finally been reduced in number after two decades of prosperity. Nonetheless, the slums are far from abolished in many parts of the country.

The problems of poverty can be diminished with the maintenance of full employment and through stability of the value of the dollar; in this way people can provide for the hazards of an unknown future. Until we reach such an objective, however, public assistance and private charity will continue to relieve the burden of the poor, who are still with us in large numbers. Their standard of living has no similarity with the magazine picture of the average American family.

SOURCES OF INCOME

People earn income from four main sources. They work for hire, or they may be self-employed, in which case the net cash result of their efforts becomes their income. If they own property and make it available to others, they earn rents, dividends, or interest. Finally, their income may take the form of government pensions and similar transfer payments under the Social Security Act.

Some income may be due to windfalls, but this is not an important source of earnings. Many people hope that their name will be drawn from a hat, and that they will get a free trip to Bermuda or a new automobile, but very few ever have such an experience. Table 12-2 indicates the preponderant role human effort plays in gaining income.

TABLE 12-2.   Sources of Personal Income 1966

Source	Dollars (*billions*)	Percent of Personal Income
Wages and salaries	394.6	67.6
Business and professional income	43.2	7.4
Farm income	16.1	2.8
Dividends	21.5	3.7
Rents	19.4	3.3
Interest	42.4	7.3
Transfer Payments (social security net)	26.0	4.4
Other (mostly private pension funds)	20.8	3.5
Total personal income	584.0	100.0

SOURCE: U.S. Department of Commerce, *Survey of Current Business.*

Work is by far the most common source of income. About two-thirds of all incomes are wages and salaries. The share of income going to wage earners has changed little over the years. The relative fortunes of different groups of workers may rise or fall—income will shift when California towns are booming and New England loses factories. Rising productivity in electronics may boost the share of the workers in this industry while textile wages fail to keep pace. Every group of workers continually fights for a bigger slice of the available income, but the people as a whole can succeed in improving their position only when total personal income rises.

The incomes of doctors, lawyers, or individual storeowners on Main Street are not classified as wages, though most such earnings are the result of hard work, as is the salary of an employee. Part of the income of an independent businessman can be considered a return on his investment in his business, which explains the use of a separate category in the table for professional and business people.

Farm income is also a mixture of earnings—from work and from property—which cannot be readily separated. The relatively low figure earned by farmers is an indication of their smaller role in the nation's economy.

Dividends are paid to the stockholders of corporations when in the judgment of the board of directors the profits of the firm justify such a step. Rent is a payment for the use of property by others. Interest represents the income paid for the use of liquid funds, as we shall see in more detail later on. The high figure for social security benefits would be even more impressive at the full value of these payments, which amounted to $43.9 billion in 1966. Social security taxes deducted from workers' paychecks have reduced the amount in the table to $26.0 billion.

OCCUPATIONS AND INCOME

A young man starting his career in the business world is usually advised to work hard and diligently if he wants to advance and make his mark in the world. This advice is certainly sound, because most progress is the result of effort; the recommendation is incomplete, however. The choice of the right occupation is of equal importance to a man's future. In a fast-growing firm, a just-average fellow will be promoted; in a declining industry, even the best man finds it difficult to advance. Similarly, when a company opens a new branch store every month, a modestly qualified but hard-working employee is likely to become manager before long. In a company without these new branches, the manager's job opens up only when the boss retires.

Occupational Trends

Sixty years ago the farmers were the largest group in our population. Industry provides the greatest amount of employment now, but trade and services are offering more new jobs and are fast becoming the main source of employment for the future. The occupational trends of the last sixty-five years are illustrated by Figure 12-1.

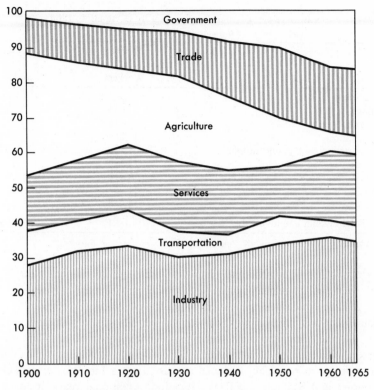

SOURCES: U.S. Department of Labor, Bureau of Labor Statistics; U.S. Bureau of the Census, *Historical Statistics of the United States.*

FIG. 12-1. Occupations in the United States
(Historical Distribution, 1900–1965)

Machines gradually take over the routine jobs in an industrial plant. The complicated marvels of modern technology require, however, expert services on an ever-increasing scale. A generation ago, the man of the house took care of his furnace in winter without too much trouble, but today he has to call a factory-trained serviceman to fix the heating and air-conditioning system when it breaks down. The increasing importance of service occupations of all kinds, including government employment, is clearly shown in Table 12-3.

The Value of Education

Is a college education worth the amount of money, time, and effort it takes to acquire? This question can hardly be answered in simple terms of dollars and cents because the improvement of man's mind, the first objective

TABLE 12-3.   Civilian Employment by Occupation, 1966
(thousands of persons)

Occupation	Number of Workers	Percent of Civil Employment
Agriculture	1,564	2.2
Mining	633	0.9
Construction	3,316	4.6
Manufacturing	19,265	26.8
Transportation and public utilities	4,180	5.8
Wholesale and retail trade	13,356	18.6
Finance, insurance, and real estate	3,116	4.4
Services	11,907	16.6
Government	14,464	20.1
Total civilian employment	71,801	100.0

SOURCE: U.S. Department of Commerce, Survey of Current Business.

of education, is intangible and cannot be measured in monetary terms any more than can the benefit gained from watching a beautiful sunset.

College graduates are much more heavily represented in the high-income groups than people whose formal education stopped earlier. However, this fact alone does not permit the conclusion that a college degree per se is the key to high income. A prosperous family may be able to help a young man to gain financial success; such a family is also likely to encourage and facilitate a college education. Additional years of education are a major financial burden for both the student and his family, and only young people of more than average means or foresight will shoulder the financial sacrifice necessary to complete their education. Men with this sort of determination would probably do well regardless of the road they chose. However, the increasing trend of business firms to require a college degree for the most desirable jobs closes the door to bright youngsters without much formal education who are not given the opportunity to demonstrate that they are just as valuable as those who come from a university.

The educational trend points toward more graduate studies. A higher level of professional education commands a sufficiently higher income to compensate for the added costs. Physicians are at the top of the income scale. The legal profession is noted for both high and low incomes. The leading lawyers are rich, but the average for the profession ranks well below medicine. Dentists and certified public accountants do very well, but teachers' salaries are lower than those of many occupations that require less training. Nurses are also poorly rewarded monetarily for the added years of preparation required for their professional competence. Many people, however, seem to be attracted to teaching and nursing because they like the nature of the work and the satisfaction of helping others, in spite of relatively smaller incomes.

HOW DO PEOPLE SPEND THEIR INCOMES?

Personal-consumption spending of the people of the United States reached $466 billion in 1966. What did they buy with their money to satisfy their wants?

Necessary Consumption

Food, clothing, and shelter have the first claim on the family income because they represent the necessities of life. In a poor country, almost the entire income is spent for such essentials; in a prosperous year people eat a little better, and in a bad year some starve. Even individuals with better than average incomes concentrate consumption on the same basic products; they probably have more food and more adequate housing, but without a mass market only a very small group of wealthy people can afford to import luxury goods. In the United States, about half of the consumer's dollar is spent on necessities.

Food. About one-fourth of total consumption is spent on food in the broadest sense. About 20 percent of the food dollar is spent on tobacco and alcohol, items not ordinarily bought for their nutritional values. The food cost also includes an increasing sum for services. Housewives no longer go to the store to buy beans or flour to be converted laboriously into a meal over a hot stove at home. Beans are purchased already cleaned, cut, frozen, and packaged attractively with instructions for the finishing touches to be applied by the user. Instead of flour, the lady buys a cake mix, or maybe rolls which lack only the brown color for serving. If we could separate the cost of nutritional calories from the value of the services included in the total price, the amount spent on just the necessary food would be surprisingly small.

Housing. Housing expenditures continue to take a large share of consumer dollars. A trend from rented apartments in large buildings toward privately owned, individual houses in the new suburbs of our cities accounts for 15 percent of consumption expenditures. Modern homes also incorporate many luxury items which only recently have come to be considered necessities. Central heating and air-conditioning systems, built-in ovens, washing machines, and other appliances raise the amount spent on housing.

Clothing. The cost of clothing is about 10 percent of total expenditures and is shrinking in comparison with other categories of consumption. Many factors are responsible for this development: The trend toward casual

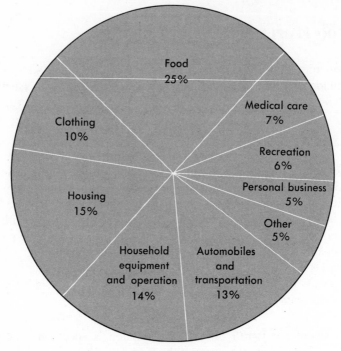

Source: U.S. Department of Commerce, *Survey of Current Business.*

Fig. 12-2.   Personal Consumption Expenditures, 1966
(by type of product)

living reduces the emphasis on dress. Clothing styles are less important for
an evening in front of the TV set than they are for a movie downtown. It is
no longer necessary to change clothes in order to compensate for varying
temperatures. When people step from their heated garage into their equally
heated automobile, they wear gloves to be fashionable rather than warm.

Postponable Consumption

Over half of all personal consumption is spent for goods and services not
immediately essential for survival. In 1966, purchases of $70 billion were
classified as durable goods—products that render service for many years,
such as automobiles, furniture, appliances, and other similar items. Producers are faced with the difficult task of forecasting with some degree of
accuracy how many units will be bought in the near future. Sales fluctuate
broadly in this category because purchases can be postponed. Every car
owner knows that he does not really have to trade in his old model so long
as it keeps running.

The amount of services bought shows a steady upward trend; it totaled $188 billion in 1966. Services include many different items. Medical, recreation, and travel services are claiming more and more of the consumer's dollar. As the length of the workweek shrinks, people gain more time for recreational activities, and this trend of current consumption is clearly illustrated by the boom in motels and motorboats throughout the country.

HOW PEOPLE SAVE

Consumers today save about 7 percent of their income and they have done so quite consistently since the end of World War II. Savings are accumulated by paying life insurance premiums, by payroll deductions for pension programs or bond-a-month plans, and by making regular payments on mortgages or other debts. This description differs considerably from the more customary view, which considers savings as a purely voluntary act like maintaining a savings account.

When savings accumulate through a contract, only the initial act is voluntary. Afterwards, a premium notice for a life insurance policy, or the bill on some other contractual payment, forces the saver to refrain from spending the same money for consumption goods.

The best method to adopt for a systematic savings program baffles many families—no simple prescription will work equally well for everyone. Life insurance is frequently the first step toward any organized saving. Unfortunately, many policyholders seem to be quite unaware of the kind of policy they are buying or of alternatives which might suit them better. Many a housewife spends more time in a grocery store deciding what brand of peas to buy than she does signing an insurance contract designed to become her chief protection in a future emergency.

To own a home is often considered a form of saving. The real estate agent assures you that it won't cost any more to own your house than to rent it. This statement is seldom correct. Repair bills and the need for renovation—which invariably accompany home ownership—are usually underestimated. But the necessity of taking care of the property withholds funds from other use, which in the long run may result in greater actual savings than would have been the case otherwise.

Some people do not want to immobilize their savings in a piece of real estate which may be hard to sell when they need cash. Is there any best method of saving? Most families will try to take advantage of all opportunities. They keep some cash in the bank for ready use and some in a savings account for next Christmas or other periodic needs. The downpayment on a house is in an account with a savings and loan association, and the premium on the life insurance policy is paid regularly. They accumulate an emergency reserve in bonds or stocks and trade their car when the last instalment is paid on the one they are driving. Each method is preferred for some specific reason, and each contributes to the welfare of the whole economy.

CONSUMER CREDIT

The similarity between consumer savings and credit is so striking that it is a surprise to note that large-scale consumer credit is essentially an innovation of the twentieth century. Savings and credit reduce the share of income available for current expenditures. They may even take the same form when they both are payments to the same bank, one a deposit in a savings account and the other a repayment on a note signed earlier. It is not uncommon for people to buy on credit when they have the money in the bank, because they want to force themselves into effecting greater savings in order to pay off the loan.

The availability of consumer credit has profoundly altered consumption decisions—they have become more flexible, and harder to predict. If exercised with due restraint, the use of instalment loans may have highly beneficial results for better want satisfaction of the people. New problems that have been arising from occasional reckless use of credit still await a satisfactory solution.

Benefits of Consumer Credit

Consumer credit enables people to buy goods when they are most needed. The young couple with small children want everything at once—a big house, a station wagon, a washing machine, furniture, and many other items. Without credit or help from their parents, they must wait until they can save enough money. In the meantime, the children grow up and leave home, and the couple are by themselves when they finally can afford the big house—twenty years too late. A modern credit system makes it possible to move in first and pay later.

An additional advantage of consumption loans is the discipline they impose on the consumer. Many people find it hard to save voluntarily but do manage to pay their monthly installments for goods bought earlier. From this viewpoint, credit exercises a steadying influence on consumer decisions.

Dangers of Consumer Credit

The negative effect of consumer credit consists in the sharp fluctuations it causes in total consumption. We have seen already that the purchase of durable goods can be postponed without much hesitation. However, if cash savings were necessary to buy such items, it would not be too difficult to estimate how many could be sold in the coming year. The consumer would have a choice only between accumulating his savings or buying goods he wants to own. The percentage of people who would succumb to the lure of new products could then be easily predicted.

The appearance of consumer credit alters the picture considerably. Consumers' decisions are no longer limited by savings. In fact, a large proportion of durable goods are bought on credit. Therefore, sales may rise suddenly when consumers feel they must have a color TV set, although they really can't afford one right now. After a period of rising indebtedness, many consumers may simultaneously hesitate to borrow more. Their choice then is not between a new vacuum cleaner or a bigger bank account, but between a new product, the cleaner, and sometimes even more desirable, a reduction in their indebtedness. The peace of mind gained from a paid-up loan may outweigh the value of any new product.

Fluctuations of Consumer Credit

The total amount of consumer credit has risen rapidly from a low point of $5.6 billion in 1945 to $93 billion in 1967. This figure does not include real estate mortgage loans.

Fluctuations in the level of consumption are influenced by the existence of a large volume of credit, as we have already seen. They are aggravated by the sharp changes in the ratio of credit to income. Table 12-4 illustrates the difference in relative indebtedness which consumers have seen fit to assume.

TABLE 12-4. Consumer Credit as a Percentage of Disposable Income

End of Year	Percent
1929	7.8
1939	10.3
1945	3.8
1948	7.7
1950	10.1
1951	9.5
1954	11.8
1959	15.2
1962	16.6
1965	18.7

SOURCE: *Federal Reserve Bulletin.*

When new credit rises faster than income, a reversal becomes inevitable, because the individual cannot assign an ever-growing share of his income to the paying of debts. When many people feel that they have used their personal credit to the limit of prudence, even a slight recession will change many consumption plans. The urge to reduce outstanding loans to a safer level becomes greater than any want for goods; this is not a buyers' strike, but merely the exercise of reasonable caution.

Composition of Consumer Credit

Consumer credit of all types is granted by financial institutions and retail stores. The largest share is provided by commercial banks; sales-finance companies are much smaller, but they are second largest in this field. Credit unions, consumer-finance companies, and retail stores provide the rest of the needed credit.

TABLE 12-5.   Composition of Consumer Credit, 1967
(*millions of dollars*)

Installment credit:	
Automobiles	30,527
Other consumer goods	19,369
Repairs and modernization	3,648
Personal loans	20,047
Total	73,591
Noninstallment credit:	
Single payment loans	7,769
Charge accounts	5,809
Service credit	5,350
Total	18,928
Total Consumer Credit	92,519

SOURCE: March 1967 data, *Federal Reserve Bulletin.*

Most consumption loans call for repayment in monthly instalments. Automobiles are the leading consumer good which people generally buy on credit; total car sales therefore exert a direct influence on the trend of consumer credit. The composition of this credit is shown in Table 12-5. People also borrow when buying or building a house. Such mortgages on private homes amounted to $225 billion at the end of 1966.[4]

Effect of Consumer Credit

Consumer credit varies with incomes. It might appear that people borrow when their income is falling and repay when it is rising. However, the opposite is the case. When the country prospers, people are optimistic and are willing to buy on credit. Prices are rising during a boom period, and the cost of borrowing seems light when the consumer feels that the price to him today is lower than it will be next year.

[4] Mortgage credit on nonfarm one- to four-family houses outstanding.

Any drop in income causes a retrenchment and a sharp drop in credit purchases, even by people whose income seems assured. They hesitate to incur more debts and prefer to wait and see, particularly when they feel sure that prices won't rise. Their firm may omit a bonus in a bad year and avoid overtime work. With cheaper prices on the horizon, more people repay old debts than are willing to engage in new financial commitments. In this way consumer credit emphasizes the ups and downs of the economy.

SUMMARY

The most striking feature of the economy of the United States is the mountain of goods consumers can afford to buy. The purchase of many of these is pleasant but not necessary and can be postponed for a long time.

Personal income fluctuates with age, education, experience, the general trend of business, or sheer luck. The average income has risen steadily and reached $6,882 per family in 1965.

Income inequality remains a problem as long as very rich and very poor live together side by side. The degree of inequality has shown a gradual reduction during the last generation, largely because the poorest group of our society has bettered its economic position.

Poverty is directly traceable to the inability of a family breadwinner to keep a job for any one of many reasons. The continued presence of poor people indicates that the wants of many people still remain unsatisfied.

The main source of people's income is their own labor. Property is another source of income, which brings in such payments as rent, dividends, or interest. In addition, pensions are also becoming a major source of income.

The chances of financial success depend to a great extent on the occupation a man picks early in life. His educational background is important for his future progress, and a college degree helps a good deal.

The largest expenditure item in a family budget is food. A house and its maintenance cost about the same. Clothing is a necessary item, but even more is spent on transportation, which includes the family car. A wide variety of services absorbs the rest of the family income.

People save when they add to a savings account, buy bonds, or pay a premium on their life insurance policy. Savings are gathered in many forms through banks, insurance companies, loan payments, and securities.

Consumer credit has made it possible to buy expensive goods when they are needed most urgently. Young couples are enabled to move into their own homes and take advantage of modern appliances long before they accumulate the savings to pay for them. This benefit is balanced by the danger of excessive debts for the individual and by a sudden drop of the consumption level when people try to repay suddenly.

Stability in the steady growth of the nation's consumption is a major factor of economic progress.

Discussion Questions

1. Why does a poor economy show little concern for the wants of consumers?
2. Why does consumption of durable goods fluctuate more than other expenditures?
3. Discuss several methods of determining income inequality; why are some more meaningful than others?
4. Why do so many families remain so poor in a rich country like ours?
5. Most people have to work for a living; what other ways are open to earn income?
6. What types of occupations show the greatest future on the basis of recent trends?
7. State the case for and against consumer credit.

Suggested Reading

BURNS, ARTHUR F., "Looking Forward." *Thirty-First Annual Report.* New York, National Bureau of Economic Research, 1951.

HARRINGTON, MICHAEL, *The Other America.* New York, Macmillan, 1962.

HEILBRONER, ROBERT L., *The Making of Economic Society.* Englewood Cliffs, N.J., Prentice-Hall, 1962.

PART III

MONEY, INCOME, AND ECONOMIC GROWTH

The economic behavior of individuals and firms has occupied the center of the stage so far. We shall now begin to look at the operations of the economic system as a whole. Is the overall performance of the economy of the United States satisfactory? Does the economy grow and does it grow enough? These are some of the main questions of Part III of this book. Our attention switches from the *microeconomics* of the firm in Part II to *macroeconomics,* the study of broad development of the aggregates or totals in the national economy.

The late John Maynard Keynes, who wrote many books on economics in the first half of the twentieth century, was the most influential contributor to the discovery and formulation of macroeconomic principles. Without going into the technical details raised by his numerous thought-provoking ideas, two major contributions are singled out here for their far-reaching importance.

Keynes helped to divert the attention of policy makers from the arid arguments about the division of the nation's output between functional groups and individuals to the more fruitful task of raising the total production of all members of the economy. He further showed that this increased output did not happen automatically, but was subject to specific influences which could be manipulated by public authorities for good or evil.

Pre-Keynesian economists were inclined to treat the nation's output as a given size. In their opinion, the amount produced would change only slowly over a long period of time as the number of workers increased and became able to add to the existing production. Suggestions to raise total output fast did not constitute a suitable basis for fruitful policy discussion. Under these circumstances, one man's gain in his share of the national wealth was necessarily another man's loss.

The economic philosophy of Karl Marx in the nineteenth century is founded implicitly on the idea that the lower classes can gain only by taking part of the national output away from wealthier population groups. According to this doctrine, a conflict of interest is inevitable and leads to a continuous class struggle that precludes cooperation.

Marx's view of the national economy can be illustrated by a pie of a fixed size split into a number of slices, with all recipients fighting continuously for a larger slice of the same pie. Keynes pointed out that the pie did not have a fixed size and that much more could and would be produced if unemployed people and other resources were usefully occupied. The pie must be enlarged as long as unemployed resources exist. The unproductive struggle among competing groups for each others' income must be replaced by a common effort to produce more through cooperation, so that all may share the greater flow of goods and services. The essence of economic progress is an ever-larger pie with bigger slices for all.

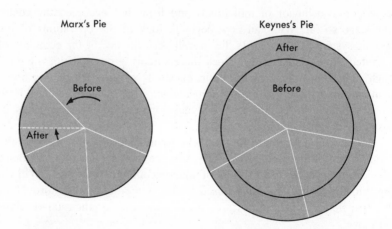

Marx's Pie   Keynes's Pie

Fig. III-1.   Two Views of the Economic Pie

Adam Smith's *invisible hand* had governed economic thought for over 150 years. With its simple rules of automatic self-adjustment according to immutable laws of nature, it had presumably protected the best interests of a free society. The mass unemployment of the thirties presented a serious challenge to the view that an economy operated at its best when left alone. Keynes demonstrated that a depression was man-made and far from inevitable. He called for deliberate policy measures by public officials to stop the waste of unemployment and provide more goods for more people.[1]

Keynes's refutation of Smith's warning against any economic activity by governmental agencies undermined his popularity with some businessmen, who failed to realize that his new theories created a constructive answer to the wave of despair following the apparent breakdown of capitalism in a depression. Today's faith in free enterprise economics is firmly built on Keynesian doctrine. There were others, of course, who had similar thoughts at the same time (or even earlier), but their formulation did not make a comparable impact on their contemporaries. Keynes's reputation as the leading economist of his era is undisputed; the following chapters could not have been written without his persuasive influence.

Chapter 13 discusses the development of money and credit, followed by a description of the banking system in the next chapter. An explanation of the meaning and measurement of national income occupies Chapter 15. The fluctuations of this income in times of prosperity and depression are the subject of Chapter 16. Public expenditures and revenues draw our attention in Chapter 17, and this leads to a controversial discussion of national policies in the final chapter of Part III.

---

[1] Keynes's most famous book, *The General Theory of Employment, Interest, and Money,* was first published during the Great Depression.

13

MONEY

Money is many things to many men; in fact, it sums up all there is to know about economics, at least for a very casual observer. Whenever business is not quite so good as it should be, a bit of tinkering with money will, in the opinion of some people, square everything promptly. Political platforms frequently show the result of monetary fads and the simple—too simple—prescriptions of money-quacks.

This book has postponed a discussion of money until this time in order to emphasize first the real aspects of economic activity. Human wants are satisfied only with goods and services; their production and distribution have been our foremost concern. However, we should not succumb to the opposite error and assume that money has no influence on economic welfare since it has only the humble function of facilitating barter. It is a potent instrument for good or evil, as this chapter sets out to show.

WHAT IS MONEY?

The basic purpose of money is to make easier the exchange of goods and services. *Money includes anything which is commonly used and widely accepted by a large number of people for the settlement of their obligations.*

Any article may serve as money as long as enough people are willing to use it for this purpose. In the areas occupied by the United States Army toward the end of World War II, cigarettes found wide acceptance as a form of money. When two little boys, however, are trading their treasures and discover that three shiny marbles are acceptable payment for a frog, neither the marbles nor the frog is money. The boys are engaged in pure barter—this swap is acceptable only to the two children involved in the deal and sets no pattern for others.

The use of money constitutes an alternative to direct barter, which is too awkward for an exchange economy. Once the social structure of society develops beyond the simple family group, money enters the picture and changes with the advancement of specialization. The more advanced an integrated economic system becomes, the more sophisticated will be the monetary arrangements that serve it. The advantages of specialization cannot be fully realized unless the economy has an adequate monetary system.

History

The use of money goes back to the dawn of history. Many commodities have served the purpose of facilitating barter. Slaves, cattle, wheat, wampum beads, and cigarettes are some of the more colorful articles used in the past. Precious metals, particularly gold and silver, have developed a long tradition of general acceptability and have become money in many nations.

The early settlers of North America were occasionally reduced to a barter system for lack of suitable money; they used an assortment of foreign coins, wampum beads, and tobacco in their exchanges, thereby causing much harm to local trade. The absence of a satisfactory monetary system and the British refusal to take timely action about it became one of the many grievances the settlers held against the Crown.

Chief Characteristics

Money differs from other commodities in one essential feature: it is normally not wanted for its own sake, but for what it can buy now or later. Therefore, the intrinsic value of the commodity adopted for monetary purposes is irrelevant. Paper currency is just as good as gold so long as people willingly accept it; a bank account is even more practical, provided most stores take checks in payment. A successful money must be generally acceptable.

The absence of intrinsic value in good money is not always understood. Many men feel that money ought to be valuable as a commodity, but in fact the opposite comes much closer to the truth. When a monetary commodity such as silver experiences a price rise, it may become unusable for its monetary purpose. The increasing demand for silver for industrial uses, particularly in photography, has exceeded the output of silver mines at 1966 prices for more than ten years. The U.S. Treasury has periodically sold silver in storage to prevent the silver price from exceeding the value of its silver coins. When the silver value contained in a quarter becomes more than 25 cents, it pays an owner to melt down his silver coins and sell them for their metallic value. To prevent the disappearance of silver coins from circulation, Congress passed a new coinage law [1] in 1965 creating coins with cheaper metal. Silver is now used only to continue the traditional appearance of our coins, but it has ceased to represent a monetary value.

Liquidity

The natural desire to accumulate cash in a bank account for the sudden needs of the future reflects a demand for *liquidity*. This concept describes

[1] Public Law 89-81, Coinage Act of 1965, July 23, 1965.

those assets which can be most readily mobilized, without loss of value, for the payment of obligations. Money qualifies best for this role of the most liquid asset.

People differ widely in their ideas of the amount of assets they wish to keep in the form of money. The demand for liquidity follows a precautionary instinct; a person wants to acquire the feeling of security that comes from building up his bank account against financial emergencies. He does not admire money for what it is, but for what it will buy when it is needed. Only a deranged old miser will sit at home counting his money. The ancient fable of King Midas points out the folly of hoarding money for the sheer pleasure of looking at it. The desire for liquidity is quite different and is a perfectly sensible safeguard.

FUNCTIONS OF MONEY

Money commonly serves four principal functions. It is not adapted to exercise all of them equally well because the requirements for these objectives are quite divergent, as we shall see now in more detail.

Means of Exchange

Money is used as a means of exchange to simplify the complicated barter transactions of a specialized economy. Thanks to this generally accepted procedure, it is possible to sell a house when leaving town, even though there may be nothing in the town we wish to buy. The money received for the house can be used elsewhere to purchase a new house, for example, or anything else we might want at that time. Without money it might be necessary to find a person moving in the opposite direction who would be willing to swap houses—a rather awkward alternative! Though the use of money introduces an added transaction into the barter between two people, it really simplifies the exchange a great deal.

An efficient means of exchange must be available wherever business takes place. Therefore, the amount of money in circulation will vary considerably with the needs of business: A small town will require more currency on market day than during the rest of the week. A merchant increases the amount of cash in his store in anticipation of the heavier volume of business on the payday of the local factory. He cashes more checks and deposits them with the bank, which in turn is equipped to handle a larger volume of money flow. In particular, the use of checks to transfer funds among members of the public makes money a very flexible means of exchange. When both parties to a transaction happen to keep their accounts in the same bank, their barter can be arranged without any actual movement of coin or paper.

Standard of Value

Trading is an exchange of one asset for another. But suppose a person wished to trade a book for a topcoat, or a topcoat for a used car. How would he know the relative values of a book and a topcoat, or of a topcoat and a car, or the relative values of any other of an endless series of pairs of items? This question brings out the need for a standard of value, a common denominator, to which relative prices can be compared.

We have seen before how prices of goods are established, how a change of mind may raise the relative value of one product in terms of another. Modern trade requires, however, that all these comparisons be accomplished in terms of one widely known and accepted product. If every state adopted its own yardstick, interstate commerce would be slowed down significantly because of the uncertainty of value standards in the next state. The trade-preventing difficulties of multiple standards can be observed clearly when we go abroad, where a dollar is not a dollar. Even in Canada a dollar may differ in value from a U.S. dollar or from any other type of yardstick.

A good standard for price reference is a rigid one which does not itself change noticeably. The very word *yardstick* implies a given length of one yard in exact and unvarying form. The lady who buys four yards of material in a dry-goods store would certainly object to a clerk measuring her purchase with an elastic yardstick which could be shortened at will! The monetary standard needs to be an equally fixed reference.

Most of the world's value standards lack the rigidity desired for efficient use. We all know that it would simply make no sense to compare dollar values of goods of grandpa's time with present prices. Most prices are much higher now; the yardstick has changed and no longer permits a valid comparison of relative values. If your house now sells for twice as much as it did when you purchased it, don't be too overjoyed until you find out what else you can buy with your money. (You may be lucky to sell it at any price, particularly if it is full of termites!)

Store of Value

Money is accepted in trade because it gives us generalized purchasing power which can be used now or later. If a man has no present plans to buy anything, he may prefer to hold his money in order to store purchasing power for the future. In this storage function, money has many advantages over other commodities, provided it retains the rigid standard of value demanded before. Prices of other goods often vary, and such commodities are therefore hazardous as means of temporary accumulation.

The great liquidity of money is a major attraction for its use in storing values. You can mobilize it for purchases without loss of time or the complicated arrangements you might encounter had you bought diamonds or famous paintings instead. The physical indestructibility and low maintenance costs of a bank account are other advantages of money for storage purposes. Valuable carpets may be eaten by moths; bank accounts never are.

Standard for Deferred Payments

A standard for deferred payments is a necessary tool for long-term credit transactions. When two parties negotiate a contract which will obligate them for several years, they need a rigid standard to express their future obligations. Money is commonly used for this purpose because of its simplicity, but its frequent loss of value over a period of time makes it an inadequate standard. If one is supposed to receive $1,000 five years later, he may expect to get the same dollars then as now; but the purchasing power of the dollar may be lower at the later date, much to his disappointment.

In bond sales and mortgage contracts, money is the common standard used for deferred payments. You can negotiate a twenty-five-year mortgage loan to buy a new house for a fixed amount of dollars only because others are willing to leave their money with the banker under the same conditions. The bank takes a chance on a "rubber dollar" as long as its depositors are willing to do the same. When the monetary standard loses value rapidly, people try to protect themselves by introducing new and more cumbersome standards for deferred payments, for example an index, with the unfortunate result that the money value of long-term contracts becomes even more uncertain.

The simplicity of the monetary standard is of such a great advantage that it outweighs the annoyance of minor changes in the value of the dollar.

WHAT MAKES MONEY GOOD?

Money has been defined as any commodity commonly used in this capacity. Its overriding feature, as mentioned already, is acceptability. Money remains money just as long as most people will accept it for this purpose.

Governments frequently make money more acceptable by declaring it "legal tender." This attribute means that a certain type of money may be used for the payment of legal debts and must be accepted regardless of the wishes of the creditor. If a man signed a promissory note ten years ago for $1,000, he can discharge his obligation now by paying the same sum. It will do the creditor no good to complain that the dollar is not worth what it used to be.

The inscription on a Federal Reserve note informs the holder that it is "redeemable in lawful money" of the United States. He may present his ten-dollar bill to a bank and receive a clean one in exchange, or two fives if he prefers, because they are the lawful money of the United States.

A declaration of legal tender boosts the acceptability of money, but the usefulness of this assurance is limited. When people no longer trust their standard of value, they will refuse to do business in a monetary commodity which has ceased to be acceptable. Legal efforts to force the population to use some specific monetary product are usually ineffective. The appearance of cigarettes as a means of exchange in the occupied zones during World War II was not the result of military orders; it evolved from the spontaneous acceptance of cigarettes as money by the local populations. A store owner would rather close shop than surrender his merchandise for lawful money he considers worthless.

Physical Qualifications

The characteristics of good money which is willingly accepted are physical as well as economic. Physical qualifications of good money are easily taken for granted because we are so familiar with them. But if we had to use cattle for money as did the ancient Romans, the complications would surprise us. The term *pecuniary transactions* for monetary dealings comes to us from the Latin word *pecus,* meaning both "money" and "cattle." At that time cattle made a fine standard of value that was widely recognized and which offered a good, steady reference for price comparisons. But animals obviously could not be used as a means of exchange for transactions of lesser value, so somewhat smaller pieces of leather or coins had to be introduced as substitutes, as tokens expressing some part of "cattle value."

Durability.   Money must be durable and not likely to deteriorate rapidly with frequent handling. Bank notes, coins, and checks do not always pass this test to perfection; they are certainly preferable to glass or apples, however.

Weight.   Money must be light in weight. From this viewpoint, paper money is far better than metal coins. Because of their weight, coins are limited to small change, where weight is no serious drawback.

Size.   Money must be small enough to be easily carried on the person, but not so tiny as to cause accidental loss. Very small gold or silver pieces were easily misplaced. On the other hand, large metallic coins presented real problems when big amounts of money had to be transferred before bank deposits came into monetary use. To an earlier generation, the stagecoach holdup was a real danger and not a popular television adventure.

Divisibility.   Money must be readily divisible into various denominations to facilitate making change. Paper money and coins accomplish this task very well. Bank deposits are even better, however, as checks can be written for the exact amount wanted at the moment.

Recognition.   To be accepted, money must be easy to recognize and familiar to most people. Try to pay your debts with a $1,000 bill! Only a banker is sufficiently familiar with such currency that he will exchange it for more customary denominations. Recognition presented a serious problem in this country when private banks issued their own currency and hundreds of different bank notes circulated simultaneously. Many cashiers would reject such notes because they failed to recognize them. Even our currency notes of today could be identified more easily if each denomination adhered to a different size or color. Similarity of all bank notes is a source of confusion, as any person realizes who has ever tried to pay a taxi driver at night!

Counterfeiting.   The temptation to manufacture his own money has challenged man as long as money has been in circulation. Elaborate precautions are taken to reduce counterfeiting as much as possible—special coloring and copy-proof ink are used to engrave watermark paper. But no amount of scientific care is likely ever to stop a daring counterfeiter completely.

Economic Qualifications

A nicely engraved piece of paper may be called money, but acceptability rests mostly on economic considerations which insure the confidence of the public and its willingness to consider a certain commodity as money. This faith is based on the belief that the commodity used will maintain its value, at least until its holder is ready to spend it again. In the long run this faith has usually been ill-rewarded, but so much money changes hands so fast that slow changes of value do not break down its acceptability.

Scarcity.   The value of money is maintained best when the amount of money in circulation remains scarce. The proper limits to the volume of money are dictated by the needs of the economy, and its issue requires central coordination and regulation. When in the past private bankers issued their own currency at a considerable profit, excessively large circulation was an ever-present danger. An unwarranted increase of the currency in circulation reduces the value of each monetary unit and destroys the faith which makes money acceptable.

Excessive scarcity can exercise an equally harmful effect. A volume of money which was sufficient in the past may prevent the expansion of trade in the future. People who are willing to produce more or buy more cannot do so without money to finance such added business. As trade is restricted by lack of money, prices change and eventually adjust to the needs of business. In the meantime, however, debtors may become bankrupt, business sales decline, and even good workers lose their jobs for want of enough money in circulation. This type of extreme scarcity is not likely to happen in a modern system, where, fortunately, such lack of money is easily avoided.

Convenience.   Money is a liquid and convenient asset which enables the owner to buy anything he desires. A sufficient bank account gives him a choice of buying a car, going to college, or spending a vacation in Bermuda. No other good is equally convenient. Once that car is bought, it can no longer be converted into a college education.

The convenience inherent in the use of money is so great that people continue to accept it even if their faith in its permanent value has been shaken. Barter is too cumbersome, and the hoarding of goods is so hazardous that money will continue to be used just because of its ease of handling.

The need for convenience can be shown by an example. In the United States, commercial bank deposits are considered money because they can be transfered readily just by writing a check. In some other countries, the law requires the user to affix a tax stamp to the check before handing it to anyone. This inconvenience has limited the use of checks to relatively few payments of large sums; bank deposits are not considered money under these circumstances, since they are not a convenient means of exchange.

PRECIOUS METALS

A widely held, popular belief considers the chief qualification of good money that it be backed by gold or silver. Unfortunately, this notion is entirely wrong. In spite of a feeling that in some vague fashion the gold stored in Fort Knox determines the value of the dollar, the fact of the matter is exactly the opposite. The dollar supports the price of gold.

Gold

The Gold Reserve Act of 1934 (as amended in 1945) restricted the ownership of monetary gold to the Treasury of the United States. It also provided that gold should no longer be coined and that "no currency of the United States shall be redeemable in gold." The lawful money of the United States is the dollar, not any specific number of grains of gold.

The law permits the Treasury to buy or sell gold for legitimate purposes at $35 per fine ounce. This standing offer to buy or sell, not only domestically but anywhere in the world, has maintained the price of gold at the same level since 1934. When other nations want dollars, they can buy them for gold at a fixed price; the same foreign central banks can dispose of any unwanted dollars in exchange for gold from the Treasury. The law freezes the gold price on a worldwide basis. It cannot fall as long as the Treasury is prepared to buy the yellow metal. Neither can it rise significantly as long as the Treasury has gold to sell.

The only connection between the national gold hoard and the money in circulation is a legal requirement that the Federal Reserve Banks must keep gold certificates issued by the Treasury—the amount of the certificates cannot be less than 25 percent of the currency in circulation. The stipulation has no practical significance since it does not cover the total money supply; in fact, our actual gold hoard has been far in excess of these requirements for a generation. A sharp reduction of the gold reserves in recent years has led to the passage of a law reducing by several billion dollars the amount of gold needed for storage.[2] Should the occasion arise, a further reduction of this storage requirement would seem to be likely.

Silver

Special legislation to support the price of domestic silver goes back to the last century. Congress continued to support the silver mines until industrial demand pushed up the price and the Treasury had to sell its hoard of silver to facilitate an orderly change to new coinage. When the Treasury finally, in 1967, gave up its role of supplying silver the price shot up 50 percent.

Value of the Dollar

The best description of the present monetary system of the United States is a matter of choice.[3] It is only essential to realize that the value of the dollar

---

[2] Public Law 89-3, March 3, 1965, is an amendment to the Federal Reserve Act which reduces the requirement of holding gold certificates.

[3] Some writers refer to our system as a "limited gold bullion standard," a description apt to confuse the issue rather than clarify it.

is determined not by a mystic link to precious metals, but by the monetary authorities of the federal government, whose decisions may increase or decrease the quantity of money in circulation. Gold continues to be used for monetary purposes only as an international means of exchange in the absence of a more practical arrangement. Its use in this connection will be discussed in more detail in Chapter 19.

THE MONEY SUPPLY OF THE UNITED STATES

The money supply of the United States consists of coins, currency, and bank deposits. The bulk of the currency is provided by the Federal Reserve Banks and is called Federal Reserve notes; their denominations range

TABLE 13-1.   Money in Circulation in the United States, 1967
(*millions of dollars*)

Coins	4,461
Federal Reserve notes	37,962
Treasury currency	940
Total currency in circulation	43,363
Demand deposits	131,100
Total money in circulation	174,463

SOURCE: March 1967 data, *Federal Reserve Bulletin*.

from $1 to $10,000. Coins are limited to the needs for making change, feeding vending machines, and stuffing piggy banks.

The largest part of the money supply consists of the deposits of families and businesses in commercial banks. Almost four-fifths of the total money supply takes the form of bank deposits. We like to think of the checks we write as money, since they serve the same purpose as dollar bills. In reality, it is not the check, but the deposit account at the bank that is the money; the distinction between the two matters only when your bank returns a check unpaid for lack of funds. You know then that a check without a deposit is as worthless as a counterfeit dollar bill.

CREDIT

All money is a form of credit. This statement may seem surprising at first glance; just because you happen to have some money in the bank or in your pocket shouldn't make you a creditor—but indeed you are! Your bank account means that the bank owes you the amount shown on its books, and you let the bank use your money or purchasing power until you are ready to buy something yourself. A debit and credit are the same transaction considered from opposite viewpoints. In the case of your bank account, you are the creditor and the bank is the debtor. If you want to spend more than you have on account, you borrow from the bank and the bank becomes the creditor.

When you carry currency in your pocket, you are a creditor of the Federal Reserve Bank, which acknowledges its liability on its books under the heading "currency in circulation." Money is the most liquid form of credit, the only one people can spend without special arrangements between creditor and debtor.

Short-Term Credit

Other forms of credit involve some delay before they can be switched to a different use. A checking account permits immediate use; a savings account requires only a trip to the bank to be converted into money. You cannot pay bills on Sunday with a savings deposit, but you may withdraw funds Monday morning. United States savings bonds can be converted into cash just as readily, provided that you have owned them for sixty days.

Long-Term Credit

Other credit instruments are not due for payment until a specified date in the future, usually called the maturity date. Most government bonds specify, for example, that the Treasury will pay $1,000 on April 15, 1984, or some other date. The owner, however, does not need to wait that long, when he wants cash instead, if he can find a buyer for his bond. He will have no trouble selling government securities, though he cannot be sure of the exact amount he will realize from a sale before the maturity date.

Relative Liquidity

Credit may be classified by its relative ease of conversion into money. Time deposits of $200 billion and securities representing the U.S. Government debt of about $320 billion can be exchanged into money with the least delay; they are, therefore, sometimes called "near-monies." Other debt certificates are not so easily sold. Life insurance policies can be converted into money without much difficulty. Bonds issued by corporations are "marketable" when they are regularly traded at an exchange. The owner of such a bond is fairly sure that he will be able to sell it when he wants to, although he cannot be sure of the price he will obtain for the security.

Still less liquid is mortgage credit on real estate, even though vast sums are involved in this type of lending operation. About $310 billion of such mortgages were outstanding in 1967. Most of these loans were granted

by financial institutions such as savings and loan associations or life insurance companies.

Merchandise sales frequently require the arrangement of credit to the
buyer. Consumer credit of $95 billion (1967) is financed by banks, stores
or other financial institutions.

TABLE 13-2.   Debt in the United States, 1966
(*billions of dollars*)

Public debt (net):		
Federal	279.9	
State	27.1	
Local	73.8	
Total		380.8
Debt of Corporations (net)		
Due within one year	264.8	
Due after one year	232.4	
Total		497.2
Debt of Individuals		
Farmers	42.1	
Mortgage loans (nonfarm)	278.5	
Commercial loans	28.8	
Financial loans	23.8	
Consumer loans	94.8	
Total		468.0
Total public and private debt		1,346.0

SOURCE: U.S. Department of Commerce, *Survey of Current Business.*

Man's economic decisions about spending or saving depend not only
on what he owns, but also on the amount he is able to borrow. Your cash
reserves can be kept much smaller when you know you can get a loan
without hesitation in case of need. An elaborate credit system helps to
time economic activity for best performance, but the mechanism is complicated, and a financial breakdown such as the one which occurred in the
thirties can do much harm. The fluctuating price of credit is a major
instrument for channeling loanable funds in the right direction.

INTEREST

The rate of interest is the price paid for the use of loanable funds. When a
person consults the commercial pages of a newspaper to find out the going
rate of interest, he encounters a bewildering variety. He should not be too
surprised, because most services are sold in different combinations and
packages. Credit is no exception. The price quoted is likely to include an
insurance premium, to compensate the lender for the risk he takes when

he makes the loan, and a charge for the cost of servicing the loan. The pure rate of interest, which is not quoted separately, represents the forces of demand and supply in the market for loanable funds.

How to Figure Interest

Interest is usually expressed as a percentage instead of a dollar amount, a technique that makes it look small and unimportant. Why should anyone hesitate to pay 6 percent interest when buying a car? If the buyer realized from the beginning that he has added several hundred dollars to the cost of the automobile, he might have either tried to borrow at a cheaper rate or waited for a while. Interest rates are usually stated on an annual basis. Beware of the lender who offers you money at 2 percent per month—you are paying 24 percent for his generous assistance!

To convert a percentage rate into a dollar figure, the rate must be multiplied with the borrowed capital amount. A loan of $600 at 5 percent costs $600 × 5/100 = $30 per year. The problem looks different, although it is not, when you want to buy a bond from someone else and try to determine how much it is worth. Let us assume this bond is a "golden cow" producing invariably and forever a yearly income of $200. If the market rate of interest happens to be 4 percent, the value of the "cow" will be $200 × 100/4 = $5,000.[4] Let us not confuse the two calculations which we have just shown. In the first case we were given the market rate of interest and the total amount of money lent out, and with this information we calculated the *annual income* in dollars. In the second case we were given the annual income and the market rate of interest, and from this we computed the *capital value*.

Why Is Interest Important?

To many consumers interest is not important. They pay cash for the goods they want when they can afford them. Others buy the goods they want whether they can afford them or not as long as the store sells on instalments. Virtually no one goes to shop for a new refrigerator determined to buy if he can borrow at 5½ percent but equally firm to do without if he has to pay 6 percent for the loan.

[4] Bond interest differs from the "golden cow" mostly because it is limited to a specific number of years. This renders the arithmetic slightly more involved, but it follows the same principle.

$$\text{Amount of income} = \text{Amount of capital} \times \frac{\text{Interest rate}}{100}$$

$$\begin{array}{l}\text{The capital value} \\ \text{of a good or service}\end{array} = \text{Amount of income} \times \frac{100}{\text{Interest rate}}$$

Businessmen are human, too, and do not act very differently from consumers. The president of a firm has seen a new machine which he feels will help reduce his production costs significantly. He arranges a loan from his banker at the best terms he can get, and his decision to buy is rarely changed because of a high rate of interest. His enthusiasm leads him to expect great results from his purchase, results which cannot be reduced to an exact interest figure. He hopes to make much more profit than anything the loan may cost.

Most users of credit seem to make their decisions to borrow regardless of the rate of interest. Why, then, does interest matter? Because of problems arising from the capitalization of income, and also because of the impact of interest on the creditor.

Capitalization of Income.   Whenever an effort is made to raise new capital, the rate of interest becomes the pivotal factor. Suppose that Jones's tool shop earns $15,000 per year and Jones wishes to raise this income to $20,000 with the installation of new equipment. He needs a financier who will provide the funds for the new machine. Jones offers a partnership consisting of a one-fourth share of his business for $100,000, the cost of the new machine. This proposition sounds fair enough since the expected increase of income will be about one quarter of future total earnings of the firm. Is Jones likely to find the financial backing?

If the market rate of interest for similar projects is 4 percent at this time, a $5,000 income represents the amount obtained from a capital investment of $125,000. Jones asks only for $100,000, which makes his offer very attractive; he will get the money. If the prospective partner, however, can get a 6-percent return on his investment in some other venture, he will not be interested in Jones's proposition. At 6 percent the capitalized value of $5,000 is only $83,333, and no investor could be expected to pay more.

Even a slight change in the rate of interest causes such a large difference in the capitalization of income that investment projects often depend on the price of funds for their execution. When the going rate of interest is high, only the most profitable projects can be financed, regardless of the confidence of the borrower about his future success. Every drop of the rate, even as little as one-half of 1 percent, will make feasible many projects which have been waiting for just this moment. Really marginal plans can be financed only when rates are low and the money supply is plentiful. The rate of interest thereby regulates the flow of investment activity.

During a period of high interest rates, such as this country experienced in 1966, many marginal projects had to be delayed because they could not be funded. Toll roads, for example, are only expected to earn enough to pay their bonds when the rate of interest is low. As the market rate rises, legislatures continue to authorize the sale of bonds for such an undertaking, but financiers are unwilling to buy them when money is hard to get.

Interest and the Creditor. Interest also has the effect of rationing out funds to the projects with the best future prospects. Suppose you decide to build your dream house. You own your lot, your plans are ready, you decide to see your banker about financing the construction. You expect to borrow $15,000 with a government-insured loan for 6 percent, with your lot as downpayment. The banker will check very carefully the location of your lot and the house plans, but he is even more interested in your earning prospects and the amount he feels you can afford to pay per month for housing. All things considered, he agrees that you can handle the type of loan you had in mind.

The rate of interest comes now into play to decide the issue. If the banker cannot get more than 6 percent from any other use of his money and he expects no upward change in rates in the foreseeable future, you get the loan and the house can be built. If conventional mortgage loans earn 7 percent for the banker, he will not be willing to lend to you at 6 percent. But you are anxious to build and ready to sign a loan for $16,000 to compensate him for the difference in interest as long as you can get the $15,000 needed.[5]

The banker may still be reluctant to agree because your income is not big enough to carry more than a $15,000 loan without trouble. A $16,000 loan would increase your monthly payments. He may advise you to either wait a little longer, until you have saved up a larger downpayment, or make the house smaller. He is not ready to give you a risky loan when he has better alternatives for the use of his funds. The borrower may not care how much interest he has to pay, but this decision may not be his to make. The lender refuses to grant the loan because he bases his judgment on the market rate of interest at the moment. Thus funds are rationed out by the interest rate to the most profitable projects.

INDEX NUMBERS

A price index is a yardstick of the changing value of money during a given time period. If you find to your dismay that your income leaves you just as short of cash by the end of the month as it did ten years ago when you earned much less, an index comparison may give you the explanation. You will discover that the purchasing power of the dollar was 20 percent higher then than now. Unless your salary has risen by a greater percentage during this period, you are really no better off.

---

[5] This is known as "discounting a loan."

The main drawback of money, as mentioned before, is its lack of rigidity as a standard for deferred payments. An index is an inflexible substitute which can be used to overcome this difficulty. It is a measuring device which finds many and varied applications. A production index can compare the changing volume of physical output or the productivity of a plant with that of its competitors; but the most common use of an index in economics is to measure the purchasing power of money.

Constructing an Index

The federal Bureau of Labor Statistics compiles some of the most widely used index number series. It collects data on the prices of goods which have major significance for the index users. The sum of the prices paid for the amount of goods usually bought during a selected "normal" (no war, no depression) year in the past is designated as the base, equal to 100. Then the prices for comparable goods in the current year are obtained. The ratio of the two sums gives us the index number for this year.

| Amount spent in current year | 1968 | $2,750 | Index | 110 |
| Amount spent in base year | 1960 | $2,500 | Index | 100 |

You divide the prices of the current year by the prices of the base year and multiply with 100 to reach the current index number:

$$\frac{2,750}{2,500} = \frac{\text{Current year index}}{100} \qquad \frac{\text{Current year}}{\text{index}} = 1.1 \times 100, \text{ or } 110$$

The accuracy of this index depends on the wisdom and skill of the men who compile it. Did they select a normal base year? Did they include the prices of the most significant goods in proper proportions? Did they choose goods in the right proportions to reflect the changes they try to measure? We shall leave these difficult problems to the statisticians and use their index for what it is worth.

Uses of Index Numbers

No single set of index numbers will suffice for all purposes. The best known index is the "cost of living index" compiled monthly by the Bureau of Labor Statistics.[6] It is widely used in wage negotiations and is selected as the official yardstick in several union-management agreements.

The "Wholesale Price Index," provided by the same statistical office,

[6] This index, officially known as the "Consumer Price Index," is prepared by the U.S. Department of Labor, Bureau of Labor Statistics. It uses prices of commonly bought consumer goods and services, "collected on a monthly basis in forty-six cities, with more than 2,500 population throughout the United States. The number of items in the index is subject to some changes and is about three hundred."

is of special interest to people concerned with the performance of the nation's economy. Wholesale prices usually change sooner than retail figures, and the index shows economic trends at an earlier stage.

Many business groups are covered by index numbers compiled for their specific needs. An index of industrial production reflects changes in industry. A farm price index compares the prices farmers receive for their crops and livestock with the cost of goods they usually buy.

The advantage of a price index is its ability to measure the changing value of money. Its use in a union contract permits the maintenance of purchasing power for the worker. If a man is entitled to an hourly wage of $3.60 and the index shows a 5-percent drop in the purchasing power of money, a wage contract based on this index will raise the wage rate to $3.78 per hour without any need for further negotiation. The index shows how much of an increase is needed to compensate for the lower value of the dollar. The major drawback of an index is its somewhat cumbersome application, which limits its use to transactions involving large amounts of money over a long period of time.

MONEY AND PRICES

The value of money is reflected by the general price level; when prices go up, the purchasing power of money shrinks, and the opposite holds true when prices drop. To maintain an unchanging value, the amount of money in circulation must vary only in accordance with the ups and downs of business transactions. The relationship between the quantity of money in circulation and the general level of prices requires further clarification.

The connection between money, prices, and the flow of business is succinctly described in this abbreviated form [7]:

$$MV = PT$$

M stands for money, or, more precisely, the quantity of money in circulation.

V shows how often the money changes hands per year (a given dollar is exchanged for goods and services) and is also called the velocity of circulation.

P represents the general price level (an index number as explained before).

T indicates the amount of business transactions during the year.

Total spending per year is represented by *MV*, the amount of money multiplied by the number of times it is used. The total monetary circulation *must* equal total transactions at some price for the same time period. If

[7] This concept is known as "the equation of exchange."

the money side of this equation is doubled, business transactions must double also, unless prices are permitted to rise. This proposition is not a guide for any specific policy, but an illustration of the way money and prices are interrelated.

When money is allowed to adjust its rate of circulation to the changes in business transactions, prices may vary very little. In an extreme boom, however, the demand for goods may increase so fast that sellers start to raise their prices. If the volume of money rises enough to accommodate both more transactions and higher prices, the purchasing power of money falls. This has happened often in the past.

During bad times, attempts to boost a sluggish economy by increasing the supply of money can cause quite surprising results. The speed of circulation may slow down and cancel the larger money supply. A ten-dollar bill used twice has the same economic impact as two ten-dollar bills exchanged only once. If the money increase actually causes a larger circulation, the result may be not more business at the old prices as hoped, but the same number of transactions at higher prices. Only if the velocity of circulation and the level of prices remain unchanged will an increase in the quantity of money stimulate the volume of transactions.

The many possible interactions between money, prices, and the level of business will continue to draw our attention in the discussion of economic growth.

SUMMARY

Money is an article commonly used and widely accepted for the purpose of facilitating exchange. Its intrinsic value as a commodity does not matter, since it is wanted only for what it can buy.

Money serves as a convenient means of exchange. As a standard of value, it expresses prices in comparable, readily understandable terms. Used as a store of value, the owner can keep assets in liquid form as long as he desires. Money serves as a yardstick for deferred payments, which are the basis of an operating credit system. In its function as a means of exchange, modern money performs extremely well; in its yardstick function it fails, at times, to maintain its purchasing power as rigidly as desired.

Good money has physical and economic features which render it more acceptable. Scarcity helps to maintain its value and assure the faith of the people who use it; convenience keeps it in circulation even when confidence is slightly shaken. Money must remain acceptable if it is to perform the assigned task effectively.

Precious metals have a long monetary tradition because of their natural scarcity. Worldwide acceptance has made gold a monetary commodity, but the only connection between gold and the dollar is a legal requirement without economic significance to the country's money supply. The notion that in order to have value money must be backed by gold is a popular misconception. The willingness of the Treasury to buy or sell gold to central banks at $35 per ounce acts as a support price for the gold mines of the world.

The value of the dollar is determined by the federal authorities in charge of controlling the money supply. This supply takes the form of coins, currency, and, for the most part, bank deposits transferable by check.

Money and short- and long-term credit instruments differ among themselves only in relative degree of liquidity. Together they act as an envelope, wrapping up all present and future trade. This complicated credit mechanism, with over $1,000 billion owned and owed at any time, is necessary for the proper functioning of our highly specialized and integrated economy.

The rate of interest is the connecting link between all forms of credit. Though users of credit may seem to disregard the price they pay, interest exerts a vital function in regulating the flow of economic activity because of the need to capitalize income at the current interest rate and because of the alternative uses of loanable funds by creditors.

The fluctuations of the purchasing power of money can be compensated for by the use of an index, which is a more rigid yardstick than money for measuring changes in value. Since its use is less convenient than money, however, application of index numbers is usually limited to transactions involving large sums payable over a long time.

The relationship between money and prices can be expressed briefly by the equation: $MV = PT$. Each one of these factors may become the cause of price changes. Attempts to influence the direction of change must take into consideration the possible effects on all variables concerned.

Discussion Questions

1. What are the functions of money? Does the dollar satisfy these functions equally well?
2. What influence does gold exercise on the value of the dollar?
3. Why is the main part of our money supply held in the form of bank deposits?
4. When would you prefer to use index numbers instead of dollar values?
5. The economy of the United States moves in an envelope of credit. Comment on this statement.
6. How can interest be important for routine transactions when so many people find it difficult to calculate the amount of interest actually due?

Suggested Reading

CHANDLER, LESTER V., *The Economics of Money and Banking,* 4th ed. New York, Harper & Row, 1964.

KENT, RAYMOND P., *Money and Banking,* 5th ed. New York, Holt, Rinehart & Winston, 1966.

ROBERTSON, D. A., *Money,* 6th ed. New York, Pitman, 1948.

SAUSE, GEORGE G., *Money, Banking, and Economic Activity.* Boston, Heath, 1966.

14

FINANCIAL INSTITUTIONS

Many and varied financial institutions serve to keep money and credit available for economic transactions. Expert management of monetary matters is essential for the most effective use of the nation's resources. *Financial intermediaries,* as they have been commonly called in recent years, carry out this function; their task is the accumulation of idle funds to be channeled to those who demand them at any time.[1]

Financial intermediaries include not only all types of banking institutions, but also other financial enterprises with the exception of holding companies. A business can be classified as financial when most of its assets consist of bonds and promissory notes.

This chapter will describe first the origin and functions of the principal financial intermediaries, followed by a brief discussion of the markets involved in their activities and the agencies which regulate them. The story then shifts to the unique characteristics of the commercial banks and explains how they create money. An outline of the organization and functions of the Federal Reserve System concludes the chapter.

FINANCIAL INTERMEDIARIES

Banking is a very old business. A glance at its historical development provides useful background information for our present institutions.

History

Early Developments. Banking history goes back to ancient civilizations. The money changers of biblical times are familiar figures to all of us. Early bankers provided a convenient storage place for valuables; these granted protection against fire and theft somewhat similar to a modern safe-deposit box in a bank vault.

Savings Banking. The banker soon learned that it was good business to pay interest to his clients if they gave him permission to use the stored

---

[1] The discussion of financial intermediaries leans heavily on the pacemaking work of Raymond W. Goldsmith, *Financial Intermediaries in the American Economy Since 1900* (Princeton, N.J., Princeton, 1958).

funds so long as they did not need them. Thus, instead of paying a storage fee to the banker, the depositor earned interest while the banker used the deposited funds to make loans at higher rates. The main function of a banker, therefore, is not to store money but to lend it. This development marked the beginning of savings-type banking.

Commercial Banking. Bankers issued storage receipts to their customers for the amounts left on deposit. People discovered that payments could be made to others by assigning these receipts to them without actually withdrawing the funds. This new technique was the start of deposit banking. The warehouse receipts eventually became bank notes, which are a banker's promise to pay on demand. When a trustworthy banker issued such notes, they were "as good as gold"—unless he went bankrupt. Banks in a modern sense can be traced back to Venice and Genoa in the Middle Ages. Martin's Bank in London was founded in 1563 and continued in operation until 1966.

Development in the United States. The Continental Congress issued $242 million in paper money between 1775 and 1780. It depreciated in value so fast that it ceased to circulate in 1781, adding to our language the well-known phrase "not worth a continental." The first permanently organized bank in the United States was the Bank of North America, chartered in 1781. By the year 1800 only a few banks had been established, most of them in New England. The first Bank of the United States, founded in 1791, was an important but short-lived institution. The Chase Manhattan Bank today still operates under a charter granted originally to The Manhattan Company in 1799.

The nineteenth century witnessed the rapid growth of commercial banking. States had chartered eighty-eight banks as early as 1811. The federal government launched the second Bank of the United States in 1816, but it became a victim of political adversity when its charter expired in 1836. By 1840 over 1,000 banks had been chartered in this country. Not all these institutions were conducted so conservatively as modern banks; failures were common whenever the country suffered an economic slump.

The financial pressure of the Civil War caused the passage of the National Bank Act of 1863, which authorized the issuance of national bank notes by nationally chartered banks. A special tax on state bank notes levied in 1865 eliminated state money from circulation. The office of the Comptroller of the Currency was created at the same time; it continues to inspect banks to this day. Life insurance companies, savings and loan associations, and personal trust companies developed rapidly during this period, but commercial banks dominated the scene as the primary source of funds, particularly for business ventures.

In the twentieth century, numerous forms of finance companies have been added, indicating the trend toward specialization in the lending function. Table 14-1 lists some of the better known financial intermediaries with their asset figures. The economic importance of various types of institutions is not fully reflected by their assets. They give, however, a general indication of their share of the financial business. The specific function of some of these institutions will now be discussed.

TABLE 14-1.   Assets of Selected Financial Intermediaries in the U.S., 1966
(billions of dollars)

Types of Financial Institution	Assets
Commercial banks	403.4
Life insurance companies	166.9
Savings and loan associations	133.9
Private pension funds	85.4
Mutual savings banks	61.0
Investment companies	46.4
Finance companies a	36.3
Credit unions	11.4
Federal land banks	5.0
a 1965	

SOURCES: Federal Reserve Bulletin and others.

Savings Institutions

Intermediaries who specialize in attracting funds from individual savers, usually involving only modest amounts per person, are organized as mutual savings banks, savings and loan associations, or as savings departments of commercial banks.

Savings accounts, or time deposits, differ from demand deposits in two essential points. Whereas the law prohibits payment of interest on checking accounts, interest is paid for amounts left in savings accounts. In the 1960's commercial banks started to issue Certificates of Deposit for fixed time periods to individual customers. These certificates usually earn higher rates of interest than normal savings accounts. Savings accounts cannot be transferred by check and are not considered to be money. Another legal distinction is mentioned occasionally. The banker may delay payment on savings accounts; a solvent banker, however, never invokes this provision, as he would promptly lose his customers.

Savings institutions differ in how they use the funds placed at their disposition. Commercial banks make loans for a wide variety of objectives: financing business needs, construction projects, consumer purchases, or college educations. Mutual savings banks have a long history of specializing in small savings accounts. Their funds are channeled into all kinds of real estate and construction ventures. Savings and loan associations concentrate almost exclusively on financing residential home construction; granting mortgage loans based on the individual family home is their main activity.

Insurance Companies

The primary objective of an insurance firm is risk protection. The pooling of risk premiums accumulates vast reserve funds, which become available for credit transactions of all types. Life insurance companies gather large sums for future payments. In the meantime, these sums are left in long-term deposits with the companies, which specialize, in fact, in long-term loans that they grant with a substantial amount of their reserves.

Personal Trust Departments

Trust departments of commercial banks and trust companies are some of the largest and oldest financial institutions. Wealthy persons furnish the funds for their operations. When a man of means feels that the members of his family do not possess the age or experience to handle large sums of money wisely, he creates a trust fund to be administered by a banker in accordance with his instructions.

The creator of the trust may start a fund during his lifetime, or arrange for it in his will to protect his widow and young children. The law regulates trust fund operations in much detail. The action of the trustees is restricted to prevent their using the funds for risky transactions which might deprive the inexperienced beneficiaries of their inheritance.

The investment of trust funds traditionally follows a conservative pattern, centering on real estate mortgages and corporate bonds. In recent decades stocks are being bought in addition to bonds, in many cases to protect the owner against the decline in the purchasing power of the dollar. Trustees may also shift from mortgages to government securities for improved liquidity.

The personal trust department must not be confused with other institutions using the same word. When a person attacks the "sugar trust," he opposes a monopolistic attempt to combine independent stockholders into a voting agreement to gain control of the industry. This type of trust agreement was outlawed by the Sherman Act of 1890.

Investment Companies

Investment companies, popularly known as "mutual funds," provide a type of service for middle-income customers comparable to the role of the trust department for the wealthy. As we have seen, in a personal trust the trustee manages the beneficiaries' funds for a fee; the bonds or stocks which the trustee buys belong to the owner of the trust. The cost of this arrangement requires large holdings of securities and would be impractical for a man with modest savings who has neither the time nor the knowledge to discover the best investment opportunities. He therefore buys shares of a mutual fund and lets the managers decide what securities offer the best opportunity for gain.

By pooling the savings of many small investors, the risk of stock ownership can be spread over more diversified holdings. Expert management of investment funds becomes possible without excessive fees for each customer. It is therefore not astonishing that this type of investment company has grown faster than have other financial institutions in the prosperous years since World War II. Mutual funds differ substantially from personal trust companies. In a mutual fund, the purchaser buys shares in the fund itself, which in turn invests the money in the stocks of other companies. The shares are always offered for sale by the fund and may be redeemed at any time.

Mutual funds were regulated by law in 1940. Their importance was insignificant because they controlled only $450 million assets all combined. In the following twelve years their assets grew to $4 billion, but their really phenomenal increase came only in the sixties. On June 30, 1966 all mutual funds reported $38.2 billion assets which made the funds and their managers influential factors in the conduct of American business. From 300,000 shareholders in 1940 the number of such investors has risen to 3.5 million in 1966. The economic impact of this new financial giant has become a subject of Congressional inquiry.[2]

Finance Companies

Some specialized credit services are considered too risky by commercial banks and are furnished, therefore, by other financial institutions. They are known as finance companies and engage in a variety of lending operations.

Sales finance companies are concerned primarily in buying contracts covering instalment sales from automobile dealers. Theirs is largely a wholesale lending operation for which they in turn must borrow needed funds. Their total assets are far larger than those of other finance companies.

Business finance companies make loans to firms that have more credits outstanding than they advance with their own funds. The finance company accepts the open accounts of its customer as collateral and provides the needed funds on this basis.

Personal finance companies are sources of individual consumer credit, supplementing the small-loan departments of commercial banks. They concentrate on making personal cash loans.

[2] The source of information about mutual funds is the report of the Securities and Exchange Commission, *The Public Policy Implications of Investment Company Growth* (89th Cong., 2nd sess., H. Rept. 2337, December 2, 1966).

Credit unions operate in the same field on a smaller scale. The modern development of consumer credit on a broad, competitive scale is less than sixty years old, but pawnbrokers have granted similar loans for many centuries; they still continue their trade today.

Investment Banking

Other financial institutions specialize in providing corporations with funds for long-term capital investments. A prominent manufacturer wants to engage in an expansion program at an estimated cost of over $100 million. Even a wealthy firm may need outside help for such a large sum. The manufacturer therefore makes an agreement with an investment banker, who will raise the funds in exchange for new securities to be issued in the name of the borrower. These are new stocks or bonds, in contrast to securities which have been previously issued and which are traded in securities markets, such as the New York Stock Exchange.

The investment banker hopes to sell these new securities promptly and at a higher price. If the borrower is not very well known, the banker may not guarantee a fixed price for the shares, but will agree to sell them as well as he can for a commission. Investment banking is limited to a few highly specialized firms located in large cities, particularly in New York. Their number of transactions is quite small, but each contract involves huge sums of money. Only a few investment bankers are needed to negotiate with corporate clients. The investment bankers are conducting a wholesale operation in mobilizing funds.

Brokers.   Brokers, on the other hand, conduct a retail operation. They sell securities to the public, in effect gathering funds on the local level. Many salesmen are needed to contact those people who want to keep some of their savings in stocks and bonds. Brokers' offices can be found in every large city in the country and in many smaller towns as well.

Brokerage firms come in many sizes. The local office may be an independent broker taking care of the needs of a few wealthy people, or part of a national chain, such as Merrill Lynch, Pierce, Fenner & Smith, Inc., who execute the orders to buy or sell for many thousands of customers every day. A firm of this size may combine both retail and wholesale functions and handle entire issues of new securities.

Many people, particularly small investors, are willing to risk their savings and buy shares of stock only because they feel sure that they will always be able to sell it, hopefully at a profit. This assurance is provided by the ability of the brokers to match "buy" and "sell" orders with each other in a nationwide network. Stock exchanges greatly facilitate their task; the most important institution of this kind is the New York Stock Exchange, where over six million shares are traded in an average day.

Stock Exchange. A stock exchange acts like a club whose actions have, however, such far-reaching impact that its operations are subject to public regulation. Only a member can transact business at the exchange, and the managing board is elected by the members. Admission is restricted, and acceptable individuals must buy a membership seat from someone willing to surrender it. A seat on the New York Stock Exchange varies in price, but it may exceed even $200,000.

Let us follow a transaction from the customer to the trading floor of the Exchange. A person who wants to buy or sell stocks which have been admitted for trading at the Stock Exchange contacts his broker and places an order. The broker, in turn, transmits this order to his New York office, which brings the order to the floor of the Exchange through a member. All orders converge there and are channeled to specialists who agree on a price which matches buying and selling instructions. When orders from the public are lopsided—for example, when everyone wants to sell—the specialist himself will buy so as to insure an orderly market without excessive fluctuations. The price of every trade on the Exchange floor is placed on a high-speed ticker tape, and the information is electronically transmitted to all the brokerage offices in the country equipped with receiving machines.

Importance of the Investment Banker. The intricate network of bankers who gather funds from many individuals and make these funds available to large corporations has contributed more to the progress of the American economy than most people realize. These bankers mobilize the initiative of free, private enterprise with an assurance of honest trading guaranteed by private and public supervision. The tremendous boost which investment banking has given to the industrialization of this country can be seen more clearly when this performance is compared with the rudimentary investment techniques still found in many less developed nations. In those countries stock ownership is confined to a few wealthy individuals who combine personal ownership with control. Smaller investors have no opportunity to share in industrial growth. Their savings consist of jewelry, gold, or real estate unless the owners invest abroad.

Government Lending Institutions

Government lending operations have become a significant factor only during the last thirty years. They are now exercised by a host of agencies specializing in loans which Congress wanted to support for various purposes. Only a few of these agencies can be mentioned here: the Farm Credit Administration, Rural Electrification Administration, Commodity Credit Corporation, Federal Crop Insurance Corporation, and the Farmers Home Administration are examples of government institutions administering credit for agriculture.

A partial list of agencies providing housing credit include Federal Housing Administration, Federal National Mortgage Association, and Public Housing Administration.

Not all of these institutions lend directly to the final borrower. In the case of the Federal Housing Administration, the government insures loans granted to individuals by private bankers in order to give low-income borrowers a chance to finance a home of their own. A report on these agencies published in 1963 covered fifty-one federal lending programs. Total loans granted under these programs reached $76 billion in 1958. Foreign lending is not included in this sum.

Commercial Banks

Commercial banks are private financial institutions authorized to accept demand deposits transferable by check. They number in excess of 13,000, with assets of over $400 billion and are the most important of the financial intermediaries. It is their unique function of *monetizing debt* which gives them their dominant position in an exchange economy.

What does monetizing debt mean? Assume that you need $500 for a trip and you do not have this amount right now. You could try to pay the motels, filling stations and stores en route with your own IOU, but you would probably not go very far. Therefore, you see your banker, who knows you and trusts you. He agrees to accept your promissory note to him and in turn he increases your bank account by $500. You can now pay your bills by writing a check against this account at will, because the banker's promise to pay is money. This distinction of the demand deposit or checking account sets it apart from all other financial operations.

Commercial banks are also engaged in various other banking activities, as we have seen already. Their diversified operations resemble a department store in the financial field. They accept time deposits (savings accounts) and have personal trust departments. Their lending operations extend to all fields. They grant loans to businesses and to consumers; they buy home mortgages and government securities. Their money-creating ability, however, is the function we shall now examine in more detail.

HOW DO BANKS CREATE MONEY?

Ask your banker how he creates money! He will probably give you a puzzled look and assure you that he does nothing of the kind. He prints no currency and never lends as much as he takes in. Still, demand deposits in private commercial banks are money. They exceeded $130 billion in 1967 and constituted four-fifths of the nation's money supply. How can we explain this apparent contradiction?

If Federal Reserve notes were the only acceptable money, banks could not create it, because in this situation only the Federal Reserve Bank could add to the circulation. Demand deposits, however, are money too. A demand deposit account can be opened for a customer in exchange for his currency; no new money is created in this case because banknotes have merely been traded for deposit money. But such accounts can also be opened in trade for the depositor's promissory note; *this transaction adds to the money supply.* The promissory note is not money, but the new deposit credited to the customer's account is.

Let us not confuse the process of money creation with the natural desire of the banker to make money in the sense of earning a profit. The earnings of a bank result from the interest paid by customers, from service charges, and from other fees. The banker's effort to earn a living has nothing to do with the creation of money.

Loan Deposits

Let us see what happens when a depositor brings $500 to a bank and opens a checking account. The banker realizes he must keep some part of it to meet his obligations; 20 percent of the $500, or $100, will do nicely, as he knows from experience. He uses the other $400 to make a loan. He accepts a promissory note from his loan customer and opens an account for him for $400. The money supply has risen, and the original $500 has become $900 because an additional deposit has been created.

A keen observer may point out that the loan deposit will not be present very long because the owner would not have borrowed from the bank unless he needed the money and planned to write checks against it immediately. This is quite true, but his checks will be deposited by the people who receive them in the same or in some other bank. The new loan money cannot simply disappear! The $400 increase in the money supply continues in existence as long as the loan remains unpaid.

In fact, the loan starts a chain reaction whereby each deposit becomes the basis of new loans, although the banker uses only the money originally left with him on deposit. When the checks for $400 are deposited, $320 can be loaned out again with the same percentage held in reserve. The total money supply reaches now $1,220. The process is likely to continue from one bank to another in a similar fashion.

Restraints to Money Creation

What prevents the banker from creating new money without limit? Three considerations keep his activity under control: the demand for currency, the action of other commercial banks, and the legal reserves required by the Federal Reserve System.

Demands for Currency.   Banks must always be prepared to satisfy a depositor who wants to cash a check and convert part of his deposit into currency. Demands for currency follow a predictable pattern for which a banker stays well prepared by keeping enough currency in storage. This amount is known as vault cash and reduces slightly the sum available for new loans.

Adverse Clearing Balances.   Assume that a small banker in a big town wants to grow quickly. He decides to lure customers away from his competitors by granting easy loans to all who ask for them. His regular deposits do not grow very fast, but he always lends the last cent the law permits, while his competitors remain much more cautious. For a million dollars total deposits, he keeps only a minimum reserve, say $150,000.

His loan customers write checks now and pay their bills. The banker expects this and figures that for every check drawn against his bank and deposited across the street he will get a new deposit from his customers who receive checks payable by competing banks. If this happens, both the deposits and the reserves remain unchanged; but our banker was daring and made comparatively more loans than his competitors. Therefore, his own new deposits will not be able to keep up with the claims from other banks that present checks for payment against his accounts.

How does this lack of balance affect the daring banker? Every banker keeps a reserve account which reflects a standard percentage of all the money deposited by his customers. Through this account move daily all the checks for deposit which are chargeable against other banks, as well as the checks written by his customers and presented by other banks for collection. When deposits and collections are of equal size, the reserve account remains unchanged and the banker keeps on lending. Because of the banker's daring lending practices in the past, however, the collections begin consistently to exceed his new deposits. Part of the newly deposited funds must now be used to replenish the reserve accounts and are no longer available for new loans.

This is likely to continue until the daring banker becomes as conservative as his competitors and a better balance has been restored to his reserve account. Claims and counterclaims in the form of checks are matched daily in the clearinghouse, and the banker's deficit is called an adverse clearing balance. When such adverse balances become chronic, the reserves will shrink and few new loans can be granted.

Legal Reserves.   The legal reserve is the percentage of member bank deposits which must be kept on deposit in an account with the Federal Reserve Bank.[3] Its size is determined by the Federal Reserve System and is beyond the control of the banker. If one-sixth of all deposits must be kept on reserve, the maximum size of the money supply will be six times this reserve. When the money supply reaches six times the amount of the original deposit, this sum will have been absorbed entirely by the reserves. Lending is limited by the excess reserves of each bank, since this process trades a bank's reserves for new loans.

FEDERAL CONTROL OF MONEY AND BANKING

After the ill-fated experiments of the first and second Banks of the United States in the early period of this country's independence, federal banking activity remained inconspicuous until the Civil War. The National Bank Act of 1863 created a truly national currency and eliminated much state influence in the monetary field.

Only in the twentieth century did the federal government exercise a controlling influence over the money supply with the creation of the Federal Reserve System in 1913. The importance of this central banking institution is so great that we shall examine it under a separate heading. The Great Crash of 1929 and the Depression which followed witnessed snowballing bank failures and a general breakdown of the credit mechanism. The financial crisis moved Congress to the creation of two new permanent agencies whose task is the prevention of similar disasters in the future. These two agencies are the Federal Deposit Insurance Corporation and the Securities and Exchange Commission.

Federal Deposit Insurance Corporation (FDIC)

By 1933 bank failures had so undermined public confidence in our financial institutions that even carefully managed banks were facing the danger of collapse. To calm the fears of depositors, Congress created the Federal Deposit Insurance Corporation, which has proven to be a most successful venture. This corporation now insures all deposits of admissible banks, both demand and savings deposits, up to $15,000. This sum is sufficient to cover most deposits in full. Nearly all banks accepting deposits from the public are insured by the FDIC and pay a modest premium for the privilege.

The result of this insurance has been spectacular. Since people are confident that their insured deposits are safe, bank runs have become a thing of the past. Even a rumor that the local bank may be shaky does not disturb its depositors too much, and their confidence makes its possible to

[3] Vault cash of a member bank is added to its reserve account balance to satisfy the legal reserve requirement.

overcome temporary difficulties due to bad management. The isolated bank failures that have occurred in the past thirty years have been generally the result of theft or embezzlement. The FDIC tries to prevent trouble by frequently inspecting those insured banks which are not members of the Federal Reserve System. Member banks are already taken care of by their own inspection staff.

Securities and Exchange Commission (SEC)

During the Great Depression, the performance of investment banking services had shown such glaring weaknesses that Congress created a regulatory agency to enforce better rules of conduct in the business. The Securities and Exchange Commission tries to prevent unethical practices in the investment banking field. It forces corporations whose shares are publicly traded to furnish much more information than was customary in the past. It also tries to make sure that the information is true and sufficiently complete to permit intelligent evaluation of the firm's position.

It will not allow a firm, for example, to omit mentioning a lawsuit which, if lost, might ruin the business, even though its present balance sheet might look rosy and optimistic.

The task of the SEC has been described as an effort to force corporations and their bankers to tell the truth. The SEC also forms a roadblock against abuse of inside information. It does not, however, try to protect the buyer of corporate stocks against losing his shirt as a result of his own bad judgment. The agency will not tell you whether or not you should buy or sell; it will not force you to take advantage of all the valuable information which becomes available. If you want to follow your hunch and the hot tip of the taxi driver who brings you downtown, you are free to lose your money in your own way.

THE FEDERAL RESERVE SYSTEM

The Federal Reserve System is the central bank of the United States. A relatively late arrival in the family of central banks, it was created by an act of Congress in December 1913. Similar institutions in Sweden, England, France, and Finland were already over a hundred years old at that time, and most other European countries had preceded us in the establishment of a central banking institution. Such institutions are charged with the management of money in the public interest.

The central bank of the United States differs in form, but not in substance, from its foreign counterparts, which maintain only one office in their respective capitals. The strong bias of the American majority against centralized control and government ownership was reflected in the creation of a decentralized institution. Twelve district banks, whose policies are harmonized by a central board, are owned, but not operated, by the member banks in each district. National monetary policy is the principal task of the entire system; its execution rests in the hands of a small group of men appointed to the direction of this organization. They are responsible to the nation, not to the stockholders.

Organizational Structure of the FRS

The Federal Reserve System is composed of the Board of Governors, the Federal Open Market Committee, the Federal Advisory Council, the Federal Reserve Banks, and the member banks.

Board of Governors. The Board of Governors is a federal institution located in Washington, D.C. It consists of seven members appointed by the President of the United States for staggered, fourteen-year terms. Each appointment must be confirmed by the Senate. The Board is responsible to Congress for national monetary policy and supervises its execution.

The Board also coordinates the operation of the entire Reserve System. The governors appoint three directors of each Federal Reserve Bank, including the chairman and his deputy. The president and first vice-president of each district bank are selected locally, but must be approved by the Board.

Federal Open Market Committee. The Federal Open Market Committee is the chief policy-making part of the system. Its twelve members include all seven governors, the president of the Federal Reserve Bank of New York and the presidents of four other district banks.

The Committee meets formally every three weeks to decide on policy changes concerning the money supply of the United States. These meetings are considered of such importance that most regional bank presidents participate, though only five of the twelve are voting members at any one time. The discussions focus on monetary reserve positions, interest rates, and instructions for the purchase and sale of federal securities. Orders are executed through the New York district bank.

Federal Advisory Council. The Federal Advisory Council is composed of one representative from each Reserve district; usually a well-known banker is selected for this responsibility, which he assumes in addition to his regular duties. The Council meets four times a year and keeps the governors informed of the financial situation in each district. The role of this group is purely advisory.

Federal Reserve Banks.   The Federal Reserve System divides the country, for administrative purposes, into twelve districts. Each district receives the services of one Federal Reserve Bank, and branch offices are established where the volume of business warrants it. District lines do not follow political subdivisions, with the result that some states are split between districts. For example, Missouri has two cities with district headquarters, Kansas City and St. Louis.

Each Federal Reserve Bank is owned by its member banks, which must buy stock when joining. Profit of operations is not the main objective of a Reserve Bank, though it never fails to earn enough to pay a 6-percent dividend. Under the law it must turn over its excess profits to the U.S. Treasury.

A Federal Reserve Bank has nine directors. Member banks elect six directors, and as mentioned before, the Board of Governors appoints three members (including the chairman). The men elected by the member banks are evenly divided between bankers and other civic leaders. Usually they are prominent citizens who accept this directorship as an additional assignment.

The district banks handle the banking business of their area, which includes many service functions, and execute financial policies determined by the central authorities of the system. Each bank, with the approval of the Board of Governors, decides on the rate of interest on loans to its members.

Member Banks.   About 6,000 private, commercial banks form the membership of the Federal Reserve System. Roughly three-fourths of these banks are national banks required by law to join the System; state-chartered banks compose the remainder. Less than half of the nation's commercial banks are members of the System, but they include all the large ones and hold almost 85 percent of all demand deposits. Nonmember banks are mostly smaller institutions which utilize the facilities of the System indirectly through arrangements with a member bank.

The obligations of membership are numerous. A member bank must maintain a legal reserve account with its district bank, comply with requirements for minimum capital, abide by all Federal Reserve regulations, and permit periodic examinations by Federal Reserve bank inspectors. The main privilege of a member bank is its ability to borrow directly from the Federal Reserve Bank. Most other important services are available to nonmembers indirectly, as our discussion of these services will now reveal.

The Service Functions of the FRS

Monetary policy is the main reason for the existence of a central bank, but the decentralized network of the Federal Reserve System has proven a useful instrument for the many services constituting the bulk of its routine daily activity. The district banks provide the currency for public circulation, keep legal reserve accounts, act as fiscal agents for the Treasury, promote the solvency of members with frequent inspections, and administer a national check-clearing system.

Currency Distribution. The amount of currency in circulation is controlled entirely by the demand of the people. Any commercial bank will gladly cash your check and hand you currency. A nonmember bank receives its supply of currency from a member bank; the member bank is supplied by its Federal Reserve Bank. A large volume of currency is stored for distribution by the Reserve Banks and is not counted as part of the money supply. When a member bank wants more currency, its reserve account is charged with the amount. The reverse takes place when the currency returns.

Legal Reserve Accounts. The law requires every member bank to keep an account with its district bank—a percentage of total deposits, determined by the Board of Governors, to be kept there in reserve. This amount is called the legal reserve, and any additional sum in the account is an excess reserve. Banks make constant use of these accounts. They send checks deposited by their customers and drawn on banks in other districts for credit to their reserve account, and these checks are balanced by those charged against the account of the member bank.

In spite of the heavy volume of business transacted with the reserve account every day, member banks try to keep sufficient reserves, and at the same time limit any excess. When they find that they do have excess reserves, they try to lend them to a bank that happens to have a deficit that day. Just a short time later the position may be reversed. These efforts to keep balances even have resulted in a lively market for "federal funds," excess reserve accounts which are transferred by check from one member to the other. Member banks may borrow directly from their Federal Reserve Bank and do so quite often, particularly when excess reserves shrink in the entire system.

Fiscal Agents. The U.S. Treasury collects and spends billions of dollars every month without any banking facilities of its own. The Federal Reserve Banks act as agents for the Treasury, keeping a multitude of Treasury accounts for different purposes. They cash Treasury checks and charge the appropriate account. Most of the deposits stem from checks sent as payment for taxes or government bonds. Some commercial banks also carry Treasury accounts under the supervision of the district bank.

Member Bank Inspections.   Federal Reserve inspectors check on the practices of member banks at frequent intervals. The early discovery of questionable activities is a service to the bank and to the entire financial system. The inspectors check not only possible violations of the law, but also any failure to conduct business in accordance with rules and directives of the Reserve Bank.

Clearinghouse.   The commercial banks in every large city maintain a clearinghouse. This is usually a room located in the financial district, where all commercial banks send their representatives to exchange checks drawn on the other banks in town. The out-of-town checks are turned over to the Reserve Bank for collection and credit to the reserve account. The Reserve Bank separates the checks by districts and mails them to the other district banks, who in turn send them to the bank on which they are drawn.

This procedure may seem cumbersome, but it keeps the cost of clearing checks low enough to furnish this service without charge. The volume of checks has increased steadily, and more than three billion pieces of paper go through the reserve clearing process each year. The need for fully automated handling is obvious, and modern equipment for sorting checks is used by most larger banks.

Policy Functions of the FRS

The demand for money rests with the people who use it. The supply of money is controlled by the Federal Reserve System and constitutes the main reason for the existence of a central bank. Our earlier discussion of prices and money has shown that changes in the money supply may cause repercussions on the price level and on the volume of business. When the economy is slowing down, the Federal Reserve Board boosts new enterprise with an "easy money" policy; during a boom the Board slows down price rises with a "tight money" policy. Money is "easy" to get when interest rates are low and bankers want to grant more loans; the same bankers charge higher interest and restrict loans when money is "tight."

We know already how money is created by commercial banks. The Reserve System puts pressure on its members to induce a fairly uniform national loan policy. How does the System go about exercising its influence?

The Board may tell the bankers that it wishes the supply raised or lowered. This technique is known as "moral suasion" and may show some results, particularly when most bankers agree that the change of policy is necessary. Other bankers, however, conform to the wishes of the System because they know that these wishes are backed by the power of more compelling action.

Persuasion alone lacks the necessary punch to keep the money supply systematically at the most desirable level. Congress has therefore provided the Federal Reserve System with more effective tools to accomplish its task. Three broad measures, when taken together, will alter the money supply in accordance with the desires of the policy makers. These techniques are the control of the discount rate, the open market operations, and the determination of reserve requirements. Let us see what happens when the Federal Reserve Board decides to reduce the money supply (the reverse procedure holds true when an increase is desired).

Discount Rate. The discount rate is the rate of interest charged by a Federal Reserve Bank for loans to its members. When the Reserve Bank wants to reduce the money supply, it raises the discount rate. Members hesitate to grant loans to their own customers when they have to borrow at rising rates.

A typical member bank, the "Friendly National Bank," may have been borrowing at a 3-percent discount rate and lending to customers at 6 percent. These customers need to pay back only after several months, in accordance with their individual loan agreements. In the meantime the discount rate rises to 3½ percent and then to 4 percent. Funds borrowed from the Federal Reserve cost more immediately upon announcement of the changed rate. The difference between the cost of the money and the return from it becomes smaller, and the "Friendly" banker is anxious to pay off his debt with the Reserve Bank. As his own customers repay their obligations, he will grant fewer new loans until his debt is wiped out.

The discount rate is not effective when the Friendly Bank is very liquid and does not need to borrow; in fact, as long as there are other member banks holding more reserves than they need for their own operations, Friendly may borrow these excess reserves from them when it happens to be short of funds for a few days. Only when all banks together experience a shortage of reserves do they feel strong pressure to borrow from Federal Reserve Banks and reduce their own loans to customers significantly. An overall shortage of reserves is usually the result of deliberate central bank policy exercised with still another tool.

Open Market Operations. The Federal Open Market Committee orders its New York agent to sell Treasury obligations in the open market. This sale has two immediate results.

1. The XYZ Corporation buys the securities from the FRS and pays for them with a check written against its account with Friendly. The Reserve bank clears the check and charges Friendly's reserve account with the full amount, $1 million.

Let us look at Friendly's situation now. It always keeps, say, 20 percent of its deposits in its reserve account. Before the Open Market sale, its reserves exceeded 20 percent by $500,000. It was not really concerned with the interest rate because it had no need to borrow. As the XYZ check clears, the deposits in the Friendly Bank drop $1 million and at the same time the need for reserves drops $200,000 (20 percent of $1 million). The balance in the reserve account drops, however, by a full million, and what was $500,000 in excess is now $300,000 short. Friendly must borrow $300,000 to maintain its customary reserves.

2. Another repercussion of the security sale is reflected in the interest rate. The Reserve Bank adds to the supply of these securities when it approaches the market. In order to reach the additional buyers needed for this sale, a higher rate of interest must be offered. The increase in the discount rate is now matched by higher rates on government securities. The cost of all other types of credit usually follows the same pattern. All loans become more expensive, and many creditors hesitate to make new loans as readily as before.

The Reserve System authorities are not concerned with the problems of a specific bank and its depositors. Even if the corporation which buys the securities keeps its accounts in a bank which can afford to clear the check entirely out of excess reserves, the sale will have the same impact on the money market. Since all banks are closely linked in their reserve position through the market for federal funds, any sizable drop in excess reserves will be felt by all of them. In 1966 the efforts of the Federal Reserve System to restrict the money supply were so effective that excess reserves gave way to a nationwide need, and banks had to borrow more than a total of $400 million.

Legal Reserve Requirements. Let us assume that "Friendly" is not the only banker with large excess reserves, but that every member bank from Boston to San Francisco has more reserves than it needs. Open market sales would have to become so large as to be impractical. In this case the third major tool of the central bank goes into action—the Board of Governors raises the reserve requirement.

Congress permits the Board to specify reserve requirements within a broad range. This tool has such a heavy impact that it is used only rarely. A 1-percent rise in reserve requirements reduces excess reserves of the banking system by over $1 billion. Such a drastic change is useful only as a last resort, and will be necessary if the reserve situation has gone virtually out of control.

Margin Requirements. The Federal Reserve System has been charged by Congress with the task of determining the percentage which may be borrowed for stock market speculation. Stock must be paid for in cash. The "margin" is the percentage of his own cash which a buyer of stocks must put up. The remainder may be borrowed from the broker. The law was intended to avoid repetition of abuses of this type of credit in the twenties, and it has, in fact, reduced excessive credit of this kind. As a tool to control the money supply, it has proven of little value.

The description of the tools of the Federal Reserve System should clarify the powerful position of the central bank. How this power can be used will be discussed in Chapter 18.

SUMMARY

Financial intermediaries are enterprises whose assets consist chiefly of intangibles or monetary claims. With total assets of more than $700 billion, they operate the exchange facilities of the economy, directing funds to the activity with the highest demand.

Many types of intermediaries specialize in different financial functions. Savings institutions gather unused funds in small amounts from many individuals. Insurance companies pool risk premiums while granting protection, and are able to assist large borrowers. Personal trust departments receive their funds, frequently in large amounts, from wealthy persons and invest them with caution. Finance companies grant loans to consumers with money borrowed from other banks. Investment bankers and brokers raise huge sums for the use of corporate enterprise by distributing securities on a nationwide scale.

Government lending institutions are numerous, with special functions in many areas, particularly in agriculture and housing.

Commercial banks have a special role as financial intermediaries, since they alone may open demand deposits transferable by check. They create money by opening loan deposits which are withdrawn and transferred from bank to bank and which do not vanish until repaid. Their ability to create money is limited only by currency withdrawals, adverse clearing balances, and legal reserve requirements.

The Federal Deposit Insurance Corporation has successfully prevented runs on banks since 1934. It insures demand and time deposits in most banks for a small premium.

The Securities and Exchange Commission protects the investor against misinformation and malpractices by persons with inside knowledge. It does not guarantee the value of stocks.

The Federal Reserve System is the central bank of the United States. It controls the nation's money supply; the demand for money depends on the public.

The System's central offices are in Washington, D.C. The Board of Governors directs its policy; the Federal Open Market Committee details policy execution, particularly in connection with securities operations. The Federal Advisory Council makes sure that the policy makers in the Capital do not lose touch with the country at large.

The decentralized operations of the System are based in twelve district banks and their branches. They manage the day-by-day banking business of their area. The member banks of the System use the facilities of their Reserve Banks while assuming the numerous obligations of membership.

The service functions of the Federal Reserve System include shipping of currency, maintaining legal reserve accounts, acting as fiscal agent for the Treasury, inspecting member banks, and clearing the ever-growing volume of checks for the banks of the entire nation.

The policy functions of the System control the money supply by determining discount rates, engaging in open market operations to buy or sell federal securities, and by regulating legal reserve requirements.

Discussion Questions

1. Why are life insurance companies considered financial intermediaries?
2. Distinguish investment bankers from trust departments in commercial banks.
3. Should a stock exchange be subject to detailed government controls?
4. No banker creates any money, but all banks together do. How?
5. Why are national banks required to keep a specific reserve with their Federal Reserve Bank?
6. What is the role of the Federal Open Market Committee?
7. What are adverse clearing balances? How do they affect a banker?
8. Distinguish the policy functions from the service functions of the Federal Reserve System. Which require more personnel? Which have more impact on the economy?
9. What is the role of mutual funds?

Suggested Reading

Commission on Money and Credit, *Federal Credit Programs*. Englewood Cliffs, N.J., Prentice-Hall, 1963.

GOLDSMITH, RAYMOND W., *Financial Intermediaries in the American Economy Since 1900*. Princeton, N.J., Princeton, 1958.

The Federal Reserve System: Its Purposes and Functions. Washington, D.C., Board of Governors of the Federal Reserve System, 1954.

TRESCOTT, PAUL B., *Financing American Enterprise*. New York, Harper & Row, 1963.

15

THE NATION'S INCOME

"Prosperity" will rank high in any list of goals selected by the American people. What makes a nation prosperous? Not the wealth enjoyed by its rich citizens, nor the castles and the jewels accumulated in the past. Prosperity results from present efforts, from the goods and services which are being added now and from the incomes paid for them. A nation's income and its change are the yardstick of economic performance.

This chapter will clarify the meaning of national income, its measurement, and its composition. The characteristics of the determinants of income and the forces influencing the level of national activity will then be discussed. Income changes and their repercussions will conclude the chapter.

WHAT IS NATIONAL INCOME?

National income in its broadest sense measures the total activity of a country over a period of time. This yardstick calculates the current flow of incomes earned by such owners of resources as workers, proprietors, and business firms; it is a *flow concept* and not a catalog of accumulated wealth. Income is not a measure of the value of oil in the ground, but of the gallons of oil pumped, refined, and sold to the consumer during a current year.

National income differs sharply from government income, the amount collected by the Internal Revenue Service to pay for federal expenditures. The income of the federal government, large as it is, represents only one small share of the total economic effort of the nation. Government income is a part of the national income.

The nation's income consists of all final goods and services produced during a given period of time. Often referred to as the gross national product (GNP), *it is the nation's output calculated at market prices* and provides the most popular yardstick of economic performance; consumers as a whole cannot possibly buy more than total output even if their incomes were to increase overnight like manna from heaven. Later in this chapter we will go into the difficulties which arise when consumers decide to buy collectively less than all the current output.

Circular Flow

Income payments and output flows create a continuous circle of goods produced and earnings received, as shown in Figure 15-1. People furnish their services to business to produce goods, which goods they in turn are eager to buy from those firms. The inner circle shows this flow of goods and services. The outer circle illustrates that people receive income for their services and spend it again to pay business for its products.

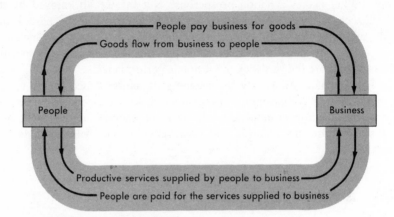

FIG. 15-1. The Circular Flow of National Income

The two flows of payments and services are identical. This definition leaves out no activity or payment. Wages, interest, and profits are all included as earnings. Assume that the businessman produces the wrong good and cannot sell it. How will the product total and the earnings total result in the same figure? If the firm cannot sell its output, the profit earned by its owner may be a loss, but the accounts are still in balance.

This equality of the two approaches is a matter of definition and does not imply that the result is good or bad. The flow of business may speed up or slow down, it may put everybody to work or leave some unemployed, but it always shows the same total for income and output.

Income Viewed as Money Earned

Income is a sum of earnings and includes all types of payments flowing to the owners of productive services. Wages and salaries make up the largest share, but money is received also for other services. For example, interest is earned for letting others use available liquid funds; rents are paid for the use of property; and profits result from sales which bring in more than total costs. If there is a loss, it is deducted. These total earnings include the profits of corporations without deduction for their taxes.

Such a method of adding up incomes can easily lead to strange results. If gross profits of corporations are included, the dividends paid to shareholders must not be counted again.

Income Viewed as Output Produced

The production of goods and services may not look like income at first glance. Let us keep in mind that all earnings result from some sort of service. People are paid for producing output. Their total earnings represent the total product of the nation. When measuring the nation's activity, we are not concerned with the problem of how hard the people work, but what they accomplish—and this means output.

How do you add the national product or output? Tons of coal, gallons of oil, baskets of apples, and carloads of refrigerators must be reduced to a common denominator so that they can be added together. The one thing they all have in common is a market price. The sum of all goods and services produced, figured at their market price, is the national product.

Total product and total income are the same in this definition. All earnings buy all products, no more, no less. Regardless of how rich we are, we cannot acquire output which has not been produced. But what about unsold output? In computing current income, the unsold output is counted as an increase in inventory. Unsold output has in a sense been sold to the producer by his suppliers and workers who expect to be paid for this contribution. The producer may not have intended to spend his income in this fashion, but he acquired the product nonetheless.

How to Figure the National Product

Value Added. The technical problems of measurement of the national product are formidable. The same product may be counted twice or three times as it changes hands from raw material to finished product. The problem is solved by counting only the value added by each producer. A steel company may sell steel to an automobile producer. He uses steel costing $200 in making a car which he sells to the dealer for $2,000; the dealer sells the car and delivers it, properly checked, to you for $2,500. The steel company reports only the value of steel in the national product; the car manufacturer reports only the value added by his firm, $1,800 in this example ($2,000 − $200); the dealer reports only the $500 added by his business.

Inventories. The flow of products on the way to the consumer is called "inventory." Inventories include raw materials, such as coal which has been mined and stored by the mine or by the steel mill that bought it. Also included in inventories is the half-finished furniture which will be ready for sale next year. The warehouses of the wholesaler and the shelves of the retailer are full of goods ready for sale but not yet transferred to the final consumer. All this mountain of products belongs to the inventory of the nation.

The total amount of goods in the process of manufacture and distribution is naturally very large because the pipelines of business must always remain filled. In the income accounts, the emphasis centers on the changes in this inventory; are we selling more from inventory than is being added, or is new production outpacing sales? Fluctuations in the size of inventories furnish an important clue for estimating economic developments in the near future. When inventories are low, production must speed up to fill the pipelines; excessively large inventories point to a slower output in the immediate future.

Money versus Real Income. Income comparisons take a long time, and the problem of unstable money values can become acute, as we have discovered earlier. The statistical information on national income is, therefore, frequently presented in two ways: "Money income" shows current data with the dollar figures actually collected at the time, while "real income" adjusts all dollar values to some base year with an index is unchanged by the vagaries of the dollar. Money income is sometimes called "current dollar income," and real income may also be shown as "constant dollar income."

INCOME STATISTICS

The term *national income,* or *national product,* has been used as a broad, generic concept. When it comes to actual measurement of the nation's economic performance, more precision is in order. The statistical problems of estimation are awesome indeed, and their discussion goes beyond the scope of this book. The details of finding reliable data can be safely left to the statisticians in the Department of Commerce, whose efforts are published periodically in their monthly publication, the *Survey of Current Business.* The information often makes the headlines of newspapers and magazines and can be quite bewildering unless the technical nomenclature is well understood.[1] We shall now clarify the meaning of their findings as they appear in Figure 15-2.

[1] Every number of the *Survey of Current Business* carries a set of fourteen tables of national income statistics, a valuable source of factual information.

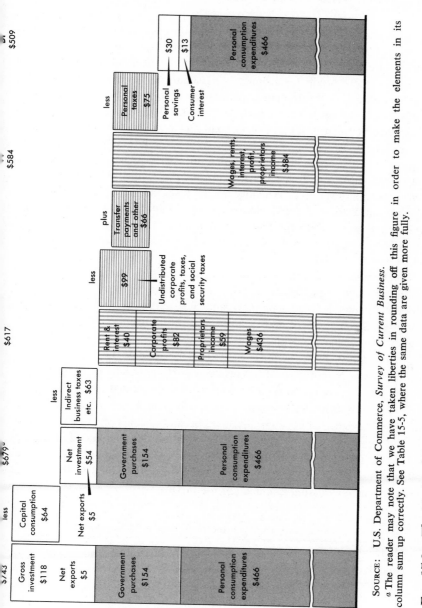

SOURCE: U.S. Department of Commerce, *Survey of Current Business.*

a The reader may note that we have taken liberties in rounding off this figure in order to make the elements in its column sum up correctly. See Table 15-5, where the same data are given more fully.

FIG. 15-2.   **The National Income Accounts, 1966**

Major Measures of Production and Income Flows

(billions of dollars)

Product Flow Versus Income Earned

The statistical information can be grouped by product flows or by income earned in accordance with the two streams of output and payment shown by the circular flow diagram. The sum of national output at market prices leads to the "product accounts." Personal consumption expenditures (abbreviated C), government expenditures (G), and investment expenditures (I) make up the total national product. We need to add the small difference between products sent abroad and goods imported in exchange; the difference is shown as "net exports." This sum is GNP, the most inclusive measurement of national economic performance. Investment expenditures include both new investments and replacements of existing goods which are no longer used. When we deduct from this gross investment figure the amount estimated for depreciation, we obtain a net investment figure which makes up NNP; the first two columns in Figure 15-2 represent the product accounts, the total output of the nation during one year $(C + I + G = GNP)$.

The same result can be obtained if we add all sources of income earned in the process of producing the output. Wages are the largest part; proprietors' income is listed separately since it is partly wages and partly other forms of earnings. Rent and interest paid to the owners of resources together with corporate profit should add up to the same amount obtained before as GNP. Profit includes here the amount paid by corporations to their owners, corporate profit taxes, and any sum saved by corporations. Profit may not always be positive, but can be represented by a loss.

The last three columns in Figure 15-2 show the result of adding incomes earned. While, logically, output and income figures must give us the same totals, the statistical differences are considerable. Let us reconcile the two approaches. Indirect business taxes and capital consumption allowances are not income payments, but they are included in the market price at which all output is added to form GNP.

TABLE 15-1.   Output Compared with Income Earned in Measuring GNP

Output Produced		Income Earned	
Personal consumption expenditures		Wages	
+ Government purchases		+ Proprietors' income	
+ Investment expenditures (gross)	$= GNP =$	+ Rent	
+ Exports (net)		+ Interest	
		+ Corporate profit	
		+ Capital consumption allowance	Nonincome
		+ Indirect business taxes	

Gross National Product (GNP)

As we noted earlier, gross national product is a rough measurement compiled by the Department of Commerce which includes all output, though some products may merely replace obsolete goods. It is a relatively simple and widely used yardstick. The general direction of economic trends is revealed by GNP estimates just as accurately as it would be by more refined series of data.

The largest component of GNP is total consumption expenditures, which were $466 billion in 1966; like other people, the government buys goods and services, both for consumption and for investment. It buys cars and airplanes, computers and typewriters, but most of all it buys the services of over two million people working in an infinite variety of public jobs. These government expenditures appear separately in the product accounts, though they become part of the various uses of income earned shown in the other statistical series. In fact, it is quite possible to distribute all government purchases between consumption and investment expenditures and eliminate the separate category for government. A study of economic performance requires, however, detailed knowledge of the behavior of the public and private sectors separately since they do not always follow the same pattern. Government purchases are a very large item in the nation's total performance; they were $154 billion in 1966.

Business expenditures of $118 billion, shown in Figure 15-2 as "investments," complete the total buying in the economy. The foreign sector, however, introduces a slight complication. Economic performance includes the production of goods sold abroad while excluding the domestic purchase of foreign goods. The total output, therefore, is adjusted for the difference between exports and imports, an export surplus in 1966 of $5 billion.

In recent years GNP has increased at a fast pace, reflecting the growth of a booming economy. From $560 billion in 1962, it has risen steadily to $743 billion in 1966.

Net National Product (NNP)

The only difference between GNP and NNP stems from the estimate of business expenditures, or investments. Estimates of net investment shown in NNP reduce the gross investment data by an amount that represents replacement of unserviceable or obsolete goods. The sum representing replacement, $64 billion in 1966, is called "capital consumption allowance" or, more commonly, "depreciation." [2] NNP in 1966 amounted to $679 billion.

[2] Capital consumption allowances differ slightly from depreciation in the statistical compilation; the distinction is unimportant for the casual user, however.

Depreciation allowance is an important concept which needs clarification. Estimates of obsolescence could become very arbitrary without specific rules. In actual use, however, depreciation represents that part of the cost of capital goods which a firm may legally deduct from current income. An example will clarify this.

Assume that a firm buys a big, new, expensive machine. It borrows some of the purchase price, because the manager of the business feels sure that the new equipment will pay for itself in a few years, thanks to its greater efficiency. The cost of this machine is so great that it would wipe out all profits if it had to be charged completely to the current expenses of the purchase year. The firm would probably not want to do this anyway, but more important is the fact that the law does not even permit such accounting practices. The firm estimates the length of the machine's useful life and charges only a proportionate share to the current cost of operations. If the cost of the machine was $50,000 and its useful life five years, $10,000 will be the amount of annual depreciation.

During a period of prosperity business firms are always interested in raising depreciation as much as the Internal Revenue Service will allow. Profits are subject to high taxation, but depreciation is considered a cost by the law and may therefore be deducted from income before profit taxes are figured. The expected length of useful life of new equipment often becomes a matter of controversy. Tax officials emphasize durability, and may claim that it takes twenty years for a machine to wear out completely and need replacement. The firm points out that technological progress renders the equipment obsolete in five years, regardless of its physical condition.

National Income (NI)

National income as a broad concept refers to all the measurements of a nation's economic performance. It is unfortunate that the term is also used in a narrow sense to indicate a specific set of statistical estimates. The statistical value of national income can be obtained by deducting indirect business taxes from NNP, or by adding the various components of income earned. Wages, rents, interest, and profit (including proprietors' income, which has some features of all the others), amounted to a total of $617 billion in 1966.

Indirect business taxes include sales and excise taxes, customs duties, and business property taxes, all of which are added to the cost of the product and thereby increase the market price beyond the amount of income earned.

Personal Income (PI)

Personal income is a statistical measure of the earnings received by people. You may feel that all business is owned by people, government is controlled by people, and that, therefore, people receive all incomes earned in the nation. As a practical matter, however, people are concerned only with that part of the nation's income which they own directly.

The difference between the personal income data and the usually larger national income series results from the fact that corporate profits and direct business taxes are included in national income but are not part of people's earnings, except for any portion paid out to owners as dividends. This difference is compensated for in part by payments from the government which add directly to individual incomes in the form of social security checks. These additions to personal income are called transfer payments; they are paid by reason of provisions of the law rather than for services rendered. Funds are transferred by the government from taxpayers to recipients entitled to these payments.

Personal income in 1966 was $584 billion. The detailed sources of personal income were shown in Table 12-2.

Interest is shown in Figure 15-2 with different amounts in all three compilations of income earned. The distinction is not important for the casual reader but is offered here for clarification. In the *NI* series, interest includes only payments for funds loaned by bankers to firms, and other similar transactions. It does not include interest paid by the government or by consumers, which is treated as a transfer payment and added to compose *PI*. Since interest payments can not be consumed or saved, consumer interest is shown alone and separately in the *DI* series.

Disposable Income (DI)

After deducting personal taxes, such as individual income taxes, from personal income, one comes to the smallest statistical measure, the disposable income. This last series reflects the amount actually available to buy the goods which satisfy individual wants; it is also the amount people may either spend or save. Disposable income in 1966 was $509 billion.

Naturally, all five sets of data follow the same trend; they go up or down together. Why do we make, then, these subtle distinctions? When the economy is booming and all signs point upward, the information makes us happy and no details are needed. But the outlook changes when the overall performance does not look prosperous, and people want action to overcome a recession. Detailed information then becomes essential before the right steps can be taken toward improvement. Some key factors will now be studied in more detail. Of particular importance to the determination of income flows are the concepts of consumption, savings, and investment.

CONSUMPTION, SAVINGS, AND INVESTMENT

A breakdown of the total output of the nation into various parts facilitates an analysis of the information. You may, for example, follow the annual changes in specific industries whose products are all part of the total income, or you may compare major categories of production activity as shown in Table 15-2. The relative size of each group, as well as its changes, is sometimes of special interest.

TABLE 15-2. GNP by Type of Product, 1966
(*billions of dollars*)

Classification	Amount
Durable goods	154.6
Nondurable goods	225.0
Services	287.2
Construction	76.5
Total GNP	743.3

SOURCE: U.S. Department of Commerce, *Survey of Current Business.*

Consumption

Personal consumption expenditures of $466 billion in 1966 constituted the largest share of total output. These were the goods and services people bought, the final products in the hands of the consumer. The money spent on consumption is a good indicator of economic performance from the viewpoint of want satisfaction.

Personal satisfaction, of course, cannot be measured by a dollar yardstick, because there is no perfect correlation between the goods people buy and their happiness. A toy that breaks on Christmas morning is an all too familiar example of this distinction; but consumption expenditures are generally assumed to satisfy the buyers and give some clue as to how well human wants are being satisfied.

During a war, GNP may shoot up considerably without satisfying consumer wants any better than before, because all the additional activity will probably be directed toward production of war material. Whether or not this additional output will divert production away from consumer goods depends on the availability of resources for war production. When many factories and people are unemployed, as was the case in the 1930's, war orders do not necessarily reduce consumption at all because the new production constitutes additional business. In any comparison of living standards, personal consumption expenditures are more meaningful than income totals.

Consumption Changes. In a poor economy nearly all income will be consumed because the entire society operates close to the starvation level. Under such circumstances, changes in consumption reflect changes in the harvest of the crops. In a wealthy economy, however, not all consumer goods are needed for survival, and many purchases may be postponed when consumers are pessimistic about their future income.

Changes in consumer behavior are seldom very noticeable, but even a shift of as little as 1 percent involves billions of dollars because total consumption is so large. Any deviation from the existing pattern becomes a significant influence on the steady flow of production.

Consumption usually exceeds 90 percent of the disposable income and is almost two-thirds of gross national product. The ratio of consumption to disposable income is relatively stable, while other components of GNP may fluctuate more readily.

The Propensity to Consume. The percentage of disposable income which is spent on consumer goods and services is called "the propensity to consume." It is a ratio or percentage comparing consumption with income. A similar comparison is calculated for savings and income and is known as "the propensity to save." A comparison of investment and income is "the propensity to invest." [3]

As personal income becomes higher, consumption will become larger as an absolute amount, but will decline as a percentage of income. It is commonly observed that wealthy people do most of the saving, while lower incomes are consumed entirely by their recipients. Although present income is of course the main determinant of current spending, expectations about the income trend in the near future have considerable influence on present consumption. When a man feels secure in his job and is sure to get a raise soon, he is willing to spend a larger share of his present income.

A rising income will naturally result in greater expenditures. Most people will spend more as their income improves, and a few may even

---

[3] The propensity to consume (abbreviated PC) must not be confused with the share of an increase or decrease in income consumed at any time. Assuming consumption equals $93 and income $100, $PC = \$93/\$100$, or 93 percent. A rise of $10 in income does not necessarily imply that $9.30 of the increase will be consumed. The share of the increase spent on consumption is called the "marginal propensity to consume" (MPC) and is likely to fluctuate more than *PC*.

splurge and spend the entire increase. The majority, however, will spend a smaller share of the additional income for some time after the increase until their consumption habits adjust to the higher level.

Savings

Assume for the moment that all income is spent promptly. In this case, business receives the consumers' money for its output and it can continue to manufacture the same goods as in the past. It cannot make any time-consuming changes because it lacks accumulated reserves; everything is absorbed as fast as it can be produced. In a modern economy, however, some income is not spent immediately but is saved instead.

Savings can take many forms. An old miser may hide dollar bills under his bed, but most people buy securities or leave their savings in a bank account. It does not matter very much to the economy which technique the saver prefers. In any case we realize that the savers will not claim the full amount of their incomes in consumption goods. The producers know this, too, and will devote part of their income on new equipment and other capital goods. If the production of capital goods accurately reflects the savings of income earners, all consumer goods are bought and all capital goods are available for future output. An excess in the output of consumption goods will not be bought by income earners who wish to save more. Total consumption, however, must be the same for both the buyers and the sellers; the unsold consumption goods become, therefore, a part of the inventory of the producer and are considered a share of his total investment, though not always a voluntary one.

We are defining as investment all goods produced but not sold to consumers, and as savings all income not spent for consumption goods. In this case, savings and investment are necessarily the same at every moment. It is easy to visualize savings as an amount of income not spent by individuals. We must distinguish, however, between personal savings, representing that part of disposable income not spent for personal outlays and total savings in the economy, which include the far larger share of income withheld from consumption by business firms. Total savings decisions are not only deliberate efforts to refrain from consumption; they also represent the residual amount left over after all bills are paid. Total, or gross, savings flow primarily from three sources, as shown in Table 15-3: personal savings, retained corporate profit, and depreciation allowance.

A difference in the figures for savings and investments is due to government accounts. Government transactions seldom balance tax collections and expenditures. A surplus in collections would be savings by government to be added statistically to the private sources of savings; a deficit

TABLE 15-3.   Sources of Savings in the U.S., 1966
(*billions of dollars*)

Source	Amount
Personal savings	29.8
Retained corporate profit (adjusted)	26.2
Depreciation allowance	63.5
Total gross private savings	119.5

SOURCE: U.S. Department of Commerce, *Survey of Current Business.*

in government tax collection results in a reduction of the figure for private savings. Any remaining difference is due to difficulties in estimating data exactly and is shown as a statistical discrepancy.

Personal Savings.   The part of disposable income which is not spent is saved. Personal consumption expenditures account for most spending; interest paid by consumers is added to consumption, though it is not spent for consumption goods. Personal savings constitute roughly 7 percent of disposable income. This ratio of savings to disposable income is the propensity to save. A slow rise in income is usually accompanied by a gradual increase not only of dollars saved, but also of the percent of income saved. A sudden drop in income has, however, some very surprising initial consequences.

The number of dollars saved from reduced incomes will, of course, be smaller. But the propensity to save, the share of disposable income saved at the beginning of a recession, for example, will often actually go up. This result seems to be quite illogical. One might expect people to continue their spending habits as long as possible and to give up saving in order to adjust to a lower income. The strange pattern of a rising share of savings at the start of a recession is sometimes called "the paradox of thrift."

This odd behavior is not as surprising as it seems, and there is a perfectly rational explanation for it. Most personal savings take the form of contractual arrangements, as we have seen already. Such contracts covering life insurance policies or installment loans, for example, usually include severe penalties for nonfulfillment. When a recession sets in, people will try to maintain these savings programs as long as they can to avoid major losses. They will refrain from buying a new TV set on installments in order to save the refrigerator which is still being paid for. The unsold TV set becomes a drop in consumption; the part of income paid to the finance company maintains the former level of savings.

Should the recession last long enough, the picture will change. Cancelled savings contracts will not be renewed while postponed consumption expenditures become more urgent, and finally a more normal pattern of spending and saving is reestablished on a lower level.

Retained Corporate Profit. The most volatile source of savings is retained profit. It jumped from $16.6 billion in 1963 to $26.2 billion in 1966. Corporations do not have to pay out all profits to their stockholders, but only that part which the board of directors declares as dividends. Most corporate managements avoid a reduction of dividends whenever possible; they declare the same dividend for many years, regardless whether the times are good or bad. Such a policy is possible only by keeping dividends low, even though profits may be high, because there is no assurance that income will stay close to a peak. The part of the net profit which is not paid to the stockholders constitutes corporate savings, or retained profit.

An example will illustrate how much this type of savings will fluctuate. Assume that the gross profit of a corporation in a good year is $8 million, and in a bad one only $4 million. The firm always pays dividends of $2 million to stockholders. Taxes are about 50 percent of the gross profit. In a good year the firm pays a tax of $4 million, plus its normal dividend of $2 million, and retains $2 million. In a bad year the taxes are cut in half to $2 million, the dividend is unchanged, but the retained savings have been wiped out completely.

Depreciation Allowance. The nature of capital consumption has been discussed earlier, but its inclusion in private savings needs clarification. Let us say that the accounts of a firm show $200,000 gross income (not profit) for the year, the entire amount of which has been spent to pay its bills. This firm appears to have accomplished absolutely nothing during the year, but we must investigate the situation more closely before we can tell for certain. If all the payments were made for materials and labor in current use, the firm is, to be sure, in a bad position. It is possible, however, that $50,000 was paid for new machines which will raise the productivity next year. This expenditure could be made with the help of the depreciation allowance on equipment bought in earlier years. Actual cost of operations was only $150,000; the remaining $50,000 did not have to be considered profit subject to taxes, but represented a true saving to the firm which could be used to pay for more machines. Substantial savings from depreciation not only reduces a firm's taxes, but also tends to encourage a steady volume of orders for new equipment to keep up to date and fully competitive.

The size of the depreciation account is an important factor in judging the profitability of a business. Suppose that two firms make the same product and show the same profit. One firm has no depreciation charges because all its equipment is so old that the costs have been fully charged long ago. The other firm has high depreciation charges because it keeps the plant constantly modern. The policy is expensive, but the increased efficiency is worth the cost, and it won't be long before the outmoded firm will find itself in real difficulties.

Investment

Financial Investment.   Investment is a very popular concept, a word with a good connotation which is approved of by most people. When a man refers to his investments, he thinks of the stocks and bonds in a safe deposit box, of the rental house he bought with some money he inherited, and the mutual fund certificate for which he is still paying. We have used the word in this sense in Chapter 14; for greater clarity, this concept is called *financial investment.*

Real Investment.   In a discussion of the national product, investment has a different meaning. It refers to that part of total production which is not intended for immediate consumption, to the output of the capital goods sector of economic activity. From the viewpoint of the economy, the acquisition of a hundred shares of stock is not an investment; a piece of paper has changed hands, but no new goods have been added to the total product of the economy. When a corporation spends funds to build a factory or install new machines, *real investment* in the economic sense takes place.

Total private investment in 1966 reached $118 billion and consisted largely of new construction and purchases of more modern machinery. Twenty-four billion was invested by the government in the construction of new buildings, bridges, and similar structures.

Investment Categories.   All goods and services produced and not sold to consumers are counted as part of real investments. The special role of government is disregarded in this definition because its purchases may well be classified for the moment as consumption, or investment spending. Investments consist of (1) new capital goods such as a turbine in a power plant, or the whole plant itself; (2) changes in the value of unfinished goods which are filling the pipelines of industry, such as steel bars, car fenders, or sheets of aluminum; and (3) additions to the inventories of consumer goods which are being held for sale.

The percentage of income invested is called the propensity to invest, similar to the consumption and savings propensities. However, changes in investment decisions show a markedly different pattern, with a tendency to rise and fall more rapidly due to their peculiar nature.

Investment Decisions.   Investment decisions are made primarily by businessmen. Of course, individuals build houses or start business activities— for example, they use their own savings to buy a truck and haul goods—but the bulk of all investment depends on a relatively small number of men who decide the fate of large corporations. These individuals are exposed to similar information; they proceed logically and often reach the same conclusions as a result. Therefore, business generally expands or retrenches as a whole.

Investment decisions depend on many different influences. Some of these are economic; others are largely psychological. Wars, for example, have a profound impact on investment because they create expectations of rising demand and shortages in many areas. Firms realize that it is wise to expand while materials are still available. Experience has shown that in wartime prices are likely to rise, an expectation that makes current investments always look cheap.

Investment Determinants.   The current trend of income exerts a powerful economic influence on investments. Rising incomes promote investments because the demand for most goods is increasing and requires expanded facilities. Larger business incomes help firms accumulate more savings and facilitate the financing of new projects. A broad upward trend causes optimistic expectations for the future and gives the appearance of probable success even to risky investments. A general expansion in an industry may force reluctant businessmen to invest in modernization in spite of their private misgivings; they fear they will be left behind and lose their market if they fail to follow the trend. In addition, new inventions and improved technology are a strong influence on investment decisions. Population growth also stimulates new business and favors an optimistic view of the future.

Investment Fluctuations.   Income and investments interact. Higher incomes cause more investments, which in turn increases activity and raises incomes even more. Unfortunately, this spiral effect holds equally true when investments and incomes are shrinking. Pessimism can also be contagious. Why build a newer and better plant when only half the present capacity is in use and the operations are showing a loss? Only few leaders of business dare to swim against the tide and commit the fate of their enterprises to a gamble based on personal optimism. Even the slightest recession shifts many expansion projects from immediate execution to a wait-and-see category.

Volatility is the chief characteristic of investments; all investors base their decisions on expectations. And since they all receive substantially the same information, both optimism and pessimism spread rapidly, causing similar changes in the investment patterns of many firms.

Investment Stabilization.   Changes in total investment figures do not seem to occur nearly as quickly as do the sudden swings in new investment decisions. The execution of investment plans take time. New orders for steel may pour in suddenly, but new steel mills are still years away from completion. In the meantime, existing facilities can be used to capacity; this change in pace is accomplished much sooner. Immediate deliveries, however, can be increased only from existing inventories.

Any sudden change in business outlook will be cushioned by fluctuations in inventories. The normal amount of goods in the pipelines of business is so large that inventory changes may amount to billions of dollars. A sudden rise in demand will be accommodated first by a drop in inventories. When consumers quit buying, inventories will rise until plants can adjust to the new situation and lower their output. Steel production, for example, continues as scheduled, though some steel orders are canceled and new orders do not arrive at the expected rate of speed. As finished steel starts piling up, the steel makers gradually revise their production schedule and order a cutback.

This stabilizing function of inventories, however, is limited to a very short time span. As inventories rise, more goods remain unsold. Unless this trend is reversed promptly, factories will shut down and people will be laid off as firms seek to bring their inventories in line with their lower expectations. The shrinking volume of business requires a smaller stock on hand and sugests a reduction of inventories which were considered normal before. The swollen accumulation of goods already in existence looks even larger under these conditions and discourages additional activity. New production will drop not only to the level of current business, but even below this mark in order to remove the excessive inventory on hand; this effort to compensate actually aggravates a difficult situation and makes fast-changing inventories the weather vane of business fluctuations.

HOW DOES INCOME CHANGE?

The nation's income is the yardstick used to measure the changing performance of the economy over a period of time. It would be nice to imagine a high level of economic activity which could be frozen into position, with everything the same ever after. We can dream about it, but we would not like the result, apart from the fact that it is just not possible.

Two reasons make a growing income necessary: the population is rising, with more goods and services needed to provide the same level of satisfaction; and people always want more tomorrow than they do today. The lady who stands in front of her clothes closet, quite unhappy because she "doesn't have a thing to wear," represents the typical attitude of humanity. Few people prefer the same old thing for long. Change is inevitable, though it is not always an improvement.

The fluctuations of national income have many causes; they express themselves in changes of consumption, savings, and investment. The spotlight thus focuses once again on these determinants of income change.

Savings = Investments

The circular flow of income has shown us the identity of output and earnings. The total product of the nation is composed of goods which are sold to consumers and producers.[4] What is not sold to consumers is invested in accordance with the definition offered earlier. We may summarize this information in abbreviated form:

$$\text{Consumption } (C) + \text{Investment } (I) = \text{Income } (Y)$$

Total earnings are either spent on the purchase of consumption goods, or they are used in another way. If not spent for consumption, they are saved in line with our earlier definition:

$$\text{Consumption } (C) + \text{Savings } (S) = \text{Income } (Y)$$

If we combine the information in the equations, we notice that consumption and income are identical in both cases, which leads to the simple, logical conclusion:

$$\text{Savings } (S) = \text{Investments } (I)$$

This algebraic truism may seem rather startling. Savers and investors are different groups of the population, and savings do not fluctuate nearly so much as investments. Moreover, many people save, but only a few take care of the investing. A small part of investment funds is saved by the investors themselves; a larger share of savings is gathered by financiers and loaned to investors. Savings and investment decisions are quite independent from each other.

In the absence of any desire to match savings and investments, and in view of their very different characteristics, it is surprising to find that the two concepts are identical. How does it come about?

Plans and Achievements

Let us break into the circular flow of production and income and assume that business wants to produce exactly as much in the future as it produces in the current period. Unfortunately, the consumers no longer desire the same amount of consumption goods, and some products remain unsold, becoming part of the inventory of business firms. At this moment the consumers are spending less and saving more, probably using their extra

----

[4] Government purchases are included in this very broad and all-inclusive breakdown and will not be treated separately in the interests of simplicity.

cash to reduce their debts on the house and the car. The increase in savings is matched by greater investments in the form of unsold inventories.

The repercussions will not be long in coming. The output of consumer goods will be reduced promptly, some workers will lose their jobs, others will stop working overtime, and the lower income payments will force wage earners to reduce their purchases. Savings will drop at the same time, since consumers can no longer afford them, and total savings become equal to the now lower level of actual investment.

This description of a beginning downward spiral clarifies the distinction between the *actual* level of savings and investment, which are always identical, and the *plans* for future periods, which may differ considerably. When the plans for future output optimistically exceed current production, an upward spiral is in the making. When the current savings level is higher than planned investments, a downward trend must be expected.

Verbal Description of the Adjustment Process.   Let us assume that investment plans are far more ambitious than the expected level of savings will permit. What is likely to happen in such a case?

The businessmen who want to build new plants and buy new equipment will place their orders as they have planned. If these orders go to firms whose factories are only partially in use, and if enough unemployed workers can be hired to fill these new orders, the result will be pleasant indeed. Payrolls rise, boosting both consumption and savings; profits increase to raise business savings; and inventories shrink as most firms make use of them to fill orders while new production is under way. The result shows that both savings and investments actually rise together in a gradual and steady upward trend.

The outcome will be different if no unemployed workers or plants are available to handle all the new orders received. In this case the optimistic investment plans will not be completed. Much will be heard about bottlenecks in steel and copper, or in concrete and aluminum. The businessmen are assured that the investments will be completed all right with just a few months' delay. The newspapers are likely to inform you that the economy is going through "a stretchout period." Savings do not rise substantially, but investments remain close to the previous level and more ambitious plans are delayed.

Should many businessmen insist that their project must not be delayed, they may offer more money to anyone lucky enough to receive the scarce material now. If the practice becomes widespread, the same limited amount of goods will be traded at higher prices, which may give the impression of greater savings and investments than before, at least in monetary terms.

The opposite will hold true if investment projects remain below the expected level of savings. The lack of new orders will lead to layoffs and lower incomes; savings will be reduced to the level of actual investments.

Numerical Description of the Adjustment Process.   A numerical example will illustrate the previous description in simple terms. Assume an income of $500, consumption of $450, and savings of $50 in the first year. Plans for the second year call for investments of $65, an increase of $15. How will these plans affect income? The following table will help to clarify the problem.

TABLE 15-4.   The Income Adjustment Process

	Y	C	S	I	PC	PS
Year 1	$500	$450	$50	$50	$450/$500 = 90%	$50/$500 = 10%
Difference between						
Years 1 and 2	$ 75			$15		20%
Year 2	$575			$65		11.3%

How has the income in Year 2 been obtained? The use of the table is intended to facilitate the estimates of change. We are assuming that the economy in Year 1 had still-unused capacity and that income and investment were able to grow. Without unemployed resources, the investment plans could not be executed completely; the table shows the expected rise of investments with the full amount planned. The rising investment requires an equal rise in savings, which was not planned. To bring about the larger amount of savings, income must rise. How much greater the income must become depends on the rate of savings. If the propensity to save remained constant at 10 percent, it would take an additional income of $150 to save the $15 needed for the investment plans. In the table we have assumed that people will save a larger share from their increase than they would from a smaller income. A rate of additional savings of 20 percent implies that for every dollar saved the income rises by $5 because savings are one-fifth of additional income. To save $15, income must rise $75. The amount of additional savings must be the same as the rise in investments. Since not all additional income is saved, the increase in income must be larger than the increase in savings. If half the additional income is saved and half is consumed, the rise in income must be twice as large as the rise in savings. If additional savings are only one-fifth of the additional income, the dollar amount added to income must be five times the dollars saved.

SKETCH OF INCOME CHANGE

The process of income change encompasses many, sometimes bewildering, alternatives, as the explanations of the adjustment process have indicated. For the reader who likes a systematic description of all possible (including some highly unlikely) alternatives, the principles governing income change can be reduced schematically to the following simplified solutions.

Investment Plans Exceed Expected Savings

Investment plans are assumed to be greater than expected savings for the same period, a fact which can be stated more briefly: $I > S$. The change caused by these plans will lead to one of three results:

1. If income (Y) remains steady and the propensity to save (PS) does not change, investment (I) will not reach its expected level and will remain at the original level of savings (S).

2. If Y remains steady and the planned higher I is to be reached, the PS will increase because more savings are needed than before from the same size income.

3. If the PS remains unchanged from the original percentage, the higher level of I will cause the income to rise sufficiently to permit the needed savings.

Case 1 leads to incomplete investments caused by bottlenecks and delays of all types. It implies that there is simply not enough steel, copper, and trained technicians available to complete all projects according to the planned schedule. The actual investments will not exceed savings, and the original plans will be frustrated and may be completed only after some delay.

In Case 2 the propensities to save and consume change. This possibility is quite farfetched and is mentioned only to offer a complete picture. In time of war it may happen that the government will insist on increasing the share of the income devoted to the investment in capital goods. The level of output of consumer goods will be restricted by law; the incomes which have nothing to buy will be absorbed by higher taxes and strong propaganda to buy more bonds.

Case 3 is particularly interesting because it causes income to rise. This increase is considerably greater than the increase in savings. Since the share of income saved remains unchanged, a rise in the amount saved necessitates a multiple increase in income.

Two possible consequences of a higher income for the economy in general must be distinguished:

a. The economy may have been operating far below its capacity, with men and machines idle and available to return to work. In this case the demand for more investments creates more employment, higher production rates, and a rise in the accumulation of real savings. This increase is a sign of favorable developments and gives hope for a return to prosperity.

b. The economy may have been operating close to its capacity level at full employment. In this case a rising income cannot take the form of greater output, because the economy already is producing as much as it can turn out at the time. If more steel is needed for an investment project, it cannot come from the steel mills, whose output is sold for months in advance. The new customer will buy the steel from another user who has some and is willing to wait, as long as he can make a profit from selling it. The result will be an increase in the price of steel and of all other goods in short supply; this will lead to inflationary price increases. The income has reached a higher level in monetary terms only; the production of real goods and services has not improved. The economy of the United States in 1966 provided an excellent illustration of this situation.

Expected Savings Exceed Investment Plans

The opposite assumption starts out with savings expectations greater than planned investments $(S > I)$. The results can again be analyzed three ways:

1. If income and the propensity to save are held to the original plans, actual investments must rise to a higher level. Such a result is improbable but can happen if managers change their minds and take a more optimistic view, or if they simply fail to slow down on production.

2. If income remains steady though investments drop to a planned lower level (a highly unlikely assumption), the propensity to save must drop. Increased consumption and correspondingly lower savings will maintain the level of savings equal to investments. Such an event might occur right after a war, when consumers want to buy all they can get and new construction drops temporarily during the changeover from war to peace. In normal times, such a combination of circumstances would probably never occur.

3. If investments are reduced as planned and the propensity to save remains unchanged, the income will shrink to the point where the old percentage of savings produces only the lower dollar amount which new investments will absorb. This is the case of a dropping national income causing less than capacity operations and unemployment. Regardless of the level of economic activity at the outset, such a recession is not desirable for a healthy economy.

The changes in the nation's income are naturally much more involved than this simple sketch indicates. Investments, savings, and consumption will all change simultaneously and reach some compromise far from any extreme result. For simplicity, however, the principles of income change can now be reduced to the abbreviated form shown on the next page.

$$I > S$$

Result $\begin{cases} \text{1. With } Y \text{ and } PS \text{ firm: } I \text{ drops.} \\ \text{2. With } Y \text{ and } I \text{ firm: } PS \text{ rises.} \\ \text{3. With } I \text{ and } PS \text{ firm: } Y \text{ rises. Effects:} \end{cases}$

          a. Starting from unemployment: causes rise of real income, or prosperity.

          b. Starting from full employment: causes rise of money income, or inflation.

$$S < I$$

Result $\begin{cases} \text{1. With } Y \text{ and } PS \text{ firm: } I \text{ rises.} \\ \text{2. With } Y \text{ and } I \text{ firm: } PS \text{ drops.} \\ \text{3. With } I \text{ and } PS \text{ firm: } Y \text{ drops. Effect:} \end{cases}$

          Regardless of conditions at the start: causes a drop in real income, or recession.

SUMMARY

National income is the sum of all incomes earned by the residents of a country over a given period of time. Its main use is to serve as a yardstick of economic activity.

National income can be pictured as a circular flow of firms and people trading goods and services in a continuous stream of dollars. Income earned and output produced are identical by definition.

The statistical description of the nation's income in five different series is summarized by Table 15-5.

TABLE 15-5. **Relationship of Statistical Series Measuring National Income, 1966**
(*billions of dollars*)

Gross national product	743.3
Less: Capital consumption allowance	− 63.5
Net national product	679.8
Less: Indirect business taxes, etc.	− 63.1
National income	616.7
Less: Corporate profits taxes, social security taxes, and undistributed corporate profits	− 98.9
Plus: Transfer payments	+ 43.9
Interest paid by government and consumer	+ 22.3
Personal income	584.0
Less: Personal taxes	− 75.2
Disposable personal income	508.8

SOURCE: U.S. Department of Commerce, *Survey of Current Business.*

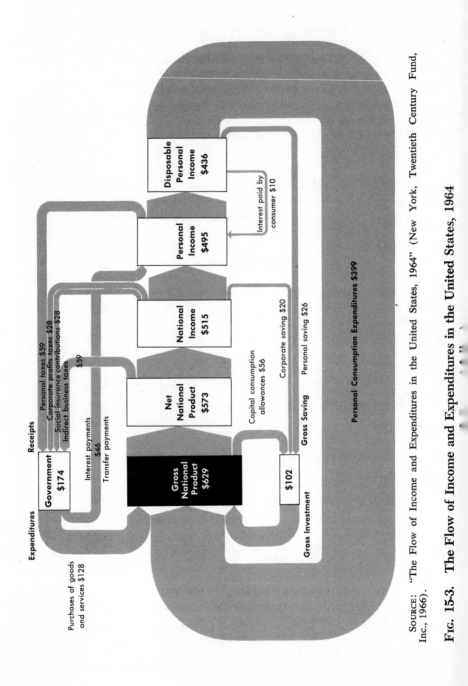

SOURCE: "The Flow of Income and Expenditures in the United States, 1964" (New York, Twentieth Century Fund, Inc., 1966).

FIG. 15-3.   The Flow of Income and Expenditures in the United States, 1964

The entire flow of income can be followed on Figure 15-3, which shows total GNP and its various components.

National income is often analyzed by its main determinants, which are consumption, savings, and investment. For policy purposes, it is quite helpful to consider government as a separate component, consisting of both consumption and investment.

Investments are the most volatile component of income, as they are easily influenced by noneconomic pressures as well as by economic factors.

Planned investments and savings differ frequently, but the actual amounts saved are necessarily the same as actual investments. To accomplish this result, all economic magnitudes are subject to continuous change. These adjustments determine the size of the fluctuating national income.

The impact of higher or lower incomes on the nation's economy forms the subject of the following chapter.

Discussion Questions

1. Compare two ways of figuring national income.
2. What is the meaning of inventories in national income calculations?
3. What is meant by retained profits, indirect business taxes, and personal taxes?
4. Can a country save too much?
5. What is the propensity to consume?
6. How can savings equal investment when they are controlled by different people whose interests may clash?
7. What is meant by the volatility of investment decisions?

Suggested Reading

HEILBRONER, ROBERT L., *Understanding Macroeconomics.* Englewood Cliffs, N.J., Prentice-Hall, 1965.

KEYNES, JOHN MAYNARD, *The General Theory of Employment, Interest, and Money.* London, Macmillan, 1936.

PETERSON, WALLACE C., *Income, Employment, and Economic Growth.* New York, Norton, 1962.

SHERMAN, HOWARD J., *Elementary Aggregate Economics.* New York, Appleton-Century-Crofts, 1966.

16

BUSINESS FLUCTUATIONS AND ECONOMIC GROWTH

The mechanical description of income change in the previous chapter presents a challenge. Once the process of economic change is understood, it should be possible to utilize this knowledge for the maintenance of a steady increase in the nation's well-being. A brief glance at the facts of economic life over the last generation will make it clear that no such happy state of affairs has yet been reached. Progress comes in sharp upward thrusts, which are interrupted by marked downturns. The end result is a modest upward movement averaging less than 3 percent annually over the years.

No one growth rate is just right for any economy; a goal of 5 percent per year has no better claim to being normal than one of 3 percent. But the existing level of economic activity of the United States in peacetime could certainly be raised, and with popular approval, by using the ample unused capacity of the people and of their factories.

This chapter will describe the dangers which lurk in the path of steady growth. It will look at the record of depressions and inflations, and their disastrous consequences; and it will end on a note of hope for prosperity and growth in the future.

Business will fluctuate. Changes in the flow of goods and services do not follow a simple pattern, which in the past was described as a business cycle. Small fluctuations cannot be avoided, but there is no law of nature that prescribes periodic depressions. The goal of prosperity and stable growth is within our reach; it has become as possible as the long and healthy life which modern medicine grants to a large majority of twentieth-century Americans.

Prosperity describes a trend of business where incomes point higher, prices remain stable, and most workers can find a job. Within these trend lines structural changes constantly occur, and some industries gain while others lose. Unfortunately, some minority groups in our midst have failed to share in the benefits which economic growth has brought to the rest of the population. Their difficulties have not been overcome by a general boom in business and require instead special efforts.

298

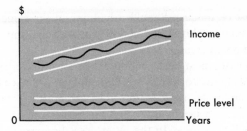

FIG. 16-1.   The Pattern of Prosperity

THE PATTERN OF BUSINESS FLUCTUATIONS

Instability in the national economy is the result of many factors inseparably woven together without beginning or end. Numerous influences are constantly at work to push the economy up or down and thereby shape the outcome. To simplify the problem, let us study the impact of one isolated event on a small town which remains otherwise unchanged.

A new building will be erected in this community of 5,000 inhabitants. Its costs are expected to reach $10 million, and construction will take over a year to complete. What repercussions can be expected from the announcement of this project? The impact will certainly be great; there will be inevitable changes of all kinds in the lives and fortunes of the citizens of Happytown, as we shall call our community.

The total income of Happytown will rise. Will its business increase more than $10 million, or will it be less; when the building is finished, will prosperity stay at the new level, or revert to its former pattern? Clearly, not all the money for the building will be spent in town. Steel girders, bricks, and roofing material are not locally available and will have to be brought in; but the construction crew moves in and spends its payroll, and the local motel is booked to capacity. Contractors hastily erect some new houses to take care of the overflow of people who don't want to commute or live in trailers. The grocery store expands its facilities, and three new filling stations spring up overnight.

The Snowball Effect of Change

Chances are that the project will boost the income of Happytown far more than the cost of the building itself. The actual size of the overall increase cannot be predicted, but specific cases can be estimated on the basis of detailed, full knowledge of pertinent facts. It will be most important to know what sort of building is under construction. If the project is a gigantic storage warehouse, expectations for a long-run, permanent improvement of

Happytown must be modest. Should a building of the same size become a factory with steady employment for 500 workers, the impact on the local economy will be much greater.

In the first case, most construction workers will have to stay in trailers because the local contractors are not willing to take a chance on a lot of new houses which cannot be rented after the warehouse is finished. A new factory causes no such hesitation; when the construction crew moves out, plant workers will take over. In the latter case the expected growth of the community is more certain, and this immediately causes a faster rate of economic activity.

The above description of Happytown presents an untidy picture. We know for certain only that because of all the added activities of its citizens, the construction project will raise the local income far higher than the actual amount of money spent on it directly in town. The size of the increase depends on future expectations and can be maintained only when the additional flow of income continues—when construction workers are replaced by permanent employees. The town has adjusted to a larger number of consumers each month, and a sudden reversal of this trend would cause serious repercussions on the local economy.

The example of Happytown illustrates a principle which permits broad application. Just as a snowball rolls down a mountainside and gains in size on the way, the injection of new money into an economic system causes repercussions far in excess of the amount of money originally spent; the size of the effect depends on the specific undertaking and its impact on the community. Economists call this phenomenon the multiplier effect.[1]

The Impact of Stimulants

The use of economic stimulants can be well suited to the promotion of growth if their application is handled wisely. Most policy arguments occur when the wisdom of a specific measure is debated.

A billion-dollar expenditure will have different results, depending on various factors.

1. Congress may declare a veterans' bonus of this size, thereby creating a consumption multiplier. The effect of this measure is likely to be disappointing. People will realize that a bonus is not a continuing improvement and will not expand their facilities in spite of the temporary spurt in business. They may be inclined to use this windfall to reduce inventories and pay debts, without pushing the economy to a permanently higher level.

---

[1] In more technical economic terms, a multiplier is the numerical coefficient which indicates how much income increases as a result of an increase in spending. An acceleration effect is also present in this example. To avoid needless complexity, it will not be treated separately.

2. Congress may authorize the construction of new post offices with automated facilities throughout the whole country, hoping as a result to create an investment multiplier. The outcome is likely to be uneven. Factories producing the right type of equipment will want to expand since they are sure of substantial orders for some years ahead; this will cause a significant multiplier effect in areas directly connected with their activity. However, the communities where the new post offices are built will not be stimulated to any real degree, since no permanent increase in local business can be expected. Indirect effects of this type of rise in public investment tend to spread slowly through the entire economy, but their impact is hard to judge.

3. Congress may reduce business taxes for firms willing to increase their investments. The multiplier effect of such a measure, which attempts to modify private decisions, is particularly hard to predict. It may be very favorable if well received, or it may be a failure should it not lead to a substantial change in business plans.

Limits to Stimulating Effects

Multiplier effects do not continue to boost the economy forever. The first doses of new activity have a strong impact, but slowly the economy adjusts to the higher level. This new plateau of relative affluence requires, periodically, a similar shot in the arm to continue on the level already achieved. The added payroll no longer causes an increase; the homes have been built; the stores have expanded; the adjustment is complete. The larger population keeps the new facilities in use, but it takes a steady trickle of *new* business to keep the contractors busy and to avoid a local recession.

Business no longer moves upward. In fact, only the all-out effort of the community to bring in supplementary activities makes it possible to maintain the established pace of the economy. Its boosters find themselves in the position of Alice in Wonderland, who discovered that it took all the running she could do to stay in the same place.

Once the steady flow of business stimulants comes to a halt, a downward effect is set in motion. It spirals downward the same way it did on the way up and may cause a chain reaction of bankruptcy and misery unless it is checked in time.

The Cause of Instability

The cause of instability should now become much clearer. People's decisions are motivated partly by hard facts and partly by intangible expectations. The restaurant owner in Happytown doubles the size of his establishment because he sees customers standing in line waiting for a table, and because he projects the present prosperity into the future, feeling optimistic and sure that his town will outpace others from now on. But he has no way of knowing precisely how much to expand.

This lack of precision causes errors. The restaurant turns out to be too big. The additional factories are not being built as fast as expected. The optimistic member of the Chamber of Commerce turns pessimistic and sees only gloom. The restaurant owner cuts back to save his own business, and his action is apt to cause other businessmen to do the same. Sales decline and pessimism spreads, further aggravating the adjustment process. A business slump sets in, and matters might get worse than they would have been without this depressing outlook.

THE PERFORMANCE OF THE U.S. ECONOMY

Figure 16-2 illustrates the actual performance of the economy of the United States since 1929. There was substantial long-run growth, but it was far from steady. The long and deep Depression of the thirties gave way to a peak effort during the war of the forties, with frequent but much smaller fluctuations thereafter. Note that the chart uses index numbers to eliminate the changes in the value of the dollar from the presentation.

Peak performances seem to be invariably connected with war periods. Unemployment finally disappeared in World War II after ten years of depression and only partial recovery. The Korean War wiped out the beginnings of unemployment which had returned to the scene. Even the prosperous sixties were afflicted by high rates of unemployment until the war in Vietnam caused an outright shortage of men and materials. Must we really fight a war to maintain a prosperous economy?

The demand for manpower rises as soon as war breaks out. This demand is not limited to skilled people, who are usually in short supply in a modern economy, but it drafts thousands of men whose lack of education makes their employment in peacetime difficult. The additional payments by the armed forces raise the demand for consumer goods at a time when unused capacity is already absorbed by purchases of war goods. This situation frequently results in an inflationary price rise, an inevitable consequence of war. This full employment level raises the living standard of those who previously had no income; but it hurts many old and retired people who must pay more for food and shelter when their incomes do not rise. The man who works two shifts and the grandmother with a welding torch are typical wartime contributions. They not only are patriotic and willing to work harder than they would in peacetime, but they are also faced with the economic necessity to raise their income.

Annual Rates
Billions of 1958 Dollars

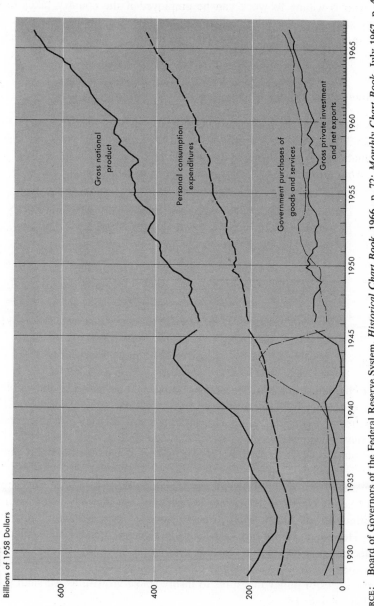

Gross national product

Personal consumption expenditures

Government purchases of goods and services

Gross private investment and net exports

SOURCE: Board of Governors of the Federal Reserve System, *Historical Chart Book*, 1966, p. 72; *Monthly Chart Book*, July 1967, p. 49.

FIG. 16-2. **Gross National Product in Constant Dollars** [a]

[a] Annually, 1929–1946; quarterly, seasonally adjusted, 1947–1965.

The need for more output is universally so great that even without war anyone who is willing to work can be employed if the country takes the necessary steps to make full employment possible. The maintenance of a steady rate of growth becomes a problem of incentives and of speedy decisions that can overcome periodic slumps in the economy.

Fluctuations Since 1920

The ups and downs of American business are depicted more clearly by Figure 16-3, in which the long-run trend has been eliminated to show only the fluctuations of business activity. The shaded areas indicate a drop in activity, while the clear parts of the chart show upward movements.

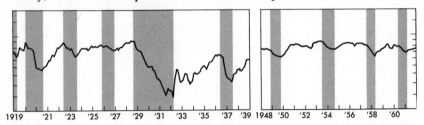

SOURCE: Julius Shiskin, *Signals of Recession and Recovery: An Experiment with Monthly Reporting*. Occasional Paper 77 (New York, National Bureau of Economic Research, Inc., 1961), p. 7.

Fig. 16-3.   Business Activity, 1919–1961

Periodic interruption of the upward movement seems to be inevitable, though a difference in the performance of the economy since World War II can be noted at a glance. Booms and recessions still alternate, but the weak months have become a smaller part of the total time period. Recessions in the last twenty years have been less severe and are spaced further apart than in the earlier period.

Nevertheless, these improvements in economic performance have not been sufficiently clear-cut to permit the interpretation that the better record will continue in the future. Any forecast based on past behavior must be hesitant. However, present-day knowledge of economic relationships should suffice to limit the downswings in business to the necessary correction of errors without incurring the calamity of a depression. The United States has adopted a series of policy measures to insure stable growth, as we shall see in detail in Chapter 18.

Control of Fluctuations

The proper timing of remedial action is essential for the control of a recession. A downward movement must be prevented from getting out of hand by maintaining total consumption expenditures in spite of layoffs in industries with excess inventories. Limited action taken early may be sufficient; massive action taken later may not be enough. When the unfavorable trend has become widespread, even people who can still afford to buy as much as before begin to hesitate. Fears of the future trigger the spiral effect of the downward multiplier and are likely to cause uncontrollable harm. In an advanced state of recession, public and private efforts to reverse the trend may prove to be too little and too late.

The downward phase of the business cycle has all the features of a big fire. Unless it is contained and brought under control in its early stages, it will burn everything in its path before the lack of further combustible material will finally snuff it out.

DEPRESSION

Younger readers of these pages have never experienced a severe depression, and stories told by their parents are not likely to convey the full impact of such an unmitigated disaster. Not unlike the Black Death of the Middle Ages, the Great Depression reached this country in 1929, mowing down all before it for over three long years, and lingered on for the rest of the decade. Only the beginning of a world war in Europe in 1939 brushed away the remaining traces of unemployment and pessimism which had been the hallmark of the thirties. To many surviving victims of this economic holocaust, war held fewer fears. To the long-time unemployed, even the possibility of death from an enemy bullet appeared to be a less terrifying alternative than the slow strangulation of joblessness and the gnawing want of a seemingly endless depression. Those who lived through it harbor the earnest hope that it will never happen again.

Causes of the Great Depression

What caused the Great Depression? Many things had to combine and interact to fashion a downturn of such magnitude. The previous boom had overreached itself. Business climbed to its peak on rising prices and higher hopes, sustained at the climax more by speculative credit and financial excesses than by actual performance. When the bubble burst and credit was sharply cut back, the ruin of overextended speculators carried their creditors, suppliers, and workers down with them into insolvency.

Prices and incomes crashed together. After four depression years, the wholesale price index had fallen to only about half its previous peak, while GNP had dropped from $104 billion in 1929 to $56 billion in 1933. Only in 1940 did GNP reach the $100 billion level again. Private and public efforts at stabilization remained unsuccessful.

The decline of business, the collapse of the banking system, and the resulting spread of pessimism interacted to worsen the depression. The entire banking system was riddled by insolvencies and shaken by unpredictable runs on bank deposits; money and credit markets were engulfed in a general feeling of distrust. Bankers could not grant credit to enterprising optimists with sick-looking balance sheets, and the sharp drops in prices made most business statements appear exceedingly pale. The year's operating profits were often wiped out by customers who failed to pay their bills and by the reductions in the value of a firm's inventories. The universal appearance of red ink and excess capacity discouraged investments both in new production facilities and in the modernization of old ones.

The state of economic knowledge at the time was so tentative that all efforts to aid recovery proceeded on a trial-and-error basis. Large-scale use of federal power to help the economy did not swing into action until 1932. President Hoover called belatedly for the creation of the RFC (Reconstruction Finance Corporation) to prevent further bankruptcies in railroads.

The major effort to turn the tide came with Franklin Roosevelt's New Deal. Reforms were started in many areas, and large-scale measures to aid recovery were initiated with great speed. Much of the new legislation was temporary—designed to get people back to work—but a large share of the country's social legislation, which has become part of our life today, dates back to the New Deal era. Unfortunately, the experimental nature of early legislation during the Roosevelt period failed to inspire broad confidence, particularly in the business community, and confidence was essential to the achievement of an early recovery.

Some of the economic legislation of the New Deal has proven to be of lasting benefit. Particularly, the extensive banking laws of the thirties have rendered the credit system less vulnerable to runs by the public; they have also strengthened its overall health. Social security laws provide some protection against economic disasters.

Legal efforts intended to restrain a boom from overreaching itself will help to mitigate a downward trend in the future. The fear of a depression is in itself a bulwark against its reappearance. At the first sign of a downturn, people tend to demand immediate counteraction, even at the risk of pushing the economy to the opposite extreme and causing an inflation.

Depression Results

Almost everyone loses in a depression. People without jobs are hurt the most, but businessmen who have had a series of losses in succession are also driven to despair. The reduced output satisfies fewer wants overall. While not all people are hurt with equal intensity, most of them find themselves financially weakened.

Prices drop as business shrinks; they may not tumble as fast as income, but they will collapse eventually. Wages are maintained for a while, but only for those who still have jobs, and even their total income is somewhat cut. Overtime disappears, special bonuses are eliminated, and shorter working hours become the rule. If the depression lasts long enough, even the hourly rates will be reduced in order to keep the employer in business.

There are very few winners in a depression. The fixed income earners discover that their fixed salary will probably not be paid in full, despite the assurance of a contract to the contrary. The same happens to many pensioners. Their pensions are guaranteed, but the pension fund depends on income from "safe" securities—which turn out to be quite worthless. The fund will have to reduce its payments, reluctantly and with embarrassment to be sure, but reduce them all the same.

The smart businessman who realizes the opportunity of investing at these low prices can become very rich, but most businessmen no longer have liquid funds for investments and their credit is not as strong as it used to be. Few people are in any position to take advantage of depression bargains.

INFLATION

Inflation has been a serious threat to American prosperity for twenty years, but its danger is not yet fully understood because the early symptoms of an inflation do not differ very much from the pleasant characteristics of growth and prosperity. A depression is spotted early and feared tremendously because of the personal experience of most older Americans. Inflation has also been with us; but because it has not been equally extreme, its full danger is not completely realized.

What Is Inflation?

Inflation is a general, prolonged rise in prices. The term *inflation* is often used more loosely when people refer to any rise in the general price level, however small. When small increases in prices alternate with occasional drops, we prefer to call such periods years of price stability, reserving the concept of inflation for the one-sided, continuous upward trend of prices in general.

Increases of some specific prices are not necessarily inflationary. If steaks are a nickel more on your meat counter, the change may be due to the weather, to the market conditions at the nearest stockyard, or to the greater popularity of outdoor cooking; it is not a sure sign of inflation, however.

Index Trends.   Even a rise in a price index will not always mean inflation. Your newspaper may announce in bold headlines "Prices Peak, Inflation Threatens!" A closer look shows that the price increase from the previous month was one-tenth of 1 percent. It would clarify the issue to call this price "stable," but it would not lend itself to a good headline.

Professor Haberler illustrates the meaning of inflation in the following words: "An average price rise of 2 or 3 percent a year, if continued several years, cannot be called negligible. It is not serious if it lasts only a few years and follows, or is followed by, a price decline of the same order of magnitude, or at least by a prolonged period of stable prices. But, if there are no reversals of the price rise and only short spans of stable prices, even an annual price rise of 2 or 3 percent is bound to become a serious problem." [2]

Rising prices should be called inflation only when most prices are moving up, when the increases are not limited to just a small area or to isolated industries, and when they persist over some time without interruption by a downward movement. Ideally, prices should reflect supply and demand conditions by fluctuating freely in both directions. If prices periodically rise but never fall, the long-run trend can only be upward; in fact, the essence of inflation consists in the absence of downward revisions. Gradually, people learn to expect that prices have only one way to go, upward. Relative prices will continue to change; the slow-selling product will not increase in price as quickly as something more in demand, but prices will not drop.

The possible extent of extreme inflation becomes clear when we look at some of the hyperinflations of recent history. After World War I, the German Republic inflated the mark until $1.00 became the equivalent of 4.2 trillion marks in 1923. At this point the printing presses were unable to cope with the daily loss of purchasing power, and merchants refused to sell goods in exchange for worthless pieces of paper.

In more recent years, examples of such hyperinflation abroad are quite numerous. In Brazil, the value of the cruzeiro in 1948 was eighteen to the dollar. By 1966, $1.00 bought 2,200 cruzeiros before the government decided to convert its currency into a "new cruzeiro" at a rate of one new for 1,000 old.

The rising prices triggered by the cost of the war effort in Vietnam became a cause for concern in 1965. Prices in 1966 rose about 3 percent, indicating an inflationary trend which could no longer be ignored.

A Little Inflation?   Some writers consider "a little inflation a good thing," referring to an annual price rise of perhaps 1 to 2 percent. A "little infla-

---

[2] Gottfried Haberler, *Inflation, Its Causes and Cures,* rev. ed. (Washington, D.C., American Enterprise Association, 1966), p. 55.

tion" may be thought to stimulate full employment. But this approach overlooks the expectations that are apt to set in; an unbroken upward movement of prices on an ever-broadening front causes more and more people to expect this development to continue. They will change from their normal spending-saving pattern to an acceleration of expenditures, in an attempt to use their money before prices rise any further. As their ranks grow, prices rise faster and cannot be held to 1 or 2 percent per year.

No exact percentage of price increase can be clearly labeled inflation. A price rise of 1 percent during an entire year is a sign of stability. Without occasional dips in the price level, the increase could not have been kept so small. Even a sharper upswing in one year may not become inflationary if a break occurs and prices occasionally drop a little. Over the decades however, the secular trend for prices points upward. This long-run pattern is sometimes called "creeping inflation." Unless it becomes sufficiently pronounced to affect people's decisions, this trend lacks the disastrous characteristics of a true inflation. It may, however, gradually reduce the purchasing power of the dollar and lead to a substantial loss of value after several decades.

Similarly, price recovery from a recession low is a normal situation and should not be confused with a real inflation, in which records for a new high are set month after month. After a short period of inflation during the Korean war, slow but steady price increases caused continuing concern until the price level was successfully stabilized in 1958. The following period of stability proved to be the longest in a generation and was maintained until the beginning of the Vietnam war inflation in 1965.

Causes of Inflation

When inflation becomes a threat to prosperity, the cause of rising prices becomes a matter for heated discussion. A public official may blame the housewife for endangering the economy through her extravagant purchases. Businessmen blame labor unions for causing the increase with their unreasonable demands for higher wages. Unions accuse management of profiteering when prices of goods reflect greater market demand by rising. The President may issue guidelines to prevent people from acting in response to market forces, but experience shows that such guidelines are ineffective. The following discussion of "demand-pull" versus "cost-push" inflation must not obscure the basic fact that all inflation has its origin in public action or inaction. No private citizen or group can command more credit, higher wages, or rising prices unless growing public expenditures and a rising money supply are supported by the federal authorities entrusted with their control.

Inflation usually develops during a period of rising incomes. Men are being returned to their jobs as business recovers from a lull, and incomes in general are going up. Overtime pay and better profits combine to create a feeling of prosperity. This is the setting for a boom. Optimistic expectations speed up demand and advance prices on a broad front. The economy approaches full employment. This is the time when prosperity is threatened by inflation.

Demand-Pull Inflation.   The traditional view of inflation points a finger at the rising demand of the public for goods of all types, a demand which pulls prices up and thereby rations the available supply. The rise in demand can be caused by more money in circulation. It is also possible that a given amount of money can be used much faster than is customary, but experience tells us that spending habits do not change easily and are speeded up only after an inflation has been in progress for some time. Accordingly, the added demand comes principally from additional money being placed into circulation.

In its early stages, demand inflation is caused by "too much money chasing too few goods." This excessive money supply cannot develop without the cooperation of the United States Treasury and the Federal Reserve System. Optimism during a boom period leads to greater willingness to spend for everything, including new investments. Investment plans depend on the banking system for their realization, and even the most optimistic banker will refuse additional loans when the Federal Reserve Bank severely restricts credit to its members. "There is no record in the economic history . . . of a serious and prolonged inflation which has not been accompanied and made possible, if not directly caused, by a large increase in the quantity of money." [3]

Why would public authorities permit such a rise in the money supply? During a boom some prices will go up automatically as the demand outpaces the supply. The governors of the Federal Reserve System will view the situation with concern, but they may hesitate to take action because prosperity is very popular.

A Treasury deficit may become the cause of inflation. During a recession, a budget deficit helps to boost current consumption. Excess savings of the public are channeled into federal expenditures through bond sales. When business is booming and private investments use all available savings, a Treasury deficit competes with business firms for the same funds. Consequently, many economists recommend a budget deficit during a recession and oppose it when incomes are rising.

In December 1965, the Board of Governors of the Federal Reserve System took the very unpopular step of raising interest rates. They continued this tight money policy during the following year, until the cost of credit rose to a level not experienced in this country for a generation. These

[3] *Ibid.,* p. 61.

drastic measures slowed down the demand for new money and caused severe cutbacks, particularly in the construction industry. City and state investment projects had to be postponed when they needed to be financed with new bond issues. In spite of these efforts by the Federal Reserve authorities, money in circulation continued to expand. A steady flow of new orders for war goods, combined with the inflationary psychology which developed in the absence of any breaking action by the Treasury or by Congress, led to yet more borrowing and a greater money supply, in spite of rising interest rates.

Cost-Push inflation. In recent years, much has been written about a "new" type of inflation, called a "cost-push" inflation, in which costs rise first and push the prices of consumer goods upward. In particular, labor costs under union influence have been accused of causing inflationary price rises. "Unwarranted" price increases of basic raw materials such as steel or aluminum have provoked immediate public interference in order to prevent inflation.

The evidence suggests that rising wage costs are a more serious threat to the economy during a recession than in an upswing. When times are bad, the unions' opposition to any reduction in hourly wages is more determined than is their demand for increases during a boom. When output must be reduced, the worker on the assembly line can no longer be employed with the same efficiency as before. Labor cost per unit of output will rise because part of a worker's cost, such as the fringe benefits mentioned earlier, cannot be reduced proportionately. The employer will therefore drop as many workers from his payroll as possible, a step which aggravates the unemployment situation.

With rising incomes and better plant use, wage demands can be absorbed more easily through a more productive use of labor. These costs are reflected in higher prices only when the pattern is favorable for such increases. Without *rising demand supported by more credit,* no amount of cost pressure can cause an inflation. If the wage claims persist beyond the economy's power of absorption, the result may be unemployment and recession, but not a general price rise without a larger money flow.

Similarly, a higher price for steel will trigger a whole round of increases only when the time is right and the demand for products is keen enough to warrant the rise. The ill-timed price increase of steel in 1962 would probably have been revised by the industry, even without political pressure, because of a lack of steel orders which, a few months later, forced prices even below the unsatisfactory level which the industry attempted to raise before. The steel price increase in 1966 reflected the increased market demand and was not reversed.

If demand is rising, the cost increase whether of labor or of steel may appear to cause inflation. Actually, however, the root cause will have been the rising supply of money and credit which made it possible to pass the cost increase on to the customer in the form of higher prices. Thus "cost-push" inflation appears to be possible only if there is an accompanying "demand-pull."

The Case for Inflation

Inflation would not be a serious threat to the economy if the majority of the people were in whole-hearted opposition to it. Too much credit and a swollen money supply can be cut back directly. In this respect, inflation is easier to control than depression, because although you cannot make people exercise new initiative and ask for more credit to overcome a depression, you certainly can slow their enthusiasm by applying brakes when a boom gets out of hand.

Wage Earners.   The danger of inflation lies in the benefits many people see in rising wages. The average person wants to get a raise in pay every year. If his productivity does not increase, and this holds true in many cases, his desire cannot be granted unless all price tags have been raised simultaneously. The higher income will not buy more goods than before, but it makes installment payments for past purchases easier to meet.

Businessmen.   Many businessmen, including farmers, like a little inflation. They want to do better than last year, and this goal can be achieved more readily at higher prices. The same sales volume produces record earnings and profits, and any weaknesses in the business structure are nicely covered up by positive results. Inflation camouflages business errors and permits the postponement of unpleasant decisions.

Consumers.   Consumers, who normally are hurt by inflation, may not object to it in its early stages. They like to buy things sooner than they can afford them, and rising prices are a perfect excuse to do so "before prices go up." A staggering number of monthly bills are made to appear lighter in view of the expected wage increase next month or next year. A bad purchase at excessive cost looks better after six months of rising prices.

Less Developed Countries.   Even economists have occasionally given an approving nod in favor of a little inflation, particularly for less developed countries. They argue that a country which is so poor that it cannot save enough will improve its lot with inflation. Wages do not rise as fast as prices, and the difference is, in effect, a forced saving imposed on the local workers.

A famous practitioner [4] answered this argument by pointing out that people get wise to this technique very soon. "When that happens, not only will the 'forced savings' disappear, but the normal flow of voluntary savings will also be diminished and be increasingly diverted to speculation in real estate and other ventures. Then the game is up, for without a ready flow of savings no economic progress can be sustained."

The initial effect of inflation has all the attributes of a habit-forming drug. It makes the user feel good, and forgetful of the inevitable disaster lurking in the future. A little more money in the pocket or in the bank is heady stuff, and few people realize that they may become the victims of this disease.

The Effects of Inflation

The results of inflation can be as disastrous as those of a depression. Since World War II, neither the upward nor the downward swings of the business cycle has gone out of control, and the extreme type of inflation is only history to most of us. The early days of American independence witnessed the worst inflation in the nation's past. The money authorized by the Continental Congress became totally worthless.

Total Effect. Inflation hurts the nation by causing inefficient use of resources; inflation redistributes the wealth of the people and favors a few at the expense of many. Creditors lose and debtors gain. The spendthrift is proven wise and the careful provider is found wrong; the speculator is smart, while the owner of government bonds loses his savings. Consumers are, on balance, the major creditors of our economy, while governments, business firms, and farmers are the debtors. The bad consequences of inflation can be avoided successfully by those who understand its gradual progress and are in a position to take precautionary action. As the value of money continues to shrink, economic self-preservation becomes the main goal of the population. Let us look at the impact of an inflation more closely.

Effect on Retired People. The largest category of pure creditors consists of retired people who live on the savings of the past. Most of their income no longer changes dollar value; it flows from pension funds, from annuities, and from safe and sound bonds issued at fixed amounts by government and private corporations. Everything they own pays a given, unchangeable

---

[4] Per Jacobsson, the late managing director of the International Monetary Fund, in an address to the meeting of the IMF in September, 1959; reported in *Summary Proceedings of the Fourteenth Annual Meeting of the Board of Governors of the International Monetary Fund* (Washington, D.C., 1959), pp. 22–23.

number of dollars. They do not want and cannot afford to speculate in their old age; inflation renders them helpless, causing hardship, if not ruin, to those who can afford it least.

Effect on Debtors.   Pure debtors, who gain the most, are quite rare. A man normally must own some sort of property before he can borrow much. Some gambler-type individuals are able to talk financiers into granting substantial loans unmatched by any apparent collateral. Although these are the largest profiteers from an inflation, their number is small. More significant as a debtor group are business corporations and farmers. Land is good collateral for loans because it will not lose value during an inflation, while the borrowed money will be easier to repay as commodity prices increase.

Speculating businessmen are a rather small group, but they stand to gain heavily in an inflation. Businessmen in general are in a position to borrow on a much larger scale than other people and to buy up property offered for sale by the victims of the inflation. The pensioners sacrifice their accumulated wealth of houses or jewelry to meet the needs of current consumption, and men who can command enough credit buy it all up.

Effect on Wage Earners.   The position of the wage earner is less clear. Salaries will rise with living costs, but not at the same speed for all groups. Wages of salesmen based largely on a percentage of sales are not affected by changing prices. Low income groups hold no savings which can lose their value. If they are unionized, their hourly rates will come closer to keeping in step with rising prices than in nonunion jobs, where rates are increased much later. People with fixed salaries which are changed only once every couple of years, such as civil servants or school teachers, stand to lose heavily during an inflation, when their modest income is hopelessly left behind by rising prices.

The Effect on the Middle Class.   The largest group of losers in an inflation is that broad segment of the population frequently referred to as the middle class. These people, who form the backbone of American society, will be particularly hard hit by an inflation. They do not object for a long time because they fail to realize what is happening to them.

They are unaware of the fact that they actually are creditors. They own a life insurance policy, government bonds, an account with a savings and loan company, a checking account, and a special savings account for emergencies. None of these is very large, but together they total far more than the debts left on an old mortgage on their house or the unpaid installments on the car. They like to see their incomes go up while their monthly payments are unchanged and hence no longer so burdensome. They fail to remember, however, that their old-age protection, their life insurance, and their pension plan are fading away as the value of their savings is destroyed. They may have paid for eighteen years to accumulate enough to see Junior through college, only to learn too late that costs have risen so much that they must borrow money before his studies can be completed.

The Redistribution of Wealth.   The results of inflation can now be summed up as favoring debtors over creditors, the rich over the poor, the gambler over the cautious, the business firm over the consumer, and the farmer over the city wage earner. Most of all, it punishes the old, the widows, the orphans, and the sick, who are no longer active income producers and who can least afford the loss. This redistribution of the nation's income certainly does not follow any pattern which a Congressional majority would ever approve, and its burdens far outweigh any temporary benefits some people see in an inflation.

The End of Inflation

A steady, uninterrupted price rise will eventually snowball out of control. Shrewd observers discover early that it pays to buy in advance and pay later. They sell their bonds and all other assets with a fixed dollar value and buy, instead, common stocks and real estate. Every round of higher prices increases the number of people who try to protect themselves against inflation in the same way. They buy stocks which are no longer cheap. Eventually most everyone is trying to do the same thing, only to discover that business transactions require both buyers and sellers for the same merchandise. The Treasury finds it difficult to sell new bonds to the public; they finance public expenditures by raising the money supply even more and thus help to increase the inflationary trend.

Inflation has run its course when people start buying goods they do not want, solely for the purpose of getting rid of money in order to protect themselves against its loss of value. The monetary unit is no longer a usable means of exchange, and the economy must start all over again. This is the logical end of hyperinflation.

Public authority can stop this collapse much earlier through its control of government spending and the money supply. People can demand such action because they know that inflation is not an act of God and can be avoided by appropriate steps at the right time.

UNEMPLOYMENT

The desire for full employment is a generally accepted goal of society. Recessions are always marked by rising unemployment, but even in good times four million people will be without jobs, as for example in 1965. Unemployment statistics may exaggerate the problem—some people listed as unemployed cannot keep a job, do not want a job, or are in the process of switching jobs. Let us not jump to the conclusion, however, that the 5 percent of the labor force listed as unemployed during a boom are all a bunch of loafers!

The unemployment problem has three facets, and it clarifies the issue to distinguish between frictional unemployment, cyclical, or aggregative, unemployment, and structural unemployment.

Frictional Unemployment

Some people without jobs are temporarily not working because they are switching employment or moving to a new location. Until the new job becomes actually available, they are registered as unemployed. The number of people in such a position is not known, but it is likely to exceed one million. This type of frictional unemployment is an inevitable aspect of a mobile society where no one is chained to his job. No major problems are created by this temporary joblessness.

Cyclical Unemployment

During a business recession, many people lose their jobs in all kinds of occupations and in many parts of the country. Of course, not all workers are hurt with equal severity; unskilled workers are laid off first, and minority groups feel the impact of joblessness sooner than others. The remedy for this general, or aggregative, type of unemployment is to be found in the area of fiscal policy, where it will receive more detailed attention.

Structural Unemployment

Structural unemployment refers to the fact that some industries may experience a shortage of skilled workers while at the same time unemployment exists in other occupations. A shortage of electronic workers in California may drive up prices in electronics; on the other hand, there may be persistent unemployment in the West Virginia coal mines. Moving miners to California obviously is no answer, because they lack the needed skills.

Past efforts to tackle the structural unemployment problem have failed because they did not recognize that the primary obstacle is inflexibility of manpower. Governmental efforts to retrain the unemployed have not yet been successful; the training frequently proves to be futile when there is no assurance of a new job to follow. For the same reason, families hesitate to move without real hope of employment on arrival, and firms do not want to recruit workers from faraway places because they cannot be sure that the man will fit the job.

The "war on poverty" has recognized that much needs to be done to eradicate this serious defect from the record of accomplishment of the free enterprise system. Its emphasis on education of unskilled labor and training of school dropouts is certainly a step in the right direction. The most important hindrance to full employment has not yet been recognized, a fact which renders all present attempts less effective than they might be. Existing laws and contracts force employers to lay workers off rather than retrain them. If the firm fires a man, the unemployment service takes over with no further cost to the employer. Should the employer decide to retrain his workers despite these obstacles, he must pay full wages and taxes during this period. He may also have difficulty assigning a retrained miner to a job which is claimed by a different union. A firm usually cannot employ a man as a welder when union welders are looking for jobs, even though he may have learned welding very well.

SUMMARY

Economic growth is not a simple target. Brave statements that we must achieve a greater percentage of growth are largely meaningless. Using the income yardstick, most people will agree that our economy is doing quite well, although it could do much better.

The obstacles to growth are numerous. The spiral effect of change enlarges the swings in economic activity, both up and down. The additional repercussions of every new undertaking vary widely and are hard to predict. Stable growth, therefore, becomes difficult to achieve.

The record of business fluctuations in this country shows steady improvement with regard to containing the severity and length of the downward cycle. We are still far from achieving complete stability, however; indeed, we may never reach this goal.

Economic progress comes in spurts, interrupted by periods when human errors must be corrected before further growth can be achieved. An early discovery and correction of mistakes avoids the need for later sharp inventory reductions which aggravate every recession. Maintenance of consumption helps to shorten the time required for such corrections.

The Depression of the thirties proved to be a grim lesson for the nation as a whole. For the most part it left losers in its wake who still remember their experience and want no repetition of this disaster.

The dangers of inflation are equally serious, but less generally understood. The initial stage of the disease looks so much like prosperity that few people object when they see prices on a steady rise. This pattern must be broken in time, before it degenerates into a serious inflation with its inevitable ruin for the majority of the American people.

Growth is slowed down needlessly by chronic unemployment, a condition which is not even eliminated during the most prosperous years. Lack of flexibility of the labor force due to technology, legal, and contractual arrangements is at the root of this disease.

In spite of all human errors, growth has been taking place during recent decades, though with sharp variations from one year to the next. As we endeavor to eliminate the remaining weaknesses of the system, the economy should be able to improve on its past performance.

Discussion Questions

1. Can business fluctuations be avoided?
2. Could the U.S. economy grow faster than it does? Should it? Point out the implications of fast growth as an overriding economic goal.
3. Will the Great Depression be repeated? What made it such a terrible experience?
4. Inflation is an ever-present danger to the health of our economic system, but many people feel that "a little inflation is a good thing." Can you explain this contradiction?
5. Why does unemployment continue to plague us even in times of prosperity?
6. Discuss the causes of the inflation of 1966.

Suggested Reading

BURNS, ARTHUR F., *Prosperity Without Inflation*. New York, Fordham Press, 1958.

COLLERY, ARNOLD, *National Income and Employment Analysis*. New York, Wiley, 1966.

GALBRAITH, JOHN KENNEDY, *The Great Crash, 1929*. Boston, Houghton Mifflin, 1961.

HABERLER, GOTTFRIED, *Inflation, Its Causes and Cures*, rev. ed. Washington, D.C., American Enterprise Association, 1966.

————, *Prosperity and Depression*, 4th ed. Cambridge, Mass., Harvard Press, 1958.

SHANNON, DAVID A., *The Great Depression*. Englewood Cliffs, N.J., Prentice-Hall, 1960.

17

PUBLIC FINANCE

The importance of the role of government in a free enterprise economy has become evident from every chapter in this book. In particular, the growth of public action in the twentieth century was shown in detail in Chapter 3. The multitude of collective tasks requires special efforts to determine the most efficient ways of providing and financing public services. A discussion of these arrangements is the purpose of the present chapter.

Public finance refers to the activity of contracting expenditures for collective services and providing the means of paying for them. The citizen influences the trend of government activity through his vote and through his expression of opinion to elected representatives. It is, therefore, particularly important that he be aware of the principles involved in public finance.

The problem of the best level of collective action is not nearly as simple as the extremes of public opinion will have it. Some public expenditures are rated by the majority as desirable over individual expenditures. Road building and better schools may benefit a community far beyond their costs, but not every idea for a publicly financed project belongs in this category. The late Professor Slichter expressed this problem of a modern economy most vividly in the following terms:

> In a dynamic society the demand for services from the government is constantly growing—not only for the traditional services but also for new services. In such a society it may actually be wise to step up, not cut down, what we spend on government. For government is not merely an expense, it is also a service-rendering organization that can repay its costs many-fold in the services it gives.
>
> To many people the expansion of government activities is a cause for alarm. They fear the effects of its growing costs on our economy. They fear that the expanding activity of the government will undermine our traditional philosophy of life by weakening the spirit of self-reliance and will imperil our political liberties by making us unduly subject to influence by the holders of public office.[1]

We shall now discuss the principles and procedures of controlling public expenditures and revenues, and will follow with a description of the main features of some widely used taxes. A look at actual expenditures and revenues of federal, state, and local governments will conclude the chapter.

[1] S. H. Slichter, "Government Spending Can Reduce Taxes," *Harvard Business Review,* July 1957, p. 100.

PRINCIPLES OF PUBLIC EXPENDITURES

The main characteristics of collective expenditures can be classified in several ways; efficiency and equity are two useful criteria which are often applied.

Efficiency

The need for efficiency in the management of collective services has been magnified by the growing impact of public action. When the total cost of government was an insignificant share of the national income, it was nice to see efficiency in government; and any harm from waste was mitigated in its effects because the amounts involved were small. With more than one out of four dollars spent by public officials today, however, inefficient use of public funds may jeopardize the growth of the economy.

Technological Efficiency.   Technological progress often determines the nature of a public service. Supervision of air lanes and airwaves furnishes a typical example of centralized services needed to permit each citizen the enjoyment of air transportation or television. A population which moves quickly and in large numbers requires broad standardizations; and the numerous license tags often found on trucks moving in several states bear witness to the need for more efficient handling of the problem.

Centralized Versus Decentralized Operations.   Any discussion of federal expenditures as compared with state expenditures is likely to create more heat than light. The trend during this century has been clearly toward more federal responsibilities, owing in part to the technological changes we have just mentioned. In many instances, federal action is more efficient even when the service can be provided on the state level. One set of centralized files for a Federal Bureau of Investigation costs less and is infinitely more efficient than fifty sets of state criminal files.

The trend toward federal expenditures is most pronounced in times of war—hot or cold—when national defense, foreign relations, and space explorations overshadow other demands on the public purse. When world tensions calm down again, the accumulated backlog of more localized demands for service will then try to catch up. A larger share of the public dollar will be devoted to schoolhouses and roads. Figure 17-1 shows recent trends in federal expenditures as compared with those of state and local governments.

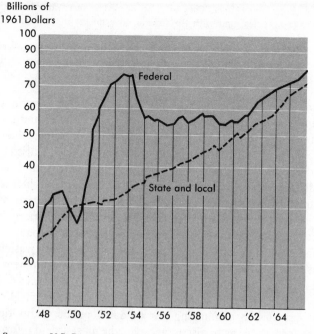

SOURCE: U.S. Bureau of the Census.

FIG. 17-1. **Trend of Government Purchases of Goods and Services, 1948–1965**

The advantages of decentralized services can be significant as priorities when specific expenditures are established. When the federal government engages in road construction, it will favor the interstate highway, even though the improvement of local roads may be a more urgent desire of the people living in certain areas. A big, modern, federal veterans hospital is a poor substitute for an urgently needed improvement of medical facilities which all citizens of a town can use.

From the viewpoint of efficiency, decentralized public services are seldom better than central control. The popular idea of defenders of states' rights that every dollar sent to Washington is half wasted would be hard to prove in very many instances. In the opinion of the Committee for Economic Development, the position of local government would be vastly improved if

. . . existing patterns of local government can be drastically revised, to encourage local policy decision-making and to permit effective management of local affairs. This will not be easy, for major structural adjustments are required if we are to preserve the fundamental values in local self-government. But competent local units, responsive to the requirements of an enlightened public, can serve two primary purposes. They can identify local problems and opportunities, and then plan and execute programs with optimum effect. They are also needed to serve in an effective partnership with state agencies, and with the federal government in its expanding fields of activity.

. . . most American communities lack any instrumentality of government with legal powers, geographic jurisdiction, and independent revenue sources necessary to conduct local self-government in any valid sense.[2]

Too Many Small Governments.   The general cost of government operations below the national level is a high one. The number and size of these governing bodies is dictated by historical accident rather than by managerial efficiency. Overlapping authority and divided jurisdiction have produced a bewildering array of frequently ineffective public authorities. School districts are still furnishing minimum standards of literacy to rural communities of the nineteenth century. Moreover, a modern high school requires several hundred students in order to afford the specialized teaching services needed for the best instruction of the youth of today.

Road construction by county commissioners is a very wasteful method because of the needless duplication of facilities; heavy equipment cannot be amortized by occasional use in only one county. A centralized state highway department is easily justified by its greater efficiency. However, the political obstacles to eliminating our outdated public authorities are frequently so formidable as to discourage even the most ardent reformers.

In the same policy statement advocating the modernization of local government, the Committee for Economic Development comments as follows:

American institutions of local government are under severe and increasing strain. Well designed, by and large, to meet the simpler needs of earlier times, they are poorly suited to cope with new burdens imposed on all governments by the complex conditions of modern life. Adaptation to change has been so slow, so limited, and so reluctant that the future role—even the continued viability—of these institutions is now in grave doubt.

The costs of local government are rising steeply. Direct expenditures by all municipalities, counties, New England towns, townships, independent school districts, and special districts rose from 20.1 billion in 1952 to $45.1 billion in 1962 . . . partly because of evidences of waste, injustice, and occasional corruption—popular discontent with both quantity and quality of services rendered by the nation's 80,000 separate local governments is greater today than it was ten, or twenty, or fifty years ago. . . .

The nation's courthouses and city halls have often seemed to lack the vision and dedication—as well as the financial resources—to diagnose conditions, devise solutions, and make vigorous response. New functions needed to meet new situations are neglected by most local units, and old functions are conducted without benefit of new techniques. By default, initiatives have commonly been left to more resourceful federal forces. Cast in an archaic mold, unable to cope with new issues, many—if not most—local governments are centers of strenuous resistance to change of any kind.[3]

2 *Modernizing Local Government* (New York, Committee for Economic Development, 1966), pp. 14–15.
3 *Ibid.,* p. 8–9.

Equity

The question of equity, or justice, is a difficult one, since different people will have different opinions as to what it comprises. Some people feel that services should be closely related to the share contributed by the taxpayers. Others want to use public authority to even out the inequalities between areas, districts, and income levels. A third group favors a compromise which offers public facilities regardless of wealth, but which encourages the greatest effort of all.

The Benefit Principle. Some citizens feel that the principles by which we judge public services are merely an extension of the same maxims which apply to the acquisition of private services for the purpose of satisfying individual wants. When a man wants a new car, he goes out and buys it; when he wants a new highway, he can buy it only collectively, but he ought to be held responsible for his share through fees or taxes which match the benefits received. Toll roads and gasoline taxes reflect this viewpoint. According to this philosophy, public services are favored only when they are clearly more efficient than private action.

In concept, the benefit principle has the advantage of great simplicity. The implications of this approach, however, are not always fully realized. The cost of national defense cannot be meaningfully allocated on the basis of benefits received. Should the cost of the space race to the moon be charged only to those who favor it? On a local basis, this philosophy would abolish public recreation facilities, because wealthy men own private estates and swimming pools and poor men cannot afford the full cost of public facilities. A poor community that offers inadequate salaries will have bad public schools because it cannot attract good teachers; the rich suburb will have excellent public facilities because it can afford them. Consequently, the poor areas remain condemned to exist under eternal slum conditions.

The defenders of this concept of equity will point out that liberal benefits for poorer sections of the state or the country encourage a letdown in efforts to collect local taxes and makes these areas wards of the central government. In addition, they charge that such outside help leads to increased dependence and promotes laziness, both traits which must be discouraged. The opposition will claim that public neglect of the less fortunate in our midst widens the gap between the rich and the poor, a result which can hardly be considered a reasonable standard of equity.

Redistribution of Income. Some people feel that equity in public expenditures must be obtained by the opposite extreme. Collective services, they argue, should give the underprivileged areas what the richer sectors can obtain without help. They favor the use of public funds for slum clearance, urban renewal, and other public facilities. They prefer centralized control for activities where poor states are falling behind, such as area redevelopment laws that extend federal help to depressed counties.

The proponents of this philosophy consider equity as an opportunity to redistribute income and give all men a chance for improvement regardless of their past record. Public assistance payments are part of this theory, which holds that the state has the moral duty to rectify the injustices caused by the private sector of the economy.

Matching Funds.   The third alternative represents a compromise. It refuses to condemn poor areas to increasing misery, but it also encourages self-reliance. The outgrowth of this philosophy is an arrangement whereby local efforts are boosted with centrally controlled matching funds. Poor districts receive some help with their expenditures from wealthier areas, but only on the condition that the backward sector makes a determined effort to help itself.

This concept of equity appeals to many people, but its realization in practice may lead to severe conflicts in specific cases. The matching of funds is widely used in connection with urban renewal, highway legislation, and public assistance. Some states follow a similar technique to apportion school expenditures.

Matching funds requires cooperation and compromise; delays will inevitably result when two sets of public authorities must approve a project. Though far from ideal, this system seems to be acceptable to a large number of citizens. The matching arrangements differ a great deal, depending on the law covering a project. In some cases the U.S. Treasury contributes only a small share, but in the case of interstate highways, for example, it pays 90 percent of the cost.

THE BUDGET OF THE FEDERAL GOVERNMENT

Legislative bodies have the duty to formulate programs which assign some order of priority to competing demands for public services. The citizens influence with their votes the type of services they receive; new programs are often the result of popular demand. Within the broad political mandate conferred by the people, the relative importance of each service is decided by the legislature upon the recommendation of the executive officer. This approach holds true for most public authorities such as state governors, mayors of towns, and other local administrators. The federal government's, however, is the most important budget to the national economy; it deserves more detailed consideration.

Historical Background

In 1789 Alexander Hamilton, the first Secretary of the Treasury, favored a policy of strong, centralized control for the purpose of promoting public services and economic growth. This active role of the federal government was rejected in an era when the prevailing philosophy limited public authority to a minor role. Congress handled all fiscal policy. The total volume of public spending was so small that a senator had no difficulty keeping fully informed about all major tasks of the federal establishment.

As federal programs grew in size and number, Congress delegated fiscal legislation to various committees. The increase in the federal role caused by World War I demonstrated the need for better fiscal arrangements. The Budget and Accounting Act of 1921 for the first time charged the President with the task of preparing a unified budget.

Budget Preparation

Ideally, the President and Congress decide on the relative importance of various federal services, assign each program to its proper department, and let the department prepare the administrative details for accomplishing its objectives. In practice, however, this procedure does not exist. The federal budget is prepared from the bottom up; each administrator decides what his office wants to do in the future and requests the necessary funds.

The Bureau of the Budget. The Bureau of the Budget is directly responsible to the President. It reviews, revises, and consolidates, then modifies and coordinates the myriad proposals for action which stream in after many months of internal struggle in the departments or agencies where they originated. The result is a haggling over dollars instead of an objective appraisal of the value of each program. The Bureau of the Budget could be transformed into an executive office with broad program and overall appraisal authority, but it does not occupy this position now.

The President of the United States eventually becomes the final arbiter of all competing requests included in the budget. In January he sends the final proposal to Congress with his annual budget message for appropriation of funds to be used at the beginning of the following fiscal year on July 1.[4] Federal budget estimates for 1968 are shown in Figure 17-2.

The General Accounting Office (GAO). In 1921 Congress created an office to assist in the unwieldy job of maintaining its constitutional control

[4] The "fiscal year" is the government accounting period; it starts and ends six months earlier than the corresponding calendar year.

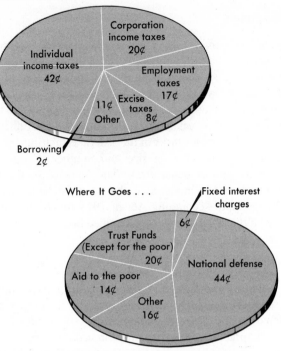

Where It Comes From . . .

Where It Goes . . .

SOURCE: The Budget of the United States Government, 1968.

FIG. 17-2.   **The Federal Budget, 1968**
(Consolidated Cash Statement, fiscal year estimate)

over federal spending. The General Accounting Office could be of great help in supervising and improving the efficiency of national programs. Unfortunately, its actual task is far more modest. Concerned largely with accounting procedures, the office makes sure that expenditures are legal, without challenging their wisdom or the efficiency of federal use of resources.

Departments and Agencies.   Within the executive branch of the federal government there are twelve departments, each headed by a Cabinet secretary, and over sixty independent agencies. They lead their own separate existence, and the organizational task of avoiding duplication and overlapping jurisdiction among them is truly formidable. When a new popular objective can be identified, several agencies are sure to battle for "a piece of the action." When the "war on poverty" was launched, the execution went to a new agency, the Office of Economic Opportunity. But others as well were quick to participate in such a popular program. Several departments came forward with their own projects to help the poor; and the Department of Health, Education, and Welfare launched several educational programs in support of the new goal. The coordination of these multiple efforts is often spotty and the cost to the taxpayer may be needlessly large as a result.

The Role of Congress

The Constitution assigns to Congress the power of the purse; only the elected representatives of the people determine national objectives and assign the means of execution. In practice, however, these lofty goals defy achievement. Congress receives the budget from the President; the sheer size of the document causes real complications, and attempts to discuss it meaningfully as a unit have failed in the past. Instead, many committees deal with one section and legislate in their area without much coordination of total expenditures. Dissatisfaction with existing Congressional budgetary procedures is widespread, the Committee for Economic Development lists the following criticisms: ". . . (1) failure to debate and decide national fiscal policy on broad, over-all terms, (2) a piecemeal approach to appropriations, (3) undue attention to short-term authorizations rather than longer-range considerations, (4) emphasis on things and services to be purchased rather than on functions performed or purposes served, (5) excessive delegation of authority to subcommittees and to their chairmen, and (6) improper interference with administrative operations." [5]

Authorization. New programs must be authorized before any funds can be made available. It has been customary for Congress to authorize programs without time limit, as an expression of its desire to pursue some specific objectives. If Congress wants to subsidize housing in slum areas, one authorization should be sufficient to do so. More and more projects, however, have been authorized in recent years for a limited time, quite often for as little as one year. Foreign aid, for example, is usually authorized for a year at a time, though many projects require a longer period for effective planning and execution. Authorization of a program is a prerequisite of Congressional approval, but provides no funds for the actual financing of a service. Lack of funds may in practice nullify a prior authorization of a project.

Appropriation. The executive branch of the federal government may pay out funds only pursuant to an appropriation voted by Congress. Conceivably, a majority of lawmakers could refuse payments for services rendered, but Congress is always under pressure to appropriate funds needed for

[5] *Budgeting for National Objectives* (New York, Committee for Economic Development, 1966), p. 42.

previously authorized services. This arrangement considerably reduces the discretionary power of the legislature. Any project which has been authorized and put into operation will need to be continued to its conclusion in order to avoid excessive waste. A new river dam project may have been authorized on the basis of low cost estimates and construction already begun. After several years of low appropriations, the project becomes more expensive than planned, and a refusal to authorize funds for the completion of the project would reduce past expenditures to a total loss.

Evaluation. The role of Congress in the evaluation of existing programs is far more limited than it could be. The GAO is directly responsible to Congress in its supervision of expenditures by the executive departments. It should not be too difficult to widen the horizon of this office so that it may scrutinize expenditures not only for their legality, but also for their continued usefulness.

Budget Measures

Federal finances are generally discussed in terms of three different budget measures. They are known as the "administrative budget," the "consolidated cash statement," and the "federal sector of the national income accounts." A comparison of the three budget measures is shown in Table 17-1.

Administrative Budget. The administrative budget is the oldest and best-known measure of federal finances. It represents the request for appropriations by the President and includes all funds requiring Congressional approval. The figures which make the newspaper headlines are usually taken from the administrative budget. Unfortunately, this well-known yardstick today covers less than 80 percent of federal transactions. A full picture of federal finances is provided by the following budget measure.

Consolidated Cash Statement. Total federal receipts from and payments to the public are shown in the consolidated cash statement. It is the best available measure of the cash flow between the federal government and its citizens and provides a more accurate financial picture than the administrative budget. Included in it is the operation of the trust funds that have been authorized by Congress on a continuing basis without need for annual appropriations. Trust funds have specific obligations for which they make payments stipulated by law; they receive the necessary cash from special taxes assigned to this purpose. Social security taxes flow directly into the fund which pays retired people and others entitled to receive such pensions. The Highway Trust Fund is supported by gasoline taxes and makes match-

TABLE 17-1.   Comparison of Federal Budgets for Selected Years
(Fiscal years, billions of dollars)

	1958	1962	1965	1968 (Estimate)
Federal Receipts				
Administrative budget receipts:	68.6	81.4	93.1	126.9
Trust fund receipts	+16.3	+ 24.3	+ 31.0	+ 48.2
Intragovernmental transactions and other adjustments	− 2.9	− 3.8	− 4.4	− 7.0
Total cash receipts from the public	82.0	101.9	119.7	168.1
Loan receipts, etc.	− 2.9	− .8	− .9	− 1.4
Timing difference	− 1.2	+ 3.1	+ 1.8	+ .4
National income accounts, receipts	77.9	104.2	120.6	167.1
Federal Payments				
Administrative budget expenditures:	71.4	87.8	96.5	135.0
Trust fund expenditures	+16.1	+ 25.2	+ 29.6	+ 44.5
Intragovernmental transactions and other adjustments	− 2.9	− 5.3	− 3.7	− 7.1
Total cash payments to the public	84.6	107.7	122.4	172.4
Loan Payments, etc.	− 3.0	− 4.2	− 6.7	− 3.6
Timing difference	+ 1.2	+ 2.9	+ 2.6	+ .4
National income accounts, payments	82.8	106.4	118.3	169.2

SOURCE: The Budget of the United States Government, 1968.

ing payments to states for road building. Mortgage loan activities by the Federal National Mortgage Association (FNMA) are partly covered by a fund. Figure 17-3 shows the extent of federal trust fund activities estimated for 1968.

National Income Budget.   We have earlier encountered the important role played by government expenditures in the composition of the national product. The measure of the federal sector of the national income accounts covers all federal transactions included in the consolidated cash statement. It excludes, however, purely financial transactions such as loans, and it differs in the timing of its receipts and payments. Therefore, it is always similar to the cash budget, though never exactly the same. Estimates of future budget expenditures have a tendency to be too low, causing often a "surprise" of unexpectedly large deficits.

RAISING GOVERNMENT REVENUE

Payment must be made for government services. Where does the money come from? There are four main techniques for raising the needed funds:

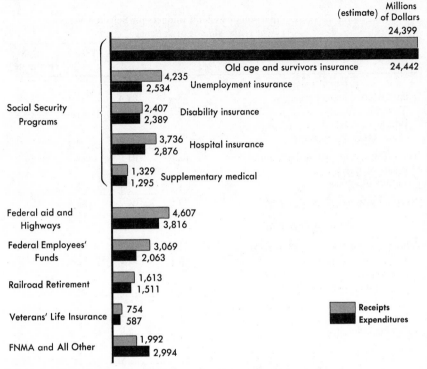

Source: The Budget of the United States Government, 1968.

Fig. 17-3.   Trust Fund Receipts and Expenditures, 1968

services are sold for a fee; bond sales raise funds from people who buy them
voluntarily; taxes are levied to bring in money by legal compulsion; and
finally, issues of new money (inflation) provide funds not raised by the
other three methods.

Four Ways of Raising Revenue

The four methods of raising enough revenue to meet government expenditures do not exclude each other but are often used together. The question
which concerns the citizen is frequently one of emphasis on one fund-
raising technique rather than another. Let us look at their relative merits.

Fee Payments.   Some types of collective services can be treated much like
those of the private sector. Local and state governments raise a significant
amount of money from sales of specific services. Water plants not only pay
for themselves, but often raise a surplus for other uses. Hunting licenses,
admission fees to state parks, inspection dues, and student fees in state
universities pay, at least in part, for the cost of services rendered.

This technique of raising money is based on the benefit principle, which has been discussed earlier. The applicability of this principle is narrowly limited. In many cases, services are rendered collectively because too many persons could not, or would not, buy them if they had a choice. The maintenance of public schools is the best example of a type of service to which the benefit principle is not applied.

Bond Sales. The government may raise funds by borrowing from the public. To do so, it offers bonds for sale with the promise of periodic interest payments and eventual return of the loaned funds. The main advantage of this method is the lack of compulsion; the purchase of bonds is voluntary. But considering the volume of funds needed by the government every year, it is quite obvious that voluntary means of fund raising cannot provide as much as needed. The bonds sold by the United States Treasury form the national debt, which will be discussed in the next chapter.

Taxes. Taxes have always been the principal source of public revenue. The right to levy taxes is the traditional function of a governing body. Indeed, the real powers of government authority are directly related to its ability to raise taxes. To tax fairly, to collect funds honestly and effectively, and to refrain from abuse of this power are the marks of good government. The main principles of taxation will be described below.

Inflation. Inflation is generally considered the most harmful method of raising needed revenue. Despite the inevitable damage wrought by inflationary methods, their popularity with legislatures has been long established. Raising tax rates is unpopular, but higher prices and incomes will boost tax revenue just as effectively at the old rates. Such an inflation may be started by the issue of new money to pay due bills, or by the sale of bonds to banks, which in turn increases the money in circulation.

Assume that a man earns $10,000 per year and pays $1,000 in taxes. If inflation drives up prices and incomes 20 percent, the same man will earn $12,000, which does not buy any more goods than his lower income did before. His tax bill rises even more, and he now owes $1,300, because his additional income puts him in a higher tax bracket. The effect of this inflationary move is, therefore, the same as the result of a direct tax-rate increase. Since not all people realize the outcome fully, it is a great temptation to vote against an open increase in taxes and to favor a hidden one.

PRINCIPLES OF TAXATION

What features make for a good tax? Some people will call this question self-contradictory because they feel that all taxes are bad. However, some taxes are worse than others, the worst being one that irritates everybody and collects nothing.

Every tax will change the distribution and use of income, because it forces the taxpayer to hand over to the government money which he would otherwise spend according to his own preference. Taxes may profoundly alter private economic goals; they can destroy business ventures and completely change traditional patterns of living. If a tax is levied on sugarcoated cereal, the business of sugarcoating cereal will suffer.

The principles of taxation provide guidance in reducing distortions caused by taxes to a level which the majority of the people will accept. A tax must be able to raise funds without undue costs for collection; it must be applied equitably; and it should promote stability and growth of the economic system.

The Ability to Raise Funds

The first objective of a tax is to raise revenue. This statement does not exclude the use of taxes for quite different purposes. A federal tax on professional gambling helps the police more than it does the revenue collector. A special tax on oleomargarine represented for many years the unsuccessful attempt of dairy interests to eliminate a new, competitive product.

Broad Base.   To raise huge sums, a tax must reach the largest possible number of citizens. This type of taxation, which includes broadly based income taxes and general sales taxes, causes the most vociferous opposition, since no individual can hope to escape its impact entirely. Legislators have far less to fear from their constituents when they levy special taxes concerning only a few people; the revenue from such a tax, however, will not be large.

Tax Avoidance.   A tax should be designed so that the taxpayer cannot avoid it. Avoidance is a legal and legitimate device of individuals to reduce their tax payments. For example, a tax on specific products, such as leather pocketbooks, can be avoided by the use of an untaxed substitute, such as imitation leather or plastic. When an industrial plant moves to Puerto Rico to avoid federal taxes, the economic impact of taxes becomes quite clear. The process of tax avoidance illustrates a major type of economic distortion caused by taxation.

Tax Evasion.   Avoidance of a tax must not be confused with evasion of taxes, which is the illegal refusal to pay the taxes required by law. A clearly written tax law combined with effective enforcement action can keep evasion to a minimum. Widespread tax evasion stems from a feeling that tax laws are capricious, unfair, and favor a minority. Such weaknesses can undermine the entire system of revenue collection when jurors are no longer willing to convict evaders because the crime has become so common that anyone, including the jurors themselves, might be indicted tomorrow.

Tax Incidence. Who pays the tax? The man who sends his check to the revenue collector is not always the one who pays. A cigarette manufacturer buys the tax stamps required by law and adds their full cost to each package. The consumer appears to be the one who pays the tax. But this, too, is not always the case. If the consumer cannot be induced to pay a higher price, the retailers or wholesalers may have to pay the tax out of their profits. A vending-machine firm may find, for example, that its customers will buy goods for a dime but not for 11 cents. A new 1-cent tax will have to be paid by the firm. The "incidence" of the tax, as the problem is called by economists, rests with someone in the chain from producer to consumer who is not able to shift the burden to someone else. The difficulty of predicting who will finally bear the brunt of a tax change greatly adds to the problems of writing wise tax laws.

The Cost of Tax Collection

The administrative burden of collecting a tax may seem of minor importance, but an efficient method of revenue collection keeps costs to a small fraction of the amount raised. The need for enforcement must also be taken into consideration when collection problems are discussed.

Administration is simplified when the collector needs to contact only a few people and when he is able to render the tax self-enforcing. Cigarette taxes, for example, have both advantages. The manufacturer's excise tax makes the producer a tax collector; the firm buys tax stamps and uses them to seal every package. Whenever a metering device can measure taxable amounts mechanically, the problem of collection is relatively simple.

Taxing a truck on the basis of actual loads carried would cost too much for the enforcement to be worth the effort. The effective collection of high income taxes from many millions of small taxpayers necessitated the introduction of the withholding principle. Most of the tax due is deducted by the employer and never reaches the income earner.

The Ability to Pay

A law could be imagined which would order every family in the nation to pay $500 per year. Such a measure would arouse a storm of protest for two reasons: most people would consider this tax grossly unfair, and many families would not be able to pay the required amount. A taxpayer's ability to pay is an important consideration in the formulation of revenue laws. This ability is hard to measure and to enforce in an acceptable manner.

A levy of heavy taxes on luxury goods which only the rich would buy presumably follows the ability-to-pay principle. But no two people are likely to agree on any list of luxury products. A mink coat may be sheer luxury for a housewife who lives in a warm climate, and a real necessity for the aspiring movie star who wants to give the impression of success. Yesterday's luxuries frequently become the necessities of tomorrow.

Income as a Tax Base.   A man's ability to pay largely depends on his current income; past income is an unrealistic measure. Levies on accumulated wealth are, therefore, likely to do great harm. The widow who continues to live in the once high-priced house of her younger years must move to new surroundings because the taxes on the house are too high for her modest pension.

Income taxes are broadly based on the ability to pay. A man with a $20,000 income may be asked to pay twice as much as one whose income is $10,000. Such a proportional tax considers the wealthy man's greater ability to pay. Usually the higher income will not only demand a greater amount of taxes, but will be taxed at a higher rate as well. The reason for the rate increase is the belief that higher income earners have less need for their money than do poor people. An effort to achieve greater income equality by taking from the rich and giving to the poor is part of the philosophy which favors progressive rates.

Progressive, Proportional, and Regressive Taxes.   A progressive tax levies higher percentage rates on higher income. A proportional tax collects different dollar amounts for different incomes, but at the same rate. A regressive tax often imposes the same dollar levy on all citizens regardless of their income. In this situation the ratio of taxes to incomes decreases as incomes increase. Let's assume, for example, that a $5,000 income pays $500 tax. If a $10,000 income pays $2,000 in taxes, the rate is progressive; if only $1,000 is due, the rate is proportional; and if the higher income pays only $500, the tax is regressive. An example of the progressive type is the personal income tax; the poll tax, which charged every voter the same amount, was regressive. Is a three-percent sales tax proportional? Before you answer in the affirmative, remember that the three percent is figured on your purchases, not on your income. Rich or poor pay the same amount of sales tax for the same purchase, an indication of regressiveness.

Most tax systems combine progressive and regressive taxes in an effort to extract as much revenue as possible. No tax law will ever be likely to satisfy all people. The majority may agree that tax laws should refrain from adhering to the extremes of progressiveness or its opposite, but they will differ violently on the right mixture. The problem of a fair distribution of the tax burden becomes more serious as the need for raising funds grows and tends to raise the rates of all taxes. High rates will stimulate new techniques for tax avoidance and create rising pressures for special exemptions and legal loopholes.

The best tax system is a matter of personal opinion rather than of scientific determination. In practice, taxes will reflect a compromise of many conflicting political pressures.

Revenue Versus Stabilization

Taxes may be introduced to counteract business fluctuations. A progressive tax collects much more when many incomes are moving into higher rate brackets; this is one way of slowing down the rise of private expenditures when business is booming. On the other hand, in a recession, when tax collections drop faster than incomes, more money remains available for consumption. This leveling effect is highly desirable to reduce fluctuations, but the job of the Treasury is complicated with bills to pay all the time.

A tax can raise a steady flow of revenue if it is levied without consideration of taxpayers' income and ability to pay. A "bread tax" would illustrate an effort to collect the same revenue in prosperity and depression.[6] From most other viewpoints, however, such a tax would be most objectionable.

Promoting Economic Growth

The use of taxation to raise revenue or to redistribute income is generally accepted; the possibility of using tax laws to promote economic growth, however, has been neglected far too long. In fact, disregard of the growth-retarding influence of some taxes must take its share of the blame for the slow development of the American economy in recent years.

Growth will be slowed down when normal business profits are taxed away. Such taxes discourage new investments and hurt small firms, particularly when these businessmen are most successful and trying to expand. They need all their profits for further investments, since they cannot yet command enough credit to use much loan capital. Any tax which penalizes the success of growing firms is an anti-growth tax.

High income taxes are frequently accused of destroying a man's in-

[6] The processing tax on grain imposed by the Food and Agriculture Act of 1965 has been called a "bread tax" by its opponents.

centive. A person may tell you that an increase in his salary would be worthless because it would place him in a higher tax bracket. Such a statement is never true; even in the highest bracket, some part of the added income will be left to the taxpayer.

In fact, studies have shown that for most people high income tax rates have no significant effect on their desire to work. Low income earners cannot afford to relax; they may even have to make greater efforts to support their families and pay their taxes. In the high tax brackets most income recipients enjoy their work sufficiently that taxes do not influence their efforts. The corporation president wants to see his firm grow and prosper as a matter of personal satisfaction, regardless of his financial reward.

High income taxes have, however, a detrimental effect on economic growth for quite different reasons. These levies channel too much effort of the best minds into the wasteful occupation of searching for schemes to avoid high taxes. Moreover, the direction of the work of high income earners may be dictated primarily by tax advantages, rather than by more productive considerations. The movie star who is willing to do a bad movie in Europe instead of a good one in Hollywood is prompted by the tax advantages to be gained abroad.

The unfavorable effect of high income tax rates becomes most disturbing when it comes to financing a risky venture. Chances of losing are great in this case, but they are balanced by an opportunity for unusually high profit. To the rich person who is able to take a chance and finance such a gamble, the prospect of a high rate of return holds no appeal. He feels like a man who is fighting loaded dice. If he loses, all his investment is gone; his risk is 100 percent. If he wins, his profit will be reduced sharply by the high income tax. No wonder he declines putting his money on an untried project! Instead, he buys a tax-exempt, low-interest-bearing municipal bond with very little risk, and he receives about the same net income.

Growth can be stimulated when tax laws permit some portion of the expense of new investments to be deducted from payments; such incentives may induce the most profitable firms with the highest taxes to expand their business and provide new economic opportunities. The effectiveness of such measures depends, of course, on the attractiveness of the incentive.

As a result of the tax reduction of 1964,[7] much has been learned about the effect of taxes in stimulating the growth of the economy. An increase in business deductions from profits for depreciation purposes in 1963 was an earlier stimulus to a then sluggish economy. This change was accomplished by executive order and did not require the approval of Congress. Its beneficial effect became apparent after a few months, when new investment by business showed a definite increase. The reduction of per-

---

[7] Revenue Act of 1964, February 26, 1964.

sonal and corporation income tax rates gave an added boost to the economy. Further, special investment credits were allowed to firms that decided on new investment spending. The results of these measures were as beneficial as expected and led to a healthy upswing, before the war in Vietnam overshadowed the normal development of the national economy.

Characteristics of Specific Taxes

How do our taxes stand up in the light of the principles we have discussed? Let us look at the five taxes which collect most of the public revenue in this country.

Personal Income Tax.   The largest amount of revenue is collected by the personal income tax. Its rates are steeply progressive and still very high, with numerous exceptions for special situations. The administration of the tax is difficult and involves much legal litigation. One of its best features is its sharp rise in collections during prosperity and the immediate drop of revenue when business falls.

Income tax rates rise so high that it is virtually impossible to become a millionaire from earning income. Many newly rich people owe their wealth to the avoidance of the dangerous word "income" and the substitution instead of "capital gains." Capital gains with a maximum tax rate of 25 percent (as opposed to 70 percent for income) are the magic words that allow people to continue accumulating great wealth. The details of converting high-taxed income into low-taxed capital gain are the domain of tax lawyers and cannot entertain us here, but their inventiveness has rendered the top income tax rates quite harmless. The marked progressiveness of the rate structure clearly has an equalizing effect, a result approved or deplored by many citizens.

Corporation Income Tax.   The corporate income tax is levied on the profit of corporations. It has rates reaching up to 48 percent for all firms showing good profits. Revenue collections shift more drastically with changes in business than for any other tax. The greatest virtues of the tax are high revenues in good times and a marked stabilizing effect which counteracts business fluctuations.

The major weakness of the tax is claimed to be its deterrence of economic growth. Small, adventurous new firms are hard hit by the way it operates; only large, stable enterprises can balance profits and losses internally to avoid high taxable income. A small firm lacks this opportunity. The tax has no effect on growth when it becomes part of the cost of the product, because it can then be shifted to the final consumer in the form of higher prices.

Employment Taxes. Taxes levied on employment are deducted from the payroll and placed directly into the social security trust fund to maintain the flow of benefits provided by law. Such taxes are regressive, since they are levied only on the lower part of a person's income; nevertheless, a steady revenue is assured unless the number of employed workers fluctuates sharply.

An employment tax offers few collection problems and does not interfere with economic growth. It helps to stabilize the economy, bringing in less revenue in bad times than in good ones. Rising rates of this tax do, however, exert an unfavorable effect on employment; when wages exceed $6,600 per year, additional amounts are not subject to payroll taxes. Therefore, it is more advantageous for a firm to employ one man for twice the hours than it is to hire two people.

Excise and Sales Taxes. Taxes levied on the sales price of a product are called excise or sales taxes. Excise taxes specify the exact product subject to the impost, for example cigarettes or automobiles, while sales taxes are general and cover all but exempt products, such as food in some states. Since rates are not related to income, these taxes are usually considered regressive.

General sales taxes are the main source of revenue of state governments. Although their administration is cumbersome, the revenue remains fairly stable since consumption does not usually change as fast as income. Excise taxes collect revenue for the federal government and for other public authorities. They are popular with the tax collector because they are simple to administer, but the arbitrariness of their impact marks them for lack of equity, particularly when rates differ for each product.

Property Taxes. Real property taxes remain the chief source of funds for local governments in spite of their glaring shortcomings. The management of these taxes is notoriously inefficient.

The value of property is established by an assessment procedure. Very often the value estimate of a house by the official assessor has little apparent relationship to the price of the building. Assessment may be based only on outside dimensions with total disregard of the nature or quality of the interior. In some states, once a house has been assessed its official value will never be changed, regardless of changes that may occur in the neighborhood or in market values. The result is a lack of equity when newer, but inexpensive, houses in a recent development pay higher taxes than a mansion which was built some years earlier.

GOVERNMENT EXPENDITURES IN THE UNITED STATES

The Cooperation of Governments

Federal, state, and local expenditure patterns are separately determined, though all levels of government cooperate in many public functions. Federal payments to state and local governments reached $14.8 billion in 1966. When federal grants contribute to a service, the central government frequently assures the maintenance of specific standards of performance throughout the entire country. Federal inspection may exercise considerable influence on the type of services rendered by the states; the uniformity of the interstate highway system shows the results of identical federal standards.

State payments to local governments for 1965 covered over 20 percent of all local expenditures and were estimated at $14 billion. Although the high cost of education is largely managed on a local level, it includes a heavy contribution of state funds.

Federal Expenditures

Table 17-2 shows all payments of the federal government for the years 1962 and 1965, as well as the estimates for 1968. The amounts include payments by trust funds, which have been mentioned before. Pension checks

TABLE 17-2.   Federal Payments to the Public by Function,
Fiscal years, 1962, 1965, and 1968
(*millions of dollars*)

Function	1962	1965	1968 (Estimate)
National defense	51,462	50,790	76,828
Welfare, health, and labor	23,918	28,191	46,609
Interest (net)	6,940	8,605	10,509
Commerce, transportation, and housing	7,178	8,329	8,725
Veterans benefits and services	6,092	6,080	6,664
Space research and technology	1,257	5,093	5,302
International affairs and finance	4,198	4,794	4,988
Agriculture and agricultural resources	4,177	5,142	4,076
Natural resources	2,339	2,921	3,538
Education	1,052	1,497	2,738
General government	1,837	2,341	2,729
Total federal payments	110,450	123,783	172,706

SOURCE: The Budget of the United States Government, 1968.

for retired people exceed $30 billion in 1968 and are still rising. New programs under the Economic Opportunity Act of 1964 add significantly to the cost of labor and education.

A large share of the expenditures for commerce and transportation is incurred by the highway construction fund, which paid about $4 billion in 1968. The cost of the veterans' services is increased by almost $1 billion due to pension benefits paid by a trust fund.

Defense. More than half of all federal expenditures are caused by past or future wars. People will agree generally that no amount of sacrifice is too great to keep the country strong and free; appropriation requests for the Defense Department are seldom reduced by Congress in any significant amount. This willingness of the American people to bear the costly burden of worldwide defenses places a heavy responsibility on the President, who must decide the nature and size of our military involvement. It should be noted that any sizable reduction of federal expenditures is unlikely as long as the cost of defense continues to rise.

Interest and Veterans. Payments for interest on the national debt and for veterans' benefits can be properly considered a cost of past wars. The large size of the interest payments is due to the rapid rise of the national debt in World War II. This cost is virtually beyond the control of administrators, as a refusal to pay this obligation would be tantamount to a declaration of bankruptcy.

Veterans' benefits are a national obligation to any soldier whose health was impaired in the service of his country. The extension of benefits to free medical services for the dependents of healthy ex-servicemen introduces, however, a situation of publicly supported medicine for an arbitrarily selected group. In view of the long-standing refusal of Congress to grant similar privileges to other groups, this arrangement seems strangely inconsistent and renders the program vulnerable to attack.

Agriculture. The cost of the farm program is reflected in the expenditures for agriculture. The dwindling representation of the farmers in Congress invites growing opposition from other taxpayers who protest against burdensome subsidies for one segment of the population. The conservation of natural resources is partly linked to farm programs. It includes also new dams for flood control or water power.

Commerce and Space. Until 1961, space expenditures were so insignificant in the federal budget that they were included in transportation. Total outlay for space in 1958 reached $89 million, in 1962 $1.3 billion, and estimates for 1968 expect space expenditures of $5.3 billion.

The cost of housing and community development, which includes slum clearance, public housing, and area redevelopment projects, has also risen in recent years and now exceeds $1 billion.

General Government and Other Expenditures. Expenditures for general government, such as the federal courts or Congress itself, do not appear to be nearly so large when compared with other national functions.

International affairs includes the cost of helping our friends abroad, except for purely military outlays provided by the Defense Department. This expenditure fluctuates considerably, depending upon the prospects for peace around the world.

State and Local Expenditures

Table 17-3 details the nature and cost of public expenditures not associated with the federal government. Education and highways are by far the costliest services for states and local governments. Not all activities are covered in the table, because many services are rendered on a fee basis or by public corporations and are not included in local expenditure budgets; public utilities are the main example of this type of service.

TABLE 17-3. State and Local Government Expenditures by Function, Fiscal Year 1965

Function	State	Local	Total	Percent of Total
	(millions of dollars)			
Education	6,181	22,382	28,563	38.3
Highways	8,214	4,007	12,221	16.4
Public welfare	2,998	3,317	6,315	8.5
Health and sanitation	2,701	5,021	7,722	10.4
Safety (police and fire)	348	3,507	3,855	5.2
Resources, recreation, housing, and urban renewal	1,235	2,849	4,084	5.5
Interest	822	1,668	2,490	3.3
General administration	1,405	1,825	3,230	4.3
All other	2,238	3,829	6,067	8.1
Total expenditures	26,142	48,405	74,547	100.0

SOURCE: U.S. Bureau of the Census, *Governmental Finances in 1964–1965.*

GOVERNMENT REVENUE IN THE UNITED STATES

Federal and state governments may raise revenue without coordinating their efforts. Duplication of taxes is not uncommon. In general, the federal government relies primarily on income taxes, which contribute over 60 percent of its total revenue. States emphasize general sales taxes, and communities depend on the revenue from property taxes.

Federal Revenue

A glance at Table 17-4 reveals the main sources of federal income. In the early days of the nation, customs collections were the only major source of federal funds. Today they are quite negligible in comparison with the four taxes which bring in the bulk of federal funds: individual and corporate income taxes, excise taxes, and employment taxes.

The critical importance of the individual income tax for a sufficient flow of federal revenue is amply illustrated by the figures. While tax rates rise steeply with higher incomes to a maximum of 70 percent, the rates above 50 percent produce little revenue since most taxpayers belong to the lower income brackets. Even a small, though always popular, reduction of the lowest tax rates causes a heavy loss of revenue and usually meets with strong objections from Treasury officials.

TABLE 17-4.   Federal Revenue, Fiscal Years 1962, 1965, and 1968
(millions of dollars)

Revenue Source	1962	1965	1968 (Estimate)
Individual income tax	45,571	48,792	73,200
Corporation income tax	20,523	25,461	33,900
Excise taxes	12,534	14,570	13,746
Employment taxes	12,561	16,905	28,392
Estate and gift taxes	2,016	2,716	3,100
Customs collections	1,142	1,442	2,100
All other receipts	7,518	9,814	13,668
Total receipts	101,865	119,700	168,106

SOURCE: The Budget of the United States Government, 1968.

The top rate of 48 percent of the corporation income tax makes the federal Treasury an almost equal partner in the fortunes of all profitable firms. A recession causes a drastic drop in this tax revenue, leaving federal finances operating at a deficit. Federal excise taxes include taxes on liquor, tobacco, and certain other goods and services, such as automobiles and phone calls. A long list of excise taxes which defied logical explanation was repealed in 1965. Such taxes will become less important as sources of federal revenue, particularly when the often postponed tax reduction on automobiles and communication services becomes effective.[8]

[8] Excise Tax Reduction Act of 1965, June 21, 1965; Tax Adjustment Act of 1966, March 15, 1966.

Employment taxes have been rising rapidly and are now a major source of revenue. Their fast increase is due to higher rates applicable on larger amounts, and to more wage earners. The full impact of this tax in the light of its new importance will need further scrutiny.

State and Local Government Revenues

The largest revenue producer at the lower levels of government is traditionally the tax on real estate. Table 17-5 reveals that almost half of all local revenue depends on this property tax.

The states collect the largest proportion of their funds from a general sales tax; most state governments use rates of not more than 5 percent. Special excise taxes include those on alcohol, cigarettes, and gasoline— favorite targets of the state tax collector.

State income taxes often duplicate the federal personal income taxes, only at lower rates. They are usually levied on the amount of income remaining after the owner has paid his federal taxes. This avoids a situation in which a person might owe the tax collector more than his total income.

TABLE 17-5. **State and Local Government Revenue, Fiscal Year 1965**

Revenue Source	State	Local	Total	Percent of Total
		(millions of dollars)		
Property tax	766	21,817	22,583	30.5
Sales tax	15,059	2,059	17,118	23.1
Income taxes	5,586	433	6,019	8.1
Other taxes	4,714	807	5,521	7.5
Fees, licenses, etc.	3,123	5,278	8,401	11.4
Miscellaneous receipts	1,361	1,968	3,329	4.5
From the federal government	9,874	1,155	11,029	14.9
From state to local governments	−13,563	+13,563	—	—
Total receipts	26,920	47,080	74,000	100.0

SOURCE: U.S. Bureau of the Census, *Governmental Finances in 1964–1965.*

Revenues from granting licenses and from services rendered for specific fees are a significant share of the receipts of state and local governments. Cities boost their income substantially by the operation of commercial enterprises at a profit, particularly in the public utilities field. Many medium-sized towns sell their own water and electricity at rates which make additional local taxes less necessary. In spite of the local popularity of this tax substitute, the economic efficiency of such small plants is often doubtful.

SUMMARY

Government functions have grown more rapidly than those in the private sector of the economy. Particularly the role of the federal authorities has been vastly enlarged in the twentieth century. The accelerated rise in recent years of services provided by states and towns demonstrates the continued vitality of the lower levels of government.

The total outlay for all public services exceeds $200 billion, accounting for almost 30 percent of the total national income. The most expensive services of the government are in the area of national defense. Next in cost and in importance are three fundamental needs for collective action: social security, education, and highways.

Public funds can be collected by means of fee payments, voluntary bond sales, compulsory tax levies, or inflationary price increases. While all these alternatives have been used in the past, we rely chiefly on taxes to provide needed revenue.

The federal government depends primarily on personal and corporate income taxes, followed by employment and excise levies. States consider the sales tax most important, while towns rely on property taxes and on financial help from the state and federal authorities.

Taxes may be designed to apply the benefit principle, but more often they are based on the ability of the individual to pay. For this purpose, progressive rates, which rise with growing incomes, are used. But the steepness of income tax rates leads to the creation of loopholes, and it distorts the incentive of high income earners. The sharp impact of corporate taxes penalizes young and growing business firms and may tend to slow down economic growth.

The use of federal finances not only to pay bills due, but to influence the national economy toward greater stability and growth, will be the subject of the next chapter.

Discussion Questions

1. A tax may be considered good or bad depending on the particular problem to be solved. Apply this principle to some specific taxes.
2. Why has the demand for federal services grown faster than other areas of the nation's economy?
3. Comment on the statement that most federal expenditures are caused by past, present, and future wars.
4. The financial position of state and local governments differs in substance from the situation in the federal government. Why?
5. Should a federal sales tax be substituted for the high income tax rates?
6. Property taxes need to be modernized. Comment.

7. "High income taxes hurt the incentive to work." This statement is heatedly debated. Can you defend all sides of this issue?
8. Why would a "bread tax" collect a similar amount of revenue in good or bad times? What are the objections to such a tax?

Suggested Reading

Budgeting for National Objectives. New York, Committee for Economic Development, 1966.

DUE, JOHN F., *Government Finance: An Economic Analysis,* 3rd ed. Homewood, Ill., Irwin, Inc., 1963.

ECKSTEIN, OTTO, *Public Finance.* Englewood Cliffs, N.J., Prentice-Hall, 1964.

Modernizing Local Government. New York, Committee for Economic Development, 1966.

SHARP, ANSEL M., and BERNARD F. SLIGER, *Public Finance: An Introduction to the Study of the Public Economy,* Homewood, Ill., Irwin, Inc., Dorsey Press, 1964.

18

MONETARY AND FISCAL POLICY

The preceding chapters on national income and economic performance have explained the nature of the problems of steady growth. As the analysis showed quite clearly, Adam Smith's happy thought that all will be well if we just quit interfering with the economy is not supported by the facts. The same information now reaches everybody, and this leads to large-scale bursts of optimism and despair that can cause wild swings in the business cycle, chaos in the monetary system, and widespread unemployment. The federal government today has the task of avoiding these undesirable results and instead promoting healthy economic growth and full employment of human resources.

The introduction of this role for public authority makes it imperative that positive policy measures be formulated in order to reach the objectives demanded by the majority. This chapter will outline some of the more widely debated policy issues of our times. Economists are in broad agreement on the main outlines of the analyses in preceding chapters, though details are always subject to different interpretations. In a discussion of policy, however, no broad agreement should be expected. Once policies receive unanimous approval, they are no longer the object of interest or discussion.

Much of the disagreement on policy stems from the difficulty of reconciling contradictory objectives. Most people want the economy to provide a stable dollar, full employment, rising consumption and investment, more goods, and growing incomes. Conflict arises because of the fundamental need to economize and the impossibility of attaining all goals at the same time. The relative importance of each goal is a matter of personal opinion, and policy measures will vary with the priority assigned to it. To illustrate the point, if full employment becomes the overriding objective, price levels are not likely to remain stable. The writer, of course, has his own ideas about these controversial subjects. He will nonetheless try to refrain from taking sides, and to present the conflicting suggestions on some leading issues without indicating his "approved" answer.

Economic policy is usually divided into monetary and fiscal policy. The demarcation line between the two categories, however, remains uncertain. Several policies may be able to accomplish the same result with different means. There is controversy over methods in such cases; the pleasanter cure is frequently far more expensive and presents a difficult choice, somewhat akin to the case of a man recovering from a bout of pneumonia who may either go back to work part time or take a month's vacation in Bermuda.

Public policy decisions on economic questions are shared by Congress and the President. Many agencies represent strong economic interests, and coordinating their conflicting efforts is hard. For a total view of the economy, the President meets often with four key advisors who have specific competence in this field. The Secretary of the Treasury, who must pay the bills of the federal establishment, is joined by the chairman of the Board of Governors of the Federal Reserve System, who controls the money supply. The director of the Bureau of the Budget exercises his influence on overall federal spending, while the chairman of the Council of Economic Advisors continuously probes the trends of the economy and suggests timely adjustments in policy. When all these advisors agree in their view, and both the President and Congress act according to it, economic development can be regulated within reasonable limits. Economic decisions are of a political nature, however, and agreement among the decision makers is frequently lacking.

MONETARY POLICY

Monetary policy includes all measures to control the supply of money and credit within the broader framework of economic policy. Primary responsibility for the formulation of monetary policy has been assigned by Congress to the Federal Reserve System, and rests particularly with the Board of Governors and the Federal Open Market Committee. The arsenal of tools at the disposal of these authorities was described in detail in Chapter 14.[1]

Why has the dollar failed to remain stable during the last twenty years? Other goals have been permitted to override the objective of maintaining the value of the dollar, and other agencies influence the money supply without reference to overall stability. The result is a compromise where the control of the credit level sometimes comes out only second best.

Conflicting Objectives

The control of the money supply encounters two obstacles: (1) When total spending is not sufficient to keep the economy prosperous, monetary

---

[1] The reader may want to refresh his memory by reviewing the operation of the tools of the Federal Reserve System before he embarks on the policy analysis which follows.

policy is hampered by the difficulty of finding suitable borrowers of available funds; (2) When total spending rises too fast and credit restraints are in order, the prospective borrowers will marshal many good reasons why such a tight money policy should be abandoned.

Too Little Money Spent.   During a depression, banks are very liquid and they want to grant more credit. They are encouraged by a permissive policy on the part of the central bank, which gladly lends more reserve funds at low rates if demanded. Bankers, however, are traditionally inclined toward caution in granting loans. In bad times, their best customers do not want more credit because the need for funds is closely related to the volume of business. Since sales are falling, they try to pay back loans and do not contract new ones, and this causes the amount of money in circulation to fall.

Some daring but unestablished individuals will try their hand at new investments even in bad times. However, the banker regards these men as highly questionable credit risks. Some economists have suggested taxing the unused funds of bankers to encourage more liberal loan policies, but such a radical departure from the traditionally conservative loan policy has not yet been given serious consideration.

Too Much Money Spent.   Most commonly, controversy surrounds the efforts of federal authorities to curtail the flow of money. The central bank will try to restrain credit when a period of prosperity appears to be heading toward broad price increases and a rapid rise in the money supply. But these restraints will inevitably be greeted by violent opposition in and out of Congress.

The opponents point out that credit restrictions will kill prosperity and growth at a time when the economy is just going into high gear. They claim that credit, though high, is not excessive because a booming nation needs a rising money supply. They emphasize the remaining pockets of unemployment which have so far been untouched by the wave of prosperity. Some areas of the country have been left far behind more prosperous states in development, but the opponents of credit restraints hope that eventually the boom will spill over and put the unemployed back to work.

Industries which usually use credit heavily, such as construction businesses, protest against the rising costs of liquid funds and claim that higher interest rates cause inflationary price increases because they drive up building costs. This statement may sound plausible but it is clearly in error. Higher interest rates have the usual rationing effect in this case and will force firms to postpone some building plans until scarce materials become more readily available and credit eases.

The conflict between the goals of full employment and a stable dollar remains unresolved. The economy needs to develop greater flexibility and new methods of adjusting to fast-changing technological requirements in production. An inflationary boom absorbs many unemployed people temporarily, similarly to a shooting war. But few people would advocate starting a war in order to wipe out unemployment. A policy of inflation to increase employment is likely to turn out to be equally harmful, but it will find many more adherents.

Credit control measures must also take into account the country's position in relation to other nations. Wide differences in nations' interest rate levels lead to the movement of liquid funds from one financial center to another. Such marked changes in the amount of credit available are not welcome, and federal policy will try to counteract them. For example, the Federal Reserve Bank of New York may want to reduce its discount rate, but dares not do so because too many deposits might be shifted to London where they will earn interest at a higher rate.

Conflicts Between Policy-Makers

The role of the Federal Reserve System in controlling the money supply is primary but not unique. Congress has created several independent agencies with the power to grant credit for specific purposes. Housing agencies, land banks, and veterans' agencies are major sources of federal credit. Their policies have a noticeable influence on the total money supply, but they are not coordinated with the broader objectives of maintaining a stable dollar.

Independent Agencies.   Specialized agencies formulate policy within the narrow mandate of their Congressional appropriations. When Congress makes a given amount of dollars available to such a body with instructions to spend the funds during a prescribed time period, the agency's management will do its best to place loans accordingly. The effect on the economy depends on the source of these funds. If they are taken away from others, no effect may be noticed in the amount of money in circulation. But the Congressional mandate may add $100 million a month to the money supply and thus frustrate the efforts of the Federal Reserve authorities to restrain new credit by this amount. The agency is interested in placing loans on schedule in order to demonstrate its effectiveness in a specialized field and to qualify for new appropriations the following year; the overall impact of its actions does not concern it.

The actions of various policy-making agencies may not only conflict but may actually cancel each other. When the tight money policy of the Federal Reserve System caused a sharp drop in the construction business in 1966, as was to be expected, Congress promptly authorized the Federal National Mortgage Association to add more than $4 billion of new mortgage loans in order to contravene the restrictive effect of the monetary policy.

Policies of the U.S. Treasury. Economic policies are most effective when monetary authorities and the federal Treasury cooperate closely. This was the case during World War II. The Treasury was able to sell bonds at very low rates of interest because the Reserve authorities supported this policy by buying bonds from banks at a fixed price when the banks needed more cash. Heavy taxes and rationing of producers and consumers helped to keep the money supply from proliferating.

After the war, the Reserve Banks were ready to resume their role of preventing a further rise of the money supply, but the Treasury wanted to maintain the easy way of selling bonds. The conflict created considerable difficulties until the two policy-making institutions reached an accord in 1951.

The year 1966 furnished a more recent example of the economic strains which result from policy differences between the Treasury and the Federal Reserve System. The demands of the war in Vietnam led to billions of dollars' worth of new orders, exceeding the economic capacity of the nation. The Treasury failed to lower nondefense spending, to take other unpopular steps which would reduce civilian purchasing power through higher taxes, or to introduce production controls. The Federal Reserve System attempted to prevent inflation singlehandedly by raising interest rates to the highest level in forty years and by increasing reserve requirements. The impact of this divided policy fell unevenly on different sectors of the economy. War goods producers were favored because prices for their products promptly reflected any increase in costs. Those segments of the civilian economy which normally use much credit became the main victims of the severe distortions introduced by this policy conflict.

FISCAL POLICY

Fiscal policy concerns the overall effects of government expenditures and taxation on the national income. Its formulation is shared by Congress, the President, and his executive departments.

What Kind of Policy?

Fiscal policy goes beyond the need to pay the bills of the federal government. It deliberately uses the flow of expenditures and revenues to influence economic activity. In the Employment Act of 1946, Congress recognized the broad function of fiscal policy; it proclaimed the responsibility of the federal government for the creation and maintenance of conditions which would achieve economic stability and maximum employment with methods promoting free, competitive enterprise.

Such a broad statement of purpose permits the use of many measures which are mutually contradictory, though each may find very distinguished advocates. Some economists fear stagnation whenever the nation's income fails to achieve new peaks. Their policy recommendations favor more federal spending, as illustrated by a former chairman of the Council of Economic Advisers who served under President Truman. During the relatively prosperous summer of 1962, he suggested:

1. Large tax reductions are needed now to increase private incomes available for spending. These cuts should be retroactive. Deferring action until further trends can be observed would only make us more "too late" than we are now. . . . Tax reduction should be applied almost entirely to middle-and low-income families, who more than others translate a large after-tax income into immediate consumer demand. . . .

2. There should be a large increase in Federal outlays for essential public needs. The task of creating enough additional demand to restore reasonably full employment is too big to be accomplished by tax cuts alone. Besides, the nation needs more schools and other publicly financed goods and services, not just more private consumer goods.[2]

During the even more prosperous winter of 1967 an equally qualified observer, who held the same position under President Eisenhower, Arthur F. Burns, commented as follows:

Unless a determined effort is made by the Congress to check the proliferation of Federal spending, the foundations of our economy may be weakened. With public revenues increasing rapidly in these good times and the public debt still growing, there is a danger that scarce resources are being applied to projects of marginal or even doubtful value. Not only that, but the recent sport in public spending is bound, sooner or later, to lead to higher taxes.[3]

The two opinions indicate a basic difference in philosophy concerning the proper level of federal spending. The conflicting advice largely reflects the social value judgments of the decision maker. For example, the increased cost of the war in Vietnam can be met by higher taxes or by a cut of domestic programs. The preferred method depends on the part of the nation's income we are willing to assign to public spending.

Another view of the future was expressed in a speech by Walter Heller, who was chairman of the Council of Economic Advisers during the Kennedy years. He introduced a new concept to justify an active fiscal policy:

I do not claim that we have, in one great leap forward, moved from the recession-prone 1950's into a new era of recession-proof 1960's and 1970's. But I am convinced that major advances in government policy and business practice are making our economy more and more recession-repellent. . . .

2 Leon H. Keyserling, "One Prescription for Unemployment," *New York Times Magazine,* August 5, 1962, p. 56. Keyserling was chairman of the Council of Economic Advisers from 1950 to 1953.

3 Arthur F. Burns, "The Federal Expenditure Explosion," *Tax Review* (New York, Tax Foundation, Inc.), March 1967, p. 10. Burns was chairman of the Council of Economic Advisers from 1953 to 1956.

The signal for swinging into action [with fiscal and monetary weapons] is no longer an expected or actual recession. Instead, it is the existence of an economic gap between what we *are* producing and what we *could* produce. To carry out the spirit as well as the letter of the mandate of the Employment Act of 1946 to achieve "maximum employment, maximum production, and maximum purchasing power" calls for positive fiscal and monetary action when economic *performance* lags behind economic *potential.*[4]

Government Action—Direct or Indirect?   A lag in economic growth can be overcome in a simple and direct way by an expenditure of more money. The very simplicity of this approach recommends it to many people. Assuming that national income ought to be some billions of dollars higher, let Congress order so much more money to be spent! Projects for more spending are always available; from passing a veterans' bonus to building new dams or post offices or moon rockets, the ways of spending know no limit. The opposite view frowns on avoidable direct federal expenditures and argues for an indirect boost to the economy through tax cuts or special incentives for private activity.

Speed is claimed as a major advantage of direct Congressional action. If the economy needs stimulating, nothing works so promptly as an immediate appropriation. Opponents point out that Congress seldom passes even emergency spending laws without a long delay, for after legal action is completed, it takes additional time to execute a project; the advantage of speed is thus more fictitious than real.

People who favor direct spending may not agree about the type of expenditure they consider best. Some look at the many desires of the population which a government can satisfy and advocate more consumption spending; others prefer public action for investments which stimulate more private activity.

Consumption Spending.   The main objection to a direct spending policy is the claim that it will not boost the economy significantly. A veterans' bonus may cause a brief rise in consumption, but the benefits will not be permanent because of the absence of any significant multiplier effect. A man who finds a new job can maintain a higher level of consumption; a one-time windfall may help him through the month or pay overdue bills, but it will not raise his consumption over a longer period.

Public Works.   Public works may cause a greater impact on the economy if they are carefully selected for their multiplier qualities. A new ordnance plant or an order for airplanes will reduce unemployment in the area where the contract is to be executed and will help many establishments in the

[4] Walter W. Heller, "The Economic Outlook for State-Local Finance," an address at the fifty-seventh Annual Governors' Conference, Minneapolis, July 27, 1965.

entire country because of the long-lasting effect of such a project. Some people will observe that airplanes should be built to meet military requirements and not to stimulate the economy. A needless airplane wastes scarce resources and cannot be defended any better than can drafting the unemployed in order to improve the statistical performance of the economy.

The case against public works points out that the timing of these projects necessarily involves such long delays that they often compete with private business at the peak of national prosperity though they were ordered much earlier to help overcome a recession. The cost of public works may by itself exert a weakening influence on the economy since people realize that they must pay for these expenditures and less money will remain for private spending.

Lower Tax Rates. Indirect action to promote economic growth is often advocated as more appropriate to a private enterprise system, and its most popular tool is tax reduction. The obvious question arises of how we pay our bills when the government cuts its income substantially. The defenders of tax reductions point with pride at the consequences of the lower income tax rates enacted by Congress in 1964. They claim the prompt upswing of the economy as proof of the wisdom of this action. They assure us that lower tax rates will stimulate private enterprise so much that business will boom and pay more tax dollars than it did before with higher rates.

It worked in 1964, but will it always be the right answer? Popular generalizations that all tax cuts will lead to higher, not lower, revenue collections are certainly not warranted. The result largely depends on the type of tax reduction enacted by Congress and the reaction of the public to such a measure. The elimination of excise taxes on many products in 1965 was favorably received for reasons of equity, but it did not increase tax collections. The possible impact of a change in taxes became clear when Congress suspended a seven-percent business investment credit in September 1966. The following drop in new investments was so pronounced that Congress found it necessary to restore the credit after less than a year. Lower taxes will boost new business but it is difficult to predict the size of the increase.

Automatic Stabilizers

Some fiscal policy measures will help to stabilize the economy without further legislation. The inevitable slowness of Congressional action prevents effective steps from being taken when they are most urgently needed. Two types of policy are preferred, therefore, to exert a beneficial effect on the economy. One group of measures operates automatically owing to the nature of existing legislation; another category depends on the discretionary judgment of the President and the executive departments.

Built-in stabilizers are those federal receipts and expenditures which tend to cause a budget deficit in response to a downturn of business activity without the need for policy decisions or actions. They have become part of the economic legislation during the last thirty years and are one of the significant changes permitting a more successful fight against depressions than was possible a generation ago. They are called *automatic* because they swing into action without any further decisions by Congress or by public officials. These stabilizers include personal and corporate income taxes and the transfer payments under the social security legislation, particularly the unemployment compensation payments.

Personal Income Tax. The steep progression of personal income tax rates has been severely criticized for many reasons, but it does exert a stabilizing influence on the economy. In a recession, income taxes drop much faster than personal incomes, and this buffer effect tends to maintain total personal expenditures during the early months of falling business, thereby facilitating a revival or an upward movement.

TABLE 18-1.   Changes in Income Tax Collections, 1946–1966
(*millions of dollars*)

Year	Individual Income Tax	Corporate Income Tax	Total	Percent Change from Previous Year
1946	18,331	12,906	31,237	−13.68
1947	19,629	9,676	29,305	− 6.18
1948	20,997	10,174	31,171	+ 6.37
1949	17,929	11,554	29,483	− 5.42
1950	17,408	10,854	28,262	− 4.14
1951	21,643	14,106	35,749	+26.49
1952	27,913	21,225	49,138	+37.45
1953	30,108	21,238	51,346	+ 4.49
1954	29,542	21,101	50,643	− 1.37
1955	28,747	17,861	46,608	− 7.97
1956	32,188	20,880	53,068	+13.86
1957	35,620	21,167	56,787	+ 7.01
1958	34,724	20,074	54,798	− 3.50
1959	36,719	17,309	54,028	− 1.41
1960	40,715	21,494	62,209	+15.14
1961	41,338	20,954	62,292	+ .13
1962	45,571	20,523	66,094	+ 6.10
1963	47,588	21,579	69,167	+ 4.65
1964	48,697	23,493	72,190	+ 4.37
1965	48,792	25,461	74,253	+ 2.9
1966	55,446	30,073	85,519	+15.2

SOURCES: The Budget of the United States Government, 1968; U.S. Bureau of the Census, *Historical Statistics of the United States.*

A major objection to this automatic action comes from persons who feel that the sudden spurt in tax collections during prosperity deprives the private sector of the economy of so much money that the growth of business is slowed down inordinately. They consider it unfortunate that the strong features of the tax during a recession will become an obstacle to rapid advance in better times. The breaking effect on a boom may turn out, however, to be helpful in restraining inflationary excesses.

Corporation Income Tax. The corporation income tax exerts the largest stabilizing effect in terms of total impact. Business profits fluctuate sharply, and the tax on these profits fully reflects the changes. Because the tax absorbs such a large share of the fluctuations, net (after tax) profits are kept more stable. Table 18-1 shows the effect of income taxation under changing conditions.

Social Security Taxes. The social security tax is a fixed percentage of payrolls, with total collections depending on the number of people employed; a rising employment means higher tax collections. Benefit payments show the opposite pattern and drop during prosperous periods. Unemployment compensation shows the sharpest fluctuations counteracting the business cycle. Retirement benefits have also a stabilizing effect, since they do not drop when earned incomes shrink in a recession. On the other hand, hard times cause some earlier retirements, and in boom periods quite a few people continue working beyond retirement age.

Discretionary Stabilizers

The discretionary power of the President to spend or to delay spending within the limits set by Congress is greater than many people realize. This power rests entirely with the executive department and influences the flow of federal funds by billions of dollars, at least in the short run.

Speeding Up Spending. The President may speed up federal spending when he feels that such a step is indicated. He can issue instructions to pay bills faster than usual or return funds due the taxpayer at an earlier date. For example, income tax refunds to individuals can be advanced or delayed by several months; they can be paid first and audited later, or vice versa. The flow of cash to the public will reflect the difference in policy. Dividend payments on government life insurance can be timed to stabilize the economy.

Slowing Down Paying. When the government wants to reduce the money supply, all its payments can be slowed down considerably. Although creditors who count on prompt payment protest against the slowness of federal red tape, the flow of funds to the public can be regulated effectively in the short run by simple administrative methods. One may argue that all bills should be paid promptly to avoid any harm to the good credit standing enjoyed by the federal authorities; but a little delay does not cause great difficulties and may well have a stabilizing influence.

Postponing Spending.   Even more important is the power of the President to delay authorized expenditures. Congress appropriates funds for new projects, but the executive branch decides when the actual contracts are awarded. Appropriations precede expenditures by many billions, and the timing of new expenditures rests with the President. It has been quite common for him to order a temporary ceiling on new contracts below the level allowed by Congress. The individual department may not like such an order, but it has no choice and must conform.

The main attack against the discretionary control by the President is based on the tradition that a Congressional mandate means prompt spending without delaying action by anyone. The actual practice of government spending, however, has never restricted the President to the point where he cannot time expenditures in the public interest.

Raising Private Consumption or Investment

The analysis of income change has shown that consumption and investment are equally capable of causing fluctuations in the nation's business. Fiscal policy may influence either or both; the adjustment mechanism itself does not identify one best method.

Underconsumption.   Some people blame deficient economic performance on lack of consumption. This idea sounds plausible and is a popular one. Most consumers like to own more goods, and most producers are able and willing to make them available. Thus, less than full production is taken as a sign of unsatisfactory performance due to the inability of the mass of consumers to buy all they want. A policy of growth will therefore maintain an ever-growing level of consumption which induces the producer to work at capacity. To raise consumption, fiscal policy must give more money, cheap credit, and lower taxes to the poor because they spend all the money they can get.

Policies of this type are usually defended by labor unions since they provide a strong basis for increasing wage rates. They are favored by politicians who want to justify spending projects, and by special-interest groups concerned with mass consumption. None of these groups, however, seem overly concerned with raising the needed revenue.

Oversaving.   Saving too much and spending too little describe essentially the same economic fact. The difference in emphasis, however, is worth noting. Underconsumption theories of business fluctuations claim in substance that the consumer does not have enough money to buy all the goods he wants and which producers would be glad to supply. Placing the emphasis on saving implies that the consumer has the money, but refuses to spend it fast enough. This latter analysis leads to a low-interest-rate policy to discourage saving and exhort the consumer to spend more and faster. It favors easier credit terms in order to reduce total savings, and direct government purchases to increase income and raise consumption.

More Investment.   Other groups, particularly those in business, favor a policy of investment incentives. They will argue that private investment with its strong leverage will restore prosperity faster than any other method. Tax reduction in the upper brackets of personal and corporate income taxes, special allowances for new investments—these and similar incentives are the right prescription from this point of view.

Arguments in favor of one or another theory are hotly debated. No clear-cut case can be made for any one remedy which would hold true under all circumstances. Only a careful analysis of each new situation as it arises can disclose the nature of the economic difficulties and suggest the best way to overcome them. A politically safe compromise which gives a little to each viewpoint is frequently ineffective and always costly, but it is often the only possible solution.

BUDGETS: BALANCED AND UNBALANCED

The balance, or imbalance, of the federal budget directly determines the size of the national debt. A budget surplus reduces the debt and a deficit increases it. The direct connection between the budget and the changes in the nation's debts does not always appear to be clearly understood by people who favor more federal expenditures *and* a debt reduction. Until the Great Depression, a budget deficit was an unusual event, limited generally to military emergencies and deplored by all right-minded citizens. Even Franklin D. Roosevelt campaigned in 1932 on a platform promise of a balanced budget. Only Keynes's writings a few years later made a budget deficit respectable, at least in depression years.

More recently, budget deficits have not been confined to periods of business slumps. The past twenty-five years of reasonable prosperity have witnessed nineteen deficits in the federal budget. In spite of this seemingly reckless approach to public spending, the nation's economy has survived the deficits and appears to have prospered in the process.

The size of federal expenditures is so gigantic today that any change in policy will add or deduct billions of dollars from the income stream. A multibillion-dollar change in spending, such as was introduced by the cost of the war in Vietnam, is bound to have a serious impact on the economy. Even if the budget had remained in balance after the sharp increase in defense expenditures, the multiplier effect of such a stream of new orders would be bound to lead to painful distortions in the economy. As raw materials are moved to war-production plants, civilian construction faces a crisis. Some workers can be shifted to new occupations, but the small-town residential building contractor will view his lack of credit and materials with unmitigated gloom. A changeover from surplus to deficit operations is, of course, felt even more strongly.

Should We Balance Budgets?

Most citizens will not hesitate to answer this question. Their instinctive response is, undoubtedly, in the affirmative. They know that they must tailor their expenditures to their income or face bankruptcy sooner or later. How, then, does Uncle Sam's problem differ from their own?

A young man who is ready to make his mark in the business world may decide to borrow to improve and speed up his career. The cost of such a loan is offset by an even greater increase in income and is well worth the gamble. Naturally, he must also plan to repay the debt long before his earning power declines. Uncle Sam may also borrow to put more people to work and see the economy come closer to full employment; like our young man, he is still capable of much economic growth. He differs, however, from the private citizen when it comes to scheduling repayments; he does not need to worry about a future decline in earning power or a limited life span. Consequently, he does not have to reduce his debt unless he wants to do so.

To balance or not to balance ceases to be an abstract issue invariably determined for all cases. It must be decided year by year in the light of the specific circumstances of the moment. Some of the more frequent arguments on this issue will now be mentioned.

Annual Balance.   The thrifty conservative insists that the nation should not live beyond its means any more than a private family, and that the budget must be balanced every year. The comparison is not relevant, as has been shown already, but the common sense of this simple proposition attracts many followers, particularly in circles which have not been faced with the need for extensive borrowing in recent years.

Compensating Balance.   A widely accepted doctrine wants the budget to compensate for the ups and downs created by the private sector during a business cycle. This viewpoint suggests that a drop in private spending be counteracted by a budget deficit, and that the reverse hold for a period of expansion. Presumably, the budget would then balance over each full business cycle. The idea sounds fine, and in fact the automatic stabilizers operate on this principle. In practice, however, it is far easier to show a deficit than it is to establish a surplus. Too many citizens demand that Congress vote for their own favorite project when times are good and "we can afford it." Therefore, the deficit years far outnumber the surplus years, and thus cause a steady rise in the national debt.

Long-Run Balance.   A more controversial approach to the balancing problem points to the war years, when deficits are huge, but unemployment disappears; notwithstanding the mental anguish due to the dangers of the fighting and the separation of families, there is often improvement in living standards. Based on this precedent, some people suggest that we forget the old-fashioned concern for balancing budgets and get on with the real business of an economy—to grow, to prosper, and to keep the people occupied.

The defenders of a chronic budget deficit point out that the business stimulus added to the economy will raise not only incomes but also income taxes and thus eventually permit the budget to balance. They also explain that a rising level of private economic activity will support greater federal expenditures. In fact, even the giant budget of 1966 was not as large a share

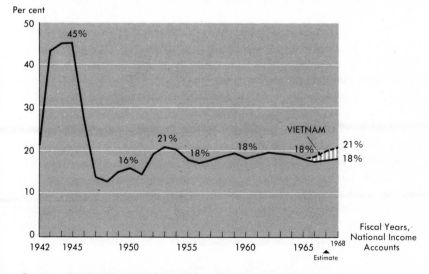

SOURCE: The Budgets of the United States Government, 1968.

FIG. 18-1.   **Federal Expenditures as a Percent of Gross National Product, 1942–1968**

of economic activity as were the much smaller payments at the end of the Korean war; Figure 18-1 pictures the budget in relation to GNP.

The opponents claim that a string of uninterrupted deficit years will lead to inflationary price rises, undermine the will to save, render the nation's debt unmanageable, and generally lead to all the disasters commonly associated with inflation. Economists usually shun the extremes and show that a budget deficit is likely to produce different results in different circumstances.[5]

The Effect of Unbalanced Budgets

Federal deficits are not all alike regardless of impressions to the contrary. The effect of deficit spending depends on the circumstances of each case, and we shall discuss these deficits in some detail. The exact opposite would hold true for a budget surplus, but the likelihood of a string of substantial surplus years is so remote that no further discussion of this possibility seems warranted.

Federal Deficits During a Recession. Budget deficits are most likely to occur during a recession. Revenue estimates in a federal budget never assume a drop in tax income, but even a small recession reduces tax revenue significantly because of the sudden drop in corporate profits. At the same time the automatic stabilizers make sure that federal payments rise even higher than estimates.

The Treasury can easily borrow from its citizens and from bankers all the money it needs, because the slowdown of business leaves savers and bankers with unused funds. As the Treasury spends these funds, they are returned to circulation and help to maintain a higher income level than would be the case if they remained idle. The deficit will prove beneficial and cushion the downward trend of the economy.

Just how beneficial will excess federal spending become? Can we really spend ourselves rich? The answer to this question, unfortunately, is far from simple, because the return to prosperity is not just a matter of spending a given number of dollars. If federal spending encourages private initiative and reawakens the citizens' optimism and his will to invest, this may well trigger the start of a new boom. If, however, federal authorities limit their spending to unproductive projects in an atmosphere which discourages private initiative, it may be hard to see any beneficial effects of the deficit.

Federal Deficits During Prosperity. Additional government spending tends to be politically popular, especially in the areas that benefit as a

---

[5] The view supporting growth with long-run balance is eloquently defended by Walter W. Heller in *New Dimensions of Political Economy* (Cambridge, Mass., Harvard University Press, 1966).

result. Projects which have been advocated during a recession to stimulate the economy will be promoted just as hard during good times because of the current availability of the funds. What is the effect of a deficit at this stage of economic activity?

The defenders of a deficit will claim that the economy is not really very prosperous. They can always point to areas and industries with unemployed workers and idle factories, because some of this blight is not erased by a general upswing of business. They can compare actual economic performance with a theoretical peak which is never reached. Such claims are sure to confuse the issue for many people who think that prosperity means a steady and universal upswing of the national income.

There are several obstacles to financing a deficit in good times. Funds are not plentiful and the Treasury is likely to be competing with private firms for scarce funds. Should the Treasury prevail on the Federal Reserve System to finance its deficit *in addition to* the private demand for funds rather than *in lieu of* it, the inflow of new money will be used to bid up the prices of many critical products and bring on inflationary results.

Federal Deficits During War.   A hot war involving many men and billions of dollars of material has been the experience of the United States three times in less than thirty years. The gigantic effort required in World War II made budget deficits unavoidable. Higher taxes, rationing, and production controls were all needed to win the war. The deficit remaining had the expected inflationary consequences, but the loss of value of the dollar was less pronounced than in the other countries involved in the war.

The deficits during the war in Korea caused inflationary price rises in the absence of restrictive measures. The early effects of the war in Vietnam point in the same direction. The demands of a war economy are too large to be supplied in addition to rising consumer demands of a booming economy. Civilian consumption must be curtailed to the amounts of available products. Less federal nondefense spending, higher taxes, or rationing are the necessary sacrifices in fighting a war. An unchecked federal deficit will cause inflation under these circumstances.

THE NATIONAL DEBT

The national debt consists of all promissory notes issued by the Federal Treasury. It arises from the need of meeting expenditures for which not enough tax revenue has been collected. The debt must not be confused with the total obligations of all the citizens of the country. Government debts, though large, are only a small share of this total.

The development of the public debt is shown in Table 18-2. The surplus or deficit of the budget in any year is not immediately reflected in

TABLE 18-2.   The Federal Administrative Budget and the Public Debt
for Selected Years, 1900–1967
(*billions of dollars*)

Fiscal Year	Budget Receipts	Budget Expenditures	Surplus or Deficit	Public Debt at End of Year	Percent of GNP
1900	.567	.521	+ .05	1.3	—
1914	.725	.725	—	1.2	—
1919	5.08	18.45	−13.4	25.5	—
1929	3.86	3.13	+ .7	16.9	16.2
1933	2.0	4.6	− 2.6	22.5	40.2
1939	5.0	8.8	− 3.8	45.9	64.9
1945	44.4	98.3	−53.9	259.1	119.5
1949	37.7	39.5	− 1.8	252.8	97.2
1953	64.7	74.1	− 9.4	266.1	74.1
1956	67.9	66.2	+ 1.7	272.8	66.6
1959	67.9	80.3	−12.4	284.8	60.7
1962	81.4	87.8	− 6.4	298.6	55.1
1964	89.5	97.7	− 8.2	312.5	51.3
1965	93.1	96.5	− 3.4	317.9	49.0
1966	104.7	107.0	− 2.3	320.4	45.0
1967	117.0	126.7	− 9.7	327.3	42.9

SOURCE: The Budget of the United States Government, 1968.

the debt changes. The cash flow of the trust funds must be added to the administrative budget to indicate the need for new borrowing. The level of the deposit accounts maintained by the Treasury is also subject to change.

The debt was insignificant before World War I and reached its first peak during the war. The prosperous twenties caused sharp reductions in the size of the debt, which continued until the Depression reversed the trend. World War II multiplied the national debt to levels never considered possible before that time. The postwar years witnessed a modest reduction, but the heavy national defense expenditures associated with the Korean war and the cold war arrested the downswing. A new uptrend set in, and for the past fifteen years the national debt has continued to rise without any significant interruption. It now exceeds $330 billion.

While the debt has increased steadily for almost twenty years, its rise has been much slower than the growth of the nation's income. From an all-time high in 1946 when the debt reached 134 percent of GNP, the weight of this burden has been steadily reduced until it dropped below 50 percent of GNP in 1965.

Both the trend and the size of federal debts have been the cause of extreme public reaction. One group feels sure that the burden of this gigantic debt will ruin our economy, while the opposition claims that the size of the debt is irrelevant insofar as its steady rise has not produced unusual hardships. Some of these views will now be discussed.

Is the National Debt Too High?

Almost every year Congress revises the official debt ceiling, which is the amount of bonds and other debt certificates the Treasury may owe directly at any time. This ceiling is a political, not an economic, limit.

Some people claim that the debt can never be too high because the Federal Reserve Banks will buy bonds from the Treasury when there are no other purchasers. This statement is technically correct, but those who hold this view seem to forget that the first task of the Federal Reserve authorities is the maintenance of a stable dollar. If the Federal Reserve always buys government bonds, there will be more and more purchasing power put into circulation, with inflation the end result.

It has been argued that the Treasury can always sell its debt certificates to the public without any help from Federal Reserve authorities, provided it offers a high rate of interest. No attempt has ever been made to fully test this statement. The flood of war bonds sold in World War II was carried out with the active help of the bankers, who wisely considered the financing of the war their main task. The resulting inflation that engulfed the country after the cessation of hostilities was the price we had to pay for the war-born debt.

When the Reserve authorities restrict credit to bankers, the banks will neither desire nor be able to hold more Treasury securities. The cost of borrowing will rise, but the high price of money is not apt to reduce federal expenditures during a war. Therefore, no useful purpose is served by high interest rates in time of war.

We learn from war experience that the economy will adjust to any debt level in a short time. If the usual purchasers of federal debt certificates do not wish to hold more than $50 billion, but the Treasury sells $100 billion, inflation then drives up all prices until the $100 billion is no longer a larger share of the nation's business than the $50 billion was earlier. This cost to the nation is too high in peacetime.

We are now prepared to answer the question, Can the national debt be too high? in the affirmative. Our criterion for the proper ceiling of the debt in peacetime is the need to avoid inflationary price rises due to excessive increases in the debt level, not any specific debt amount.

The Composition of the National Debt

A large debt requires careful management. For practical purposes, the major part of the national debt is permanent, but the financial tradition of the Treasury discourages the issue of debt certificates without specified time limits. Other nations such as Great Britain have for many years issued permanent debt certificates with no maturity date, but United States bonds always carry a definite time limit.

The debt is called short-term when it must be repaid within twelve months or less. Most of the short-term debt consists of ninety-day treasury bills which are sold at auction every week. This part of the debt amounts to nearly $100 billion. Intermediate-term debt is sold by means of "treasury certificates" which mature between one and five years. Debt with a maturity date of more than five years is called long-term debt and consists of government bonds. As any part of the debt comes due, the Treasury sells new IOU's to raise the funds needed for repayment on time. For all practical purposes, the total debt is a permanent obligation, though all debt certificates are paid punctually.

The Ownership of the National Debt

Who owns the national debt? Table 18-3 shows the distribution of ownership for three selected years.

TABLE 18-3.   The Ownership of the National Debt
(billions of dollars)

Owners	1947	1959	1967
Individuals	65.6	69.4	75.9
Commercial banks	68.7	60.3	57.4
Federal Reserve	22.6	26.6	43.5
State and local governments	7.3	18.0	23.4
Corporations	14.1	21.4	14.9
Insurance companies	23.9	12.5	9.5
U.S. Government agencies and trust funds	34.4	53.7	68.2
Foreign accounts	2.7	12.0	14.0
Other investors [a]	17.7	17.0	22.4
Totals	257.0	290.9	329.2

SOURCE: *Federal Reserve Bulletin.*
[a] Includes savings institutions, dealers and brokers, mutual savings banks, corporate pension funds, and nonprofit institutions.

Commercial banks own most of the short-term treasury bills, as they are a convenient means for keeping reserves. Individuals have greatly increased their savings, but the amount of government bonds, in their hands has increased slowly during the last twenty years. All other private bond buyers —corporations, insurance companies, or bankers—have added little or actually reduced their holdings of federal debt in spite of the large rise in the total funds controlled. Various governmental agencies keep their rising volume of liquid funds in federal debt certificates and account for the total increase. Foreign central bankers, in particular, have purchased an increasing share of the federal debt in the last fifteen years.

A popular argument suggests that we forget the national debt because "we all owe it to ourselves." If we own bonds directly as individuals or indirectly through a life insurance policy or bank account, it may appear that as taxpayers we provide the interest payments for ourselves, the bondholders. It should be obvious, however, that there is no direct link between bonds owned and tax payments. If we cancelled all bonds and reduced tax payments by the amount saved in interest, the economy would be in a different situation, and a weaker one. Bond owners gain a feeling of security because they own a nest egg which can be readily converted into cash in case of need.

Shifting the Debt Burden.   Opponents of a large debt will claim that the weight of interest payments shifts the burden of current expenditures to the following generation. They fail to realize that the real burden consists in the surrender of goods from private to public use which takes place when the deficit arises. Interest payments may force the people without bonds to pay taxes for honoring obligations to bondholders in the future. We may disagree with the wisdom or the equity of such transfers of funds, but the overall impact of these transactions does not change the total national income.

Internal Versus External Debt.   Some people are willing to accept a large national debt provided it is sold entirely at home, as was the case with our debt until recently. They will, however, view with alarm any appearance of foreign obligations. The distinction is unfounded. A rise in foreign ownership of our national debt is the manifestation of a deficit in our international accounts which is being settled by borrowing. Any concern over debts abroad must come to grips with the imbalance of our foreign accounts, not with the resulting shift in the ownership of the debt. This problem forms the subject of the following chapter.

SUMMARY

Questions of policy remain most controversial because people assign different priorities to desirable but conflicting goals.

Monetary policy describes the measures used for the control of the money supply and is determined primarily, but not exclusively, by the Federal Reserve System. The central bank tries to steer a policy course which carefully avoids too little or too much credit.

Monetary policy is most effective when the action of the Federal Reserve Banks, the independent agencies, and the Treasury are carefully coordinated to achieve the same objectives. This cooperation has not always been achieved in the past.

Fiscal policy considers the effects of government expenditure and revenue on the entire economic system; it involves public activities to promote stability and growth under conditions of full employment.

Conflicts arise between policy makers who favor a direct spending approach with higher Congressional appropriations and others who feel that an indirect method of tax incentives will bring better results. A similar controversy ensues when one group wants to promote consumption by lowering income taxes in the lowest brackets while others want to stimulate investment by reducing high-bracket personal taxes and levies on corporate profits.

Public works are often advocated as a suitable way to stimulate employment; opponents of this view consider them an indefensible and ill-timed waste of resources.

Automatic stabilizers have become an important method of avoiding depressions since their introduction in the last thirty years. They swing into operation without direct Congressional or executive action, through sharp changes in tax collections and the leveling influence of social security payments.

The power of the President in speeding up, slowing down, or postponing expenditures is an important tool of fiscal policy. His ability to influence the flow of federal funds may exert a powerful stabilizing effect when executive action is well timed.

Federal budgets used to be traditionally in balance every year. The last generation adopted the principle of compensatory budgets with deficits in bad years and surpluses in good ones. Some economists go beyond the idea of balancing the budget over a business cycle and suggest the use of deficits to promote full employment and economic growth.

The effect of budget deficits depends on the source of the funds, their use, and the timing of federal action. When federal expenditures use idle funds, the effect on the economy is beneficial. Should the government finance its deficits with new money from the banking system during a time of full employment, the consequences are inflationary.

The size of the national debt has become a matter of concern for many citizens. No fixed amount can be considered an absolute maximum, but an inflationary rise of the money supply must be avoided.

The use of monetary and fiscal policy has a powerful impact on the economy. It can promote steady, stable growth when managed wisely, and it can lead to disaster when it becomes a tool of irresponsible political action. There is hope that a better understanding of alternative policies will lead federal action to the effective promotion of stable growth.

Discussion Questions

1. Why can the Federal Reserve System not guarantee the stable value of the dollar?
2. Why does the United States today require a positive fiscal policy?
3. What is the cost of war?
4. State the case for and against a balanced budget.
5. Is the nation going bankrupt if it fails to reduce the national debt?
6. Will automatic stabilizers prevent another depression?
7. Should we reduce tax rates in the interest of economic growth? What taxes? High or low rate brackets?
8. Should the government attempt to boost consumption or investments?

Suggested Reading

BUCHANAN, JAMES M., *Public Principles of Public Debt.* Homewood, Ill., Irwin, 1958.

HELLER, WALTER W., *New Dimensions of Political Economy.* Cambridge, Mass., Harvard, 1966.

LEE, MAURICE W., *Toward Economic Stability.* New York, Wiley, 1966.

LEWIS, WILFRED, JR., *Federal Fiscal Policy in the Postwar Recessions.* Washington, D.C., The Brookings Institution, 1962.

OKUN, ARTHUR M., *The Battle against Unemployment.* New York, Norton, 1965.

PART IV

THE UNITED STATES AND THE WORLD ECONOMY

Today's world does not permit anyone, not even the largest and strongest nation, to indulge in isolationist policies. The domestic economy, dealing with both individual and national problems, has acquired a third dimension in its international involvements.

The problems of a world economy have much in common with those observed from a purely domestic viewpoint. They differ, however, not only in detail, but also in some basic principles.

The fundamental distinction between foreign and domestic economic problems can be traced directly to the nationalistic attitude of mankind in the twentieth century. When the domestic economy is discussed, we realize that measures which help the economy in general will eventually be good for each of us individually in the form of better jobs, more sales, more goods, and better opportunities. We know instinctively that in a modern, interdependent economy we are all in the same boat. A depression in Pittsburgh or Detroit is bound to have unfavorable repercussions in Tulsa and San Francisco.

In our international relations, there is no such feeling of solidarity. A famine in India is deplorable but of no direct economic concern to most people in the United States. A business boom in Europe is an interesting newspaper item; what we really want to know, however, is whether or not this expanded foreign economy will help or hurt our future sales here and abroad. In our minds this earth is not yet one world. We make this subtle differentiation almost subconsciously when we refer to the problems of the domestic economy as "ours" while the rest of the world has "theirs."

The specific distinctions which give rise to the following chapters flow directly from this basically nationalistic attitude of those of the world's people who shape the behavior of nations. Separate currencies, manipulated by central banks in the interests of domestic policy objectives, create the problem of balancing international payments. This is the subject of Chapter 19. The rationale for foreign trade in the national interest will be discussed in Chapter 20. The question of economic assistance to underdeveloped countries will occupy Chapter 21. The influence of ideological contrasts on economic systems is the topic of Chapter 22.

19

INTERNATIONAL PAYMENTS

The Federal Reserve Bank of Kansas City may be a creditor or debtor of the Federal Reserve Bank of Dallas at this moment. Very few people know or would care about such a technicality—of concern to no one except the accountants of the two banks. A dollar is a dollar in Kansas City and in Dallas; it has the same value, commands as much confidence, and remains totally indistinguishable in both cities. Periodically, one bank grants credit to the other because of an increased demand in its area, and shortly thereafter the situation may be reversed. The national economy remains unaffected by these transactions.

Internationally, there is no common currency; instead, there are numerous nationally controlled monetary systems. Efforts to keep these currencies stable, so that their values in comparison to each other do not change, have been relatively unsuccessful for many decades. This lack of stability of national currencies adds a new dimension of risk to international transactions. A concept of major importance is the status of a nation's international credit as revealed by its balance of payments.

THE BALANCE OF PAYMENTS

A balance of payments is an accounting statement which reflects all the transactions that take place during a specified period of time between a country (and its residents) and the rest of the world. The time span covered by this statement is usually one year.[1]

Let us look at the United States balance of payments more closely. Accounting statements can present the reader with varying degrees of detail. The quarterly presentation by the Department of Commerce is a forbidding-looking document to everyone but the specialist, but the highlights of our foreign economic affairs can be presented quite simply, as seen in Table 19-1.

The meaning of the terms used needs some explanation. A plus (+) balance indicates that U.S. receipts were larger than payments due. These

[1] All modern nations prepare such statements, which are published monthly in *International Financial Statistics* (Washington, D.C., International Monetary Fund). The U.S. balance of payments is presented in detail quarterly by the Department of Commerce in the *Survey of Current Business.*

TABLE 19-1.   The Balance of Payments of the United States, 1966
(*millions of dollars*)

I. Balance of private current transactions	+7,684
II. Balance of private long-term capital transactions	−1,664
III. Balance of government activity transactions	−6,766
Surplus or deficit of the balance of payments	− 746
IV. Financial adjustments:	
Short-term claims and liabilities	+ 767
Official United States government reserves	+ 568
Unrecorded transactions	− 589
Total adjustments	+ 746

SOURCE: U.S. Department of Commerce, *Survey of Current Business.*

receipts are also called "credits," while payments are considered "debits." When we export goods, we acquire a credit; when we import a product instead, we must pay for it, and we call this import a debit, or a minus (−) balance.

The balance sheet indicates that the United States has a comfortable surplus in its current business (Table 19-1, entry I). Part of this surplus is spent on investments of many types all over the world (entry II); these continuing private investments assure our leading role in world business for years to come. The worldwide obligations of our government are expensive and add a heavy minus (−) figure to the accounts (entry III). The sum of the three balances leads to a deficit of less than $1 billion in 1966. The United States has had a deficit for seventeen years with the exception of 1958, which had a slight surplus. These chronic deficits are a matter of public concern and have been amply discussed in the press.

How do we pay for a deficit? Business firms and bankers, together with a few wealthy citizens, are constantly shifting funds from country to country, to where they are safest or are most needed, and where they can earn the highest returns. The movement of private funds is hard to predict, because the safety of money is often in conflict with its ability to earn interest. A rising rate of interest may attract funds from abroad; but it can also be interpreted as a danger signal, a sign of impending financial trouble, at which point cautious investors take their money elsewhere. In 1966 changes in claims and liabilities helped to reduce the deficit (entry IV, first item).

The United States government has to arrange for the payment of any remaining deficit. It may borrow abroad or perhaps persuade a foreign government to keep more dollars. Ultimately, the Treasury sells gold to any foreign central bank that asks for it (entry IV, second item). In 1966 it sold $571 million in gold, much of it to France, whose president had expressed his distrust in the dollar.

"Unrecorded transactions" (entry IV, third item) are not a sign of careless accounting. Goods shipped abroad are recorded when they leave our borders, but financial transactions cannot always be readily identified. A bank may not know all transactions actually involving foreign residents; domestic checks may be sent abroad and become a debit in the balance; and other transactions can fail to be included in reported accounts. We might expect that unrecorded receipts and payments will cancel each other; when the balance in this account is large, it reveals broad movements of funds into the country or away from it. Of course, the total balance of payments must always be zero—unless someone has made a mistake.

Components of the Balance of Payments

Each one of the balances shown in the table is the result of many transactions. Some of them will now be examined.

Private Current Transactions. Exports and imports of merchandise represent the trade balance. The United States has had a surplus in the trade balance since 1873, though it changes considerably in size over the years. The continued presence of a substantial export surplus is a reasonably good indication that our manufacturers remain competitive and can hold their own in world trade.

It has not been customary to break down merchandise transactions

TABLE 19-2. Private Current Transactions in the U.S. Balance of Payments, 1966
(millions of dollars)

Account	Receipts (*Credits*)	Payments (*Debits*)
1. Merchandise:		
a. Exports	29,180	
b. Imports		25,507
2. Services:		
a. Exports	11,907	
b. Imports		7,267
3. Private remittances (net)		629
Total Private Current transactions	41,087	33,403
Balance as shown in Table 19-1, entry I	7,684	
Details of service accounts: (2a. and b. above)		
(1) Transportation of goods	2,585	2,903
(2) Travel	1,417	2,623
(3) Dividends and interest earned	5,585	1,311
(4) Other services (fees, insurance, royalties)	2,320	430
Total services as shown above	11,907	7,267

SOURCE: U.S. Department of Commerce, *Survey of Current Business.*

into specific industry accounts, but services are always represented in some detail, as shown in Table 19-2. The consequences of this accounting procedure have been most unfortunate for the travel industry, which has been singled out for legislative attacks by federal authorities because of its normal state of deficit. This deficit is not surprising; it reflects the relatively great wealth of this country, whose people can afford to travel abroad in greater numbers than the citizens of other nations.

Dividends or interest payments produce a large surplus for the United States because our firms own factories and branch offices all over the world. This service account reveals the measure of the benefits which accrue from the ownership of foreign investments. Other services include not only insurance payments, but also royalties, license fees for the use of inventions, and other items.

Private remittances are usually gifts to foreigners by citizens. This account is a net figure, from which all cash gifts to the United States have been deducted.

Private Long-Term Capital Transactions.   Long-term capital transactions are movements of funds among countries intended for periods of more than one year. *Direct investments* have the purpose of providing control of a foreign enterprise; *portfolio investments* are attempts to earn higher rates of interest abroad. When an American insurance company buys a Canadian bond, it makes a portfolio investment. An example of direct investments is the construction of an oil refinery in Venezuela by an American oil company, or the purchase of a small plant in Belgium by an American competitor who hopes to use the plant as a base for expansion in Europe. For-

TABLE 19-3.   Private Long-Term Capital Transactions in
the U.S. Balance of Payments, 1966
(millions of dollars)

Accounts	Receipts (*Credits*)	Payments (*Debits*)
4. U.S. residents' investments abroad (net):		
a. Direct investment		3,363
b. Portfolio investment		1,105
c. Repayments of investments	405	
d. Other changes in U.S. assets abroad	487	
5. Foreign investments in U.S. (net):		
a. Direct investment		21
b. Portfolio investment	881	
c. Other changes in foreign assets in the U.S.	1,052	
Total private long-term capital transactions	2,825	4,489
Balance as shown in Table 19-1, entry II		1,664

SOURCE: U.S. Department of Commerce, *Survey of Current Business.*

eign firms, in turn, build or buy factories in the United States. One such transaction was the purchase of Underwood by Olivetti from Italy. American direct investments abroad are usually more than $3 billion annually, because our far-flung interests all over the world require steady modernization and expansion to stay ahead of the competition. This annual cost on our part is far greater than any repayments of foreign investments here, but is not so high as the current income from the investments made in the past; compare Table 19-3, entry 4.a, with Table 19-2, entry 2(3).

The low figures in Table 19-3 could be misleading. Data for individual financial transactions are not available, and the balance sheet for all accounts reflects only the net difference reported by banks and others at the end of the year. The total flow of funds to and from the United States is the largest of any country. We can afford to invest more than other nations, and the financial market in New York is the world center for raising huge sums of money. Our traditional freedom in worldwide financial transactions, combined with the relatively greater stability of the value of the dollar, has been responsible for the leading position of this nation in world finance.

Government Activity Transactions. The heavy deficit incurred by our government in its international transactions reflects the political involvement of this country in every corner of the earth. The pattern of this deficit has been consistent since World War II. Our officials try, however, to reduce the impact our government's foreign transactions have on the balance of

TABLE 19-4. Government Activity Transactions in the U.S.
Balance of Payments, 1966
(*millions of dollars*)

Accounts	Receipts (*Credits*)	Payments (*Debits*)
6. Grants, nonmilitary (net)		1,915
7. Loans:		
a. Loans granted		2,592
b. Repayments received	1,286	
c. Subscriptions to international organizations	100	
8. Military transactions:		
a. Sales	908	
b. Purchases		3,649
9. Pensions		363
10. Other government transactions:		
a. Income from services	915	
b. Payments for services		1,456
Total government activities	3,209	9,975
Balance as shown in Table 19-1, entry III		6,766

SOURCE: U.S. Department of Commerce, *Survey of Current Business.*

payments. Gifts and loans to other nations are used to buy American goods whenever possible. Military grants are not shown in Table 19-4; these are gifts of American equipment which involve no cost overseas. Nonmilitary gifts and loans seem large, but official estimates inform us that $3.8 billion of this total has been spent on goods and services in the United States.

TABLE 19-5.   Summary of the Balance of Payments of the United States, 1966
(*millions of dollars*)

Accounts	Receipts (*Credits*)	Payments (*Debits*)
I. Private current transactions:		
1. Merchandise exports and imports	29,180	25,507
2. Services exports and imports	11,907	7,267
3. Private remittances (net)		629
Totals	41,087	33,403
II. Private long-term capital transactions (net):		
4. U.S. residents' investments abroad:		
a. Direct investments		3,363
b. Portfolio investments		1,105
c. Repayments of investments	405	
d. Other changes in U.S. assets abroad	487	
5. Foreign investments in the U.S.:		
a. Direct investments		21
b. Portfolio investments	881	
c. Other changes in foreign assets in the U.S.	1,052	
Totals	2,825	4,489
III. Government activity transactions:		
6. Grants (excluding military) (net)		1,915
7. Loan disbursals and repayments	1,386	2,592
8. Military sales and expenditures	908	3,649
9. Pensions		363
10. Others (services)	915	1,456
Totals	3,209	9,975
Totals, entries I–III	47,121	47,867
IV. Short-term financial transactions (net):		
11. Short-term claims and liabilities	1,102	335
12. U.S. government gold holdings	571	
13. U.S. government holdings of convertible currencies and IMF reserves	537	540
14. Unrecorded transactions		589
Totals	2,210	1,464
Totals, entries I–IV	49,331	49,331

SOURCE: U.S. Department of Commerce, *Survey of Current Business.*

The largest deficit item involves military transactions by the government. Sales of arms to many nations partly offset the huge cost of keeping armies all over the world. The defense department rents or builds barracks with local labor; it constructs roads and airstrips; it buys local construction material, crushed rock, for example, and perishable consumer goods. In 1966, the total bill reached almost $4 billion. Until our armies abroad can be reduced in number, no substantial improvement of this particular deficit can be expected.

We can now present the information contained in the various sections of the balance sheet together in a more detailed statement of the entire balance of payments. The same facts are assembled in Table 19-5.

Analysis of the Balance Sheet

The study of the balance of payments drives home the lesson of the worldwide interdependence of trade and services, the interactions in the flow of goods and money, and the connection of internal and international economic policies. No single account shows the same amount of payments and receipts; in fact, no account should balance. This statement contradicts the popular view that the flow of trade ought to be the same in both directions. Only a world of straight barter without credit could produce a balance of this type. Every country has some normal surplus and deficit accounts; the United States has a surplus from selling jet planes and a deficit from buying bananas. Therefore, we must not blame any single account for the deficit in the overall balance. It makes no better sense to campaign against eating bananas than it would to attack the airplane industry because it failed to export twice what it does. How can we economize and remove our persistent deficit without cutting specific expenditures?

Raise Exports. Some people suggest that none of our foreign expenditures can be reduced; therefore, the United States must export more and earn enough to pay its bills. This demand for more receipts defies easy translation into practice, when already our exports of goods exceed our imports by about 20 percent. Additional exports depend more on the willingness of the customers to buy than on the exporters' desire to sell abroad on a larger scale.

Reduce Imports. Domestic firms with foreign competitors will advocate restrictions on imports in order to improve the balance of payments. Their seemingly patriotic gesture may be more helpful to their own interests than to the nation. The United States always exports more than it brings in, and it cannot afford to restrict its imports because of our broad vulnerability to retaliation. A mutual reduction of barriers is more likely to increase our exports by a greater amount than our imports, and thus of more benefit than further restrictions would be.

Reduce Government Spending Abroad.   Many businessmen are justly proud of their export accomplishments, and they also read with pleasure that our domestic wheat surplus has finally been eliminated with the help of record sales abroad. They seem to forget that these exports are often paid for with grants and loans to the buyers from the U.S. Treasury. The temptation is great to blame all our difficulties on the huge deficit caused by federal spending abroad and to forcefully oppose "useless foreign giveaway projects." No one defends unnecessary expenditures, but a drop in foreign aid might not improve the deficit in our balance nearly so much as advocates of such a change expect.

Reduce Foreign Investments.   The isolationist citizen has his counterpart in the public official who knows that the government would not approve of unjustified foreign expenditures and therefore feels sure that they cannot be reduced. He protests, instead, against unnecessary private travel and ignores the planes we sell abroad to carry tourists from the United States. He persuades Congress to reduce the deficit by passing laws against foreign investments, without realizing the damage such a move will do—not only to our income from foreign dividends, but also to our exports of equipment which so often fill our foreign factories.

An unbroken stretch of foreign deficits has been our experience for too many years, and official measures to reverse the trend have so far been hesitant and ineffective. Ultimately, Congress will be forced to come to a sober reevaluation of our worldwide commitments. We must carefully weigh the benefits of yet another division stationed abroad against the possible harm resulting from an impression that the dollar is weak and that prudent people should keep their funds elsewhere.

The United States as the World's Banker

The financial problems of the United States differ in substance from those of most other nations. Our unique position is due to the fact that the U.S. dollar has become the world currency and New York its financial center. Only Great Britain in defending her long tradition of ruling world finances maintains the pound sterling as an international money, but England's economic weakness in the last twenty years leaves the pound at best in a position of supplementary currency, which can be used only as long as the United States will protect its value.

The role of world banker has some favorable aspects, but they are offset by definite obligations. The main advantage of a banker is the happy fact that he can use his own IOU to buy many goods and services he needs. In the case of the United States, almost $30 billion were held abroad in

1967 which we were able to use for the purchase of foreign goods and services. International banking also brought added business to this country, particularly to New York.

A banker also encounters some important obligations. A banking business exists on faith. We know already that no banker keeps enough currency to pay all his depositors at once. He uses most of his deposits for loans to other people, keeping only enough cash to supply the everyday demands of his customers. As long as they trust him, he has no problems, but he must behave in such a manner that his actions do not cause doubt or suspicion.

The United States is in a comparable position as the banker of the world. Our solvency is so strong that the position of the dollar can be defended with ease. Table 19-6 shows the international assets and liabilities of

TABLE 19-6. International Funds of the United States, 1950 and 1965
(*Year-end estimates in millions of dollars*)

	1950	1966
Assets		
Private direct investments abroad	11,788	54,562
Private portfolio investments abroad	5,700	21,003
Private short-term claims	1,516	10,670
U.S. Government long-term claims	10,768	21,182
U.S. Government short-term claims	1,767	4,457
U.S. Government gold stock	22,820	13,235
Total assets	54,359	125,109
Liabilities		
Direct investments by foreigners in the U.S.	3,391	9,054
Portfolio investments by foreigners in the U.S.	4,606	17,946
Dollar obligations held by foreign governments	4,382	17,921
Dollar obligations held privately	5,256	15,468
Total liabilities	17,635	60,389
Excess of assets over liabilities	36,724	64,720

SOURCE: U.S. Department of Commerce, *Survey of Current Business.*

this country. In the long period of yearly deficits from 1950 to the present, our assets have grown faster than our liabilities. We did not leave more dollars abroad, but we used these dollars well for the purchase of growing and profitable investments in many countries. *A nation is solvent when international assets exceed its liabilities;* it may not, however, be liquid.

Liquidity refers to a nation's ability to pay cash on demand to all who ask for it. Foreign holders of dollars and short-term dollar obligations, such as ninety-day Treasury bills, are in the same position as a bank's depositors. They may exchange their dollars for francs or marks or pesos at will, but they have no intention of doing so as long as they trust Uncle Sam's financial policy. We must preserve this confidence to avoid a liquidity crisis. In 1965 foreigners held over $33 billion payable at short notice. Uncle Sam had only $17.7 billion worth of assets which could be turned into cash immediately (last two asset items in Table 19-6).

The willingness of residents of other countries to accept additional dollars is the first balancing factor in the United States' balance of payments. If they want to exchange their dollar accounts for American goods and services, no harm will come to our balance. A drop in the credit account will be matched by a rise in exports when our firms deliver the goods ordered. Should, however, the foreign owners of dollars begin to doubt the determination of the monetary policy makers of this country to defend the stability of our money, they may sell dollars in exchange for other currencies, such as Swiss francs or British pounds.

The annual deficit in the balance of payments becomes disturbing only when it seeds thoughts of disbelief in the minds of dollar owners. Official statements of alarm do not improve our position. Inflationary price rises which might reduce the competitive advantage of the American exporter are a luxury the world's banker cannot afford. We must avoid triggering a run on the dollar, a situation in which all our permanent assets would be of little help. Many proposals for reducing this danger have been discussed by the leading financiers of the western world, but no far-reaching changes in the system of international payments have yet been attempted.

Shortages in Underdeveloped Nations

A quite different balance of payments problem is faced by underdeveloped countries, whose difficulties result directly from their limitless appetite for imports they cannot afford. They are not concerned with foreigners holding their currencies, as they transact all international business in some better known monetary unit. In the absence of sufficient credits to buy everything desired, the governments of these nations frequently ration foreign purchases in order to channel imports according to a nationally approved plan.

FOREIGN EXCHANGE

Foreign exchange is the name given to all monies of other countries; the *exchange rate* is the price of these currencies. A key currency is one which is used widely by other nations for international transactions. United States dollars and pounds sterling, the monetary unit of Great Britain, are favored along with a few others, because of the belief that their values are maintained without change. How are the values of world currencies determined?

Freely Fluctuating Exchange Rates

Exchange rates are prices, and they will fluctuate. In a well-organized market where many currencies can be traded for each other without interference, demand and supply of each monetary unit determine its price. When many people want to buy dollars, the price of dollars will rise; the price will fall when people want to sell.

Few countries permit free fluctuations in the market price of their currency. Canada allowed her currency to fluctuate within rather wide limits for some years before she abandoned the experiment in 1962 and returned to maintaining a fixed price for the Canadian dollar.

As a yardstick, a currency must be rigid; otherwise it is quite useless for comparison purposes. When the price of a national currency fluctuates too freely, the currency will no longer be used for international transactions—people will find safer ways of doing business.

Fixed Exchange Rates

Exchange rates are usually determined by a national government, which announces the price of gold or of some other major currency in terms of its own money. The State acts here very much like the monopolist in Chapter 8, who announces a sales price for his merchandise and adjusts the supply to the market demand. The result of this arrangement depends on the skill or the good luck of choosing an exchange rate which is neither too high nor too low. Such a rate must permit the largest flow of international transactions within the limits imposed by the balance of payments.

What happens when the fixed exchange rate is not right? Let us assume there is a rate of $1.00 for 100 francs when prices in the two countries would justify a rate of 200 francs per dollar. The dollar country will buy virtually nothing abroad because all franc merchandise is too expensive. The people in the franc country buy cheap dollars and import all they can. This lopsided arrangement cannot last forever.

The Treasury in the dollar country must accept more and more francs for its dollar or the price will change. The importers will protest vigorously because their business is being ruined. Only the exporters in the dollar country think that they are great salesmen and that these are wonderful times. The exporters in the franc country protest to their government against the unfair dollar competition. Eventually, the conflicting actions of the two governments must lead to a compromise, or to a breakdown in trade relations.

For the opposite case, we assume that the dollar, exchanged for 100 francs, is worth only 50. The result will be even more unfortunate. People will want to buy foreign goods priced in francs because they are so cheap. The Treasury will sell all the francs it owns or can afford to purchase; but its reserves will not last forever and it must correct the exchange rate in time.

A fixed rate of exchange can be maintained only as long as it happens to represent a workable compromise of many conflicting interests. A country can undertake a deliberate policy of domestic deflation to prevent a forced revision of the exchange rate; indeed, Great Britain decided on this rare and painful course of action in 1966. In most cases such drastic steps against prosperity and full employment at home are considered politically impractical, and a national treasury faced by a heavy demand for other currencies, which it can satisfy only for a limited time, must choose between two equally difficult alternatives: it may impose exchange controls or it may depreciate the value of its currency.

Exchange Controls

An exchange-control system is created by law and assigns to a government institution monopoly rights over all economic transactions with foreign countries. Such state monopolies were widely used by most nations before 1958, when they agreed to restore freedom of private action to world trade and payments; the United States avoided the use of these controls during the entire period. The shortcomings of such a cumbersome system far outweigh any possible benefits. In 1965, with the use of guidelines without legislative approval, we came closer to the spirit of exchange controls than we had at any time in the past during peacetime. Informal pressure was exerted on several hundred large firms to refrain from foreign investments unless approved by federal authorities.

Currency Depreciation

A country may avoid exchange controls by raising the price of all foreign currencies to the point where fewer people want to buy them. Such a step is usually called a depreciation, or a devaluation, of the currency. People who want to buy francs because they are considered cheap (100 francs for one unit of their own currency) will change their minds when they have to pay two units of their own money for the same 100 francs; to state it differently, their own monetary unit now buys only 50 francs.

The British government in 1949 reduced the amount of dollars paid for one pound of sterling from $4.03 to $2.80. To the pound owner, dollars had suddenly become much more expensive, and the demand for dollars at this new price promptly dropped. Some people who had bought dollars earlier were now ready to sell them again for sterling.

Depreciation can be a successful method of improving a nation's balance of payments if other countries are willing to cooperate and refrain from reducing the value of their currency at the same time. When everyone tries to change the price of their currencies by the same percentage, no one is any better off than before.

Depreciation is ineffective when the outflow of funds is caused by a nation's losing its major export business. A small country with a tradition of specializing in the foreign sale of ostrich feathers faces a crisis when the fashion changes and people no longer want ostrich feathers at any price. A currency depreciation will not help in this case, thus a substantial adjustment of the whole structure of the existing economy becomes necessary. Unless the nation is able to revamp its export business to fit new world demands, its living standards will inevitably be reduced. Financial reserves may temporarily bridge the gap in foreign payments while the country adjusts to the new situation, but depreciation will not help.

THE INTERNATIONAL GOLD STANDARD

The function of gold as a means of international payments can be traced back many centuries. Particularly in Western Europe, where it has never been found in significant quantities, the natural scarcity of gold has guaranteed its value over long periods of time. The lesser coins produced by most rulers compared unfavorably with gold, because the issue of currency was frequently increased to help a local government pay heavy debts. People learned from bitter experience to trust only in gold for the maintenance of stable values. Contracts between nationals of different countries were expressed in gold, and payments in other currencies were acceptable only at the going rate of exchange of that currency for gold. All countries adhering to the gold standard were in fact using one common world currency—gold—equally valuable to all of them.

How Does the Gold Standard Operate?

The operation of a gold standard can be sketched very simply. If currency A is valued at five units per ounce of gold and currency B trades at ten units per ounce of gold, prices in A must be about half as much as in B. If A prices, however, are as high as B prices, people will buy B and sell the A currency for gold. The flow of gold and business away from A toward B will depress prices in A and raise them in B until they reflect the gold rate of the two currencies.

The Rules of the Game. The functioning of a gold standard depends on the willingness of the participating countries to adhere to the strict rules of the game. These rules need to be understood in order to realize why modern governments are reluctant to tie their countries to this standard.

1. A country must subordinate its domestic economic policy to the requirements of its international financial obligations. Domestic interest rates, for example, must not be influenced by the monetary authorities to a point where they are much higher or lower than in other gold-standard countries. If they are too low, financiers will move their funds abroad, and the resulting shortage of credit will raise the rates again. If interest rates are too high, foreigners will supply more funds and bring the rates down.

2. The prices in all gold-standard countries are determined by the nation with the lowest price level. No nation can afford to raise prices alone. The effect of this limitation can be very depressing on the domestic economy. If a government wants to boost prices and stimulate a low level of business, it cannot do so, because higher prices will raise imports and reduce exports unless the cheaper countries are willing to cooperate.

3. An isolated domestic boom cannot be sustained. An increase in business stimulates imports and leads to payments of gold. The outflow of gold restricts credit, depresses the price level, and kills the boom.

4. The central bank must refrain from independent action in controlling the money supply. Changes in available funds simply reflect the flow of gold from one nation to another.

Breakdown of the Gold Standard.   These rules of the game should explain quite clearly why modern nations no longer adhere to a gold standard. They deprive a country of the opportunity to make most of the decisions usually entrusted to national authorities. Historically, the gold-standard rules were no heavy burden for nations whose economies were effectively isolated from each other by high transportation costs and by little knowledge of each other. Most business in the past was of a local or regional character, immune to foreign influences; the flow of international trade was largely limited to products which were unavailable locally at any price. Where price comparisons entered the picture, the high cost, great risk, and loss of time inherent in transportation difficulties prevented even the most efficient producers from effectively competing far away.

The use of the gold standard was limited, therefore, to a fairly small number of internationally traded products and to neighboring countries. The inevitable difficulties of the system were mitigated by the concentration of credit facilities in the city of London and by the exclusive use of the British currency for international transactions. None of these conditions holds true today.

A domestic full-employment policy is considered more important than the rules of the gold standard. The availability of gold itself has failed to expand as fast as the needs of a rapidly growing world commerce. World credit is no longer controlled from one center, and liquid funds are therefore apt to shift from country to country at the slightest provocation.

The Gold Standard Today

The international value of gold today is derived in substance from its relationship to the United States dollar. Under American law, the United States Treasury will buy gold at $35 per ounce. The world market price of gold does not deviate much from this rate as long as the United States chooses to maintain it. Other countries are willing to accept gold at the same price because they can convert the metal into dollars; therefore, the dollar-gold combination provides a usable international currency.[2]

The operation of this dollar-gold standard depends on the maintenance of a fixed rate. The gold reserves of the United States, which are still the largest in the world, must remain impressive enough to strengthen everyone's faith in the existing arrangement and withstand all possible challenges of our ability to maintain this rate. A continued deficit in the United States' balance of payments has caused a reduction of the gold reserve and may, in time, sufficiently undermine world confidence in the dollar price of gold to require a new set of rules for international payments.

FINANCIAL INSTITUTIONS

Two international institutions are now operating toward the goal of facilitating world payments. The older one is the Bank for International Settlements (BIS) in Basle, Switzerland, which was founded to help in the liquidation of the payments difficulties arising from German reparations after World War I. The other institution is the International Monetary Fund (IMF), created at the end of World War II for the purpose of improving international financial relations.

The Bank for International Settlements

The Bank for International Settlements was an outgrowth of the Young Plan;[3] it commenced operation in 1930. Its first task was to assist in the settlement of the German reparations remaining from World War I. This assignment soon lost its importance because reparations payments were

[2] The arrangement whereby some countries keep their reserves in currencies which in turn have a fixed gold price is sometimes called a gold-exchange standard.

[3] Owen D. Young was the American chairman of an international committee of experts that negotiated an agreement for the final settlement of the problem of German reparations; the report of the committee was signed on June 7, 1929. It recommended the creation of the BIS in Part VI of its report.

suspended. The bank's main function today is "to promote the cooperation of central banks and to provide additional facilities for international financial operations." [4]

The BIS is essentially a European bank, which maintains, however, close contact with the Federal Reserve System. Its limited membership emphasizes the financial problems of industrialized countries.

The board of directors holds monthly meetings and determines the nature of the operations of the institution. These meetings are a major source of strength of the BIS. They make possible a high degree of informal cooperation among the central bankers, who face similar problems in maintaining stable currencies. They may even arrange temporary loans to each other in order to help stabilize the international monetary system. The techniques of the BIS are very flexible and adapt quickly to the ever-changing needs of world finance.

The volume of actual financial transactions, though considerable in recent years, fails to reflect the real importance of this institution. Its major influence stems from the monthly contacts it provides for the leading central bankers of the world. The United States, though not a member, is always represented at these meetings by a top-ranking official.

The International Monetary Fund

The International Monetary Fund was created at the Conference of Bretton Woods in 1944 for the purpose of promoting exchange stability, a goal approached through the pooling of additional currency reserves provided by all the member nations. These monies can be loaned for a short time (sold, in the terms of the agreement) to those nations which need them most.

The membership of the IMF includes over 100 countries and is much broader than the BIS. Most members of the United Nations join the IMF, with the exception of the countries of the Communist Bloc. The influence of the membership is weighed on the basis of relative economic importance, which leaves a strong vote in the hands of the nations with the largest shares in international commerce.

In its short history, the evolution of the IMF has firmly established its usefulness in world finance. From the start it has promoted international monetary cooperation, assisting several countries in the reconstruction of their domestic currency systems after World War II. The rather limited funds at its disposal have necessitated the IMF's adopting a cautious policy in the use of its currencies. A member can receive financial help only when its difficulties promise to be short-lived and when he has initiated the

[4] Article 3 of the Statutes of the Bank for International Settlements.

necessary steps to reverse the trend which required the aid. The financial assistance of the IMF is not a giveaway program.

The capital resources of the Fund have been expanded gradually and are now in excess of $20 billion. Not all of this sum has actually been paid, since the mere assurance of IMF help is frequently sufficient to stabilize a currency which is experiencing a crisis of confidence. The added support of the IMF induced some important Western countries in 1958 to abandon their exchange-control systems, which had remained an unwanted legacy of depression and war. The free movement of currencies, now operative among over twenty nations, has strengthened the Fund and the international exchange system. While the world still has a long way to go before a move from pesos to liras, or dollars to pounds, will elicit as little excitement as a shift of credit from Atlanta to Dallas, the rehabilitation of an international payments system has shown encouraging progress in recent years.

SUMMARY

The lack of a common world currency makes it necessary to maintain a credit system which balances international payments over short periods of time, in spite of a natural tendency toward broad fluctuations.

The balance of payments is an accounting statement which registers a country's international transactions with all other nations. The relative impact of the various accounts in the statement is an indication of the present position of the country in the world economy.

The components of the balance of payments can be grouped into many categories. A distinction between current and long-term transactions permits better evaluation of coming changes. A separation of trade and financial accounts is primarily due to different accounting methods. Separate treatment of the government accounts puts the spotlight on those payments which public policy can control most directly. Balancing items receive separate treatment because of their critical importance in maintaining worldwide financial stability.

The balance of payments of the United States shows a long-standing surplus in merchandise trade boosted by a steady income from past investments in foreign countries. Part of this surplus is reinvested abroad by private financiers, who always discover new opportunities in foreign lands for fast growth or high profits.

The surplus of the United States' balance of payments has given way to deficits for seventeen years. Balance is maintained only by the willingness of foreigners to hold dollar obligations and by gold sales of the Treasury.

No deficit can be allowed to become chronic. The United States can eliminate this undesirable result by a public policy which limits total commitments to the funds available.

Foreign exchange rates are the prices for other nations' currencies. Their stability is a necessary requirement for confidence in international transactions.

When exchange rates are no longer stable, the government may resort to exchange controls or devaluation of the currency. After wide use for many years, the serious shortcomings of exchange controls have led to their abolishment in many countries.

Devaluation of a currency is an alternative to exchange controls. It will bring stability only when it can count on the cooperation of other nations and avoid inflationary policies at home thereafter.

The gold standard has a long monetary tradition based on the natural scarcity of the metal. All countries on the gold standard use the same currency—gold—and must adhere to certain rules of the game. These rules require subordination of domestic economic policy to the requirements of international balance.

Modern governments no longer adhere to the rules of the traditional gold standard. The value of gold today is the result of United States policy, which supports the world gold price at $35 per ounce. The dollar-gold standard is a usable world currency as long as confidence in its fixed rate can be maintained. The stock of gold of the United States had dropped below $14 billion by the end of 1966.

The Bank for International Settlements has provided an opportunity for regular meetings of the central bankers of Western Europe and the United States for over thirty years. Their frequent discussions have facilitated understanding and cooperation toward greater stability of member currencies, a result far more important than the actual banking transactions of this institution.

The International Monetary Fund has promoted greater stability of world currencies through advice and additional reserves furnished to its members. Its basic goal of a stable world currency has not yet been reached, but much progress in that direction permits one to be cautiously optimistic.

Discussion Questions

1. When does a balance of payments show a deficit?
2. What accounts in the United States' balance statement always show more receipts, and what others always show more payments? Why?
3. How can the federal government help to reduce the deficit of the balance of payments?
4. Should exchange rates be allowed to fluctuate?
5. Gold is at the center of all economic activity, and what this country needs is a return to the gold standard. Comment on this statement.

6. Why is gold a balancing factor in international payments?
7. Does a payments deficit mean that a country is necessarily broke? Explain.
8. What is the function of the IMF?

Suggested Reading

BALASSA, BELA, ed., *Changing Patterns in Foreign Trade and Payments.* New York, Norton, 1964.

JACOBSSON, PER, *The Market Economy in the World of Today.* Philadelphia, American Philosophical Society, 1963.

TRIFFIN, ROBERT, *Gold and the Dollar Crisis.* New Haven, Conn., Yale, 1960.

YEAGER, LELAND B., *International Monetary Relations.* New York, Harper & Row, 1966.

20

FOREIGN TRADE

The balance of payments reflects the international financial position of a country. It imposes restraints on policy makers and helps to prevent domestic measures which might undermine the credit worthiness and the competitive position of the nation's traders.

Foreign trade will now draw our attention. The desirability of trading abroad is generally acknowledged, but the men who represent the forces of protection against imported merchandise are traditionally strong in the halls of Congress. Their influence causes restrictive legislation which sometimes directly conflicts with trade agreements intended to reduce the obstacles to free trade. A recent creation of significant impact upon world trade is the European Common Market; a discussion of its implications will conclude this chapter.

A NATION'S PLACE IN WORLD TRADE

What economic information is most revealing in a comparison of the relative position of the world's nations? Each country emphasizes different features geared to impress others with its great strength; for example, it may point out a wealth of raw materials or food crops, a growth in industrial capacity, a heavy volume of exports, or even a fact as irrelevant as the number of telephones installed. There are, however, more basic data with which to draw a reasonably accurate picture of the international standing of a nation's economy—data which indicate the share and composition of its national income earned in foreign trade, the concentration of this trade on specific commodities and countries, and its influence on the trade of the rest of the world.

Nationalistic spokesmen like to pronounce the complete independence of their country from the rest of the world. Frequently their statements fail to include the fact that such independence would inflict poverty on the people. The economic position of different lands varies, but an objective evaluation can make a good guess at the nature of the sacrifice when political leaders demand from their citizens that the country must "go it alone." The independence of a hermit is not the sort of life most people hope to achieve.

Share of World Trade

Few countries control a large enough share of world trade to exert any noticeable influence on others. Most nations contribute less than 5 percent of a total of over $180 billion per year. No one nation occupies a monopoly position for any essential raw material.

The foreign trade of the United States, with about $29 billion worth of exports in 1966, is the largest single share of world business, approaching 17 percent of the total. Germany and the United Kingdom each hold about 10 percent, with France, Canada, and Japan accounting for over 6 percent apiece. All industrial countries [1] together handled more than two-thirds of the world's trade.

Other nations find that they must adjust their economic policies to the pattern set by the advanced nations unless they can create larger units with a positive influence of their own.

Foreign Trade and National Income

The size of a country and its industrial advancement are reflected in the share of national income which accrues from foreign trade. For a small nation like Denmark, much of its trade lies abroad. Any small, industrialized country relies heavily on foreign customers and suppliers, because the domestic market is not large enough for the efficient use of even one low-cost plant for many types of business.

Foreign trade constitutes only a small share of our GNP but is at the same time a large part of world commerce. This apparent contradiction is resolved when we consider that the national output of the United States is almost four times as large as the international trade of the world. Our exports seldom exceed 5 percent of GNP; our imports are usually less.

We must not be misled by the low percentage that foreign trade occupies in the total United States output. Most business transactions are purely domestic, but a firm producing for export or using imported equipment depends on foreign trade quite heavily. Let us consider for a moment how much the average consumer relies on imported goods. For breakfast, he eats a banana from Guatemala with his cereal, served in a china bowl from Germany; he sips coffee from Brazil, sweetened with sugar from the Philippines, while reading the morning paper produced from Canadian woodpulp. He goes to his office in an overcoat made from Australian wool (with an Italian hat on his head), and drives a car rolling on tires of Malayan rubber, fueled by gasoline refined from Venezuelan crude oil. He

---

[1] Industrial countries include the United States, the United Kingdom, industrial Europe, Canada, and Japan; see *International Financial Statistics* (Washington, D.C., International Monetary Fund, August 1967).

turns on his radio made in Japan and listens to a sharp attack against unnecessary imports. At this point, he is ready to reach for an imported pill to rid himself of a purely home-grown headache.

Of course, some of these products are also produced in this country—sugar, for example. But the total domestic production of these goods is not large enough for our demand, or, if made exclusively at home, would become more expensive.

Composition of Foreign Trade

The foreign trade of the United States is fairly well balanced among raw materials, foodstuffs, and manufactured products. The exports of a highly industrialized nation are naturally concentrated in the output of its factories, but raw materials and foodstuffs still constitute an important element of total sales abroad.

Commodity Distribution of Foreign Trade

Some nations' foreign trade centers heavily on a few types of products or commodities. A country comes to depend increasingly on others when all of its income from selling abroad is concentrated on one product. A bad crop year or a sudden change in demand may reduce earnings so much that the country can no longer pay for its imports and must depend on whatever credit other nations are willing to grant. Arabian oil, Brazilian coffee, and Malayan rubber illustrate the problems of one-commodity export countries.

The export commodities of the United States consist of a very long and varied list. In Table 20-1, only the products with the highest export values are listed separately.

TABLE 20-1.   What the United States Sold Abroad, 1966
(millions of dollars)

Commodity	Value
Grains (wheat, corn)	3,189
Soybeans	760
Chemicals	2,676
Automobiles, trucks, and buses	2,387
Aircraft	1,101
Nonferrous metals	735
Electrical machinery	1,899
Construction machinery	971
Farm machinery	628
Other machinery	3,948
All other commodities	10,886
Total exports	29,180

SOURCE: U.S. Bureau of the Census, 1967.

U.S. Exports.   Export categories are broadly drawn and include the products of many different manufacturers. Machinery of all types accounts for a large share of this outflow because it frequently represents the results of research and technology, a key feature of industrial progress. Modern equipment is sold largely to the progressive nations of Western Europe. The specific items under this heading vary continuously with the fast-changing picture of technical advancement.

Wheat remains the leading farm export commodity. Cotton fluctuates sharply from year to year, tobacco and rice exports are smaller in dollar volume. The importance of foreign shipments for all four of these crops must not be underestimated. Domestic surpluses are reduced sharply when over 30 percent of the annual crop is sold abroad. The American farmer is a big exporter, but he usually fails to recognize the extent of his international involvement. The special efforts made by the Department of Agriculture to distribute farm commodities abroad under the provisions of Public Law 480 have been discussed in Chapter 11.

Mass production goods depend on exports more than their dollar volume of output would reveal. Because of the heavy overhead cost of automated operations, a continuous flow of sales is necessary for profit. The home market may absorb the largest share of this assembly line and still just manage to break even. However, the sales boost from exports adds enough volume to permit more efficient use of plant facilities without increasing costs unduly. The result is a significant improvement in profits.

Foreign markets become particularly helpful when a domestic recession shrinks sales at home while world business continues to move upward.

U.S. Imports.   United States imports concentrate heavily on raw materials not available in sufficient quantity here, and on tropical farm products which we are unable to produce economically. The list of high dollar-volume imports in Table 20-2 includes paper, coffee, copper, and aluminum. These commodities may be broadly called noncompeting goods. Of course, substantial domestic production exists in some of these products, but the home-grown output remains far below the needed minimum supply.

The purchase abroad of goods in direct competition with domestic products causes much opposition. Petroleum imports are an excellent example, since the value of these products is so great, and the heavy flow of this commodity is caused partly by the fact that the foreign oil is American owned. United States companies pump oil wherever they control it and find it cheapest, utilizing their resources both here and abroad.

Automobiles compete in a field subject to sudden change. The United States' export surplus of cars and trucks is traditionally large. During the peak of the small-car boom, however, the United States imported more

TABLE 20-2.   What the United States Bought Abroad, 1966
(*millions of dollars*)

Commodity	Value
Petroleum and its products	2,127
Nonferrous metals (copper, aluminum, etc.)	1,552
Iron and steel products	1,305
Automobiles (new passenger cars)	1,237
Coffee	1,067
Electrical machinery (radio, TV, etc.)	1,016
Paper	986
Chemicals	957
Textile fabrics	908
All other commodities	14,352
Total imports	25,507

SOURCE: U.S. Bureau of the Census, 1967.

automobiles than it sold abroad. They have dropped again to a more normal level, but still remain a big import product. Steel products have always been exported on a large scale. In recent years, however, we have brought in far more steel than we have sold abroad, and it is now one of our largest import items.

Almost half of the imports to the United States consist of crude and partly manufactured materials. Finished consumer goods in competition with domestic products constitute one-third of the total. Some people may be surprised to discover that the foreign competitors for our domestic

TABLE 20-3.   U.S. Imports Representing over 90 Percent
of Total Supply, 1963

Commodity	Percent of Supply Imported	Value of Imports (*millions*)
Coffee	100	$954.9
Crude rubber	100	201.3
Crude diamonds	100	179.6
Cocoa	100	135.2
Bananas	100	83.1
Carpet wool	100	65.8
Tea	100	58.2
Copra	100	38.1
Silk	100	27.2
Chromium	100	20.1
Jute	100	13.1
Columbium and tantalum	100	5.5
Tin ore	100	3.1
Cryolite	100	1.8
Manganese	94	67.6
Asbestos	92	61.7

SOURCE: U.S. Bureau of the Census, 1966.

textile fabrics, watches, wooden clothespins, or handblown glassware do not furnish most of our imports. Producers of these specialized items have in the past asked for more protection against foreign competition.

Dependence on Imports.   The dependence of the nation on imported products cannot be measured by dollar values alone. Rare metals and minerals with unique characteristics may be needed only in small amounts, but for their specific purpose they are vitally necessary. The heat shield which protects a satellite capsule upon reentry into the atmosphere requires imported ingredients for satisfactory qualities of heat resistance. Such items do not loom large in the import statistics, but they are essential to progress in the exploration of the universe.

A complete list of commodities whose imports exceed 80 percent of our total domestic needs in recent years would include over eighty-five items. The United States' dependence on imports amounting to over 90 percent of our total supply is illustrated in Table 20-3.

Geographic Distribution of Foreign Trade

The foreign trade of a nation is often concentrated on exchanging goods with neighbors and a few other countries linked by special historical ties. The British Commonwealth's trade is a good example of such a tradition. A nation whose trade is heavily concentrated in one or two other countries can hardly conduct a national policy in conflict with those nations. Hos-

TABLE 20-4.   Geographic Distribution of U.S. Foreign Trade, 1966

Country	U.S. Exports		U.S. Imports	
	Dollars (*millions*)	Percent	Dollars (*millions*)	Percent
Canada	6,661	22.8	6,106	23.9
EEC *a*	5,332	18.3	4.098	16.1
United Kingdom	1,737	5.9	1,761	6.9
Japan	2,365	8.1	2,948	11.5
Other Asian Countries	4,362	14.9	2,264	8.9
Mexico	1,180	4.1	705	2.8
Venezuela	598	2.1	1,025	4.0
Other Latin America	2,415	8.3	2,213	8.7
Africa	1,349	4.6	999	3.9
All others	3,181	10.9	3,388	13.3
Totals	29,180	100.0	25,507	100.0

a The European Economic Community (EEC) comprises France, Italy, West Germany, Belgium, the Netherlands, and Luxembourg.
SOURCE: U.S. Bureau of the Census, 1967.

tility might mean a loss of the best source of supply or of their chief customer.

The best customer of the United States is Canada. As shown in Table 20-4, the six nations of Western Europe which make up the developing European Common Market buy together more goods from us than any other single country except Canada. Africa is less important as a customer for United States exports; this continent has limitless desires, but its ability to pay for a large volume of imports is restricted. Japan buys a great deal from the United States, as do Mexico and Venezuela.

United States imports are heaviest from Canada, followed again by Western Europe's Common Market, Japan, and England. Cuba used to occupy a prominent role in our foreign trade before political difficulties interrupted the normal flow of goods between neighbors. The entire trade position of the United States is pictured in Figure 20-1.

WHY TRADE ABROAD?

Foreign trade is based on the same reasoning which underlies domestic trade. Modern technology causes specialization; the advantages of specialization become real only when a smoothly working system of trade permits people to exchange the fruits of their labor for the numerous needs of human life. This reasoning does not stop at the water's edge. If domestic trade increases wealth, business should not remain confined within arbitrary boundaries simply because it is easier to avoid foreign entanglements.

A country can always remain self-sufficient if it is willing to pay the price in the form of a lower standard of living. We can get along without coffee, but we won't like the sacrifice. The Great Wall of China restricted to her own people the accomplishments of an advanced civilization. It kept out the foreigner and his innovations, until the progress of the rest of the world had passed by a sealed-off culture which had become stagnant.

Comparative Advantage

World trade thrives on the uneven distribution of people, of their skills and knowledge, and of natural advantages. Men do not move abroad as readily as the goods they make. Every group finds something it can do better or cheaper than others, which it can trade for foreign products. How does a nation trade with others when it does everything better than they do? The question may seem far-fetched, but it was answered in the beginning of the nineteenth century by David Ricardo in his famous doctrine of

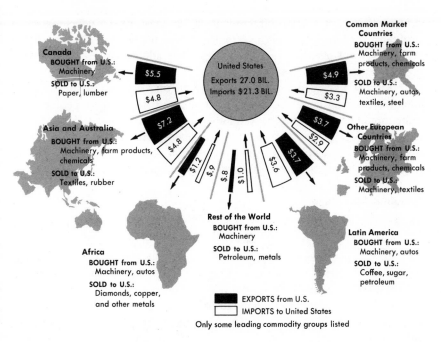

Canada
BOUGHT from U.S.:
Machinery
SOLD to U.S.:
Paper, lumber

United States
Exports 27.0 BIL.
Imports $21.3 BIL.

Common Market
Countries
BOUGHT from U.S.:
Machinery, farm
products, chemicals
SOLD to U.S.:
Machinery, autos,
textiles, steel

Asia and Australia
BOUGHT from U.S.:
Machinery, farm products,
chemicals
SOLD to U.S.:
Textiles, rubber

Other European
Countries
BOUGHT from U.S.:
Machinery, farm
products, chemicals
SOLD to U.S.:
Machinery, textiles

$5.5 $4.8 $4.9 $3.3 $7.2 $4.8 $3.7 $2.9 $1.2 $.9 $.8 $1.0 $3.6 $3.7

Rest of the World
BOUGHT from U.S.:
Machinery
SOLD to U.S.:
Petroleum, metals

Latin America
BOUGHT from U.S.:
Machinery, autos
SOLD to U.S.:
Coffee, sugar,
petroleum

Africa
BOUGHT from U.S.:
Machinery, autos
SOLD to U.S.:
Diamonds, copper,
and other metals

EXPORTS from U.S.
IMPORTS to United States
Only some leading commodity groups listed

Source: U.S. Bureau of the Census.

Fig. 20-1. Where the U.S. Traded in 1965
(*billions of dollars*)

comparative advantage. Since it continues to be invoked as a basis of policy decisions, it is briefly mentioned here.

Ricardo suggested that international specialization is always helpful. Even the most advanced nation cannot do everything, because her people do not have the time to handle completely all the things in which they excel; therefore, she must compare her relative advantage over other nations in making shirts or sugar and concentrate on those activities where her advantage is the greatest. If you have the time to make only one of two products, though you may be more skilled than all other people in making both, you should concentrate on the one item where your skill advantage is most pronounced and let the other be produced at higher cost by those who have the time.

A simple example will clarify the meaning of this theory. When the world's champion typist goes to law school and receives a law degree, he has time to handle his new law business and type his own briefs. As he becomes also the best lawyer in town, he finds it impossible to accept all the legal business offered and at the same time continue to do his own typing. He decides that he is better off specializing in legal work, which is more profitable for him, and hires a secretary to type his briefs, even though her typing may not be nearly so good as his. His advantage is comparatively greater in his legal business.

Ricardo excluded the possibility of moving workers to the country where everything could be done better, because he thought people were quite immobile when transfer to another nation was involved. A significant increase in the output of a country was hampered by the inflexibility of operations in Ricardo's era. A man on a seventy-two-hour work week could not be induced to do much more work at any price.

Absolute Advantage

Most foreign trade is based on an absolute advantage. We can usually produce more goods if we can do one thing better than others; also, we do not face Ricardo's problem of being better in so many things that we lack the time to do them all. Our purchases abroad are limited to merchandise we cannot produce at home, or could produce only at prohibitive costs.

Under conditions of absolute advantage, we sell abroad everything we can do better than others and buy from them the goods which they are superior in producing.

Why, then, do people object so often to the free flow of trade when this is clearly the best system for reaping the benefits of specialization? Businessmen all over the world hate to admit that others have become more efficient than they and can operate more cheaply. When the successful competitor lives abroad, the temptation to exert political pressure at home becomes the natural reaction of a firm in trouble. It is often easier to remove the threat to a domestic firm and its traditional way of making a living by invoking government action that it is to improve business operations.

TRADE RESTRAINTS

The restrictions to world trade in the national interest are still based on the ancient pronouncements of mercantilistic doctrine. The businessmen in the year 1600 fought imports from abroad with the same arguments advanced today when industry representatives face Congressional committees. A strongly nationalistic spirit supports the selfish demands of local firms against foreign competitors.

The native producer unhappily accepts the challenge to his position from a domestic competitor because he has no choice in the matter, but he is not ready to grant foreigners equal access to his own market. The attitude of many businessmen toward foreign competition can be summed up in a simple guideline for their Congressmen: "When in doubt, keep it out."

Forms of Protection

Restraints on importation can take many forms. In current practice, three methods of interference with trade are most common. Tariff duties are best known, but quota restrictions have become increasingly important in recent years, at least in the United States. Seldom mentioned, but quite effective, is a system of administrative restraints which discourages attempts to import some types of merchandise.

Tariffs. A tariff is a tax. This tax can be applied to collect revenue, and it is frequently used for this purpose. We call it a *revenue tariff*.

Today a tariff is widely applied for a different purpose. It is also a barrier against imports of goods from other countries. Such a barrier is called a *protective tariff*.

The goal of protection directly contradicts any efforts to collect revenue. A good revenue tariff has low enough duty rates to maintain a large flow of imports as well as heavy collections. The best protection is achieved, however, when duty rates are so high that nothing is imported and no revenue is collected.

Quota Restrictions. Some national firms would like to be protected even though their limited output can satisfy only a small part of the demand. When a large share of a product necessarily comes from abroad, a few domestic competitors cannot command a fully protective tariff, but prefer a system of quota restrictions.

Quota restrictions are limitations on the total volume of specific imports for a given period of time. Congress authorizes the use of restrictions and delegates to an administrator the task of determining the exact quantity to be admitted to this country. The administrator considers the normal requirements of the nation and makes an estimate of probable domestic supply. The difference will be permitted to enter the country; determination of demand based on world market prices may or may not influence the decision.

A tariff erects a wall that grants only limited shelter to domestic producers. Foreign firms may try to scale this wall by paying the required duty. A quota restriction, however, is far more restrictive. We may look at it as a door in the solid wall of restrictions, opened just enough to permit entry to a trickle of needed goods. As soon as they pass, the door shuts tight and no foreign willingness to compete or to pay duty will add to the imports.

The United States traditionally frowns on the use of quotas, but this principle has been systematically violated in recent decades. Quotas were first introduced in agriculture during Depression days, and Congress later extended them to include several raw materials. Lead and zinc came first, and textile and oil producers have since received quotas of increasing restrictiveness.

Quota restrictions reduce competition from foreigners and leave international trade relations exposed to every kind of political pressure. They can be used as a tool to discriminate between supplier countries or as an instrument of economic warfare. If we want to favor Country X, which wishes to sell us lemons, we grant it a lemon quota. The indiscriminate use of such devices in peacetime leads to a reciprocal reduction in foreign trade to the detriment of all countries concerned.

In some countries, exchange controls have been used for the same restrictive purposes. When a firm needs a permit to pay for foreign merchandise, refusal to grant such permission restricts imports just as effectively as a quota. The United States does not use this particular technique.

Administrative Protection.   Administrative protection is seldom mentioned in spite of its effective use as a restraint to imports of consumer goods. This device consists of such a formidable amount of red tape that it discourages attempts to import some products. The United States tariff distinguishes about 5,000 different product classifications and the importer can seldom be sure how his latest purchase will be classified. He may have thought to import handkerchiefs subject to a low duty rate, but the customs official disagrees and labels them linen scarfs or ornamental embroidery, which calls for different rates. The uncertainty of interpretation, combined with a traditional reluctance to give the importer the benefit of the doubt, discourages attempts to import products where the profit can be wiped out by a high duty assessment.

The Case for Protection

The arguments for the protection of domestic producers against their foreign competitors have followed the same pattern for generations. Several will be presented here because of their wide popularity. However, none of them is valid in the present position of the United States, as will be shown in each case.

The Infant Industry Argument.   One of the oldest arguments is the infant industry argument. It says in substance that a new domestic industry will be able to become competitive and efficient if it is permitted enough time to learn its business. In the meantime, the government should keep competing products out of the country in order to allow the industry to establish itself and grow up.

This argument is quite plausible and logically sound. In practice, however, no industry receives government aid until it is sufficiently well established to fight vigorously and expensively in the halls of Congress. The infants protected by tariffs are no small industries but large, influential firms, in some cases established for generations. Once they have reached the shelter which protects them against competitive imports, they will not willingly give up their duty protection.

The real infant industries of the United States do not ask for protection because they do not need it; though young in years, they have already become formidable competitors without fear of imports from other countries. A demand for help comes more often from industries which have grown stale over the years. They are unable to progress as fast as their competitors and are too inefficient to maintain their established position at home. While the argument for infant industry protection is good, the practice actually supports the outdated methods of business firms that have failed to keep abreast of the times.

The National Defense Argument.   Another popular argument urges that some industries be protected in the interest of national defense. Such an argument is perfectly sound—whenever it can be truthfully applied.

There is a sharp difference of opinion between the producers of a commodity and its users about how essential their production process is to the country. Few industrial operations can benefit the nation if they are so weak in peacetime that only government help can keep them alive. It may be more in the national interest to stockpile essential products and keep them in storage for use in the event of war than to depend on the continued operation of an industry no longer able to stand on its own feet. Some industrial claims of defense importance are even contradicted by the defense authorities themselves.

The Cheap Labor Argument.   Industry spokesmen often tell Congress that they cannot compete with "coolie labor." The statement implies that foreign firms pay such low hourly wages that American firms cannot compete while paying high salaries to their own workers. If the domestic and the foreign firms used identical manufacturing techniques and if these techniques were to include a significant share of human labor, the complaining firm would be correct that it cannot compete successfully.

In fact, the firm should not even try to compete on these terms. If a U.S. producer cannot use his labor force more efficiently than a competitor operating in a country where capital equipment is too costly to replace human labor on a large scale, our employer needs to modernize. He either fails to use up-to-date methods, or his business has not progressed enough to afford the expensive labor employed by more modern industries. A United States worker produces many times more than his foreign counterpart because he operates with better equipment, which renders his efforts more efficient. An American employer must always find more efficient ways to use expensive human labor. When he fails to do so, he can no longer justify his operation.

The Employment Argument.   Another popular argument wants to discourage buying foreign products in order to provide domestic employment. The maintenance of the highest feasible rate of employment in this country is certainly a worthy goal, but tariff barriers are not the best way to accomplish it.

Inefficient use of manpower does not serve the full employment goal. It is easy enough to keep everybody busy. The simplest approach consists in drafting all unemployed persons into government service, military or civilian; but the goal of the economy is want satisfaction, not just keeping busy. Producing goods inefficiently at home is no more justifiable than drafting people for useless activity. When workers are engaged in outdated, noncompetitive tasks, jobs must be created which will use their skills for want-satisfying production rather than waste their efforts on a perpetuation of obsolete occupations.

Closing an inefficient domestic plant is generally a hard blow for the community involved, especially when the town is small and offers little alternative employment. The loss of employment, however, must be measured on a national scale against the gain of new jobs in the firms which import the product and distribute it at a lower price in larger volume. Naturally, Congressmen are more likely to hear from the town in trouble than from the firms which thrive on new imports.

This list of arguments in favor of protection is by no means complete,[2] but it should suffice to indicate the fallacy of trade restrictions for a country in the dominant position occupied by the United States. For almost a century this country has exported more goods than it has bought from abroad. Any attempt on our part to increase the barriers against imports can find swift retaliation from other nations with an import surplus. In view of the traditional competitiveness of American business, this country is served best with the fewest possible barriers to world trade.

[2] A retaliation argument favors tariffs to increase the bargaining power in bringing down foreign restrictions. An argument to "keep the money at home" is popularized by a remark attributed to Abraham Lincoln: "I do not know much about the tariff, but I know this much, when we buy manufactured goods abroad, we get the goods and the foreigner gets the money. When we buy the manufactured goods at home, we get both the goods and the money." The only true part of this argument rests in the first eight words.

TRADE LEGISLATION

The economic position of the United States today demands broad freedom of trade. A bipartisan Congressional majority will, however, continue to favor protectionist policies. The explanation for this apparent contradiction is largely historical.

The History of U.S. Tariffs

The first Congress of the United States passed the first tariff law in its first session. The country has never been without one since that time. The original tariff law was a revenue measure to provide the federal government with the funds needed for all its activities.

From the beginning however, the protectionist philosophy found strong champions. Alexander Hamilton's Report on Manufactures (1791) was a classic expression of the mercantilistic viewpoint, well suited to a new, fast-growing nation bent on commercial rivalry with the established firms of the old world. By 1824, protectionist views prevailed and some of the tariff duties were intended to reduce foreign competition. Frequent changes in duty levels gave way to a solidly protectionist tariff during the Civil War.

By 1873 United States exports began to exceed imports, a pattern which has been maintained ever since. A protectionist majority of Northern and Central States with newly established industries continued to control tariff legislation. Several revisions of the law led in 1930 to the Hawley-Smoot tariff, which contained the highest duty rates in United States history and which remains today, much amended, the basic tariff law of this country. It reflected a hostile attitude to all imports, an attitude which was the natural outgrowth of depression fears.

The Reciprocal Trade Agreements System

The extremely high rates of 1930 proved so detrimental to the foreign trade of the nation that broad reductions became necessary. The President hesitated, however, to ask Congress for a completely new tariff law, which was politically difficult to obtain; he initiated instead a different technique of tariff changes with the Reciprocal Trade Agreements Act of 1934.

The RTA Act of 1934. The new law authorized the President of the United States to alter duty rates in exchange for similar concessions by other countries without submitting such agreements to the United States Senate for approval. His authority to negotiate was limited by several provisions. The most stringent limitation proved to be the short duration of the authorization. As the law contained a definite expiration date, the President had to return to Congress every few years and ask for a renewal of his authority. Congress has never refused, but every renewal increasingly restricted the executive freedom to negotiate.

Peril Point and Escape Clause. After World War II, the law was amended to include peril point provisions and escape clauses, which eventually rendered the President's negotiating authority virtually ineffective. A *peril point* is defined as the lowest duty level which will keep domestic competitors of an imported product from being hurt by excessive imports. A special committee listens to all arguments from importers and competing producers and decides, *before* a trade agreement is negotiated, on the exact peril point. Our negotiators try to avoid granting duty reductions to other nations when they drop below the peril point level.

An *escape clause* refers to the situation which occurs *after* completion of a trade agreement. When duty rates have been reduced and a domestic competitor discovers that his business has been hurt by the reduction, he may file a complaint with the United States Tariff Commission, which will investigate the case. If the Commission feels that the complaint is justified, it will recommend a cancellation of the duty reductions, which will enable the domestic firm to "escape" the detrimental effects of the agreement on its business. Other nations frown on this technique because it wipes out any substantial advantage they may have gained from a trade treaty with the United States.

The Trade Expansion Act of 1962

Following the intiative of President Kennedy, Congress passed the Trade Expansion Act of 1962. This law allowed him for five years to negotiate a broad new treaty with many nations in order to reduce trade barriers uniformly for entire product categories, such as chemicals. The so-called Kennedy Round of negotiations ended in an agreement on the last day before the negotiating authority expired. Many tariff rates will be reduced in five equal annual stages starting January 1968. Total reductions at the end of this period are scheduled to approximate thirty percent of present rates.

THE EUROPEAN ECONOMIC COMMUNITY

A high living standard for the entire population of a country is based on low-cost mass production, which enhances the productivity of every worker.

Mass production requires easy access to raw materials and broad markets for standardized products. The United States has long been the prototype for this kind of modern economy.

Western Europe matches the United States in total population and resources. Europe's historical division into frequently warring, independent nations has prevented it from matching the economic achievements of the United States in the twentieth century. Prior to World War II, the European answer to these problems was the creation of gigantic colonial empires. When these structures collapsed with the political emancipation of Asia and Africa, Western Europe was finally forced to tackle the arduous task of unifying a multitude of small nations.

Beginning with Benelux and followed by the European Coal and Steel Community, the integration process has now reached the stage of a European Economic Community. The final goal of transforming the concept of "Europe" from a geographic expression into a politico-economic entity is not yet in sight, and many pitfalls still wait on the road to its achievement.

Benelux

Benelux is the name given to the economic union of Belgium, the Netherlands, and tiny Luxembourg, created under the impact of World War II by Belgian and Dutch authorities exiled in London during the German occupation of their countries. Immediately after their liberation, the three separate economies began to integrate. Tariff schedules for imports from other countries were unified first; internal trade barriers came down next; and finally, full freedom for business operations could be established within the entire territory of the three nations.

The European Coal and Steel Community

Benelux was far from complete, but after five years it clearly showed the right way toward European prosperity. Under the inspired leadership of Jean Monnet of France, three large countries—France, Italy, and Germany —joined the three Benelux nations in a broadened effort to integrate their economies. They agreed to the creation of new, common institutions aimed at the unification of the coal and steel business, which was at the core of their industrial efforts. The venture was launched in 1950 as the European Coal and Steel Community (ECSC).

The new rules governing coal and steel gave the entire economies of the six nations a big boost from the beginning. The general rise in business eased the needed adjustments and the inevitable hardships which are a

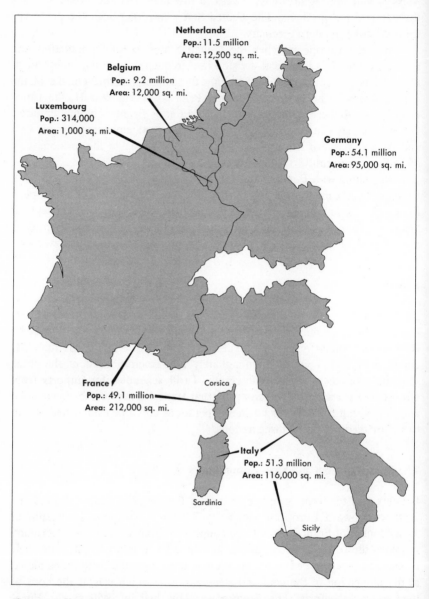

SOURCE: *How Is the Common Market Faring Today?* French Affairs Series, no. 198 (New York, French Embassy, Press and Information Division, November 1966), p. 12.

FIG. 20-2. The Six Nations of the European Economic Community

part of such radical changes. It was a novel and arduous venture, but a sufficiently successful one to break down the walls of traditional hostility and lead the founders of Europe toward more ambitious goals of economic integration.

The European Common Market

The Treaty of Rome in 1957 established the European Common Market for the economies of the six countries which had joined before in the unification of coal and steel. The European Economic Community (EEC), as the group is formally known, comprises a population comparable to that of the United States and contains most raw materials of importance to modern industry.

The unification of the area was scheduled to proceed by stages, reducing internal trade barriers (tariffs and quotas) by 10 percent every year; a common external tariff was also introduced. Workers may take jobs in any area included in the agreement and enjoy the same protection as the citizens of the country. Corporations will all be treated alike under the law, as a maze of legislation hostile to foreigners is gradually being revised with respect to the other members of the Common Market.

The original treaty provided for the elimination of customs barriers and quota restrictions within the market area by 1970. The results of the early tariff reductions were so favorable that the member nations agreed to complete the dismantling of all internal trade barriers by July 1, 1968. At the same time, the duties levied on imports from nonmember countries will be the same in every nation of the Community.

The Common Market is the result of many compromises. Unification of duties on industrial products turned out to be easier than the creation of a common farm policy. In fact, several crises occurred during the negotiations concerning agricultural prices and policies; they were finally settled by the end of 1966.

Some manufacturers, who have operated for decades according to an unchanging pattern in a small country, find the winds of change and competition irksome and hard to take. New firms, however, have sprung up promptly and are profiting from the opportunities of the broader market. The overall effect has been most beneficial, raising the economic standards of the six member nations faster than those of the neighboring countries who are not part of the new market area.

During the early years of transition, trade among Common Market members grew rapidly and accounted for a larger percentage of total foreign trade for each member nation. This favorable result is the main reason the new Community is likely to withstand all attacks and crises.

TABLE 20-5.   Value and Percentage of Intracommunity Trade
(*in millions*)

	1958		1964	
	Dollars	Percent	Dollars	Percent
Intracommunity imports:				
Germany	1,896	25.8	5,098	34.9
France	1,227	21.9	3,762	37.4
Italy	687	21.4	2,365	32.7
Netherlands	1,518	41.9	3,671	52.0
Belgium and Luxembourg	1,462	46.6	3,145	53.3
Totals	6,790	29.6	18,041	40.2
Intracommunity exports:				
Germany	2,406	27.3	5,910	36.5
France	1,136	22.2	3,487	38.8
Italy	608	23.6	2,266	38.0
Netherlands	1,337	41.6	3,233	55.7
Belgium and Luxembourg	1,377	45.1	3,494	62.6
Totals	6,864	30.1	18,390	43.2

SOURCE: *How Is the Common Market Faring Today?* French Affairs Series no. 198 (New York, French Embassy, Press and Information Division, November 1966), p. 4.

The Impact on the Other European Nations.   The remaining countries of Western Europe did not join the new Community at the start for various reasons of both historical or political origin. Mostly, however, they did not expect the new system to be very successful.

After a few years, it had become apparent to all that the rate of growth of the Common Market nations far exceeded the progress of their independent neighbors. This unfavorable comparison placed the governments of the nonaffiliated countries under pressure to join the new Community. Great Britain, as the largest, had preferred her traditional Commonwealth agreements to the uncertain dream of a European economy. Some of her major trading partners had maintained their links to Britain. By 1961, however, it had become obvious that a unified Europe had a better potential than the British tradition. The United Kingdom applied for admission to the Common Market, but the negotiations for entry broke down in 1963. In May 1967 England applied again, hoping that conditions had changed sufficiently to make admission possible. Negotiations are likely to be prolonged.

Greece joined as an associate member in 1962, and Turkey was added on the same basis in 1964. Associate members are smaller nations that are also less developed industrially and are, therefore, given permission to adopt Common Market rules at a slower pace. Other nations would like to join on a similar basis.

When the Common Market is fully integrated and approaches its goal of complete economic unification, it should become less difficult to add new members to the group. The initial effectiveness of the Community's institutions is largely due to the determination of its founders to create more than a free trade area and to establish unified economic policies for all members. Until this goal is reached, a small membership is a real advantage.

Impact on the United States. The United States supported the creation of an integrated European economy from the beginning, since the existence of strong partners and prosperous customers favors our best interests. The immediate impact on this country is one of change in many lines of business. We are witnessing the growth of a powerful competitor. The United States has imported more steel in recent years than it has exported—contrary to its traditional role—and this reversal forced domestic steel producers to renovate their plants and modernize their operations much faster than planned.

This new spirit of worldwide competition combined with reciprocal tariff reductions creates new opportunities for our most progressive manufacturers, who have contributed to posting new records for United States exports in the sixties. The flow of American investments to Europe brings pressure to our balance of payments now, but it insures the profitable participation of United States industry in the European progress.

Impact on Others. Some former French colonies in Africa have negotiated commercial treaties with the Common Market, which gives preferred status to their exports of tropical products. South America has been unhappy over this commercial advantage arranged for its competitors. The nations of Latin America decided, in turn, to create an all-inclusive customs union of their own, the Latin American Common Market. It has not yet shown any real accomplishments and demonstrates the inherent weakness of an international organization with too many members whose interests differ widely.

The Future of the EEC. The task of unifying six nationalistic states that have long been suspicious of each other is long and arduous. The first phase gradually brought a customs union into being; it has been completed ahead of its original schedule. The second phase is one in which common policies are being worked out; many difficult compromises have been reached and accepted. The third phase, which assumes that these independent nations act as one country, is just beginning. The prospects for the future of the Common Market have been assessed by its own governing commission in these terms:

In the first two stages of the transitional period, the principal commitments undertaken in the Treaty have been fulfilled. The results have often gone beyond what the sponsors of the Treaty could have hoped for. While this progress has been going on, differences have arisen between the Member States in political matters not covered by the Treaty of Rome. Serious and disquieting though they may be, these disagreements have not, however, affected the life and development of the Community. . . . The outside world makes no mistake about this and regards the Community henceforth as a determining factor in world economy.

The task of building a united Europe is a long way from finished. Much still remains to be done to execute the program outlined in the Treaty of Rome. . . . But the first eight years have already brought to our endeavour such success and dynamism that there can no longer be any doubt that we are on the right road.[3]

SUMMARY

A nation's place in the world economy can be determined by some fundamental comparisons. A country whose foreign trade is a high percentage of its national income depends more on others than does one where this ratio is low. A lopsided concentration of trade on raw materials or finished goods leads only to increased dependence.

One-commodity-export nations are in a weak international position; so are countries that transact most foreign business with one or two neighbors. If a nation combines several of these weaknesses with a tiny share of the world's trade, it is economically independent in name only.

The United States is in a most advantageous position from every one of these viewpoints. This country is the world's most important trading nation even though foreign trade occupies only a small share of the national product.

Foreign trade is based on expanding specialization requiring a widening network of distribution and exchange which does not stop at the water's edge. World trade flourishes because skilled people and their resources are not evenly distributed around the world.

Restraints to foreign trade have a long history, since established firms often invoke governmental protection against foreigners who become more competitive. This attitude prevailed in the mercantilistic period many centuries ago; the same arguments are still advanced today regardless of their lack of applicability to current trade problems.

Protectionist devices may take the traditional form of tariff duties, or they may restrict trade more severely with rigid quota restrictions. Administrative red tape can exert a powerful deterrent on the importation of some categories of consumer goods which cannot afford to chance the uncertainties of customs evaluation.

The United States tariff is as old as the country. It reached its highest

---

[3] European Economic Community Commission: *Eighth General Report on the Activities of the Community* (June 1965), pp. 21–22.

rates with the Hawley-Smoot tariff of 1930. Since that time, rates have been reduced piecemeal through the machinery of the Reciprocal Trade Agreements System. Congress passed new legislation in 1962 to permit across-the-board reductions of duty rates when matched by similar concessions abroad.

The European Economic Community, begun by six nations, is the result of efforts toward economic integration since World War II. The ambitious and strenuous task of transforming separate, small countries into one modern industrial community encounters limitless obstacles, which the founders of the movement hope to conquer in one generation. The many accomplishments to date have given their efforts so much momentum that the seemingly impossible dream of an integrated, prosperous Europe may yet come true in our time.

The new nations of the world that have just achieved their independence after years of struggle watch in astonishment the spectacle of their old colonial masters voluntarily surrendering large segments of independent decision making to an integrated economic system. They are not ready to do likewise, but this lesson on the best road to prosperity will not be lost. It can usefully be applied to the problems of underdevelopment, which will occupy the following chapter.

Discussion Questions

1. How economically independent can a small Central American republic become?
2. Should the United States abolish its traditional tariff protection?
3. Distinguish tariffs from quota restrictions.
4. Should the United States favor or fight the European Common Market?
5. Why should we encourage international trade?
6. What are the main provisions of the tariff legislation of the United States?

Suggested Reading

INGRAM, JAMES C., *International Economic Problems*. New York, Wiley, 1966.

JENSEN, FINN B., and INGO WALTER, *The Common Market*. Philadelphia, Pa., Lippincott, 1965.

MAYNE, RICHARD, *The Community of Europe*. New York, Norton, 1963.

RICARDO, DAVID, *The Principles of Political Economy and Taxation*. New York, Dutton, 1933; Everyman's Library, No. 590.

SNIDER, DELBERT A., *Introduction to International Economics,* 4th ed. Homewood, Ill., Irwin, 1967.

21

ECONOMIC DEVELOPMENT

All economies need to grow and to develop. In this chapter we shall concentrate on those nations whose development has not kept pace with the advancement of Western Europe and North America. Most of these countries would like to reach in just a few years the state of advanced economic development which the Western world has attained only after centuries of effort. The first question of interest here is the cause of this sudden desire for economic advancement by the less-developed nations; the second question, intimately connected with the first, is why the people of the United States should concern themselves with the problems of the less-developed world.

The obstacles to a better life for most of the world's people are formidable. They will be sketched briefly; following this will be a discussion of some commonly suggested methods to overcome these difficulties. An outline of the assistance efforts in progress by the United States and by international institutions will conclude the chapter.

THE HOPES OF UNDERDEVELOPED NATIONS

Humanity has lived in conditions of extreme poverty for as long as historical records can be found. A few well-managed families usually emerge above their fellowmen and discover that life on earth can be bountiful, but they have always been the first to realize that the existing scarcity of economic goods reserves such an exalted position to a few. The traditions, the law, and even the religions of mankind have attempted to reconcile the masses to their poverty. Since living standards could not be raised appreciably above the starvation level, it behooved the wise men to convince the majority that misery was part and parcel of nature, that this life was inevitably a vale of tears, and that hope must focus on the hereafter.

The West's own struggle for enlightenment took generations before living standards improved in the wake of technological advancement and efficient mass production. Only in the twentieth century did the news of a better life for all spread beyond the confines of Western Europe and North America. Greeted with skepticism in the beginning, the far-flung

412

operations of World War II brought the message of a new life to every corner of the earth.

Jet transportation and electronic communications have upset the ideas and the traditional ways of life of the great majority of the world's people. This revolution of thought and of hope goes far deeper than most of the upheavals in history. It is commonly called today "the revolution of rising expectations." "The 1.3 billion people living in less-developed countries and territories will not be satisfied with promises of progress. One way or another they will try to achieve quickly at least a little of what you and I already enjoy." [1]

Economic development represents hope for a better tomorrow, for a giant vault across decades, if not centuries, by means of large-scale industrialization with the help of foreign capital.

The characteristics of underdevelopment differ widely among nations, but their common feature is a very low national output, created in large measure by peasants in agricultural pursuits. Specific dividing lines are arbitrary; for example, some areas in the United States remain so far behind others that they might well be called backward, but the squalor which accompanies an annual per-capita income of $200 or less clearly marks some countries as underdeveloped.

These nations include most of Asia and Africa, and there are vast stretches of Latin America which still await the arrival of the economic revolution. Other nations have progressed a little further, but still live far below the common experience of the average North American, whose economic standards have become the ambitious dream of the underdeveloped world. Eighty percent of their population produce the food needed to keep themselves and the remaining 20 percent from starving. In the United States, 10 percent of the people grow more than the whole country can use.

The over-ambitious hopes of impatient millions have created a world in turmoil. The traditional leaders in many nations long for the peaceful past, when every man had his place and generations followed each other without much change. The clock, however, cannot be turned back. We have shown the world what can be done; humanity is now convinced that disease, poverty, and starvation are not God given, but man made. The uprooting of traditional thought patterns has caused pressures which leave no alternatives. "Only more economic development offers any hope of escape from the problems which economic development itself has already brought forth." [2]

[1] Paul G. Hoffman, *World Without Want* (New York, Harper & Row, 1962), p. 7.
[2] Eugene R. Black, *The Diplomacy of Economic Development* (Cambridge, Mass., Harvard, 1960), p. 16.

ADVANCED NATIONS AND UNDERDEVELOPMENT

Since the end of World War II, the United States government has spent on the average more than $4 billion annually on international pursuits. To be sure, not all of this outpouring of funds has been directed toward economic development, but this enormous steady flow of funds raises the question more urgently every year: What do we expect to accomplish with this effort?

No clear-cut answer has appeared, and even thoughtful and broad-minded citizens are left in a questioning and impatient mood, making it increasingly difficult for Congress to pass an annual appropriation for the support of our foreign policy.

The real cause for concern with the world's backward nations goes deeper than a simple political answer. "We must give them money because otherwise the Russians will do it" is a negative and unconvincing approach to the problem. Friendship cannot be bought, and political bribery will not develop an economy. A form of international blackmail is not only bad economics, but equally short-sighted politics.

On the opposite end of the spectrum, the idea of development becomes a moral issue. Some people feel like their brothers' keeper and consider it a moral obligation to aid weaker countries. The flow of private missionaries has long been sponsored and supported by those who regard it as their duty. These necessarily limited efforts may command our sympathy, but they cannot qualify as a basis for governmental policy. The task of abolishing poverty the world over dwarfs even the great resources of the West. To raise false hopes which are soon to be disappointed would be a grave disservice to everyone involved.

The two most obvious reasons—outbidding the Russians dollar for dollar, or helping these peoples as a moral obligation—need to be challenged. There *is* a true element of competition which compels the advanced nations to be concerned with the fate of the poor, but it goes far beyond the question of the next cash loan. The poor nations, and many of them are also new nations, are aroused; they demand change and action; they expect to see prompt results, and they feel frustrated when their economy does not grow like magic. They will listen to many voices, and the insidious advice from the Communists to tear down the past and the present sounds very tempting to leaders who discover that the road to the summit is rocky and slow.

In the struggle between East and West, the Communists have long proclaimed the need for leveling the socioeconomic order before a new system can be started. The West supports more economic equality and hopes to achieve it by raising incomes in the lowest sector. Since the negative start of the left-wing program is easily executed, the West has to demonstrate that its hopeful philosophy can produce practical results. The struggle for men's minds can be won by the positive solutions of the West if it can nurture with effective action the tender plant of hope for economic progress without the coercion and ruthlessness of its opponents.

The world's people want better standards of consumption now. If all current output is consumed, nothing is left for the creation of new capital goods to serve a better tomorrow. Poor people do not feel they can afford to save. Therefore, they fall easy prey to the voice of the Soviets assuring them that only the strong force of dictatorship can make people divert their efforts toward more investment in the future and sacrifice some consumption of the present generation. The West must show the underdeveloped world that it offers a workable alternative to this cynical formula of pressure before the suppressed masses of the earth engulf us all in a wave of desperate destruction.

ROADBLOCKS TO DEVELOPMENT

Several thousand years were needed to transform the human animal into modern man, but new nations today need not look forward to an equally slow development process. They know that a systematic growth effort will succeed, as they have already seen happen in many places; they merely must bring it about by adapting their own situation to the model of the West. Copying is easier and can save much time. The remaining obstacles to development, however, are still formidable.

Fast-growing populations eat up growing food supplies like locusts, leaving no surplus for next year. A high rate of illiteracy often makes it difficult to use the available labor supply for all but the most primitive tasks. Management skills are very scarce, and they are badly needed in the organization of a modern economy. Nationalism, inevitable and sometimes necessary for new countries, often prevents the most effective use of foreign assistance. The lack of capital is frequently invoked to explain slow progress. All these obstacles will now be discussed in more detail.

The Population Explosion

The conspicuous effectiveness of modern medicine in reducing infant mortality is a wonderful accomplishment, but it has greatly aggravated the task of the economist. If he had reached the scene before the physician did, development efforts might have been more fruitful. In the overpopulated lands of Asia, starvation has traditionally limited the number of those who survive infancy. A rise of economic output keeps more people from starving, but it spreads the added goods among so many more mouths to feed that the per-capita income shows no progress.

Development efforts are frustrated when even a sharp rise in output is nullified by an equally fast rise in the number of people. Efforts to popularize birth control have failed to reestablish a better balance between population and food supply. An historical observation may permit hope for the future, however, as the birth rate seems to adjust eventually to economic conditions. A high birth rate was necessary when few newly born infants survived, and the traditional pattern of the overcrowded nations has not yet been able to adjust to the new reality of many living children.

An improved food supply will render adults more vigorous and better able to shoulder the arduous tasks of a modern economy. As the life expectancy increases, men of working age will outnumber dependent children more and more.

Education

A high rate of illiteracy is often blamed for some of the difficulties in starting economic growth. Idle men are abundant, but in their present state of illiteracy they are not suitable manpower for industry. An industrialized, urban existence requires more education than does primitive life in rural surroundings.

An insufficient number of teachers now and inadequate training facilities for the teachers of tomorrow create a gap in learning that must be bridged. The cost of education may have appeared to be unjustifiably high in the past when there was no demand for literate workers and where education, as most other good things in life, was a luxury for the few. The special effort of the United States in the training of better teachers is a constructive contribution toward accelerating the educational improvement of poor nations.

Management

Managerial ability is the by-product of an industrialized, competitive society. In an underdeveloped nation, the task of management is one of the responsibilities of the well born. Its execution is often amateurish and inefficient, but the large, inherited wealth of the owners allows for waste and squandering of resources. No competitors threaten the holders of large estates. Even inept management produces enough to maintain the traditional family position, though the peasant workers may suffer when there is little left for them.

Foreign observers often wonder why so many upper-class young men study the humanities and the law when their natural position of leadership designates them for top management positions. Familiarity with the law is helpful for aspiring political leaders, and wealthy families seldom avoid political involvement. The revenue from their estates finances this type of life, even with the weakest management.

The economic repercussions of this system are serious. Inefficiency wastes the nation's meager resources. A managerial middle class is missing, since a trained manager cannot find employment unless he owns the enterprise. Industrialization is held back because the wealthy estate owners realize that the financial opportunities of modern manufacturing need constant managerial attention and involve risks which they are ill prepared to take. Government leaders are ready to move into this vacuum with public investments but managerial skills are too scarce to adequately staff the new bureaucracy. This vicious circle creates real difficulties for rapid economic development.

Nationalism

A strong national spirit, a love for one's own country, is a fine sentiment. This is the sort of nationalism that finds general approval. Many underdeveloped nations, however, adhere to a rather extreme form of nationalism. Particularly, the countries that have won their independence only in the last two decades, after long periods of colonial rule, seem to feel that the essence of patriotism is a hatred for everything foreign.

Economic progress welcomes patriotism as a motivating force in underdeveloped nations which have suffered frequently from the absence of a national consciousness on the part of the wealthy. All too often, the very rich invested their profits abroad and treated their own country more like a piece of property than a homeland. The desire of a ruling class to see the economy of its people grow and prosper is the first precondition of development.

Nationalism as a constructive force is easily perverted into an instrument of monopoly control and of political power. Foreigners provide wonderful scapegoats for every kind of domestic trouble and mismanagement; they furnish a needed escape valve for the repressed anger born of misery and disappointment.

This hostile attitude may sometimes backfire, as a simple example will illustrate. Assume that the local power company is foreign owned. The government exerts its right to keep rates extremely low, so low in fact that the power company makes no profit. Naturally, the firm refuses to expand its facilities while losing money; it cuts costs by firing workers whose task has been to give better service to the customer. At this point, the nationalistic political leaders may blame the "foreign exploiters" for the power shortage and expropriate their property! This all-too-common procedure will not help the economy. Service before was bad; now, inefficient politically controlled management is added to the existing difficulties and the service becomes even worse. New industrial projects, patiently negotiated over the years, are abandoned by foreign investors. The precedent of expropriation discourages their efforts; besides, the new plant requires a dependable supply of electricity, which is now beyond their reach.

This sort of behavior on the part of leaders is often a calculated effort to slow the winds of change. Every government will give lip service to economic progress in our time; it could not do less. The power groups of the nation, however, have no intention of permitting a new society of businessmen, manufacturers, and professional specialists to take over. The living standard of the population is therefore sacrificed to the power struggle of the rulers—all in the name of national independence.

Lack of Capital

Every underdeveloped country complains about a lack of money capital for the many new investments needed. Poverty does not permit saving; without saving, there can be no new investment; without investment, poverty will become even worse. Consequently, the need for capital is proclaimed to be the most critical bottleneck in the development effort.

Domestic Capital.   This justification for capital requirements sounds plausible enough, but it is frequently an excuse and not the main obstacle in the path of development. The poor cannot save, to be sure, but the poorest countries usually have a wealthy upper class. What do the rich do with their money? Much of it is wasted through bad management, as mentioned earlier, but what remains would still be sufficient for some economic growth, if it became available for investment in new industry. Unfortunately, a large share of this wealth is not used for such a purpose.

Judging from the experience of an industrialized nation, we can too easily assume that saving takes advantage of all opportunities to earn more, and that an efficient network of finance channels the available savings into investment. Such a chain of events is not the typical pattern of an underdeveloped country. The financial system of a growing country does not usually command much confidence in the stability of its currency. Therefore, people do not leave their funds in any form where they receive a fixed amount of their currency later on. Savings accounts, bonds, mortgages, and similar forms of savings are not wise methods of keeping money. Small savers especially have no opportunity to leave their funds in a way which would be useful to the country. The large savers, or rich men, could turn investors themselves and create their own industries. For reasons discussed earlier, they seldom chose to do so.

The alternative to saving is hoarding. While saving is a constructive way of refraining from consuming too much, hoarding is a simple attempt to protect oneself against total loss. The hoarding instinct finds many ingenious ways of satisfaction, but hoarding typically takes three forms: (1) Small savers buy something durable, preferably jewelry, gold, or silver, which is believed to keep its value and can also be easily hidden; (2) More prosperous savers buy real estate, which is probably very much overpriced, but still preferable to a bank account; (3) The wealthiest and most sophisticated savers place most of their funds abroad.

To overcome the shortage of domestic savings, some governments establish a gradual inflation. This is intended to force the people to save, in as much as their wages will buy fewer consumer goods, and thus leave more resources available for capital goods. This reasoning is erroneous, because it is the very fear of inflation which motivates the resource owners to hoard and not to save.

Hoarding is caused by distrust of the government and by a steady dose of inflation which justifies this lack of faith. The shrinking purchasing power of domestic money convinces the hoarder of his wisdom when he withdraws all his funds and converts them into foreign currencies. What little savings inflation may forcibly collect from the poor by lowering their purchasing power is more than compensated for by encouraging the rich to hoard. Inflation is a danger, and not an aid, to a poor country.

In spite of the harm done by inflation, the depreciation of the world's currencies continues unchecked. During the decade 1956–1966 only two nations out of 45 surveyed maintained 90 percent of their currencies original value, whereas ten countries, all less developed, lost over half their monetary value.[3]

Foreign Capital. Capital is very mobile and can be attracted from abroad with a friendly attitude. Many capital-starved nations complain that foreign funds are unavailable for their development efforts. Invariably, the complaining governments have created an inhospitable atmosphere for foreigners and their investments. To be sure, the bankers and industrialists are invited to bring their money; beyond this elementary point, however, the laws are all against them. They may not invest in the more profitable industries, nor in the more important ones; they must hire local managers regardless of their availability, and use domestic labor whether or not it is suitable.

Should they earn a profit in spite of all this harrassment, they pay taxes; often they are not permitted to send dividends to their own country. Instead, they are encouraged to put their profits in more local investments

[3] From the annual survey of comparative rates of shrinkage in the value of money, *First National City Bank of New York Monthly Economic Letter,* July 1967.

as directed by the government. In view of all these restrictions, it is a real miracle that some private investors still persist in taking a chance on future improvements in such unfriendly surroundings.

The often-repeated accusation that private foreign investors cannot or will not provide sufficient investment capital for underdeveloped nations clearly misses the point. The few spots on earth with a healthy climate for investment have never been short of funds for promising ventures.

Some expensive public projects may not be suitable for private investors. Harbor installations, road building, irrigation, or flood control may be needed before private enterprise can exercise its initiative. The capital for such social overhead projects can be borrowed from several international institutions or from foreign governments. Lack of funds may be an excuse, but it is seldom the real stumbling block to economic development.

Out of the three M's—**m**en, **m**aterial, and **m**oney—which hinder the growth of the poor nations, men are by far the most important hurdle. Raw materials may be found at home or bought abroad; money is mobile and can be attracted; but men must change ancient habits, and the human mind with its old ways of thinking must learn to adjust to the new ways of the machine age. National attitudes must be changed and ancient traditions abandoned. The structure of authority must be revised; indeed, the whole ruling class needs to reform or be removed from power if reform is not forthcoming. The process of changing men's minds is long and difficult, a course not completed in a hurry.

DEVELOPMENT METHODS

The successful development of advanced nations becomes the model for the efforts of new countries. The techniques of the nineteenth century, however, do not fit the conditions of today, and the methods used by the more recent arrivals are necessarily quite different.

Industrialization

All advanced countries are heavily industrialized. The Russians followed the traditional pattern of oppression, long familiar to their people, in order to build a modern industrial empire. They sacrificed an entire generation's dreams of a better life to the creation of capital goods, so that a future generation may produce higher living standards.

Canada's approach was exactly the opposite. Her people proved hospitable to foreign investors and created a new industrial empire in cooperation with British and American capitalists—without much central guidance and in an atmosphere of great freedom. The high educational standards of the country greatly simplified the task for the developers.

Japan reached her goal with some foreign help, but largely through her own efforts, making skillful use of the fruits of foreign experimentation and of the rehabilitation efforts of the United States in the last two decades.

Many underdeveloped nations want to follow these examples. "Industrialize and you will be rich" describes the simple faith of impatient countries. They may want to import a big steel plant from abroad without realizing the intermediate steps that must be taken before a steel plant can help their economy.

More modest goals of industrialization should accompany most development attempts. As small plants grow, managers are learning for the bigger tasks ahead. These plants absorb surplus, unskilled labor in the production of badly needed consumer goods, such as clothing.

Improvement in agriculture, with the help of simple tools and better techniques, is often an essential step that precedes industry. Urban workers must be fed; the land must be made to yield added output. In addition, the traditional methods of farming are in urgent need of reform, although peasants are often the least willing to introduce change.

Planning

All new countries draft formal development plans. Some follow the Soviet example, outlining projects in great detail for a five-year period, only to discover later that some projects are not feasible and the plan cannot be executed. Others remain more flexible so that they need not acknowledge failure.

Organization of the development effort is obviously necessary. A rigid plan which reserves all major activities for government enterprise usually remains a wishful dream. Even nations such as India, who proclaim their faith in socialistic organization, have a smaller share of their output produced by the public sector than is the case in the United States. A planning board with innumerable officials must employ so much of that very scarce managerial talent that little remains for the construction and operation of new plants.

Flexible plans, limited to establishing priority goals for various types of industries, are likely to prove more fruitful. When such plans can be adapted to channel private initiative toward objectives supported by public encouragement, the results will be better.

One of the major drawbacks encountered by public planning is political in origin. A public administrator cannot concentrate the expenditure of funds on one project or on one small area of the country; unless he is a strongly entrenched dictator, he must try to keep most voters reasonably happy. Most less-developed nations have one or a few modern urban centers, often seaports. The new industrial civilization radiates slowly from these centers, and the faraway interior may not see the advent of modern times for a generation. The planners are fully aware that new factories should be built close to the large centers of population with easy access to existing roads, power plants, and so forth. But for political reasons, every area must have its own project, which places a great burden on the nation's meager resources and slows down the progress of the entire economy.

DEVELOPMENT ASSISTANCE

Institutions in increasing numbers have been created for the specific purpose of helping underdeveloped nations. The list is far too long for complete coverage here, so only the most important organizations will be discussed. This country has sponsored its own organizations to function abroad. The United States also has a leading role in international administrative bodies and in special regional groupings.

Direct Assistance by the U.S. Government

Help from the United States to other nations utilizes many different channels. The Department of Agriculture sends abroad its own salesmen, who dispose of surplus commodities under arrangements which are most favorable to the buyer. Defense officials prepare technical agreements for the mutual protection of the participating nations. The main assistance effort is channeled through the Export-Import Bank of Washington and through the Agency for International Development.

The Export-Import Bank of Washington, D.C. (Eximbank). The Eximbank was created by Congress during depression days (1934) with the specific assignment of helping United States exporters. During World War II, the Bank converted to the demands of economic warfare. Since that time, many new assignments have been placed in the hands of the able management of this financial institution.

The Eximbank today concentrates on two different tasks of major importance:

1. It acts as an insurance company somewhat similar to the FNMA in the field of domestic housing. In this capacity, it guarantees exporters or their bankers against undue risks on overseas sales. The insured pays a modest premium for this protection which, because it includes political risks, would not be available through private channels.

2. The Bank engages in long-term loans abroad in support of the foreign policy of the United States. These loans help the development of the recipient countries, but they also support the exports of this country in that all loans granted by the Bank must be spent on American products.

In its foreign lending capacity, the Eximbank avoids competition with private bankers; it may grant a loan which is too risky for private financing and even support the sale of weapons by the Defense Department to foreign nations whose identity remains unknown to the Bank. In view of the political orientation of its financial decisions, defaults of payments have been much smaller than might be expected.

Aggregate authorizations of the Bank during its life have exceeded $16 billion. It is a government corporation with a capital of $1 billion and permission to borrow from the U.S. Treasury up to $6 billion. It may not have more than $13.5 billion outstanding in loans, guarantees, and insurance at any one time. During its lifetime, it has been able to pay to the Treasury over $1 billion in dividends and interest on borrowed funds, and it has built a reserve of over $1 billion to protect itself against future losses. As the figures indicate, the Eximbank, though financed by appropriated funds, has served the taxpayer well.

The Agency for International Development (AID). Under the label of AID the United States government distributes low-interest loans and grants to some sixty countries all over the world. After suffering innumerable changes since its creation, this agency is now part of the State Department. Its original purpose was the administration of the European Recovery Program in 1949. During seventeen years of operation under different names, AID has disbursed about $40 billion to underdeveloped nations. About three-fourths of this assistance took the form of grants, while the other 25 percent are low-interest loans with liberal repayment provisions.

The European Recovery Program in the late forties proved tremendously successful in restoring the economies of our European Allies to prewar strength. The program was administered by a temporary administrative organization intended only for a four-year period. But the early success of the agency prompted Congress to keep it in existence with frequently changing directives and chief administrators who had an average tenure of about eighteen months. AID still operates under a heavy turnover of personnel, and many of its experts are on temporary assignment.

The bulk of economic assistance has been concentrated in recent years on a smaller number of countries where the need is greatest or the chances of accomplishment look best. Eighty-seven percent of direct assistance was intended for sixteen nations in 1968. These loans and grants cover a broad spectrum, from wheat to fertilizer, and from trucks to the services of university specialists. The emphasis now focuses on improvements in agriculture, on health programs, and on better education.

The improvement of education is assigned to a special division of AID. Its origin goes back to President Truman's inaugural address (1949). He proclaimed in his "point four" the intention of the United States to assist the peoples of economically underdeveloped areas to help themselves. Since its modest beginning, the Point Four program has sent thousands of teachers and technicians to most of the developing nations in order to train native instructors and to introduce modern methods, particularly in agriculture. Participating in technical assistance abroad are 126 American colleges and universities.

The cost of this program is modest since there are only a limited number of well-qualified instructors willing to undertake these pioneering assignments. Its effectiveness in convincing leaders in new nations of the advantages of the free enterprise system can be measured only when the next generation takes over the political control of these countries.

The Peace Corps.   The Peace Corps is a relative newcomer in the field of foreign aid. Created by the Kennedy Administration, it aims to tap the resources of idealism and the venturesome spirit so typical of young men and women in their early twenties. Its tasks are mostly educational, similar to AID training projects; Peace Corps workers are frequently required to live in intimate contact with the native population of a country, at the very edge of civilized existence.

International Development Institutions

A host of international agencies concerned with underdeveloped nations has come into existence during the past twenty years. United Nations commissions or affiliates sponsor improvements and loans for several aspects of development. The Food and Agriculture Organization (FAO) promotes better farming methods and price stability for the crops on which the nonindustrial nations rely.

The chief financial institutions of a truly international character are those which were chartered at the Bretton Woods Conference. The International Monetary Fund was created at that meeting and has been discussed before (Chapter 19). The International Bank for Reconstruction and Development (IBRD) more commonly known as the World Bank, also received its charter at that time.

The IMF and IBRD cooperate with each other; the members of the World Bank also belong to the Fund. The tasks of the two institutions, however, differ sharply. The Fund grants *short-term* loans to boost, temporarily, the exchange reserves of members who have deficits in their balance of payments; the Bank makes *long-term* loans for economic development projects.

The World Bank.   The World Bank is not a giveaway institution. Every borrower is carefully investigated to insure the feasibility and usefulness of the project; equally important, the evaluation must indicate that the borrower will be able to repay the loan. This detailed study covers not only the engineering and financial aspects of a project, but it includes as well a scrutiny of the management personnel. The Bank also provides for regular inspection, and for reports during the actual construction and throughout the life of its loan. The Bank never lends the total cost of the project, but requires local financial participation in order to insure the continuing interest of the borrower in efficient operations.

The World Bank makes loans in cases where private capital is not available on reasonable terms. Its lending is restricted to production projects related to reconstruction or development in member countries, but since 1948 all lending has been for purposes of development. Since its beginnings, the far-flung operations of the Bank have helped to finance over 900 projects in eighty-two countries for which it has lent over $10 billion. Public utilities and transportation projects claim two-thirds of the loan funds. Railroads, highways, and harbor installations are strongly supported by the Bank, as shown in the table below. Education projects have only recently been accepted as suitable because of the difficulty of earning foreign exchange to repay the debt that results from this type of project.

TABLE 21-1. **Purposes of World Bank Loans, 1967**
(*millions of U.S. dollars*)

Electric Power	3,589
Transportation	3,446
Industry	1,597
Agriculture and forestry	802
Reconstruction	497
General development	205
Communications	128
Others	178
Total	10,442

SOURCE: Annual Report of the World Bank.

The funds needed for this task are gathered from five different sources:

1. The capital subscribed by its members exceeds $22 billion; about $2.2 billion of this amount is paid in and can be used for lending purposes. The remainder is in the form of a guarantee fund to assure creditors that the Bank will meet its obligations. To date the Bank has encountered no defaults on the loans, and is not likely to have to call for additional payments of capital.

2. The Bank sells its own bonds and notes in the major capital markets of the world to raise a part of the funds needed by its clients. In the beginning, these bonds were usually sold in the United States. As the Bank's good name became better known and Europe recovered from the war, more bonds were sold in Switzerland, Germany, and other countries. The total amount owed by the Bank exceeds the equivalent of $3 billion.

3. The fine reputation of the Bank for careful screening of its projects made it possible to interest other investors in direct participation in new loans and in the purchase of existing loans. It has become customary practice for the World Bank to sell parts of its loans to private banks, insurance companies, and other institutions. Initially, IBRD guaranteed the repayment of the loan to the purchasers, a practice which is no longer used. The total amount of loans sold to other investors added over $2 billion in development funds.

4. Repayment of old loans furnishes a steady flow of funds for new investments. To June 30, 1967, repayments have aggregated $1.3 billion.

5. Earnings have accumulated faster than the founders of the Bank expected, and have contributed a sizable amount to the funds available for lending purposes. In the fiscal year 1967, the Bank reported a net income of $170 million. A summary of the funds raised is shown in Table 21-2.

TABLE 21-2.   Sources of Funds of the World Bank, 1967
(*millions of U.S. dollars*)

Borrowed funds (still outstanding)	3,075
Paid-in capital	2,285
Loans sold to other investors	2,035
Repayments of loans to the Bank	1,263
Reserves (income earned from operations)	1,183
Total	9,841

SOURCE: Annual Report of the World Bank.

The total investments of this agency may not seem too large in view of the world's unlimited needs. The pace-setting characteristics of many Bank loans, however, have created a standard of achievement which goes far beyond the mere raising of funds.

The International Finance Corporation.   Occasionally, the World Bank encounters financing proposals suitable for private enterprise, for example, a sawmill. The mill owners are not sufficiently well known to receive credit abroad for expansion or modernization. Their need for funds is satisfied by the International Finance Corporation (IFC), which was founded in 1956 by the World Bank for this particular type of lending. IFC shares its administration with the Bank and follows similar investment principles. Although its total operations are modest, it occasionally fills an important need. In its first eight years IFC had committed only $137 million, but it is now able to draw on much larger sums if needed.

The International Development Association (IDA).   IDA is the latest (1960) creation of the World Bank. Many nations found themselves in situations where new loans proved commercially impossible, even when a project was considered highly desirable by both borrower and lender. The country in question was simply "loaned up"; it could not afford any further foreign debts until its international earnings improved significantly. Under these circumstances a new loan would necessarily be more in the line of a gift, and the World Bank was not a charity institution. The Bank agreed, however, to administer any voluntary contributions by its members and use such funds for interest-free loans, allowing fifty years for repayment. These special funds are administered separately by IDA, an affiliate created for this purpose. The evaluation of high-priority projects by the Bank and IDA is combined to permit financing together when the cost is too high for either one alone.

The cooperation of the two institutions has been so successful that by 1966 members had made available to IDA $1.6 billion, with the hope of continued future contributions. IDA has already granted eighty-nine credits to thirty-two countries for almost $1.4 billion. Most of the agency's funds are drawn from the wealthier member nations, and the size and effectiveness of its operation depends entirely on their willingness to continue to provide.

The Alliance for Progress

The Alliance for Progress was established in 1961, when the United States and nineteen Latin American Republics agreed on a vast cooperative effort to foster economic growth at an accelerated speed. The ambitious objectives of the Alliance include faster industrialization, land reform, better systems of taxation, and improvement of public health, housing, and education.

The United States government pledged $10 billion to the program over a ten-year period. These funds will be channeled largely through the Inter-American Development Bank (IDB) founded in 1959, also under the sponsorship of the United States. IDB uses the contribution of the United States as a special fund from which low-interest loans can be granted. It supports a wide variety of projects, such as completion of a highway from Chile across the Andes, low-cost housing construction, or irrigation in Colombia.

The results of this ambitious effort still belong to the future. The cooperation of participating nations foreseen by the charter of the Alliance has not yet wholly taken place. Currency disorders, expropriation, and nationalistic restrictions by local governments do not provide the fertile ground which is needed if the seeds of foreign aid are to be brought to full flower. The ultimate success of this venture will largely depend on what Latin America does for itself.

SUMMARY

Economic development of the majority of the world's people has become an urgent problem; the poor no longer accept their dismal fate without protest, and their rising expectations cannot be stopped.

The system of free enterprise must show that it provides a workable alternative for poor nations. They have been told by others that only coercion will produce the savings needed for new investments, and that the freedom of the rich is a luxury they cannot afford.

Development efforts are impaired by a birth rate adjusted to high infant mortality rather than to the new expectation of survival. The change in social customs is slower than the progress of modern medicine.

Lack of the education needed for industrial work makes nonutilized farm labor hard to employ. The absence of managerial training causes scarce resources to be largely wasted.

Nationalism as a constructive force initiates efforts to invest in the future of the homeland. It will, however, slow down progress when it turns to the extreme of hostility to foreigners and their investments in the development of the country.

The lack of capital is often considered the biggest obstacle to development. This is true under existing conditions. In order to overcome this situation, all that is needed is stable financial management at home and a friendly climate for foreign investors.

Industrialization is the first step of a developing nation. Its beginnings are slow and modest; capital-intensive, heavy industry is the final result only of long efforts. One glamorous prestige project contributes little to the welfare of the people.

Central planning has become a standard approach to development efforts. Plans which are too ambitious, too rigid, or too dependent on execution by public agencies seldom lead to effective action. A plan which flexibly organizes individual initiative and orients private efforts toward priority objectives may prove more beneficial to the nation.

Many United States organizations support developing countries. The Export-Import Bank grants loans and guarantees to assist American efforts in foreign countries. The Agency for International Development grants aid to friendly nations and supports their desire for education and training. The Peace Corps enlists the idealism of American youth and directs it toward the same objectives.

The World Bank with its affiliates, the IFC and IDA, has granted over $10 billion in development loans to member nations. Its careful scrutiny of every project and its nonpolitical approach to secure the efficient use of scarce resources serve as a model for effective development planning. The operations of the Bank are setting a standard of excellence for the execution of new projects in many countries. Its splendid example points the way to true economic progress.

Discussion Questions

1. Should the United States continue to grant foreign aid?
2. What is the task of the Point Four program?
3. Should we help India build a steel mill?
4. What obstacles to development are most difficult to overcome? Why?
5. "The road to riches goes through a schoolhouse." Comment.
6. Distinguish the functions of AID, IDA, IMF, IFC, Eximbank, IDB, and IBRD.
7. Why can nationalism become a force for good or evil when a country wants to speed up its development?
8. People are the chief reason for lack of development. Why?
9. How does the World Bank finance its projects?

Suggested Reading

HAGEN, EVERETT E., *On the Theory of Social Change.* Homewood, Ill., Irwin, Dorsey Press, 1962.

HOFFMAN, PAUL G., *World Without Want.* New York, Harper & Row, 1962.

KRAUSE, WALTER, *Economic Development.* Englewood Cliffs, N.J., Prentice-Hall, 1961.

WARD, BARBARA, *The Rich Nations and the Poor Nations.* New York, W. W. Norton & Company, 1962.

22

RUSSIA AND THE WEST

A glance at the underdeveloped regions of the globe has made us aware of different ways to solve, or not to solve, the problems of economic scarcity. Heilbroner has aptly classified the numerous techniques used to satisfy economic wants into three groups: "Looking not only over the diversity of contemporary societies, but back over the sweep of all history, the economist sees that man has succeeded in solving the production and distribution problems in but three ways. . . These great systemic types can be called economies run by Tradition, economies run by Command, and economies run by the Market. . . ."[1]

In many nations, the methods of economizing still follow the time-honored path of ancient tradition with unchanging rules of production and consumption. Dismal poverty is the consequence of such an approach to economic life, and modern development efforts try to liberate the long-suffering majority of mankind from its fate.

The market system is represented by the United States and has been described in some detail in this book. Its main virtues and shortcomings will be accented by a brief comparison with the Russian system, the outstanding example of an economy run by Command.

THE RUSSIAN ECONOMY

Russian production figures in the twenties were as low as they were a hundred years earlier during the regime of the Czars. Today, the U.S.S.R. is firmly established as a large industrial power second only to the United States. In fact, the Soviet Union is challenging our leadership with the announced purpose of winning the production race by 1970.

In the last forty years, the Soviets transformed the vastness of Eastern Europe and much of Asia into the industrialized Russian empire of today. How did they do it? How does their technique of economic decision making differ from our own?

[1] Robert L. Heilbroner, *The Making of Economic Society* (Englewood Cliffs, N.J., Prentice-Hall, Inc., 1962), p. 9.

Central Planning

The decision of what to produce is the necessary first step in any production process. The Russians delegate this decision to the highest level of political authority; a central planning office fixes broad goals of essential production. The United States had a first-hand acquaintance with similar methods when the War Production Board of World War II made the major output decisions for the country.

The main advantage of a centrally planned system of output is the absence of interference by the consumer, whom we ordinarily consider as the most important figure in the economy. Central planning in a dictatorship can safely disregard the consumer unless he starts a revolution. This lack of consumer influence was a most important factor in the rapid transformation of Russia into an industrialized nation. It made possible the use of a much larger share of national resources for the production of capital goods than is generally allocated in free market economies. After one generation of deliberate planning, an industrial revolution has reached its basic objective at the expense of the Russian consumer, whose wishes were sacrificed.

The planning of how to produce is much more difficult. Waste must be avoided, but how does anyone know what is the most efficient technique to produce any specific good? A free economy has a clear advantage in this respect through its pricing system, which registers the relative efficiency of several alternatives at the same time. The Russians also use a form of prices in the determination of production costs, but they do not permit the impact of prices to extend to the level of distribution. One of the consequences of such a partial use of pricing is the tendency of factories to be located close to their raw material, regardless of the cost of shipping the finished product. Such a production pattern leads to an excessive load for the transportation system, which has, in fact, remained a bottleneck to Russian industry for many years.

A production technique which is aimed uniquely at the goal of fulfilling an output quota can lead to some very peculiar results in terms of consumer satisfaction. The story has been told of a Russian factory which produced light fixtures. The monthly quota of fixtures was very large and could be completed only by reducing the amount of material used in each fixture. As a result, the flimsy product promptly broke down in routine service. In response to the complaints of the users, the quota from the plant was changed. The management would now be judged not by the numbers of items, but by the tons of material used and shipped to stores. The factory adjusted to the new demands by producing huge, heavy chandeliers which in some cases brought the ceiling down with their weight.

Other inefficiencies are introduced in the Plan due to the difficulties of comparing the relative cost of repairing old equipment with the advantage of replacing it with something more modern. A competitive price warns the management of a firm that they must replace obsolete equipment, though they may be reluctant to do so. In a central plan, however, decisions to build new factories are made on a higher level of bureaucracy than are decisions to repair. As a result, Soviet production has a tendency to maintain obsolete plants far beyond the time when they should have been replaced.

Incentives

Every economic system develops a set of incentives, which are usually a combination of positive rewards and negative penalties. The incentives for corporate managers in the United States are not too unlike those of their Soviet counterparts, who are state officials. In both countries the managerial group is well compensated in comparison with their fellow citizens.

The Russian plant director does not own his home, because private property has been abolished. But his job entitles him to the use of a house which is probably comparable to that of an American in a similar managerial position. Of course, the house lacks all the appliances that we consider standard equipment, for which the Soviets have substituted a maid.

The manager's salary is high, but his main incentives are a chance to be promoted for good performance and a bonus for fulfilling the Plan. The emphasis on complying with a goal dictated by a superior is similar to the technique of many American corporations. Here, a sales quota, which must be filled in order to qualify for a reward, looks very much like the quota assigned by a central Plan; the main difference is the Russian insistence on more production rather than on more sales.

The similarity of the two incentive systems ends with a comparison of positive managerial awards. The negative incentives are very different. Penalties for an unimaginative managerial performance in an American corporation are not very harsh. The firm must experience a serious crisis before a member of long standing in the corporate hierarchy is summarily dismissed. This threat, and much more severe consequences, is vivid and ever present for a Soviet official. If the Plan runs into difficulties, scapegoats must be found, and the selection of victims can be arbitrary. We witness, therefore, the frantic attempt of the Russian manager to always meet the assigned minimum, even if product quality is sacrificed in the process to the extent that the output becomes unserviceable.

Incentives for workers are largely monetary and differ more sharply within the same plant than they would in the United States. Pay scales are strongly based on actual performance, rather than on time spent on the job. The worker must produce so many units per hour, and the hourly wage changes when he completes more or less than the assigned quota.

The strongest incentive for hard work, however, is a negative one, of a kind that is thoroughly repulsive to an American. Each Soviet worker has a labor book containing a complete history of his personal qualifications and performance. The employer takes custody of this book, and without it no worker can find new employment. Therefore, the worker cannot resign his job any more than a soldier can quit the army. If his performance is poor or if he fails to be on time for work, he may be severely penalized or even jailed.

The absence of profit as a reward for risk-taking marks an important difference in incentive systems. Progress is the result of innumerable small innovations. American businessmen experiment with small changes every day. They may succeed or they may fail, but the chance for profit is sufficient for them to take the risk.

This type of incentive is essentially missing in the Soviet system, and the economy suffers the consequences. The absence of profits does not matter in the introduction of major innovations. A gamble on a new type of moon rocket becomes a policy decision of top officials; but the endless small improvements which we leave to the initiative of the individual are largely absent in the Soviet technique. In fact, the Russians have become increasingly impressed with the advantages of a profit mechanism and may actually make some effort to incorporate it into their economy.

Growth and the Consumer

The success of Russia's economic growth has been achieved at the expense of the consumer—the forgotten man in their story of rising output. The officials decide that rockets receive priority, because they enhance the power of the rulers and their international prestige. A country used to generations of dictatorship and oppression by central governments abides by such decisions more readily than would a free nation. The view of the role of government makes Russia's rulers fitting successors to the czars of old. The decisions are still made by a small group in power; only the emphasis has shifted from agriculture to industry.

Compared to the miserable living standard of the past, the Russian consumer in the sixties has never been so well off. Residential construction remained neglected for decades, and the erection of new, large apartment houses now is felt to be a real improvement, in spite of leaking roofs and bad plumbing. When a family has lived in one room for twenty years, a move to a new two-room apartment brings pure joy. The renters will gripe about the poor quality of the construction, but they would not want to return to the past—which is their only meaningful comparison.

The Soviet economy has demonstrated that economic growth can be achieved by an underdeveloped country whose ruthless leadership is able to command the compliance of most of its population. As Russia reduces the output gap which still separates it from the United States, it may be able to satisfy the consumer more than in the past. Such a shift of objectives would certainly change the techniques of the economic planners to methods which are more comparable to our own.

AN EVALUATION OF THE AMERICAN ECONOMY

How good is our economic system? No human institution is ever perfect, but the review of the American economy has been an optimistic story. With all its shortcomings, our system of free enterprise has produced the highest living standard for the majority of the people of any civilization in the history of mankind.

The pricing mechanism promotes efficiency; indeed, no system has ever been more efficient. The use of prices for profit incentive develops initiative, innovation, and risk-taking, which are essential ingredients for economic progress. The pressure needed to prevent laziness is applied by competition, which forces men to work harder than they might otherwise like. The pricing system is the brightest tool of a free economy.

The American economy continues to grow, as our income yardstick clearly shows, but it has not grown fast enough to use all the people and their resources as fully as possible. The incentives for growth are not yet as effective as those for greater efficiency. No agreement has been reached concerning the best methods of abolishing involuntary unemployment. Public authority will occupy a key role in the promotion and maintenance of stable growth, though we are not yet certain what this role should be. The Russian example offers us no help, because we are not prepared to sacrifice personal freedom and consumer sovereignty on the altar of economic growth.

Since the dark days of the Great Depression, we have learned so much about the operation of an economic system that future depressions can be avoided. We have, in fact, strengthened the exchange mechanism and introduced stabilizers which would suffice to prevent the worst. However, we have not yet determined the proper course to achieve the best.

The success story of the American economy holds the bright promise of prosperity and better want satisfaction for the future. No economic system, however, can operate better than the people who make it work. The institutions of free enterprise, with all their great record of achievement, are always under attack. Profits are popular but losses are not; competition can never be taken for granted; the power of public authority may be abused; the pricing mechanism can become rigid or distorted; and the forces of monopoly—be it private or public—are ever present. We can never let down our guard; the price of freedom is eternal vigilance.

Suggested Reading

CAMPBELL, ROBERT W., *Soviet Economic Power.* 2d ed. Boston, Houghton Mifflin, 1966.
SHAFFER, HARRY G., *The Soviet Economy.* New York, Appleton-Century-Crofts, 1963.
SPULBER, NICHOLAS, *The Soviet Economy.* New York, Norton, 1962.

INDEX